Exploring Developmental Psychology

Exploring Developmental Psychology
Understanding Theory and Methods

Margaret Harris

SAGE Publications
Los Angeles · London · New Delhi · Singapore

First published 2008

SAGE Publications Ltd
1 Oliver's Yard
55 City Road
London EC1Y 1SP

SAGE Publications Inc.
2455 Teller Road
Thousand Oaks, California 91320

SAGE Publications India Pvt Ltd
B 1/I 1 Mohan Cooperative Industrial Area
Mathura Road
New Delhi 110 044

SAGE Publications Asia-Pacific Pte Ltd
33 Pekin Street #02-01
Far East Square
Singapore 048763

Library of Congress Control Number: 2007941934

British Library Cataloguing in Publication data

A catalogue record for this book is available from the British Library

ISBN 978-1-4129-0334-9
ISBN 978-1-4129-0335-6 (pbk)

Typeset by C&M Digitals (P) Ltd., Chennai, India
Printed in Great Britain by The Cromwell Press Ltd, Trowbridge, Wiltshire
Printed on paper from sustainable resources

For Franni with love

CONTENTS

LIST OF FIGURES

PREFACE

Why I wrote this book and how you can get the most out of reading it

Having taught undergraduate and postgraduate students for many years, and supervised innumerable final year research projects and MSc dissertations, I know that many students are keen to do research in developmental psychology but often know little about how to do it. In part this is because traditional courses in psychology research design and statistics tend to devote little or no time to the practicalities of research involving children or to the complexities of analysing and interpreting developmental data. I could have attempted to remedy this situation by writing a textbook about developmental psychology research. Instead I have chosen to do something rather different although you might not realise this if you only look at the first two chapters of this book. These explain some of the underlying issues in developmental psychology such as the nature of developmental change and the kinds of theories that are used to explain how and why change occurs; and I also discuss different ways in which development can be studied.

The first two chapters are intended to set the scene for the major part of the book which has a quite different format, consisting of articles from developmental psychology journals. These articles have been carefully chosen to reflect widely differing approaches to the study of children's development. My reason for focusing on journal articles is that I think the best way to learn about developmental psychology research – apart from actually going out and doing it – is to read recent articles to see how researchers develop and test hypotheses, collect and analyse data and interpret their findings. This approach might sound daunting if you are a student because developmental psychology articles are often difficult to read unless you are already an experienced researcher. This is not because they are badly written but because the underlying theory, the methodology and the data analysis they report are complex. So what I have done in this book is to give you a helping hand.

Each of the 13 papers in the book has a commentary that explains issues you may find difficult to understand. The commentary will guide you through the underlying theory, the hypotheses, the methodology, the statistical analysis and the interpretation of the data. I explain the background to each paper and help you to understand why researchers carried out each study in the way that they did. The points I make in the commentary have arisen from my experience of the kind of questions that my own students ask about journal articles.

This book does not teach you how to do statistics but it does show you how developmental psychologists use statistics in their research and, where I think it would be helpful, there are notes to guide you through the analysis and results section of a paper. However, I am assuming that you already know something about research design and that you are likely to have already carried out some experiments in practical classes, probably using other students as your participants. You do not need to have had any practical experience of research involving children but I am assuming that you are familiar with basic statistical tests such as *t*-tests, analysis of variance, correlation and regression.

Articles are grouped into chapters according to the age of the children being studied, or the type of methodology being used, or the kind of population that is being studied. You may well find that some chapters are more relevant to your particular interests than others and there is no need to read every article. However you will get the most out of this book if you read each article alongside my comments. Articles are reproduced in full with the exception of the abstract and references. We have omitted these so that my commentary can be interwoven more easily with the text.

You will also find a list of questions on Table 2.1 (p. 28) that you can use as a general guide when reading the articles. These list the kinds of questions you should ask yourself as you read each paper. Remember, it is important to understand not only what researchers found but also how they went about their research and why they made the choices they did.

I hope you will come away from reading this book with two important things. The first is a better understanding of the kinds of hypotheses that are tested by developmental psychology researchers, the methods they use and the conclusions they draw about the nature of development. The second is that you have a framework for understanding new journal articles. If you feel confident to browse through the latest issue of a developmental psychology journal then I know that I have succeeded in my task.

Margaret Harris
May 2007
Oxford

PUBLISHER'S ACKNOWLEDGEMENTS

The authors and publishers wish to thank the following for permission to use copyright material:

We thank the American Psychological Society for granting us permission to use the following article:

Deak, G. O., Flom, R. A., & Pick, A. D. (2000). Effects of gesture and target on 12- and 18-month-olds' joint visual attention to objects in front of or behind them. *Developmental Psychology, 36*(4), 511–523.

We thank the British Psychological Society for granting us permission to use the following articles:

Benenson, J. F., & Schinazi, J. (2004). Sex differences in reactions to outperforming same-sex friends. *British Journal of Developmental Psychology, 22*, 317–333.

Bradmetz, J., & Schneider, R. (1999). Is Little Red Riding Hood afraid of her grandmother? Cognitive vs. emotional response to a false belief. *British Journal of Developmental Psychology, 17*(4), 501–514.

Cain, K. (1999). Ways of reading: How knowledge and use of strategies are related to reading comprehension. *British Journal of Developmental Psychology, 17*, 295–312.

We thank Blackwell Publishing for granting us permission to use the following articles:

Christophe, A., & Morton, J. (1998). Is Dutch native English? Linguistic analysis by 2-month-olds. *Developmental Science, 1*, 215–219.

Hughes, C., Oksanen, H., Taylor, A., Jackson, J., Murray, L., Caspi, A., et al. (2002). 'I'm gonna beat you!' SNAP!: an observational paradigm for assessing young children's disruptive behaviour in competitive play. *Journal of Child Psychology and Psychiatry, 43*(4), 507–516.

Karmiloff-Smith, A., Thomas, M., Annaz, D., Humphreys, K., Ewing, S., Brace, N., et al. (2004). Exploring the Williams syndrome face-processing debate: the importance of building developmental trajectories. *Journal of Child Psychology and Psychiatry, 45*(7), 1258–1274.

Meins, E., Fernyhough, C., Wainwright, R., Das Gupta, M., Fradley, E., & Tuckey, M. (2002a). Maternal mind-mindedness and attachment security as predictors of Theory of Mind understanding. *Child Development, 73,* 1715–1726.

Savage, R., & Carless, S. (2005). Phoneme manipulation not onset-rime manipulation ability is a unique predictor of early reading. *Journal of Child Psychology and Psychiatry, 46*(4), 1297–1308.

Woolfe, T., Want, S. C., & Siegal, M. (2002). Signposts to development: Theory of mind in deaf children. *Child Development, 73,* 768–778.

We thank Elsevier for granting us permission to use the following articles:

Bailey, T. M., & Plunkett, K. (2002). Phonological specificity in early words. *Cognitive Development, 17,* 1265–1282.

Milgrom, J., Westley, D. T., & Gemmill, A. W. (2004). The mediating role of maternal responsiveness in longer term effects of postnatal depression on infant development. *Infant Behavior and Development, 27,* 443–454.

Muldoon, K., Lewis, C., & Towse, J. N. (2005). Because it's there! Why some children count, rather than infer numerical relationships. *Cognitive Development, 20*(3), 472–491.

While every effort has been made to trace the owners of copyright material, in a few cases this has proved difficult and we take this opportunity to offer our apologies to any copyright holder whose rights we have unwittingly infringed.

1

THE NATURE OF DEVELOPMENT

The aim of this book is to explore different ways of thinking about and studying children's development. As in any other science, research in developmental psychology aims both to describe and explain the phenomena under investigation: the particular aim of developmental psychology is to describe and explain developmental change.

It is worth taking a moment to clarify the special nature of developmental change. Change occurs all the time and at many different levels, and it can be both positive and negative. Change in a positive direction, that is towards greater accuracy and better organisation, is regarded as being 'development'. So, in speaking of developmental change, I am talking about change that can be seen as part of the process by which, over time, children move from a less mature to a more mature way of thinking and behaving where greater maturity is seen as being more adult-like. It is worth noting, however, that developmental change does not always show a smooth trajectory from lesser to greater maturity, as we see later in this chapter. This has implications for both the description and explanation of development.

Describing developmental change is considerably easier than explaining why it occurs. An overview of models of development (Valsiner, 1998) draws the rather pessimistic conclusion that:

> Child psychology today is surprisingly free of interest in building models of general development. The discipline is filled with hyperactive attempts to accumulate data, but attempts to make sense of the data, in terms of models of basic developmental processes, are relatively rare. (Valsiner, 1998: 189)

A rather similar observation is made in the opening chapter of *Rethinking Innateness* where the authors note that:

> Ironically, in the past several decades of developmental research there has been relatively little interest in the actual mechanisms responsible for change. (Elman et al., 1996: 1)

Although description is the easier task, it is useful to begin by considering what kinds of change developmental psychologists are attempting to describe. For, as we will see later in this chapter, theories of developmental change are intimately bound up with underlying notions of the nature of change itself.

Transformational and variational change

It is useful to distinguish two major kinds of developmental change that can be described as *transformational change* and *variational change* (Overton, 1998). Transformational change refers to change over time, from conception and the prenatal period through infancy, early and middle childhood to adolescence, adulthood and old age. As children grow older, they show transformational change in almost every aspect of development. They undergo huge physical and mental changes as motor, social, emotional and cognitive skills develop. Many aspects of transformational change in different areas of development are interrelated and understanding one aspect of change (for example, in a particular cognitive skill) may also involve understanding how this relates to other changes that are occurring at the same time (for example, in social skills).

Variational change refers to variation within development at a particular point. Consider, for example, children's ability to reason. This undergoes striking transformational change from infancy to adolescence but, at any given age and developmental level of thinking, children will use a variety of different solutions to a particular problem – this is variational change. Interestingly, individual children will often not only vary from each other in their problem-solving strategies but the same child may use a different strategy from one day to the next or even from one question to the next within the same session.

All abilities – both mental and physical – are subject to transformational and variational change. However, the interrelation between the two dimensions of change is more clearly spelled out for some aspects of development than for others. One aspect of development where there has been a great deal of investigation of both dimensions of change is children's reading. In general, children become better at reading as they grow older and there are a number of different theories to explain how the nature of reading changes with age. However, some children are much better at learning to read than others. This means that understanding the processes by which children learn to read requires not only an explanation of transformational change, that is how children's reading strategies develop over time, but also an explanation of variational change, that is how the reading strategies of good readers differ from those of less good readers. Furthermore, if we consider reading as a global phenomenon, we also have to explain why the speed with which children learn to read is different in different countries; and also why there are national differences in the incidence and severity of reading difficulties.

A key aspect of understanding variational change is to be able to describe the course of development for a typically developing child so that it is then possible to identify and describe atypical progress. Thus, in the case of reading, we need to know what level of reading is age-appropriate for any given script. This, in turn, requires information about the range of variation in reading ability at a given age so that we can distinguish among good, average and below average readers and typical and atypical use of particular strategies.

A developmental systems perspective

What kinds of theory best account for both transformational and variational change? Early developmental theories tended to argue for 'either/or' accounts of the influence of genetic factors or the environment on development (Harris & Butterworth, 2002). The term 'nature-nurture' was first coined as long ago as 1869 by Francis Galton in his book, *Hereditary Genius*, but fierce arguments between nativists and empiricists continued for much of the twentieth century with developmental change being seen either as the 'mere triggering of innate knowledge' or as 'inductive learning' (Elman et al., 1996).

One vivid illustration of the opposition of these 'either/or' kinds of explanation can be seen in the controversy that surrounded the work of Margaret Mead, the celebrated anthropologist. Mead's seminal study of adolescents in Samoa (Mead, 1928) claimed that the pattern of adolescence that characterised Western societies was not evident among the population of Samoa. The forward to the book, written by Boas, an eminent anthropologist who was Mead's mentor, set out the main conclusion:

> In our own civilization the individual is beset with difficulties which we are likely to ascribe to fundamental human traits. When we speak about the difficulties of childhood and adolescence, we are thinking of them as unavoidable periods of adjustment through which everyone has to pass ... The results of [Mead's] painstaking investigation confirm the suspicion long held by anthropologists, that much of what we ascribe to human nature is no more than a reaction to the restraints put upon us by our civilisation. (Mead, 1928)

Mead's claim that adolescents in Samoa were 'gentle, uncompetitive and guilt-free' (Grosskurth, 1988) was seen as strong evidence that development was shaped by the environment, a view that chimed with the American public of the times and resulted in Mead's book becoming a bestseller.

Mead's chief critic, Derek Freeman, strongly contested this view of Samoa, arguing that Samoan adolescents displayed the same patterns of emotional extremes that were evident in Western culture (Freeman, 1983). Undoubtedly, the truth about the influences of nature and nurture on adolescence lies somewhere in between these extreme views, and, although there are differences of emphasis, modern accounts of development tend to assume that developmental change occurs both as a result of maturation and growth and through the interaction that children have with their environment. As Elman et al. (1996) note:

We believe that an interactionist view is not only the correct one, but that the field is now in a position where we can flesh out this approach in some detail. (Elman et al., 1996: xii)

One important factor in the current ascendancy of interactionist theories is that there is now a more sophisticated understanding of the way in which genetic factors operate (Gottlieb, 2007; Rutter, 2007; Westermann et al., 2007). Some of the arguments in this area are complex but, for present purposes, the key point is to recognise that there are important reciprocal influences within and between the different levels of development within an individual. Thus, genetic activity, neural activity, behaviour and the physical and socio-cultural effects of the environment all interact. I return to this issue in the next section.

Modern developmental accounts also look both at effects that operate at the level of the individual and those that are evident within a particular social group or culture. They do not, as Lerner puts it so elegantly, 'force counterproductive choices between false opposites; rather, these issues are used to gain insight into the integrations that exist among the multiple levels of organization involved in human development' (Lerner, 1998).

Of necessity, modern theories of development are complex just because they consider the interrelation of many different influences on development; and perhaps this is one reason why, as we have already noted, research often concentrates on data collection and interpretation rather than the wider implications for developmental theory.

The epigenetic landscape and beyond

To illustrate some of the issues that arise in adopting what might be described as a developmental systems perspective (Lerner, 1998) it is useful to consider one early and very influential model, Waddington's 'epigenetic landscape' (Waddington, 1975) in light of the most recent development in understanding gene-environment interactions that are discussed later in this section.

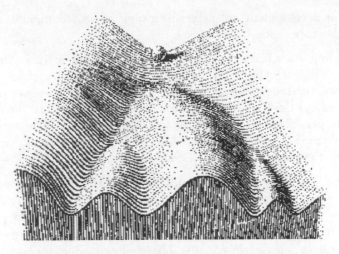

Figure 1.1   *The epigenetic landscape (based on Waddington, 1975);* from Harris & Butterworth, 2002: 38

Waddington, whose work has more recently been discussed as an underlying model for connectionism (Elman et al., 1996), was concerned with the complex relationship between the phenotype and the genotype. The phenotype, that is how an individual looks and behaves, is the result of an interaction between the genotype (the pattern of genes) and the environment. Waddington's metaphor of the epigenetic landscape was intended to explain the nature of the interaction between genotype and environment. He envisaged development as:

> a set of branching valleys in a multidimensional space that includes a time dimension, along which the valleys may extend. The development of the phenotype of an individual proceeds along a valley bottom; variations of genotype, or of epigenetic environment, may push the course of development away from the valley floor, up the neighbouring hillside, but there will be a tendency for the process to find its way back. (Waddington, 1975: 258)

The ball in Waddington's diagram represents the developing organism. The ball rolls downhill through a landscape made up of hills and valleys. These represent possible pathways that the development of an individual may take. The pathway taken by the rolling ball, as it progresses downhill, is constrained by the landscape but it is also affected by environmental events. These two factors interact. For example, if the ball is knocked off course (i.e. away from the valley floor), much greater force is required to move the ball out of a deep valley than out of a gently sloping valley. This reflects the fact that the consequences of a particular environmental factor will vary considerably according to where and when in development it occurs. Some aspects of development are very susceptible to environmental influence while others are much less so.

Another important feature of the epigenetic landscape is the incline of the valley floor into which the ball descends. All the valleys are inclined so that the ball will tend to roll forward (representing development over time) but in some valleys the floor has a gentle incline while, in others, the incline is much steeper. The ball will roll rapidly downhill in a valley where the incline is steep but progress will be slower where the incline is gentler. This represents the relative speed of development at different points.

The metaphor of the epigenetic landscape elegantly illustrates one way to think of possible pathways that development can take. It alerts us to the possibility that development can proceed along many alternative pathways that end up at the same place. It shows us that proceeding along a particular pathway early in development will have consequences for later development. It also leads us to expect that there will be important individual differences in both the rate and course of development in spite of similar end points; and, finally, it reminds us that development may not end up in the same place for all children.

Recent studies suggest that this picture of development is even more complex than the metaphor of the ball rolling downhill through the epigenetic landscape might suggest. Gottlieb (2007) introduces the notion of 'probabilistic epigenesis'. This contrasts with the traditional view of predetermined epigenesis, that is, the idea that genetic factors determine neural structures that, when mature, function in particular ways. In other words the sequence that is assumed in traditional epigenesis is:

genetic activity → structure → function

The key idea behind probabilistic epigenesis is that influences at the different levels of development are bi-directional. As Gottlieb puts it, 'neural (and other structures) begin to function before they are fully mature and this activity … plays a significant role in the developmental process' (Gottlieb, 2007: 2). These mutual, bi-directional influences are depicted in Figure 1.2.

One of the examples that Gottlieb gives to illustrate his approach is the relationship between maternal behaviour in early infancy and patterns of attachment. A common finding is that there are relationships between patterns of maternal interaction in early infancy and later patterns of infant attachment (Harris & Butterworth, 2002). Gottlieb cites the finding that mothers whose interaction is classed as 'intrusive' when their infants are 3 months old are likely to have children who are classed as 'insecurely attached', that is, they tend to stay close to their mother in an unfamiliar situation and are very upset, and not easily comforted, when she leaves

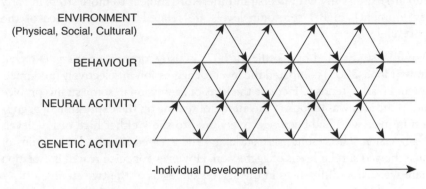

BI-DIRECTIONAL INFLUENCES

ENVIRONMENT
(Physical, Social, Cultural)

BEHAVIOUR

NEURAL ACTIVITY

GENETIC ACTIVITY

-Individual Development →

Figure 1.2   *Probabilistic epigenesis;* from Gottlieb 2007: 2

them with a stranger (Lewis, 1990). Gottlieb argues that understanding the sequence of cause and effect involves looking not only at how a mother's behaviour might affect her child's development but also considering how the mother's behaviour might be affected by her child's early behaviour. The suggestion is that mothers may be over-stimulating because their children are not socially oriented at a young age, preferring to focus on objects rather than people. With such infants, mothers are likely to be more proactive in their attempts to provoke social engagement whereas, in the case of more socially oriented babies who spontaneously send out lots of social signals such as looking at the mother and smiling, such attempts are not necessary. Indeed the most common pattern is for the mothers to be predominantly responsive to their infants rather than proactive. The suggestion is that over-stimulation – repeatedly trying to provoke a response – may then lead to insecure attachment.

One might also note that the tendency to focus on objects rather than people may well be the result of a genetic predisposition that might be present in both the infant and the mother. Thus genetic effects may also have a role in shaping the child's environment as well as working more directly.

Gottlieb illustrates the complexity of gene–environment interactions – or coactions as he prefers to call them – at other levels of development. For example, in rhesus monkeys, low serotonin metabolism is associated with higher levels of impulsivity, aggression and risk taking. In humans, low serotonin levels are associated with alcohol abuse and depression. At the genetic level, the level of serotonin metabolism is associated with the presence of a long or short allele in the serotonin transporter gene (5-HTT). Significantly, however, the genetic effects are mediated by the effects of rearing (Bennett et al., 2002). For monkeys who are reared with their mothers, seratonin levels are not related to the form of the 5-HTT gene. However, for monkeys who are reared only with peers (and therefore subject to more stress in early development), higher serotonin levels are related to the presence of the short allele.

One final study cited by Gottlieb (2007) is also worth mentioning. A recent study (Hood, 2005) compared the levels of aggression in selectively bred mice. Isolated rearing tends to increase the level of aggression in some strains of mice and so the idea was to look at the effects of rearing on the expression of aggression in mice who had been selectively bred to show either high or low levels of aggression. The results were striking. When reared socially, both strains of mice showed similar levels of aggression. However, for mice reared in isolation there were large differences in the aggression levels of the two strains.

This example clearly illustrates how aggressive behaviour in mice is the result of a gene–environment interaction. In mice, where both selective breeding and rearing can be carefully controlled, it is possible to begin to explore this interaction in ways that are not possible for humans. However, there is every reason to suppose that similar kinds of interactions and coactions operate in human development.

Are there stages in development?

The model of the epigenetic landscape might suggest that the course of development is best understood as a continuous process of change. However, the location of junctions between the valleys can be seen as representing a point of transition between one stage of development and the next. Piaget, whose own thinking was very much influenced by the work of James Mark Baldwin (Harris & Butterworth, 2002), used the concept of stages in his theory as a way of distinguishing discrete periods in development that were qualitatively distinct from one another.

There are a number of different criteria for identifying developmental stages (Flavell, Miller, & Miller, 1993). First, as I have already implied, stages are characterised by *qualitative* changes. A qualitative change is not simply a matter of being able to do more of something but of doing it differently. Qualitative changes are relatively easy to spot in some areas of development, such as gross motor skills. Most babies begin to move around by crawling (or bottom shuffling) and then, later on, they acquire the necessary co-ordination to walk. Crawling and walking are qualitatively different types of locomotion. Drawing a distinction between qualitatively different kinds of cognition such as thought and language is arguably more difficult than in the case of motor skills.

Even where there is evidence of a qualitative change this does not, on its own, provide evidence for a transition between stages. Transitions are also marked by *simultaneous* changes in a number of aspects of children's behaviour. For example, between the ages of three and four years, children show a change in their ability to carry out a number of cognitive tasks. These include tasks designed to assess Theory of Mind understanding (Wimmer & Perner, 1983), appearance-reality tasks (Flavell, Green, & Flavell, 1986), and multi-dimensional card sorting (Towse, Redbond, Houston-Price, & Cook, 2000). Simultaneous changes in the ability to do such tasks suggest that a stage change, perhaps in ability to deal with more than one representation or dimension at a time, is occurring between the ages of 3 and 4. The possibility of a wide-scale change in ability points to the importance of looking at development from a broad perspective rather than merely concentrating on a single aspect of developmental change.

A third feature of stage transitions is that they are typically *rapid*. It may be relatively easy to spot a period of rapid physical change. For example, as children move into adolescence, they often go through a growth spurt in which they gain several inches in height and several pounds in weight in a few months. Similarly rapid change can be observed in other areas, such as children's language ability. Once the first 30 or so words have been acquired, many children show a sudden increase in the rate at which they learn new words (Fenson et al., 1990).

Stage theories are very common in developmental psychology. As we have already noted, Piaget is the best known proponent of a stage theory of development but many other theorists, including Freud and Vygotsky and neo-Piagetians, such as Robbie Case (Case, 1985), have used the notion of stages. There are, however, other ways to view development as we see in the next section.

Linear and non-linear change

A rather different way of thinking about qualitative changes in development is evident in dynamic systems theory. This approach aims to produce a mathematical model describing how qualitative changes come about through the accumulation of small scale quantitative changes. In this way, dynamic systems theory accounts for qualitative change without the need to appeal to the notion of discrete stages.

The key to dynamic systems theory is that it attempts to model non-linear dynamics. There are two sorts of dynamics: *linear* and *non-linear*. The theory of linear dynamics is most obviously applied to mechanical interactions, such as a collision between two billiard balls: change is smooth and continuous and the new pathway that a ball will take after it has been hit by another ball can be precisely predicted from such factors as the angle and speed of collision. However, while linear dynamics can account for mechanical interactions, the patterns of change that occur in biological development are seldom smooth and continuous. Indeed, many apparently linear patterns of change over time come about either because only a restricted age range is considered or because researchers average data gained from a heterogeneous sample of children (Elman et al., 1996).

To take a simple example from Elman et al. (1996), if we were to plot the size of children's shoes against their age, the resulting function might well be linear if only data from children aged between 5 and 11 years were to be included. If we included data from older children, the resulting slope of the graph would no longer be linear as we would see the characteristic growth spurt in shoe size as children enter adolescence. Similarly, data collected from a large sample, containing children who come from diverse socioeconomic and ethnic groups, might appear to be linear. This is because there would be wide variation among children of the same age and this would average out into a linear increase. However, if the sample were to be restricted to children from similar backgrounds, the underlying pattern of non-linear change would emerge.

Dynamic systems theory uses non-linear dynamics to model developmental change (Thelen & Smith, 1994; van Geert, 1998). One of the strengths of dynamic systems theory is that it points to the great variety of different patterns that developmental change may take. In their analysis of what they call 'the shape of change', Elman et al. (1996) describe six different forms of change, only one of which is linear. Some of the most important patterns are shown in Figure 1.3.

The pattern of change shown in 1.3c is commonly found in developmental psychology. The example used by Elman et al. (1996) is of the relationship between age (in months) and the number of different words that children can say. Initially children learn words at a slow rate but, the more words they know, the faster the rate at which they learn new words. Other patterns of change may look more like 1.3b. Here, children initially develop at a very fast rate but, over time, the rate of development slows down. I discuss some examples of this pattern of change in the next section.

In light of our earlier discussion about developmental stages, the pattern shown in 1.3d is particularly interesting. Unlike the three other examples, this shows discontinuous change and what looks like a stage transition. However, both dynamic systems theory (van Geert, 1998) and connectionist modelling (Elman et al., 1996) show how the gradual accumulation of small changes over time can give rise to a sudden, step-like change.

Information processing approaches

Another way of looking at developmental change is through the information processing approach. Like dynamic systems theory, the information processing approach emphasises detailed analysis of the processing demands of individual

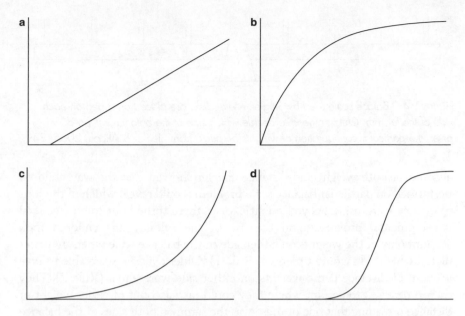

Figure 1.3 *Some examples of linear and non-linear forms of change;* adapted from Elmen et al., 1996: 176, 186, 191

tasks and their modelling in computer programs (Klahr & Wallace, 1976; Siegler, 1998). The main idea is to consider how children's abilities to meet the processing demands of a particular task change over time. One important aspect of a task is the memory load it imposes. A particular task may require a certain number of items to be held in memory at the same time and so this aspect will prove problematic for young children who can only remember a small number of items. Similarly, a particular task such as sorting cards according to their category may require a child to deal with two dimensions, such as colour and shape, that are changing independently but are interrelated (Towse et al., 2000). Children below a certain age will find it difficult when they have to take account of two dimensions simultaneously.

The most detailed information processing account of development has been developed by Siegler (Siegler, 1998; Siegler & Alibali, 2005). Some of Siegler's most influential work has looked at developmental changes in problem solving. Siegler outlined four stages that are evident in the way children attempt to solve problems involving a balance scale (see Figure 1.4). Children are shown a scale with weights placed different distances from the fulcrum and their task is to decide which side of the balance will go down. This is a difficult task because it involves taking into account both the weights on either side of the fulcrum and the distance of each weight from the fulcrum.

Siegler identified four different rules that children could use to solve balance scale problems. These rules differ in the extent to which they take

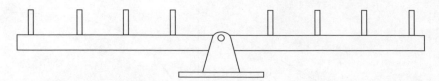

Figure 1.4 *Balace scale used by Siegler. Metal disks are placed on a peg on each side of the fulcrum. Children need to decide which side of the balance will go down, given the particular configuration of weights on pegs; from Siegler & Alibali, 2005: 349*

account of both weight and distance. Siegler showed that the way children performed on particular balance scale problems could reveal which of the four rules they were using. As you might expect, there turned out to be a general developmental progression in the use of the rules. Young children took account only of the weights on either side of the balance scale when they predicted which side would tip down (Rule 1). Older children were able to take account of distance if the weights on either side were equal (Rule 2). They then progressed to a point where they could take account of either weight or distance providing that one of these was the same on both sides of the balance (Rule 3). Siegler found that 17-year-olds were still using this latter rule much of the time even when they had learned about balance scales during science lessons. Very few children were able to take account of weight and distance simultaneously as is required to solve the most difficult balance scale problems (Rule 4).

Interestingly, Siegler discovered that a major factor in the inability of the 17-year-olds to solve the balance scale problem was that examples they had worked on in class were subtly different from the version used in the experiment:

A later conversation with a science teacher in the school proved revealing. The teacher pointed out the balance scale in the experiment was an arm balance, whereas the balance scale used in the classroom was a pan balance, in which pans with varying amounts of weight could be suspended from hooks at varying distances from the fulcrum. Retesting a few students indicated that they indeed could solve comparable problems presented on the pan balance! This limited generalization is, unfortunately, the rule rather than the exception in problem solving. (Siegler & Alibali, 2005)

The students' failure to generalise performance across tasks highlights an important issue for studying development. In making claims about children's ability to complete a task successfully, it is important to know how general a particular ability actually is. Is it limited to a single task, to a set of similar tasks or does it extend across a range of dissimilar tasks? Siegler's observations illustrate that very specific characteristics of a particular task can have a significant effect on children's performance. This is an issue that we return to in Chapter 2.

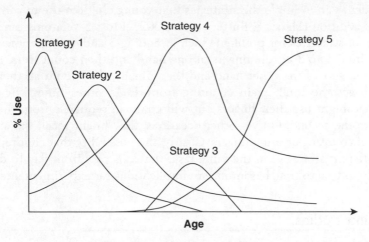

Figure 1.5   *Siegler's overlapping waves model of cognitive development;* from Siegler & Alibali, 2005: 98

Another key feature of Siegler's approach to thinking about developmental change is the idea that children can have, at any one time, a number of different ways of thinking about a particular problem. Siegler argues that children's varied ways of thinking about the same task compete with each other so that, over time, the more advanced ways are used with increasing frequency and the less advanced ways are used less frequently. In other words, children have alternative strategies for solving problems. With experience, strategies that prove effective are used more while other, less effective, strategies disappear. Figure 1.5 illustrates what Siegler describes as an overlapping waves model of development.

You will see in Siegler's model the kind of developmental trajectories noted in the previous section on non-linear dynamics. The different strategies all have a non-linear time course with the most typical pattern being an increase over time followed by a decrease. The interesting thing about the model is that it depicts multiple strategies, each with its own time course.

This kind of model is good at explaining variational change since, at any one point in time, children may have several different strategies available. As Siegler notes:

> Children's thinking is far more variable than has usually been recognised. This variability is omnipresent, occurring at all ages, in all domains, and at all points in learning. The variability is evident not just at the neural and associative levels ... but also at the level of strategies, theories and other units of higher level cognition. It is present not only between different people ... but also within a single person solving the same problem at two points close in time ... (Siegler, 2007: 104)

Consider as an example the strategies that young children use to carry out simple addition (Harris & Butterworth, 2002). Most 5-year-olds can use a variety of strategies for problems such as adding 3 and 4. Sometimes they count from 1 to 3 on the fingers of one hand and then count from 1 to 4 on the fingers of the other hand and then, finally, they count all their fingers to get the total, again counting from 1. At other times, the same children might use their fingers but will count in sequence from the first hand to the second. On yet other occasions, they might recall the answer without counting or using fingers. Clearly, the possibility that children may use different strategies in the same task, that can vary from day to day or even from trial to trial, has important implications for experimental testing.

Training studies

Siegler has been particularly interested in the effects of experience on children's development. In an early study of the balance scale (Siegler, 1976), children aged between 5 and 8 years who used Rule 1 (taking account of weight by ignoring distance) were given systematic feedback on one of three types of problem. In the feedback conditions, they were given a balance scale problem and asked which side would go down. Then the balance lock was released and children were able to see which side went down. One group of children saw only examples which they could already solve using Rule 1. The other two groups saw examples where Rule 1 would make the wrong prediction. One group saw problems that could be solved using Rule 2, that is, the weights on the two sides were equal but the distance from the fulcrum varied. Children in the other group were presented with more difficult problems in which either the weights or the distances from the fulcrum were equal. These kinds of problem can only be solved using Rule 3.

Siegler found that the type of feedback affected children's ability to solve new balance scale problems. Not surprisingly, children who had experienced only problems that could be solved using their existing rule did not show any improvement. Both 5- and 8-year-olds, who were shown Rule 2 problems (in which weight was the same but distance varied), usually advanced to Rule 2. This represents a relatively small advance on Rule 1 so it should be fairly easy for children who use Rule 1.

The behaviour of children who had been exposed to Rule 3 problems varied with age. Rule 3 is considerably more sophisticated than Rule 1 and most of the 5-year-olds did not move on from Rule 1. However, most of the 8-year-olds advanced to Rule 3. Subsequent testing showed that the 5-year-olds were only encoding weight in balance scale problems and were not paying attention to distance from the fulcrum. For this reason, they were unable to develop an understanding of Rule 3 which required them to notice how distance affected the balance of the scale. By contrast, the older children were already paying attention to both weight and distance and so were able to acquire Rule 3 with the right kind of feedback. This illustrates very clearly the interaction between new experience and current developmental state. New experience has its greatest effect when it builds on knowledge that is already in the process of developing – an idea that was first encapsulated in Vygotsky's seminal concept of the 'zone of proximal development' (Vygotsky, 1961). This idea has important implications for the design of training studies. Training is most likely to produce an effect if children can readily relate their new experience to what they already know.

Variation across tasks

Another important aspect of variation in strategy is that children may use different strategies in tasks that are only slightly different. We have already seen, in the case of the balance scale, that children may fail to generalise from one version of a task to another. Other variations in the way that a task is presented can also have an effect on children's performance.

A classic study (Bryant & Kopytnyska, 1976) compared children's use of measurement in a standard Piagetian task with measurement in a very similar task. In the standard Piagetian task, children are shown a tower of bricks standing on a high table. Children are asked to build another tower of the same height on a table that is 90 cm lower. Since the reference tower is not at the same level as the one that the children build, a direct visual comparison of height is not possible; and it is also not possible to simply count the number of bricks required as the two towers use bricks of different sizes. The way to succeed in the task is to measure the reference tower so that the constructed tower can be built to exactly the same height. A stick of the same height as the reference tower is made available for this purpose.

Piaget (Piaget, Inhelder, & Sizeminska, 1960) found that children of 5 and 6 years were reluctant to use the stick as a way of making a comparison and relied, instead, on making a direct – and unsuccessful – comparison between the height of the two towers. At this age they were often very confident about their ability to make a purely visual judgement about the height of the two towers as Piaget's detailed descriptions of the children's responses illustrate. Here is the reaction of a boy, aged 5;3:

> Looks at the model and arranges his bricks differently while making his tower the same height. Now and again he checks on his progress.
>
> [*Experimenter*] 'Is it the same height?'
> [*Child*] 'Yes.'
> [*Experimenter*] 'How do you know?'
> [*Child*] 'By looking at the blocks.'

[*Experimenter*] 'What if I told you it isn't as high?'

[*Child*] 'I can see it's the same.' He adjusts a crooked block without altering the height of the tower.

[*Experimenter*] 'Can you think of a trick to see if it's the same height?'

[*Child*] 'No, I tell you it's right!' (in a peremptory tone).

(Piaget et al., 1960)

Piaget's original observations were confirmed by Bryant and Kopytnyska (1976). However, they found that children who did not spontaneously mea-sure the height of the two towers were much more likely to use a measuring stick when it was clear that a direct visual comparison of length was not possible. In their novel task, children were given two blocks of wood with a hole drilled into the top. The children were asked to find out whether the two holes were of similar or different depth and, if the latter, which hole was deeper. The clever thing about the Bryant and Kopytnyska task was that the relative depth of the two holes could not be determined just from look-ing into them. Confronted with a task in which direct visual comparison was clearly not possible, children did use the stick to measure and compare the depth of the two holes.

There are many other instances of research showing that children can use a more sophisticated strategy to solve a task when they are supported in doing so by the way a task is structured. When and why children use one strategy rather than another is an important issue for any account of developmental change. Understanding factors that can inhibit and facilitate solutions often provides an important insight into the specific aspects of ability that are in the process of development and into the wider question of why developmental change occurs. See, for example, Bryant's discussion of whether it is conflict-ing or converging outcomes that lead children to advance to a more sophisti-cated understanding of the use of measurement (Bryant, 1982).

Investigating developmental change

So far in this chapter we have considered the different patterns that may appear in developmental change. We have seen that change may be gradual or abrupt, linear or non-linear. We have also seen that there are likely to be large differences both between individuals and even within the same indi-vidual tested on different occasions. There are also likely to be differences in the way that children respond to particular tasks. Even small differences in the structure or context of an experimental task can affect performance and, as we saw in the examples of the balance scale and measurement tasks, children may be able to solve problems involving one task but not be able to solve comparable problems involving a very similar task that varies in some critical detail.

There are several principles of good experimental design that emerge from these general observations about the nature of developmental change. Perhaps the most important is that the best studies make use of converging evidence. In other words, they use a number of different ways to assess children's performance and then look for overall consistencies in behaviour.

Another important principle is that good studies of development should enable the study of individual differences. This does not mean that children should only be studied on an individual basis. Indeed, it could be argued that data on an individual child may tell us very little about general patterns of development. What is important, however, is to strike a balance between studying both transformational and variational change. A good study, or series of studies, should reveal both how the abilities of children at different ages and stages of development change and how much individual variation there is in children's behaviour at a given point in development.

2

EXPLORING DEVELOPMENT

In this Chapter, I consider how different models of development can be tested. My main concern is with the interrelation of research methodology and particular views of development. In other words, I want to consider whether choosing any one method of collecting data presupposes an underlying model of development; and whether the choice of a particular approach constrains the nature of the conclusions that are likely to emerge.

You will probably not be at all surprised to find that these questions are difficult to answer and they are a major concern for philosophers of science. A thought-provoking analysis of the interrelation among philosophy, concepts and methodology in developmental psychology (Overton, 1998) outlines the crux of the problem:

> There is little disagreement among scientists, historians of science, and philosophers of science about where science begins – in common sense and the contradictions that show up when we begin to examine common sense – and where it leads – to refined theories and laws that explain. Science is a human knowledge-building activity designed to bring order and organization into the flux of everyday experience. Disagreement emerges only when the question is raised of exactly how, or by what route, science moves from common sense to refined knowledge. This issue – the route from common sense to science – constitutes the methodology of science. (Overton, 1998: 155)

Overton goes on to show that models and theories are closely related to observation and experimentation. In other words, the methodology that researchers adopt and the kind of observations they make are heavily influenced by their theoretical stance about the nature of development. One example that Overton discusses of this interrelation of theory and method hinges round task simplification.

Task simplification

The basic approach in task simplification, which has been used in many areas of developmental psychology, is to simplify the procedural details of a task, such as the instructions and the stimuli, in an attempt to assess more directly what children can actually do. As we will see in later chapters, reducing unnecessary complexity in task procedure and instructions can often be a good thing since there are many examples of unnecessarily complex procedures that serve to underestimate children's capability. This is particularly evident in studies that rely heavily on verbal methods as we see in Chapter 5. However, as Overton argues (Overton, 1998), there is a potential problem with indiscriminate task simplification since this may change the nature of the task itself so that it no longer assesses the same ability as the original task.

We have already considered one example of task simplification when we discussed Siegler's information processing approach (see Figure 1.5). Consider the balance scale task that Siegler used in a series of studies (see Figure 1. 4). This was an adaptation of a task originally devised by Piaget (Inhelder & Piaget, 1958) to assess a broad-based logical competence. Children were given a balance and a set of weights and were asked to position the weights so that the scale balanced. They were also asked a series of questions designed to uncover what they understood about the way that the balance scale worked. Selection of the correct position for the weights and explaining the rationale for these choices each requires a certain level of understanding of how balance is achieved. It is therefore important to ask whether the same levels of understanding are required when the format of the balance scale task is changed.

In Siegler's modification of the task (Siegler, 1976), rather than being asked to position the weights, children were presented with the balance scale already set up with a certain combination of weights placed at a given distance from the fulcrum. They were then asked to predict which of three things would happen when the scale was released: would the right hand end go down; would the left hand end go down; or would the scale remain level? It can be argued that Siegler's version of the balance scale task is a test of local problem-solving ability rather than a test of more general logical competence as intended by Piaget. Interestingly, this interpretation is consistent with Siegler's own observation that the adolescents he tested found it very difficult to generalise from a rather similar problem they had learned about in class only recently (see Figure 1.5).

As Zelazo and Müller point out (Zelazo & Müller, 2002), there is an important theoretical and empirical distinction between being able to observe and predict a relation and understanding that relation. Children who understand the underlying principles of the balance scale should be able to generalise to similar problems that exploit the same underlying rationale. Children who are merely able to predict how particular combinations of weight and distance will affect the balance of the scale will not be able to solve other problems of similar complexity.

Another striking example of task simplification centres round Piaget's tests of infants' ability to reason about hidden objects. These tests involve the infant retrieving an object whose location has been moved (see Figure 2.1). In the last two decades, tests of object permanence have evolved into

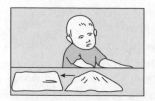  

Experimenter distracts
infant and switches the
position of a hidden object

Infant searches for a
hidden object in the
same place as before,
despite its obvious size

Infant is confused
when the hidden
object is not found

Figure 2.1   *Errors in the object search task. This 9-month-old infant looks for an object at its previous location even though the bulge under the cloth gives a strong clue to its real location;* from Harris & Butterworth, 2002: 101

perceptual habituation tasks in which infants inspect occluded arrays (Baillargeon, 1999). There is no doubt that such tasks can provide important information about the gradual development of infants' ability to take account of the perceptual characteristics of increasingly complex displays – a point I return to in the next section. However, it is important to recognise that habituation tasks do not test the same ability that Piaget originally investigated. For this reason, the fact that relatively young infants are able to succeed in habituation tasks may not provide, as is often claimed, strong evidence that Piaget underestimated the perceptual abilities of infants. One of the important features of the Piagetian A-not-B task is that it assesses infants' ability to put their understanding of object location – and relocation – into action and, as such, it assesses a more complex level of ability than is required to succeed in an habituation task.

Reliability and validity

Overton (1998) sees the tendency towards task simplification as part of a wider confusion between the reliability and validity of a method of assessment. He notes that:

...a great deal of the developmental literature carries a split message implying that validity is derivative. The claim of this message is that, if consistent behavior (i.e. reliability) is observed in an appropriately controlled setting, then validity will follow naturally. (Overton, 1998: 162)

The key issue here lies in the distinction between consistent and reliable behaviour and the theoretical interpretation of that behaviour. Presenting children of a certain age with a particular experimental task may produce a predictable pattern of behaviour but it is important to show that the observed behaviour really is a measure or marker of the phenomenon that the experimenter has assumed it to be. This is a consistent theme in the interpretation and reinterpretation of research findings and there are a number of examples in the later chapters. For the moment, let us consider one particular manifestation of the validity issue – what Flavell has described as the 'diagnosis' issue (Flavell, 1992; Flavell et al., 1993).

Flavell poses the question of how researchers who are interested in a particular cognitive entity can know, for certain, that a particular child actually 'has' that entity. Take, for example, Theory of Mind (ToM) – the ability to make inferences about the mental states of other people. The task for the researcher is to steer a careful course between, on the one hand, attributing ToM to a child who does not yet possess it and, on the other hand, failing to attribute ToM to a child who really does possess the ability.

There has been a consistent tendency to simplify the demands of tasks that are assumed to assess children's capacity to make judgments involving ToM. As might be expected, as tasks become progressively simplified, more and more children are able to complete them successfully and so ToM is attributed to children at younger and younger ages with wider and wider characteristics (Flavell, 1992). This does little to solve the diagnosis problem, that is, to distinguish false negatives from false positives.

One way of responding to the diagnosis problem is to return to the underlying question posed by developmental psychology. Is it possible to demonstrate developmental *change* in the way that children respond to a particular task? If so, it is then possible to go on and identify a developmental sequence. So, properly posed, the question is not, 'Do children possess or not possess a particular entity?' but 'What is the difference between the way that younger and older children respond to particular situations?'.

One nice illustration of the demonstration of a developmental sequence comes from the work on infant perception of object occlusion that I mentioned earlier. In an overview of her research, Baillargeon takes on a number of challenges to the claim that even young infants are able to represent and reason about objects that are hidden from view. In light of the issues I have been discussing, the most important challenge is that such a claim 'is static and non-developmental, and as such constitutes an unproductive approach to cognition' (Baillargeon, 1999).

Baillargeon's counter to this claim is to pose the question: 'Do young infants' expectations about hidden objects undergo developmental change?'. She then goes on to argue that they do. She shows that infants first form an initial concept based on a simple, all-or-none distinction. Then, with further experience, they successively identify variables that serve to elaborate and refine the initial concept. One of the examples Baillargeon discusses is infants' knowledge of what she describes as 'support events',

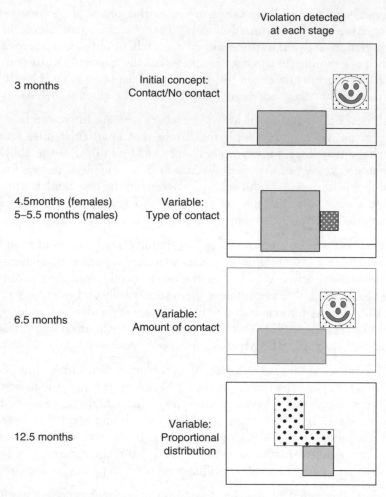

Figure 2.2   *Developmental change in infants' understanding of support events;*
from Baillargeon, 1999: 116

that is, events in which one object is released and is either supported
(so that it remains stable) or not supported by another object. The developmental progression is summarised in Figure 2.2, taken from Baillargeon
(1999).

According to Baillargeon, infants begin with a simple contact/no contact
distinction and, at around three months (Baillargeon, Needham, & DeVos,
1992), they expect an object to be stable if it is released while in contact
with another object but to fall if it is not in contact with another object. At
this initial stage, infants can recognise that the event depicted in row 1 violates this principle since the released object remains where it was even

though it is not in contact with the other object. Then, a few months later, infants show evidence of taking into account the *type* of contact between two objects and distinguish between cases where one object is released onto another object that serves to support it and cases where there is contact but not support (as in the second row of Figure 2.2 where the released object remains stable even though it is at the side of the 'supporting' object). A few months later, infants take account of the *amount* of contact as well as the type. If an object has half or more of its bottom surface resting on the supporting object, they expect it to remain stable, but otherwise they expect it to fall. At this stage, infants detect that an event like the one in the third row of Figure 2.2 violates this principle.

By the age of just over 1 year, infants are able to take into account not only the amount and type of contact but also the proportions of the object that is released. The kind of event that infants saw to test this aspect of understanding is the one in row 4 of Figure 2.2 where the released object is asymmetrical and, as a result, will not be supported even though half of its bottom surface is in contact with the supporting object. Infants of 12 months could detect that the event depicted in row 4 was implausible but younger infants could not.

The important point about Baillargeon's account, which is derived from very careful experimentation, is the evidence she provides of a clear developmental progression in the way that infants respond to the different kinds of simple events involving objects; and this is an important first step in describing and then explaining how infants develop an understanding of the way objects behave.

Longitudinal designs and individual differences

The work carried out by Baillargeon and her colleagues, like the majority of research in developmental psychology, used a cross-sectional design in which infants of different ages were compared. Such designs are very good at uncovering transformational change but they are less good at describing variational change. For this purpose, longitudinal designs, in which the same children are followed over time, are often better.

Pinpointing individual differences in development has traditionally been more of a feature in some areas of research than in others. For example, within the area of language development, there has been a long history of considering not only the similarities among children but also the extent to which they vary from one another. It is interesting to speculate about why there is greater or lesser emphasis on variation in particular aspects of development. It may be that some aspects of development are more prone to individual variation than others or that such variability is more or less easy to observe. For example, in the case of language development, researchers have been aware of the fact that, across the World, children acquire many different languages and so it has been natural to ask whether the process of acquiring a particular language is essentially the same for all languages. It has also been well documented that, even within a single language community, children show great variation in their language development. These two sources of evidence of individual variation have led to a strong focus on individual differences in child language research.

Another factor is that the traditional choice of method to study a particular aspect of development may result in more or less emphasis on individual variation. Within the study of language development, there has been a history of detailed longitudinal observation of researchers' own children (Bowerman, 1973; Grégoire, 1937; Halliday, 1975; Smith, 1973). There has also been a strong tradition, characterised by Roger Brown's seminal book, *A First Language* (Brown, 1973), of carrying out a very detailed longitudinal study of a small number of children. Both methodological approaches have tended to emphasise how much individual children vary in the speed with which and the way in which they learn to talk. Interestingly, Brown's book considered the early stages of acquiring Japanese as well as English, illustrating that both the choice of methodology and the awareness of other languages served to emphasise variation in development.

These concerns with individual variation in language development have, in turn, fed into the assessment measures that researchers use to quantify the language ability of individual children. The norms for the two MacArthur-Bates Communicative Development Inventories (Fenson et al., 1990), which have become the standard instruments for determining the size and content of spoken vocabulary in children of under 30 months, show not only the mean vocabulary scores for children at a particular age but also scores that lie one standard deviation above and below the mean and so are considered to lie within the range of 'normal' development. The point of these latter values is to indicate the very wide variation in the early language development of typically developing children. The CDI has now been standardised in a number of different versions, including Italian, Spanish, British English and American Sign Language and this has facilitated the cross-linguistic comparisons that are such an important feature of research on language development.

The microgenetic method

Another, more general, approach to the study of development that emphasises individual variation and gradual change over time is the micrognenetic method (Flynn, Pine, & Lewis, 2006). A major aim of this approach is to examine change as it occurs rather than taking a snapshot of development at different ages. This is done by taking repeated measures from the same children during that period that they are undergoing change. The difference between this approach and more traditional longitudinal studies is in the collection of data at very frequent intervals. Studies of children's early language development have often adopted this approach, collecting language data at weekly or monthly intervals. Such an approach allows researchers to define the shape of change in a particular domain. They can ask whether change is gradual or abrupt and whether the shape and rate of change are the same for all children. The microgenetic method places emphasis on the importance of studying individual variation.

Flynn et al. (2006) identify three characteristics of the microgenetic method. First, observations must span a known period of change. In other words, observation should start some time before a change is expected to occur and end only after the change has been observed in all – or, at least, the great majority – of the participants. The second feature is that the density of observations should be high in comparison to the rate of change so that there are a large number of different observations around the time that change is occurring. Finally, the observations themselves are subject to detailed and fine-grained analysis to establish the processes that underpin the changes.

As Flynn et al. point out, although there are potentially huge rewards to be derived from the adoption of a microgenetic approach, there are also potential pitfalls. One is that repeated presentation of the same task may give rise to unreliable findings as children become over-practised. Another issue is that microgenetic studies are expensive in terms of the amount of time that is required for the analyses since the amount of data generated by repeated and very detailed observation can be overwhelming. Another problem can sometimes be that, to use a familiar metaphor, this approach makes it hard to see the outline of the wood because of the detailed view of each of the individual trees. In the end, it is important to give an account of change that explains the most commonly occurring patterns in relation to the range and variation of change.

In terms of the theme of this chapter, perhaps the most important point to note is that a detailed investigation of the nature and rate of developmental change in a given domain, and across a given age-span, may provide a rather different view of the processes involved than a cross-sectional comparison. This contrast is one illustration of the more general point that any account of developmental change is constrained both by the underlying theory of the nature of change and by the methodology adopted to uncover that change. It should by now be clear that the methodological choices made by a particular researcher are implicitly or explicitly influenced by the underlying model of development that is assumed.

Ethical issues in developmental psychology research

Over the past few years, there has been an increasing emphasis on ethical issues in psychological research. Needless to say, research with children calls for scrupulous consideration of these issues. The most detailed guidelines for the ethical treatment of children in psychological investigations are provided by the Society for Research in Child Development (SRCD). Full details of the guidelines can be read on the SRCD website at www.srcd.org.

Two of the most important issues covered in the SRCD guidelines are the kind of procedures that can be ethically used with children and the way in which the informed consent of participants should be obtained. As far as the first issue is concerned, the SRCD guidelines are as follows:

The investigator should use no research procedure that may harm the child either physically or psychologically. The investigator is also obligated at all times to use the least stressful research procedure whenever possible. (SRCD Ethical Standards for Research with Children; http://www.srcd.org/ethicalstandards.html)

The principle of using the least stressful research procedure in developmental psychology research is an important one but it is not always easy to decide what might prove stressful. Presumably, all researchers would agree that the infamous procedures used by Watson (Watson, 1919; Watson & Rayner, 1920) to demonstrate that young children could be conditioned to show fear of small animals are unethical and should not be used. In one such study, having established that infants did not show any natural fear of a wide range of animals, a small dog was tossed into the pram of a 6-month-old baby in order to see how she would react. Not surprisingly, the baby became terrified and subsequently showed fear not only of dogs but even to rapidly moving toy animals. The persistence of the learned fear response was tested when, at 18 months, a tame white mouse was placed on the floor nearby. The child responded by crying and rushing into her father's arms.

Other procedures may be less clearly distressing but may also be unjustified. Considerable care has to be taken that children are not subject to loss of self-esteem, embarrassment or a feeling of exclusion. The latter can be an important factor to consider where the majority of children in a group, such as a school class, take part in a study but a small minority are excluded because, for example, they have a specific learning difficulty or English as an additional language. These issues are considered at some length in the next chapter, especially in connection with Paper 1.

The principle of informed consent applies to all research in psychology in that any participant must fully understand what is involved in a study before giving agreement to take part:

The specific issue with this important principle of informed consent is that children may not be able to fully understand what they will be required to do and so they cannot give informed consent. In such a case the study can be explained to a suitable adult – such as a parent or teacher – who can then give consent on behalf of the child:

Even when informed consent has been obtained it is still very important that children have as good an understanding of what they will be asked to do as possible and they should also, if appropriate, be given an opportunity to agree or not agree to take part. They should also be allowed to withdraw from a study part way through. In the case of infant studies it is important that the investigator abandon a study if an infant shows signs of discomfort or prolonged distress.

Evaluating research studies

Although there are many different ways of carrying out research to investigate developmental change, there are a number of issues that apply to the great majority of studies, not least the ethical issues that I have just noted. Table 2.1 summarises some key questions that should be asked at each stage of reading the report of a research study.

The papers I have chosen in the following chapters use a wide variety of experimental designs and procedures that involve the collection of rather different kinds of data. In each paper, I have chosen to focus on specific issues but it is important to note that the general questions that I have listed in Table 2.1 are also relevant even though I may not have discussed them.

Table 2.1   *Some key questions to ask about a research study*

Introduction

- What have previous studies shown?
- Why is the present study different?
- How does the general methodology compare with that of previous studies?
- Are there clear hypotheses/predictions?

Participants

- Was informed consent obtained?
- Who took part in the study?
- Were there different groups?
- If so, how were they matched?
- Is the matching appropriate?
- Are there any other key subject variables that have been ignored?
- How does this sample compare with previous studies?

Design

- What is the design of this study?
- What tasks were used?
- Are they the same as those used in previous research?
- If not, how do they differ?
- Are they appropriate for the age and type of children?

Procedure

- How and where were the children tested?
- Are there any ethical issues to consider?
- What were they asked to do?
- Did they understand the tasks?
- Are there factors (e.g. language level) that might have prevented them from completing the task?

Results

- Look at the data tables and the inferential statistics
- What did the authors find?
- Was this in line with what they predicted?
- Were any findings inconsistent with the predictions?

Discussion

- Is the summary of what the authors found accurate e.g. have they claimed a significant finding where an effect was only 'approaching significance' or 'marginally significant'?
- Do they fully justify their conclusions?
- Do they relate their discussion to their original question?
- Are there other factors that may have affected the results?

3

OBSERVATIONAL METHODS

AND QUESTIONNAIRES

Observing behaviour

The two most important decisions a researcher has to make in designing an observational study are where to carry out the observation and what kind of events to observe. As with any other kind of research, the answer to these methodological questions depends on the precise questions that the researcher is attempting to answer.

Observations can be divided into those taking place in the 'field' and those that occur in controlled settings. In the former case, the observer goes into the natural environment of the group or individual who is to be observed. The aim is to see a wide range of behaviours. In the latter case, the observer controls the observational setting with a view to observing specific kinds of behaviour. In both types of observation, however, the observer will choose to concentrate on particular aspects of behaviour that will shed light on the hypothesis under investigation. These key aspects are recorded either at the time of observation (making a record of the occurrence and duration of particular events) or are derived, at a later date, from an audio or video recording.

In order to record target behaviours in a way that is both reliable and valid, it is essential to develop coding categories that are exhaustive, mutually exclusive and reliable. A set of exhaustive categories will account for all of the observations that are to be included in a study. For example, a researcher might want to know what mothers talk to young children about. There are many different ways of categorising mothers' utterances. For example, a researcher might choose to look at utterance topics such as toys, books or food. Alternatively, a researcher may be interested in whether an utterance is child-oriented or mother-oriented. In the former case, the mother takes her lead from the child in choosing what to talk about whereas, in the latter case, she does not. These two categories are, in theory, exhaustive as mothers either talk about something that responds in some way to her child or they talk about something that is not related to anything done or said by the child.

Categories should also be mutually exclusive which means that an event can be classified as falling into only one category. For example, child-initiated utterances could be sub-divided according to the kind of event that the mother was responding to. In one of my early studies (Harris, Jones & Grant 1983), I divided child-initiated utterances into five types according to the event that led the mother to begin a new conversational topic. The five kinds of event were *child vocalisation, child gaze* (where the child turns to look at a new object or event), *child action* (where the child begins a new activity) and two combined categories of child vocalisation accompanied by gaze (*voc. + gaze*) and child vocalisation accompanied by action (*voc. + action*). These five categories accounted for all of the child-initiated utterances (and so were exhaustive) and each utterance fell into only one of the categories (and so the categories were mutually exclusive). The use of the combined categories was an important part of the coding scheme since, without them, utterances involving child vocalisation accompanied by some kind of activity would have often fallen into more than one category.

The third essential feature for coding categories is that they are reliable. This means that events can be reliably assigned to a category such that two people will independently assign each event to the same category. The chances that events will be assigned to the same category will be high if each category is clearly defined (using examples of the kinds of event that occur in each category) and the person carrying out the category coding is well trained so that all coders are applying the coding scheme in the same way.

Finally, as you will see from papers in this chapter, it is important that coding is carried out by someone who does not know the specific aims of a study or anything about the participants who are being observed. This is because observations should be as objective as possible and not prejudiced by the observer's prior expectations about the behaviour of certain participants.

Field observation

In field observation, the observer chooses a location which is frequented by members of a target group and then observes a range of behaviours that occur. This kind of observation is very common in the study of animal behaviour such as Jane Goodall's pioneering study of chimpanzees (Goodall, 1986) but relatively rare in developmental psychology.

One common environment for the observation of children is the classroom. Here a researcher will usually focus on the behaviour of a single child for a set period of time, and the interactions between the target child and others in the classroom. Since it is impossible to record or analyse all aspects of behaviour, observation is sampled either by time or by event. In time sampling, all the behaviour in pre-determined categories occurring at given times is recorded for later categorisation. In event sampling, every occurrence of a given event is recorded for a set duration such as 10 minutes.

With the widespread use of video recording, observations of this kind are invariably recorded for future analysis. However, introducing a camera into a natural setting such as a classroom is often difficult since observations are most useful when children are unaware of the camera's presence. Furthermore, filming is often not of a sufficiently high quality to allow appropriate analysis unless there is good control of such factors as lighting and camera angles.

Observation in a controlled environment

Because of difficulties in collecting reliable observational data in the field, observation in developmental psychology usually takes place in a carefully controlled setting. There are three main advantages to observation in a controlled setting. First, it allows direct comparisons of the behaviour of different children since all participants in a study are observed in an identical setting in which the same kind of events occur. Secondly, because the choice of the setting limits the number of behaviours that can occur, a small number of categories of behaviour can be selected in advance and used to quantify children's responses to the situation. Finally, and perhaps most importantly, the setting for structured observation can be chosen so that particular behaviours of interest are likely to occur.

Paper 1   Assessing disruptive behaviour in young children (Hughes et al., 2002)

In Paper 1, the authors use structured observation to assess disruptive behaviour in 5-year-old children. They observed pairs of children playing a card game that was rigged in such a way that first one child and then the other experienced a losing streak. The competitive card game was chosen for observation because the authors were interested in disruptive behaviour, the idea being that losing would provoke children into negative responses. Had the authors been interested, for example, in co-operative play they would have chosen a different setting such as a task in which children worked towards a common goal. The precise features of the observational setting are very important in research because children's behaviour will vary considerably from context to context. The key is to choose a setting that will give rise to relevant behaviours for the hypothesis under investigation.

In the introduction to the paper, the authors explain the advantages of their approach in comparison to other methods. They note that many previous studies of children's disruptive behaviour have relied on reports from adults. Such reports appear to be biased both by the specific context in which an adult knows a child (home or school) and also by the adult's knowledge of the child. For this reason, the reports of parents and teachers often show little agreement. The authors advocate observation as a more direct and, hence, reliable method of assessing children's behaviour.

Field observations, in which researchers observe a child in an uncontrolled setting, can be very time consuming not least because of the amount of time that is required to analyse children's behaviour. The authors' solution was to observe children's behaviour in a carefully standardised setting that allowed direct comparisons between different children. As we have noted, their choice of setting was very specific. Two children play a card game, SNAP, rigged so both, in turn, experience a losing streak.

The idea of the SNAP paradigm is to place both children in a situation where, for part of the time, they feel frustrated and mildly stressed. Losing at SNAP is an excellent choice for this purpose as an earlier study by the same research team had shown that young children are strongly affected by losing at a competitive game (Murray, Woolgar, Cooper, & Hipwell, 2001). That study had used the rigged SNAP game with 5-year-olds to show that the losing streak affected children's self-perceptions; and it also established that there were consistent differences in behaviour between children identified as 'hard to manage' and control children who were typically developing. The previous study had also found continuities between earlier negative behaviour in the 'hard to manage' group and negative behaviour during the SNAP task. Both findings point to the utility of the SNAP paradigm as a valid way of assessing disruptive behaviour in 5-year-olds.

One possible issue of concern with the SNAP task is that it places children in a stressful situation. This raises clear ethical concerns that are discussed in the paper.

Journal of Child Psychology and Psychiatry, 2002; 43(4), 507–516

'I'm gonna beat you!' SNAP!: an observational paradigm for assessing young children's disruptive behaviour in competitive play

Claire Hughes,[1] Henna Oksanen,[2] Alan Taylor,[3] Jan Jackson,[3] Lynne Murray,[4] Avshalom Caspi,[3,5] and Terrie E. Moffitt[3,5]

[1]University of Cambridge, Uk; [2]University of Helsinki, Finland; [3]University of London, UK; [4]University of Reading, UK; [5]University of Wisconsin, USA

Research into disruptive behaviour disorders has highlighted the importance of identifying children with behavioural problems at an early age. Early onset of behavioural problems is a strong predictor of a 'life-course persistent' prognosis (Moffitt, 1993). In addition, clinical interventions are likely to be much more successful with younger children, whose problems are not as entrenched or complex as those of older children (Carey, 1997).

How should behavioural problems in young children be assessed? Most studies rely upon questionnaire ratings provided by parents or teachers, since the self-report measures used with older children or adolescents are developmentally inappropriate and direct observations are typically time-consuming, difficult to standardise, and strongly influenced by day-to-day variability in behaviour, such that they show little or no agreement with aggregate rating scales (Epstein, 1983; Hops, Davis, & Longoria, 1995; Jones, Reid, & Patterson, 1975; Stoolmiller, Eddy, & Reid, 2000). However, it is now well recognised that parent and teacher ratings of behavioural problems show only modest agreement with each other (Loeber, Green, Lahey, & Stouthamer-Loeber, 1989), raising interesting questions about context- and informant-effects. For example, findings from several studies suggest that both maternal factors such as depression (Briggs-Gowan, Carter, & Schwab-Stone, 1996; Hay et al., 1999) and transactional effects (Masten & Curtis, 2000; Patterson, Dishion, & Chamberlain, 1993) influence mother ratings of problem behaviours. Similarly, teacher ratings are likely to be influenced by the child's reputation in the school (Realmuto, August, & Hektner, 2000).

Direct observations provide a valuable means of avoiding both informant effects and influences of past transactions on how a current behaviour is interpreted. An important research challenge is therefore the design of observational techniques that can be applied in a standardised format and that are not overly time-consuming to conduct or code. In response to this challenge, in this study we report findings from a novel dyadic play scenario for assessing individual differences in disruptive behaviour. This particular play scenario was chosen because it involves a potential threat (losing a competitive game), and several prominent theoretical accounts of disruptive behaviour focus on heightened perception of/response to threat. For example, Dodge and Frame (1982) found that aggressive children showed a 'hostile attribution bias' when presented with stories involving either neutral or ambiguous actions; this bias is particularly apparent in situations that directly involve the child (Dodge & Somberg, 1987).

The paradigm used in the present study was a competitive game of SNAP, rigged to expose both players to a mildly stressful experience (a losing streak within the game). From an adult perspective, losing a game may not seem especially frustrating or threatening, but for school-aged children success or failure in competitive play is very important. This point is highlighted by recent findings from two recent experimental investigations using rigged-game designs. In the first of theses, both self-report and filmed observations of 8- to 12-year-olds in competitive play with a child actor showed that these children found the rigged situation provoking (Underwood, Hurley, Johanson, & Mosley, 1999). Moreover, as Underwood et al. (1999) discuss, more overt displays of anxiety or frustration might be expected from children in competition with a playmate rather than an unfamiliar peer.

In the second investigation, Murray, Woolgar, Cooper, and Hipwell (2001) developed the SNAP game (used in the present study) to examine depressive cognitions among 5-year-old children of depressed mothers. As predicted, children of depressed mothers expressed significantly more hopelessness, pessimism and low self-worth during the losing streak of the game than their typically developing peers. These findings challenge previous studies of young children that failed to show associations between depressive risk status and children's self-reported depressive cognitions (Goodman, Brogan, Lynch, & Fielding, 1993; Nolen-Hoeksema, Girgus, & Seligman, 1986; Rholes, Blackwell, Jordan, & Walters, 1980). This contrast suggests that eliciting spontaneous responses within a salient and ecologically realistic context may provide a sensitive index of problems linked to young children's perception of threat.

The above findings suggest that through its inclusion of a salient and ecologically realistic threat the SNAP game might provide an ideal context for observing individual differences in disruptive behaviour. Hughes, Cutting, and Dunn (2001) explored this possibility in a longitudinal study of 40 'hard to manage' children. Each child was filmed playing the game with a friend at age five, and again at age seven. Compared with a typically developing control group, the 'hard to manage' group showed higher rates of negative behaviour at both time-points. In addition, individual differences in negative behaviour towards peers were stable between ages five and seven, and correlated ($r > .34$, $p < .05$ at both time-points) with earlier individual differences in violent pretend play (Dunn & Hughes, 2001). Together, these findings suggest that the SNAP game is a valid and reliable context in which to observe the social-interaction problems of young disruptive children.

However, a number of questions remain unanswered. For example, are there gender differences in children's disruptive behaviour in the SNAP game? Do ratings of disruptive behaviour in the SNAP game agree with adult reports of externalising problems? How reliable are observational ratings of disruptive behaviour in the SNAP game? The present study (which was part of a wider research programme) addressed these questions in the following ways.

Significant contrasts between girls and boys have been reported in the prevalence, nature and severity of behavioural problems (Zahn-Waxler, 1993). However, these studies typically rely on parental reports, and parents may well evaluate the same behaviours differently for boys and girls (Condry & Condry, 1976; Stevenson-Hinde & Glover, 1996). Direct observational studies typically involve small samples (often composed exclusively of boys), and so rarely have sufficient power to examine effects of gender. Here we report findings from

800 children (200 boy-boy pairs and 200 girl-girl pairs). Our first aim was to capitalise on this large sample to establish whether ratings from this new observational paradigm confirm the gender differences in disruptive behaviour typically reported in questionnaire-based studies.

Second, the study included parent and teacher ratings of externalising behaviour, using widely used, well-validated questionnaire measures: the Child Behaviour Check-list (Achenbach, 1991a) and Teacher Report Form (Achenbach, 1991b). This enabled us to compare our ratings of negative behaviour in the specific context of competitive play with another child with adult ratings of externalising behaviour that reflect how children behave in a wide variety of situations. Assessing the agreement between these different perspectives is important for establishing the *external validity* of the SNAP measure, as well as for deciding how these different sources of information should be combined to provide a robust multi-measure index of behavioural problems in young children.

Third, before rating began, we randomly assigned data from individual children within each pair to either the main sample (S1) or the replication sample (S2) in order to assess the *replicability* of our findings. This was an important goal, since the SNAP game used in this study takes only five minutes to administer, whereas most observational studies of disruptive behaviour involve much longer sampling periods. In addition, since the present study involved 800 children it was necessary to develop a quick and simple coding system; this had the added bonus of making clinical applications of the instrument more feasible, but did raise the question of whether the simplified coding would also be reliable.

Fourth, although the SNAP paradigm has been used successfully in two previous studies (Hughes et al., 2001; Murray et al., 2001), the question of reciprocal influences between social partners has yet to be addressed. Hughes et al. (2001) found that 7-year-olds who began with a winning streak only to have victory snatched from them showed significantly more negative behaviour than those children who began by losing but later caught up with their friend; however, this effect of winning order was non-significant among 5-year-olds. Unfortunately, the composition of child dyads in their study was very variable (some 'hard to manage' children were friends with each other, while others were friends with children in the control group, or with other children). As a result of this between-dyad variation, it was not possible to explore within-dyad reciprocal influences on disruptive behaviour. In contrast, all children in the present study were filmed playing with a same-sex, twin sibling. By bringing together data from S1 and S2 it was therefore possible to examine not only the effects of winning order, but also the reciprocal influences on disruptive behaviour.

In sum, a rigged card game was used in this study to examine individual differences in 5-year-olds' disruptive responses to competitive threat. First, we asked whether boys would show more disruptive behaviour than girls in response to the threat of losing a competitive game. Our second question concerned the external validity of ratings from this rigged situation. This issue was addressed (i) by examining the correlations between ratings of disruptive behaviour on the SNAP game and parents' and teachers' ratings of externalising problems, and (ii) by assessing whether children whose questionnaire scores indicate clinically significant levels of externalising problems showed elevated levels of disruptive behaviour in the SNAP game. Third, to examine the replicability of our results, data from individual children within each pair were randomly assigned to two different samples. In the interest of space, the results from both sets of analyses will be presented together. Fourth, effects of winning order and similarities within each pair were briefly explored.

Method

Participants

Recruitment and participant characteristics

The children in this study were all taking part in a large-scale investigation of environmental influences on early development that in turn was part of a broader programme of research using an epidemiological sample of twins born in England and Wales between 1994 and 1995 (Dale et al., 1998) Data for this study were collected during home-visits to families with same-sex twins, conducted within 60 days of the children's fifth birthday (mean age = 60 months, *SD* = 1.8). The families selected for this study were the first 400 families to receive home-visits. Because all families were seen on a schedule tightly tied to the twins' fifth birthday, the first 400 families seen are not biased by having been more compliant or eager to participate than the remainder of the cohort.[1] Limited resources precluded the inclusion of all study families; one practical aim of the study was to demonstrate the validity of the SNAP paradigm in order to attract funding to extend coding to include the full sample of children.

Participants in this study included 218 monozygotic twin pairs (106 girl–girl pairs and 112 boy–boy pairs) and 182 dizygotic twin pairs (94 girl–girl pairs and 88 boy–boy pairs). To ensure independent data points and assess the replicability of our findings, individual children in each pair were randomly assigned to either 'sample 1' (S1) or 'sample 2' (S2). Since one child from each pair was a participant in either S1 or S2, the two samples were identical in age and zygosity.

Note that children were placed in girl–girl and boy–boy pairs. There were no pairings of boys with girls. This was because the children who took part in the SNAP study were recruited as part of an ongoing study of same-sex twins. The children were observed at home, playing with their twin. They were therefore very familiar with their partner in the SNAP game.

Family background

Information about parental education and occupation was collected during an interview with the mother. Note that in the UK, CSE and GCSE exams are taken at age 16 (the former are recognised to be much less challenging than the latter); A levels are taken at age 18 and are usually required for university-entry. The distribution of family ethnicity, maternal educational and head-of-household occupation for the participants is shown separately for girls and boys in Table 1. Independent sample *t*-tests showed no gender differences in ethnicity, parental education or parental occupation.

Intellectual ability

This was assessed during individual testing of each child using the vocabulary and block-design subtests from the Wechsler Pre-school and Primary Scales of Intelligence (WPPSI) (Wechsler, 1990).

> *Children taking part in the study were given two sub-tests from the WPPSI. The two tests were chosen to assess verbal intelligence (vocabulary test) and non-verbal intelligence (block design test) since children may show different levels of performance on these two aspects of intelligence. The specific reason for administering these subtests is not explained in the paper. However, it is possible that children who show disruptive behaviour may have learning difficulties. Thus it is important to show that observed differences in the SNAP task are in addition to any differences that might be explained by intellectual differences among the children.*

Behavioural questionnaire ratings

Mothers completed the CBCL (Achenbach, 1991a) during the home-visit. With parents' consent, teachers were sent the TRF (Achenbach, 1991b) by post, together with a pre-paid response envelope and a pen. In this study we focus on mother and teacher ratings of aggression, delinquency and overall externalising problems.

> *In addition to the rigged SNAP game, adult reports about the children were collected using two questionnaires, completed by their parents and teacher. The Child Behaviour Checklist (CBCL) and Teacher's Report Form (TRF) ask about a child's activities, social relations and school performance. They are designed to pick up behavioural and emotional problems. Note that parents were asked for consent before the TRF was given to their child's teacher.*

Direct observations

Materials

The rigged SNAP game was played with two decks of 40 playing cards, each showing a picture of a farm animal. Each card was numbered, so that before the game, the decks could be arranged in the correct order to ensure the rigged pattern of animal matches and mismatches for each child. In addition, an A4-sized metal picture board with a picture of two snakes (each numbered 1–10 from head to tail) was used, so that each child could move a magnetic counter along his or her snake when he or she received a matching pair of picture cards (i.e., a 'SNAP').

The use of the snake and counters ensures that children were made aware of their success or failure at SNAP. It also makes their success or failure 'public' since the two children in the game could compare the positions of the counters on each snake.

Procedures

The SNAP game was administered at the end of a three-hour home-visit. A small Sony Camcorder was mounted on a tripod in a corner of the room at the start of the visit, so that by the time the game was played, the presence of the camera was no longer intrusive. The game was used as originally described by Murray and colleagues (2001), with two minor modifications: (i) the researcher dealt cards to each child simultaneously, rather than consecutively, and (ii) magnetic counters rather than sticky stars were used to mark each child's progress in the game. These modifications were introduced to ensure the participation of children with short attention spans, and reduced the duration of the game from approximately ten down to five minutes. Note that the key feature of the SNAP game was its rigged design, which was exactly the same as in the study by Murray et al. (2001). In all but a small minority of cases, the children played the game on the floor in a quiet room with a researcher. Full instructions for the game are given in Appendix 1. Briefly, on each deal of the game the researcher simultaneously presented each child with a pair of picture cards. If a child received a matching pair he or she was allowed to move a magnetic counter one place along a racetrack – the children were told that the first to the end was the winner. The cards were rigged so that each child received a winning streak and a losing streak, so that the children were level-pegging by the end of the game, which ended in a tie, with each child being given a prize of a colouring book. Given the potential ethical concerns of exposing children to the threat of losing, it is worth noting that post-visit feedback from families showed that the children greatly enjoyed the game and hoped for another opportunity to play soon.

The counter-balancing of the winning and losing streak enabled both children to succeed overall in the SNAP game and be awarded a prize. This manipulation was an important ethical aspect of the research because parents reported that children felt positive about the game in spite of experiencing a losing streak.

Table 1 Child and family characteristics of study participants

		Boys		Girls	
		Sample 1	Sample 2	Sample 1	Sample 2
Number	N (total)	200	200	200	200
Age	Mean in months	60	60	60	60
	(SD)	(5)	(5)	(5)	(5)
Full Scale IQ	Mean	95.71	96.37	94.32	94.81
	(SD)	(14.90)	(15.90)	(13.36)	(14.78)
Aggression	Mother – mean (/40)	12.84	13.33	11.17	11.45
	(SD)	(8.28)	(8.40)	(6.94)	(7.42)
	Teacher – mean (/40)	5.68	6.12	3.39	3.77
	(SD)	(7.50)	(8.40)	(5.26)	(5.33)
Delinquency	Mother – mean (/26)	2.84	2.80	2.85	2.24
	(SD)	(2.54)	(2.54)	(2.14)	(2.08)
	Teacher – mean (/26)	1.02	1.00	0.60	0.57
	(SD)	(1.73)	(1.85)	(1.24)	(1.16)
Externalising	Mother – mean (/66)	15.68	16.13	13.52	13.69
	(SD)	(10.31)	(10.32)	(8.47)	(8.82)
	Teacher – mean (/66)	6.64	7.16	3.99	4.35
	(SD)	(8.96)	(9.95)	(6.21)	(6.09)
Disruption	SNAP rating – mean (/10)	3.94	3.75	3.16	3.11
	(SD)	(2.11)	(2.04)	(1.51)	(1.46)
Ethnicity	Caucasian	94%	94%	93.5%	93.5%
Mothers' education	Degree or higher	9.5%	9.5%	9.5%	9.5%
	No academic qualifications	33%	33%	36%	36%
Occupational status	Professional/Managerial	52.5%	52.5%	34%	34%
	Unskilled/unemployed	16%	16%	7.5%	7.5%
Family structure	Lone parents	22%	22%	19%	19%

Coding

Coding of disruptive behaviour for each individual child was made using both a global scale and an event frequency scale (each applied from videotape across the whole session). Global ratings reflected both minor and major disruptive acts. Minor acts of disruption included surreptitiously moving counters to the wrong place, interrupting the researcher, and singing while the researcher was trying to explain the game. Major disruptive acts included: grabbing the board, knocking the board over, throwing counters, trying to snatch the researcher's cards, refusing to relinquish cards, swearing or other forms of verbal aggression, hitting the playmate or storming out of the room. The criteria for each of the ratings on the 5-point global scale were as follows:

1 = child co-operative throughout the game
2 = child not fully co-operative (e.g., responded sluggishly to a request)
3 = child failed to be co-operative more than once, or at least one minor disruption
4 = child shows one overt disruptive act, or several minor disruptive acts
5 = child's disruptive behaviour results in premature game termination

There were two levels of coding of the children's behaviour during the game. Both were carried out from video recordings made during the SNAP game. The global rating was an overall assessment of the children's behaviour during the game (on a 5-point scale). Note that the authors draw a careful and well-defined distinction between major and minor disruptive acts. There was also an event rating. This considered each child's behaviour to see if he/she had broken the rules of SNAP during the course of the game. Rule-breaking was coded on a 3-point scale which distinguished between no cases of rule-breaking, a rule being broken on one or two occasions, or more frequent rule-breaking. Although the authors do not say so, the decision about where to set the category boundaries for the extent of rule-breaking would have been influenced by the distribution of rule-breaking instances. Setting the boundaries at zero, two and more than two instances suggests that most children did not break the rules very often. Thus the difference between not breaking the rules at all and breaking them once or twice was important. Where a critical event is more frequent, the boundaries will be set in a different place. The important point is that the category boundaries should reflect the overall distribution of events within the sample of participants.

The event scale indexed the frequency of rule-violations (e.g., calling 'SNAP' without having a matching pair of cards, trying to move the counter more than one square along). Note that these incidences of rule violation (coded on a 3-point scale: 1 = not present, 3 = occurred once or twice, 5 = occurred more than twice) did not contribute to global ratings of disruptive behaviour. (The 1/3/5 rating was used rather than 0/1/2 to give equal weight to the event scale and global scale.) A trained researcher (who was unaware of the children's CBCL scores) coded the child on the left-hand side of the screen for all 400 pairs, before returning to code the child on the right-hand side of the screen. All coding was done in real time, so coding time per child equalled administration time (mean = 5.5 minutes, range = 3–15 minutes). A second researcher (who was also unaware of the children's CBCL scores) independently coded 46 randomly selected children to establish reliability, all kappa values exceeded .83, indicating a good level of inter-rater agreement.

This rating of rule-breaking was carried out by an experienced researcher who did not know about the children's behaviour at home and so could not be biased by prior knowledge. In order to demonstrate that the ratings were reliable, a second researcher also coded the rule violations of 46 randomly selected children. The lowest level of agreement between the two sets of ratings was 0.83. A kappa coefficient of 0.80 or greater is considered evidence of good inter-rater agreement.

Data reduction

Global and event ratings of disruptive behaviour in the SNAP game were significantly correlated with each other ($r(399)$ = .51, .52 for samples 1 and 2 respectively, $p < .001$ for both samples). These two scales were therefore summed to create an aggregate disruptive behaviour score. To minimise distorting effects of outliers without loss of data, all outliers were set to 2 *SD* above the group mean using gender-specific means and standard deviations.

To reduce the amount of data the global rating and the event ratings were inter-correlated to see if they were measuring similar types of behaviour. Correlations were around 0.5 for both samples of children. At one level this degree of correlation might not seem high since it only accounts for 25 per cent of the variance. However, given the large sample size, the correlations were highly significant and so the authors aggregated the two scales to give an overall score for disruptive behaviour. Where scores are clearly related, as is the case here, it is common either to use only one score or to produce an overall score. This has the advantage not only of reducing the amount of statistical analysis required, and so making it easier to interpret the results, but also of reducing the chance of a Type 1 error, that is, finding a statistically significant result that has occurred by chance. (The chances of a Type 1 error increase in line with the number of statistical comparisons that are carried out.) The data were also processed to remove outlying scores, that is, scores falling more than two standard deviations above the mean. (Note that, in the original ratings, low scores indicated full co-operation/no rule-breaking and high scores indicated severe disruption/frequent rule-breaking so scores well above the mean would indicate a child with highly disruptive behaviour.) In parametric data, outlying scores can distort measures of central tendency and dispersion so it is common to remove or standardise them in some way. Here outlying scores were standardised by reducing them to two standard deviations above the mean. Note that this was done separately for boys and girls, using specific means for each group.

Questionnaire measures

Ratings of externalising behaviour were also collected during interviews with mothers and by questionnaires from teachers using the Aggression, Delinquency and Externalising (Aggression + Delinquency) subscales of the Child Behaviour Check List (CBCL) (Achenbach, 1991a) and Teacher Report Form (TRF) (Achenbach, 1991b).

Results

Descriptive statistics

Table 1 shows the mean estimated full-scale IQ (FSIQ) separately for boys and girls in each sample. Paired *t*-tests showed no sample differences in FSIQ, and independent samples *t*-tests showed no gender difference in FSIQ.

Mean mother (CBCL) and teacher (TRF) questionnaire ratings of aggression, delinquency and externalising are presented separately by gender and sample in Table 1. Paired *t*-tests showed no differences in ratings between the two samples, but a significant effect of informant. For all three scales (aggression, delinquency and externalising), mother ratings were higher than teacher ratings, in both S1 and S2 ($t(398) > 13.85$, $p < .001$ for all six comparisons). Table 1 also shows the mean ratings of disruptive behaviour on the SNAP game, by gender and sample. Paired *t*-tests showed no sample difference in mean ratings of disruption ($t(398) = 1.08$, *ns*). Independent samples *t*-tests showed no effect of winning order on mean ratings of disruption (for both S1 and S2, $t(398) = 1.10$, *ns*). Gender differences in questionnaire and observational ratings are presented in the next section.

Gender differences in disruptive behaviour

As predicted, both mothers and teachers rated boys higher than girls for aggression, delinquency and overall externalising behaviour (for mothers, in S1 $t(398) = 2.16, 2.08, 2.29$, respectively; in S2 $t(398) = 2.37, 2.40, 2.54$ respectively, $p < .05$ for all three scales in each sample for teachers, in S1 $t(398)$ = 3.52, 2.80, 3.51, respectively, in S2, $t(398)$ = 3.32, 2.73, 3.35 respectively, $p < .01$ for all three scales in each sample). SNAP ratings of disruptive behaviour were also higher for boys than for girls ($t(398)$ = 4.29, 3.58 for S1 and S2 respectively, $p < .01$ for each sample). That is, regardless of the informant, rating method and context, boys appeared more disruptive than girls. The effect size for this gender difference ranged from .20 (mothers' ratings of externalising in S1) to .37 (SNAP ratings of disruption in S1). From Cohen (1988), $r = d/\sqrt{d^2+4}$), so corresponding r^2 values ranged form .10 to .18. That is, across all rating methods, gender accounted for 10–18 per cent of the variance in disruptive behaviour.

Validity and replicability of SNAP ratings

The external validity of disruptive behaviour ratings on the SNAP game was assessed in relation to mother (CBCL) and teacher (TRF) questionnaire ratings of aggression, delinquency and overall externalising bahaviour. First we examined the correlations between these different rating scales. Was there significant agreement between observational ratings on the SNAP game and adult-reports on these well-validated questionnaires? Next, we examined whether the sub-group of children with extreme CBCL and TRF ratings of externalising behaviour were significantly more disruptive on the SNAP game than the remaining majority of children. That is, did ratings from the SNAP game support the questionnaire-based clinical cut-off? Finally, by using co-twins as a replication sample we were also able to investigate the replicability of SNAP ratings.

Agreement with questionnaire ratings

Correlations between SNAP ratings of disruptive behaviour and mother/ teacher ratings of aggression, delinquency and overall externalising behaviour are presented in Table 2. Overall, the results showed significant agreement for 10/12 correlations. However, the magnitude of these correlations was only modest ($r(399)$ ranged from .16 to .21 for teacher ratings, and from .09 to .16 for mother ratings). For each sub-sample, mother-related delinquency was the only externalising scale that did not correlate with SNAP ratings. Mean values on this scale were very low, so the lack of correlation may simply reflect the limited variance on this scale. When the effects of FSIQ were controlled, partial correlations between SNAP ratings of disruptive behaviour and teacher ratings of aggression, delinquency and externalising remained significant (at the $p < .05$ level of higher) in both S1 and S2; partial correlations between SNAP ratings of disruptive behaviour and mother ratings of aggression and externalising remained significant in S2 but fell just below significance ($p = .09$) in S1.

Table 2 *Correlates of SNAP ratings of disruptive behaviour, by sample, gender and informant*

Measure	Sample	All (n = 400)	Boys (n = 200)	Girls (n = 200)
WISC IQ	1	−.13*	−.15*	−.13
(Block & Vocabulary)	2	−.12*	−.20**	−.02
Parental occupational status	1	.07	.04	.10
(highest value)	2	.09	.11	.05
CBCL Aggression	1	.11*	.13	.01
	2	.16**	.28**	−.06
CBCL Delinquency	1	.09	.20**	.04
	2	.11	.21**	−.11
CBCL Externalising total	1	.11*	.13	.02
	2	.16**	.28**	−.07
TRF Aggression	1	.17**	.19**	.05
	2	.20**	.23**	.10
TRF Delinquency	1	.16**	.16**	.07
	2	.16**	.18*	.07
TRF Externalising total	1	.17**	.19**	.05
	2	.21**	.23**	.09

*p < .05, **p < .01.
CBCL = mother ratings; TRF = teacher ratings.

The two subscales from the WPPSI were used to calculate an overall IQ score for each child. These scores were then used to see whether there was still a significant relationship between the SNAP scores and each of the three scales of the maternal and teacher questionnaires once the common factor of IQ had been accounted for. For the teacher ratings, correlations between all three scales and the SNAP scores remained statistically significant for both samples of children. (It will be remembered that the children in this study were recruited as part of a much larger study into the development of twins. This enabled the researchers to create two comparable samples in which one member of a twin pair was placed in one sample and the co-twin in the other sample.) For the mother's ratings, there was no significant relationship between SNAP scores and delinquency ratings. The researchers attributed this to overall low ratings on this scale by mothers. Of the two remaining scales, ratings of aggression and externalising remained significant for sample 2 but not for sample 1.

Table 2 also shows the correlations between SNAP ratings of disruptive behaviour and questionnaire ratings of aggression, delinquency and externalising behaviour separately for boys and girls. These correlations appeared stronger for boys than for girls (for whom all correlations were non-significant). However, one-tailed tests using Fisher's z-transforms showed that in S1 there were no significant gender differences in the strength of these six correlations for girls and boys; while in S2, there was a significant gender difference in the strength of the correlations between SNAP ratings and all three mother (but not teacher) questionnaire ratings (z > 1.63, 1-tailed). Since questionnaire ratings are based on typical everyday behaviour, these results indicate that the SNAP game may have somewhat greater ecological validity for boys than for girls. We will return to this issue in the discussion section.

> Further analysis separated scores for girls and boys. An important gender difference emerged in that none of the correlations was significant for girls. Furthermore, in sample 1 there were no differences in the size of the correlations for girls and boys, but in sample 2 correlations with maternal ratings (but not teacher ratings) were higher for boys than for girls. It will be remembered that there were significant partial correlations between SNAP scores and mothers' ratings in sample 2 so it may be the case that these arose because of consistencies in the behaviour of boys rather than because of consistencies in the sample as a whole.

Do 'high externalisers' show high disruption on the SNAP game?

Our second approach to assessing the validity of the SNAP game was to examine whether children rated on the questionnaires as showing extreme levels of externalising problems ($\geq$ 95th per cent) obtained significantly higher SNAP ratings of disruption than did the remaining majority of children. The children in the extreme 'high externaliser' group were all rated $\geq$ 95th per cent for externalising problems (cut-off score = 17 for boys, 15 for girls) by both mothers and teachers. Table 3 shows the mean z-scores for disruption for extreme and normal groups, for each sub-sample. These means were compared using t-tests that did not assume equal variance (using natural logarithms of the z-scores to reduce skewness). A significant difference in mean SNAP ratings of disruption was found for both S1 and S2 ($t(398) = 2.09, 3.59$, $p < .05$. $p < .001$ respectively).

> The relationship between adult ratings and behaviour in the SNAP task was also considered by comparing children who had received an extreme rating on externalising by both mothers and teachers. The cut off used to identify this group of 'high externalisers' was the top 5 per cent of the sample as a whole, using separate norms for boys and girls to allow for the fact that boys scored higher than girls.

Agreement in findings from S1 and S2

Note that the data for S1 and S2 (shown in Tables 1, 2 and 3) were remarkably similar. Admittedly, S2 cannot be considered as a full replication sample for S1, since the children in each sample were related to each other. Nevertheless, the data from the two groups showed extremely similar means and distributions. In support of the *replicability* of SNAP ratings of disruptive behaviour it is worth noting that 30/32 analyses showed very similar results in both samples. (The exceptions were the correlations between SNAP ratings and CBCL aggression and externalising that were significant for boys in S2 but not S1.)

Are our findings limited by reciprocal influences between playmates?

Finally, the data from S1 and S2 were combined to examine the within-pair correlation in SNAP ratings of disruptive behaviour. This correlation ($r(398) = .24$, $p < .001$), although significant, was lower than within-pair correlations in ratings of externalising problems made by mothers or teachers ($r(398) = .53$, $.63$ respectively, $p < .001$ for both).

Table 3   Mean (gender-specific). SNAP z scores for children with extreme vs. normal ratings of externalising problems

Sample	Measure	Extreme (≥ 95th %)	Normal (< 95th %)	Group diff. T
1	x	.47	−.03	2.09*
	SD	(1.34)	(.97)	
	N	24	376	
2	x	.81	−.05	3.50**
	SD	(.84)	(.97)	
	N	22	373	

**$p < .01$; *$p < .05$.

Recall also that there was no effect of winning order on SNAP ratings of disruption. That is, within each pair the SNAP paradigm is equally sensitive to disruptive behaviour in both children (who necessarily experienced different winning orders).[2] Taken together, these findings suggest that reciprocal influences on the SNAP game are modest, and do not limit the validity of individual-based ratings from this observational paradigm.

The final part of the analysis considered whether the behaviour of an individual child during the SNAP game had been affected by the behaviour of the other child in the pair. This is always an important question to ask in any analysis of behaviour within a dyad. The way that one member of a dyad behaves will inevitably affect the behaviour of the other dyad member so it is good practice to consider the independent contribution made by each partner. In this study, the correlation of SNAP ratings of behaviour within pairs was compared with the within-pair correlations of mother and teacher ratings of externalising behaviour. The SNAP correlation was lower than that for both ratings and, from this, the authors conclude that children were behaving independently during the game. They note that the design of the SNAP procedure, in which first one child was successful and then the other, made it more likely that the behaviour of the two children in a pair would be independent since, at any one time, one child was winning and the other losing.

Discussion

The focus of this study was a new technique for observing disruptive behaviour, involving a rigged competitive game of SNAP. Previous work (Hughes et al., 2001) with the SNAP game revealed group differences in disruptive behaviour between young 'hard to manage' children (all ≥ 90th per cent for symptoms of attention-deficit hyperactivity disorder – ADHD) and their typically developing peers (all < 50th per cent for ADHD symptoms). These differences were stable from age four to age seven, supporting the reliability of this observational paradigm. The present study extends this preliminary finding in several ways.

First, the participants in this study were filmed playing with a twin sibling at home, rather than with a friend at school. Thus the observations differed in both situational context and in social partners, providing a useful test of the *generalisability* of findings from the SNAP game. Second, this study involved a much larger and more representative sample; in addition, co-twins were allocated to two separate sub-samples, to provide an internal replication study. The data reported in this study therefore also support the *replicability* of findings form the SNAP game. Third, this study included concurrent parent and teacher ratings on standardised questionnaire measures of externalising problems. These mother and teacher ratings showed modest but significant correlations with SNAP ratings of disruptive behaviour (even when the effects of IQ were controlled), supporting the *external validity* of the SNAP game. Fourth, this study showed significant contrasts in SNAP ratings of disruptive behaviour between children with extreme (≥ 95th per cent) scores for externalising problems and the remaining majority of children. Compared with Hughes et al's (2001) study of 'hard to manage' children, the group comparisons in this study were both qualitatively different and quantitatively more conservative. The positive findings from the study therefore support the *sensitivity* of disruptive behaviour ratings form the SNAP game.

At this point it is worth considering why, although significant, correlations between direct observational ratings and adult questionnaire reports were relatively modest. Since previous studies indicate that both assessment methods are reliable, the most obvious explanation for this modest correlation is that the SNAP paradigm assesses disruptive behaviour within a specific context (competitive play with another child) at a specific time, whereas questionnaires such as the CBCL provide global ratings of everyday behaviour across a range of contexts and a time-frame of months rather than minutes. Although, as discussed in the introduction, the SNAP game provides a window onto children's behaviour in a highly salient context, numerous previous studies have highlighted both the context-specificity (Gardner, 2000; Hops et al., 1995; Stoolmiller et al., 2000) and day-to-day variability (Jones et al., 1975;

Stoolmiller et al., 2000) of disruptive behaviour. As a result, only a modest agreement with global questionnaire ratings can be expected, since each method assesses different facets of an underlying behavioural disposition (Epstein, 1983). In view of this long history of observational measures of disruptive behaviour failing validity checks, we believe that the significant correlations between SNAP ratings and adult questionnaire scores (especially teacher scores) are very encouraging.

A second extension to previous research with the SNAP paradigm comes from the fact that this study's large sample size enabled effects of gender to be explored. Significant gender differences were obtained from all three informants: parent and teacher questionnaire ratings of externalising behaviours, and researchers' direct observational ratings of disruptive behaviour in the SNAP game. Power analysis showed that gender accounted for 10–18 per cent of the variance in disruptive behaviour – this is somewhat larger than the effect sizes of gender that are typically reported in studies that adopt a traditional individual differences framework. This finding confirms Maccoby's (1998) view that gender differences become more striking when viewed through the lens of *child-child interactions*.

Note that each child in this study was filmed playing with a same-age, same-sex sibling. Evidence from several studies of a marked gender divergence in play-styles is therefore relevant. Compared with girls, boys' play is more competitive, and more often on the edge of aggression (Charlesworth & Dzur, 1987; Flannery & Watson, 1993; Smith & Boulton, 1990), while boys' speech is more power assertive (Leaper, 1991; Miller, Danaher, & Forbes, 1986). Thus the fact that only same-sex pairs were involved in this study may have heightened the observed gender difference in disruptive behaviour. Further work with mixed-sex pairs playing the SNAP game is needed to explore this possibility properly.

Gender differences have also been reported in children's relationships with adults. As toddlers, boys have been shown to be more likely than girls to ignore mothers' initial low-key remonstrances, so that mothers become more likely to resort to more forceful methods of control (Minton, Kagan, & Levine, 1971). Similar findings have been obtained in studies of adult-child interactions in nurseries (Fagot, Hagan, Leinbach, & Kronsberg, 1985) and in the first year of school (Grant, 1985). An adult researcher administered the SNAP game, and many of the examples of 'minor disruption' involved acts that were directed towards this adult (e.g., interrupting the researcher or trying to snatch the researcher's cards). To our knowledge, the extent to which contrasting attitudes and/or responsiveness to adults can explain gender differences in disruptive behaviour has not been investigated, but is an interesting avenue for future research in this field.

In addition, the competitive threat within the SNAP game (and the possibility of rule-breaking) may have been especially arousing for boys. Thorne and Luria (1986, cited in Maccoby (1998)) found that, unlike girls, boys show great excitement in rule-breaking, while Eisenberg, Fabes, Nyman, Bernzweig, and Pinuelas (1994) found that boys became more aroused than girls when watching a film that contained an element of threat. Boys' positive enjoyment of this kind of arousal has been posited as one factor contributing to early gender segregation in peer interactions (Maccoby, 1998), and so it may also be that the SNAP game was not only more exciting for boys, but also more representative of boys' everyday social interactions. This hypothesis is supported by the stronger agreement of SNAP ratings with adult ratings for boys than for girls (although this gender difference was only statistically significant for mother ratings in S2, and may simply reflect the greater variance in boys' ratings). In support of this view, careful naturalistic observations suggest that for *both* boys and girls, individual differences in response to arousing or stressful situations are valuable, since 'even by preschool age individual differences in children styles of regulating themselves ... are related to their everyday anger-related behaviours' (Eisenberg et al., 1994, p. 126).

Finally, it should also be noted that whilst the present coding system focused on male-relevant behaviours, the SNAP game is very versatile, and could equally well be applied to assess female-relevant behaviours. This point is clearly demonstrated by Murray et al.'s (2001) original use of the SNAP game to study childhood vulnerability to depression.

Taken together, the data presented in this study confirm that the SNAP game is a potentially valuable supplement to more standard questionnaire methods of assessing disruptive behaviour, as it has been shown to be for assessing depressive cognitions in young children (Murray et al., 2001). In particular, our data suggest that the adapted SNAP game is not only simple to administer and code, but also yields direct ratings of disruptive behaviour that are reliable, show significant agreement with adult questionnaire reports, and are sensitive to both gender differences and the contrast between children showing clinically significant vs. normal levels of disruptive behaviour.

Although the findings from this study are encouraging for other researchers investigating disruptive behaviour in young children, more work is needed to establish fully the reliability of the SNAP paradigm. Given the rigged nature of the game, assessing short-term test-retest reliability is likely to be problematic. However, in our future research we hope to assess the long-term predictive validity of SNAP ratings. The current data all derive from the age-five phase of this research programme; the age-seven phase is now well under way; this will enable us to analyse the SNAP paradigm's effectiveness in predicting ratings of disruptive behaviour across a two-year interval. In particular, we hope to ascertain the extent to which age-five disruptive-behaviour ratings from the SNAP game and from the CBCL/TRF predict unique or overlapping variance in disruptive behaviour at age seven. More long-term research plans with this sample include an evaluation of how well the SNAP game predicts other outcome measures such as psychiatric referral and juvenile delinquency (cf., Patterson & Forgatch, 1995). Other possible future directions require a new sample; these include comparisons of mixed-sex vs. same-sex pairs; validation of the SNAP paradigm against more traditional approaches involving longer time frames for observing disruptive behaviour; and assessing the SNAP game as a tool for assessing improvements following intervention.

Acknowledgements

The Medical Research Council funded this study. We would like to extend warm thanks to all parents, children and teachers who participated in this study.

Appendix 1
Instructions for the (revised) SNAP game

The game is conducted with two children (A and B) sitting side by side and the researcher opposite (either on the floor, or at a table), and is introduced as follows.

'Have you ever played a game called SNAP! before? Well, we're going to play a game a bit like SNAP, using these special snakes. This one is for you (A) and this one is for you (B). I'm going to give you each two cards with pictures of farm animals.' To A: 'If your cards have the same animal on them, I want you to say 'SNAP!!' To B: 'And if your cards are the same, you can say 'SNAP!!' too!' To both: 'When you get a snap, you can move your magnet ONE place along the snake.' (Give a magnet to each child.) 'NO CHEATING!! Move your magnet one place along each time you get a SNAP. The winner is the first to get to Number 10, and will get a special prize. OK, do you understand what to do? Let's have a practice first without the magnets. First I'll give two to (B). That's right, they're a SNAP. Now, in the proper game, you'd move your magnet one place, wouldn't you? Now it's (A)'s turn. Oh, so they're not the same, so you wouldn't say SNAP, would you?'

The test-phase begins when both children understand the rules of the game. On each deal of the test phase, the cards are dealt simultaneously to Child A and Child B.[3] The researcher should encourage the children to see the game as a race (e.g., by occasionally asking *'Who's going to win?'*), but should also look out for cheating (e.g., surreptitious movements of the children's counter). The cards were prearranged so that Child A won trials 1, 2, 3, 4, 6, 7, 8, 16 and 18, child B won the practice trial and trials 5, 9, 10, 11, 12, 13, 14, 15 and 17, and both children got a SNAP on the 19th (final) deal, and so emerged as joint winners.

1 Post-hoc tests comparing the 400 families in this study with the remaining 718 families showed no sample difference in ethnic background (c2 (9,1116) = 14.92, ns, 94% White in this study vs. 89% in the remaining sample) or maternal age (t(1116) = .30, ns). However, there was a non-significant trend for mothers of children in this study to have fewer educational qualifications than mothers in the remaining sample (t(1116) = 1.72, p = .09). The mothers of children in this study also showed significantly lower reading scores on the WRAT (Wide Range Achievement Test) (Wilkinson, 1993) than mothers in the remaining sample (t(1116) = 2.72, p < .01).

2 This conclusion may not hold true for all age-groups, since in a previous study Hughes et al. (2001) found no effect of winning order in 5-year-olds, but a significant effect when the children played the game again at age 7.

3 In Murray et al. (2001), the cards were dealt to the two children consecutively (except for the final deal), and progress along the snake was marked by sticky stars.

The authors raise a number of pertinent issues in their discussion. They begin by discussing the reliability of the SNAP paradigm as a measure of children's disruptive behaviour. They then go on to consider a number of other key issues. One is the difference between a situation-specific assessment of behaviour, such as the SNAP task, and the ratings made by a familiar adult which take into account behaviour over time and across a range of situations. The consistency between children's behaviour in the SNAP task and the adult ratings is, as the authors say, 'very encouraging'.

Another issue discussed by the authors is the importance of gender as a factor in interactions between two children. This is an aspect of social interaction that has received increasing attention in recent years (Leman, Ahmed, & Ozarow, 2005) and it is quite clear that boys and girls behave differently when they are in same sex and opposite sex pairs. The authors also raise the possibility that there may have been gender differences in the way that girls and boys responded to the competitive SNAP game.

Longitudinal observation in a controlled environment

Paper 2   Effects of mother's postnatal depression on infant development (Milgrom, Westley & Gemmill, 2004)

Paper 2 also uses observation in a controlled environment, in conjunction with other measures, to investigate how postnatal depression (PND) in a mother can affect her infant's development. One important feature of this study is that it is longitudinal. Babies of depressed and non-depressed mothers were recruited for the study in the first weeks of life. Then mothers and babies were followed up at intervals until the infants were 42 months old. As the authors explain, while it is clear that there are links between postnatal depression and infant development, it is less clear why or how these links come about.

Mothers who suffer from depression have been shown to interact with their infants in a less positive way than non-depressed mothers and it has been argued this has a direct effect on the cognitive and emotional development of their infants. However, as we have already seen in Paper 1, the behaviour of one member of a dyad can directly affect the behaviour of the other member so the contribution of each has to be carefully teased apart.

Teasing apart the interactions of mothers and infants is especially difficult for two reasons. First, each mother–infant pair has a long history of inter-action so the pattern of interaction at any one time will be the product of many previous interactions. Secondly, mothers and infants share both their environment and their genes in common so it is possible, for example, that a mother who is vulnerable to depression may have a child who is different in some way from the child of a mother who is not vulnerable to depression; and it may be that this genetic difference, at least in part, gives rise to observed differences in development rather than the mother's style of interaction.

A longitudinal study can provide an excellent opportunity to tease apart patterns of cause and effect in development and to distinguish the contri-butions of each partner. It is important to remember, however, that very careful use of inferential statistics is required to ensure that these patterns are interpreted in the most appropriate way.

Infant Behavior & Development, 2004, 27, 443–454

The mediating role of maternal responsiveness in some longer term effects of postnatal depression on infant development

Jeannette Milgrom [a,b], Doreen T. Westley[a], Alam W. Gemmill[a]

[a]Parent-Infant Research Institute, Department of Clinical and Health Psychology, Heidelberg Repatriation Hospital, 300 Waterdale Road, Heidelberg West, Vic. 3081, Australia
[b]Department of Psychology, School of Behavioural Science, University of Melbourne, Melbourne, Vic. 3010, Australia

1. Introduction

Postnatal depression (PND) affects around 10 per cent of all mothers. During PND, women suffer a cluster of depressive symptoms over extended periods (weeks, months or sometimes years: O'Hara & Zekoski, 1988).

The detrimental effects of PND on child development have been detailed in several small longitudinal studies (see Cooper & Murray, 1997; Milgrom, Martin, & Negri, 1999; Murray & Cooper, 1997). Meta analyses of the available published data have found small but significant effects of PND on both emotional and cognitive child outcomes at one year of age (e.g. Beck, 1998). For example, Lyons-Ruth, Zoll, Connell, and Grunebaum (1986) reported lower scores on standardized scales of mental and motor development in infants of depressed mothers. Other researchers have recorded behavioural and social adjustment difficulties up to the fifth year of life including children's behaviour towards their mothers, the presence of behavioural disturbance at home and the social patterning of play at school (Murray et al., 1999). The effects of PND may even persist into later childhood, such that 11-year-old schoolchildren whose mothers were depressed three months postpartum have been found to have lowered IQs, more attentional problems and greater difficulty with mathematical reasoning (Hay et al., 2001).

How might these effects be mediated? One strong possibility is via impairment of the early mother–infant interaction (Murray, Cooper, Wilson, & Romaniuk, 2003). Depressed mothers speak less, are less responsive, present with a 'flat' affect and express more negative emotions (Frankel & Harman, 1996; Righetti-Veltema, Conne-Perreard, Bousquet, & Manzano, 2002). Exposure to non-optimal maternal interactive behaviour may interfere not only with information processing abilities but also with the capacity to develop behavioural self-control (Tronick & Weinberg, 1997).

Recently, Cicchetti, Rogosch, and Toth (2000) reported the efficacy of a preventative psychotherapeutic intervention aimed specifically at improving the early mother–child relationship in terms of positive interaction and maternal affect. By improving these aspects of the interaction, the negative impact of PND on infant IQ was abolished. This result is consistent with the idea that impaired mother–infant interaction mediates PND's effects on cognitive development. However, a non-causal correlation between impaired mother–infant interaction and impaired child development could arise if both are (independently) correlated with PND.

Furthermore, research has consistently found a strong association between maternal depression and infant temperament (e.g. McMahon, Barnett, Kowalenko, Tennant, & Don, 2001). It has been reported that aspects of neonatal temperament can influence maternal mood and maternal interaction style (e.g. Murray, Stanley, Hooper, King, & Fiori-Cowley, 1996; see meta-analysis by Beck, 1996). Conversely, others have found that maternal depression, child-rearing practices and early life events can themselves affect aspects of child temperament (e.g. de Vries & Sameroff, 1984; Sugawara, Kitamura, Toda, & Shima, 1999).

In this paper we present an empirical test of the hypothesis that maternal responsiveness in early infancy is the primary mediator between maternal depression and specific infant developmental outcomes, namely cognitive functioning and temperament at 42 months of age. This explicit mediational model is summarized by the path diagram in Fig. 1, where *a* and *b* represent the path coefficients of interest. For simplicity, all other direct, additive and multiplicative effects of depression on IQ are here subsumed in the path coefficient labeled *c*.

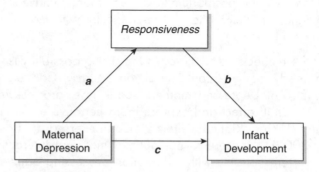

Figure 1   *Path diagram of mediation hypothesis*

Baron and Kenny (1986) have detailed the methodological requirements for identifying mediator variables in psychological data. The logic of the method relies on estimating the relationships among a series of regression coefficients. First, the potential mediator must be shown to depend on the underlying causal factor of interest (in this case, PND). Next, the causal factor must successfully predict the outcome variable (child developmental measures). Last, the variance in the outcome variable ascribable to the causal factor must be significantly reduced by inclusion of the mediating variable in the statistical model. This approach has been used successfully to test models of father–child attachment (Lundy, 2002) and has been systematized in a formal statistical test by Sobel (1982).

mediating variable it is first necessary to show, using regression analysis, that maternal depression is directly linked to maternal responsiveness. This means that maternal depression scores statistically predict maternal responsiveness or, in other words, mothers who are depressed are less responsive in interaction with their infants than those who are not depressed. The next stage is to show that the underlying causal variable (maternal depression) directly affects infant development, again using regression analysis. The final stage is to show that infant development is better predicted by the inclusion of responsiveness as well as depression as predictor variables.

2. Method

2.1 Participants

Forty, depressed, recently delivered mothers were recruited while being treated as inpatients at mother–baby psychiatric units in Victoria, Australia. A control group of 48 well mothers was recruited from community health centres in metropolitan Melbourne. Recruits came from a broad socio–geographic range. All participants were volunteers competent to give signed consent, which was obtained at the time of enrolment.

Note that written consent from all participants was given. Later on in the paper, the authors note that mothers in the depressed group were moderately depressed. Had they been severely depressed, it is arguable that they could not have given informed consent. At the time of recruitment, the mothers who were characterised as 'depressed' and their babies were inpatients in a mother-baby psychiatric unit. By the time the first observations took place, when the infants were 6 months old, the mothers were no longer being treated in the unit.

Infants were aged on average 15.8 weeks old ($SD = 7.1$) at the time of enrolment. Women were included in the 'Depressed' group if they had been diagnosed with a major depressive disorder by a psychiatrist when admitted at the relevant mother–baby unit. At enrolment and again when their infants were 6, 12, 24, and 42 months of age, all participants were assessed using the Hamilton Depression Rating Scale (HDRS; Hamilton, 1976).

2.2 Maternal responsiveness

Mother–infant interactions were observed subsequent to the acute depressive episode, when children were 6 months old. Maternal responsiveness was rated by a trained research assistant (RA) using a measure adapted by Milgrom and Burn (1988) from rating scales by Censullo, Lester, and Hoffman (1985) and by Brazelton, Koslowski, and Main (1974).

The RA was trained by watching 12h of tape from previous studies until 84 to 92 per cent inter-rater agreement with the author of the scale was consistently achieved. Maternal responsiveness is defined as the mothers' sensitivity in responding to infants' cues, i.e. if the infant is distressed the mother will soothe the infant.

Before coding the responsiveness of the mothers in the study, the research assistant carried out coding on 12 hours of videotape to the point where her coding was in high agreement with the author of the scale. Note that this is a different way of establishing coding reliability from that used in Paper 1 where a sample of videotapes was independently coded by a second rater and then agreement calculated. Arguably, checking inter-rater agreement by a second independent coding of the actual videotapes used in the study is a more robust way to establish coding reliability since it can be more or less difficult to code behaviour in particular studies according to the quality of the video recording and the visibility of the behaviours in question.

The higher the score the more frequently the mother responds to minimal verbal cues and is very sensitive to non-verbal messages. Responsiveness was rated for frequency of occurrence (0, < 30 per cent of the time; 1, 30–60 per cent of the time, and 2, > 60 per cent of the time).

Responsiveness was rated on a 3-point scale according to how often the mother responded to infant cues. As this measure is a key part of the research it is surprising that relatively little detail is given about the rating procedure. The reference for the full rating procedure is to an unpublished thesis and so not easily accessible. It is very important, in presenting the findings from a study using ratings, to describe the categories used in detail as in Paper 1.

Five, three-minute interactions were videotaped when infants were awake and alert. The same toys were used for each play session. Mothers were asked to 'play with your baby as you would normally at home'. The dyad engaged in the play session for a few minutes prior to filming, to help them feel at ease. Efforts were made to focus the video camera on the faces of mothers and babies during the interaction, while keeping the play activity in frame.

2.3 Infant outcome measures

2.3.1 Temperament

The Short Temperament Scale for Infants (STSI) and Short Temperament Scale for Toddlers (STST) are 30-item, parent-completed questionnaires eliciting information on infant temperament (Prior, Sanson, Smart, & Oberklaid, 2000). The STSI is intended for infants under 1-year-old and the STST for toddlers. They are based on factor analyses of the Revised Infant Temperament Questionnaire and the Toddler Temperament Scale, respectively (Carey & McDevitt, 1978; Fullard, McDevitt, & Carey 1984). The 30 items are averaged, generating slightly different, but overlapping, sets of subscales for the two instruments. These include approach; co-operation-manageability; persistence; rhythmicity; distractibility; irritability; and reactivity.

A global scale of child temperament, the Easy-Difficult Scale, calculated from those subscales common to the STSI and STST, was used here. The STST and STSI were administered at enrolment and at 12,24 and 42 months of age.

> The hypothesis under investigation refers to maternal responsiveness to young infants (that is, at 6 months) in relation to infant cognitive functioning and temperament three years later. The measures of cognitive functioning (WPPSI-R and Early Screening Profiles) were only obtained once, when the children were 42 months old. This is in line with the hypothesis. However, the temperament measures were collected on three different occasions (when infants were aged 12, 24 and 42 months). The authors do not explain why they did this although they also collected data on maternal depression at the same sessions. Both infant temperament and maternal depression might be expected to change over time and to be mutually influential. However, it is perhaps surprising that the authors did not also assess maternal responsiveness at these ages since, if their hypothesis is correct, responsiveness might also be expected to vary.

2.3.2 Infant IQ

The Wechsler Preschool Primary Scale of Intelligence (Revised) assesses intelligence in children aged 3 to 7 years (WPPSI-R; Wechsler, 1989). The WPPSI-R yields a Performance IQ, Verbal IQ and Full Scale IQ, has a reliability of 0.63-0.89 at 3.5 years and has good construct validity (Wechsler, 1989). A shortened form of the WPPSI-R, including seven, key, verbal and performance sub-tests, was administered at 42 months of age.

2.3.3 Infant cognition

The Early Screening Profiles (ESP) measure cognitive and language development in young children (Harrison et al., 1990). The Cognitive/Language Profile was used here, composed of 78 items yielding four sub-tests: visual discrimination; logical relations; verbal concepts; and basic school skills. Visual discrimination and logical relations make up the Cognitive Sub-scale and verbal concepts and basic school skills combine to form the Language Sub-scale.

2.3.4 Statistical analysis

Data for the temperament scales were incomplete because not all mothers were seen on each of the planned three occasions. The authors dealt with these missing data by assuming that scores from a missing session remained unchanged since the previous point at which the temperament scale had been completed. In a longitudinal study, the most appropriate way to estimate the value of missing data will depend on what is being measured. In this case, the underlying assumption is that temperament will be stable over time and so an earlier score can be used to estimate a later, missing score. A different assumption is required where a measure is expected to change over time, as is the case for any measure of children's competence (such as vocabulary knowledge) where children would be expected to score more highly with age.

Participant demographics were explored using χ^2 tests (for frequency data) and t-tests. Analysis of Variance (ANOVA) was used to test the null hypothesis of no difference between group means. The assumption of normality was confirmed graphically and by Kolmogorov–Smirnov goodness-of-fit tests. Where data were non-normally distributed, non-parametric methods were employed. In repeated-measures ANOVAs, involving STST and STSI data, missing values due to dropout were dealt with by *last-value-carried-forward*, a standard *intention-to-treat* imputation technique, and by then conducting these same ANOVAs for a second time, using only complete data, without imputation of missing values. Since the results of significance testing were qualitatively the same, and our conclusions unchanged using both methods, for ease of graphical and tabular interpretation, we report the latter analyses here.

In analysing the putative mediating effect of maternal responsiveness on Full infant IQ, we applied the test for identifying mediating variables given by Sobel (1982), deriving a z score for the path *ab* thus:

$$z = \frac{ab}{\sqrt{b^2 s_a^2 + a^2 s_b^2}}$$

Regression coefficients and their standard errors were assessed by Ordinary Least Squares (OLS) regression. We estimated the path coefficients, *a* and *b*, along with their respective standard errors, s_a and s_b, as follows. First, maternal responsiveness at six months was regressed on initial HDRS depression scores, yielding our empirical estimate of *a*. Next, 42-month Full IQ (WPPSI-R) scores were fitted as the dependent variable in a multiple regression model with initial HDRS scores and 6-month responsiveness scores as the two independent variables (giving the unstandardised regression coefficient of HDRS scores as our estimate of *b*). These estimates and their standard errors were substituted into Eq. (1).

Statistical computations were executed in SPSS version 11.5, by hand, and using the online software at http://www.quantrm2.psy.ohio-state.edu/kris/sobel/sobel.htm developed by Preacher & Leonardelli. Not all items on all psychometric questionnaires were completed by all participants at all time-points. Thus, reported sample sizes differ between some measures. Significance levels were set $\alpha = 0.05$.

> *The first stage in the analysis was to compute the relationship between maternal depression scores and maternal responsiveness (path (a) in Figure 1). Then a multiple regression was carried out in which both maternal depression and maternal responsiveness scores were entered as the predictor variables and WPPSI-R scores as the predictor variable. This gave the value of path (b) in Figure 1. Using the formula shown in the paper, a value was computed for the combined path (ab), that is maternal depression ⇒ maternal responsiveness ⇒ infant cognition. The prediction was that this path would provide the statistically strongest prediction of infant cognition.*

3. Results

3.1. Participants

Demographic data from the two groups displayed very close similarity. The mean age of mothers was depressed = 30.4 years (range 19–39); non-depressed = 31.1 years (range 20–38). Depressed and non-depressed mothers had virtually identical years of schooling (12.3 and 12.7, respectively). Infant sex ratios in both groups were very close to 1:1. Forty per cent of depressed mothers and 35 per cent of non-depressed mothers had other children. No significant differences existed between the two groups on any of these variables when assessed by χ^2 and *t*-tests ($p > 0.05$ in all four cases).

3.2. Attrition rates

Dropout rates were similar in both groups (Table 1). Of the original 88 participants enrolled, seven left the study before their child reached 12 months of age (five depressed, two control), five left after 12 months (two depressed and three control) and a further 20 dropped out after 24 months of age (10 depressed and 10 control). Thus, 23 depressed and 33 control mothers stayed in the study until 42 months making 56 'completers' in total, 65 per cent of those originally enrolled. Non-completers did not differ from

Table 1   Participant flow and timing of dropouts

Time-point	Non-depressed	Depressed	Total
Enrolment (15.8 weeks)	48	40	88
12 months	46	35	81
24 months	43	33	76
42 months	33	23	56
Non-completers	15	17	32

Table 2   Hamilton Depression Rating Scale (HDRS) scores

Time-point	Non-depressed (S.E.)	Depressed (S.E.)
Enrolment (15.8 weeks)	3.19 (2.98)	12.81 (6.74)
12 months	3.57 (3.47)	6.87 (6.08)
24 months	2.58 (2.68)	5.79 (6.42)
42 months	3.03 (3.58)	8.09 (7.63)

completers on initial HDRS scores ($p > 0.05$) or STSI scores ($p > 0.05$) and this was true of subsequent time-points.

There was a marked decrease in the mean score of depressed mothers on the Hamilton Depression Rating Scale from initial assessment at around six months to the second assessment at 12 months. Since these initial scores were used to test the prediction about the mediating effect of maternal responsiveness this may have some bearing on the results. However, the depression scores of mothers in the depressed group remained higher than scores of non-depressed mothers for the duration of the study. Note that the authors used Bonferroni corrections to adjust the alpha level for their statistical comparisons. This means that the alpha level of 0.05, which is used as the standard criterion for determining significance in psychological research, was divided by the number of comparisons being made within the same data set. Here there were four comparisons of maternal depression scores and so 0.05 was divided by 4 to give 0.0125. Thus a comparison had to generate a p value equal to or less than 0.0125 in order for an effect to be considered statistically significant.

3.3 Maternal depression

HDRS scores are given in Table 2. Initial HDRS scores among the depressed group fell in the range usually considered to reflect 'moderately' depressed mood and this is to be expected as therapeutic intervention was already underway for most of these inpatients by the time they were enrolled into the study. Presumably HDRS scores in this group would have been higher at the time of admission. The initial difference of 9.7 points [$F (1,86) = 82.3$, $p < 0.001$] narrowed by 12 months and then remained more or less stable. Despite this, HDRS scores in the two groups were significantly different at all time points, after Bonferonni adjustment of the experiment-wise Type 1 error rate to account for multiple testing ($p < 0.0125$ in all cases).

3.4 Maternal responsiveness

Responsiveness data were non-normally distributed and were analysed by Mann–Whitney U tests. The mean maternal responsiveness scores at six months postpartum (S.D. in parentheses) for each group were as follows. Depressed mothers, male infants: 1.42 (0.52); depressed mothers, female infants: 1.49 (0.48); non-depressed mothers, male infants: 1.77 (0.32); non-depressed mothers, female infants: 1.64 (0.49). Responsiveness scores differed between the depressed and non-depressed groups ($p = 0.024$), but not between the sexes ($p > 0.05$).

3.5 Infant outcome measures

The STST/STSI Easy-Difficult Scale revealed an enduring difference between the two groups over time (Fig. 2), but no differential effect of time with depressive status [main effect of depression: $F(1,34) = 5.7$, $p = 0.022$; Time × Depression interaction: ns]. Maternal 6-month responsiveness scores did not correlate with Easy-Difficult Scale scores at any time point.

Table 3 shows those WPPSI-R sub-tests that were significantly different ($p < 0.05$) between the two groups, as well as the average IQ scores at 42 months of age. Infant gender and maternal depressive status were fitted as independent factors in a two-way ANOVA of Full Scale IQ scores. Children of depressed and non-depressed mothers differed neither on Verbal IQ nor on Performance IQ ($p > 0.1$ in both cases) but did differ significantly on Full IQ score.

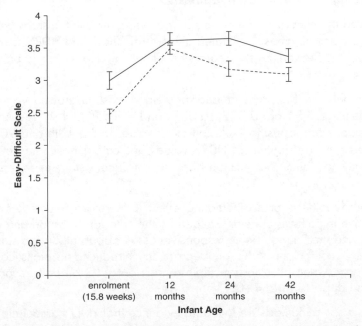

Figure 2   *Easy-Difficult Scale (STSI/STST) scores from six to 42 months of age (± 1S.E.). Solid line: depressed group; broken line: non-depressed group*

Male infants of depressed mothers had significantly lower Full Scale IQs than every other group of children. While children of depressed mothers had lower Full IQ scores per se, boys and girls were roughly equal on average, the statistical interaction of gender and depression arising solely from the disproportionate effect of depression on male infant IQ as depicted in Fig. 3 [main effect of gender: $F(1,50) = 0.37$, ns; main effect of depression: $F(1,50) = 5.59$, $p = 0.022$; Gender × Depression interaction: $F(1,50) = 3.99$, $p = 0.05$].

Early Screening Profile results are shown in Table 4. The overall Cognitive/Language Profile differed significantly between children of depressed and non-depressed mothers, as did language abilities.

Table 3   Infant IQ (WPPSI-R) scores and sub-test results at 42 months

WPPSI-R item	Depressed (S.E.)	Non-depressed (S.E.)
Geometric design*	7.39 (0.33)	8.39 (0.5)
Arithmetic*	11.09 (0.37)	12.26 (0.43)
Verbal IQ	107.35 (2.99)	113.16 (2.1)
Performance IQ	106.52 (1.9)	110.41 (2.03)
Full IQ*	106.56 (2.05)	113.16 (2.1)

Note: Only those sub-tests showing significant differences on univariate tests are tabulated here.
*$p < 0.05$

3.6 Testing the mediation hypothesis

We tested the mediation hypothesis by assessing the relationships between the child outcome measures, maternal responsiveness and HDRS scores, as described in Section 2. The regression of IQ on depression is plotted in Figure 4.

OLS models of the paths a and b yielded unstandardised regression coefficients (± S.E.) of $-0.022(\pm 0.007)$ and $+ 16.8 (\pm 4.9)$, respectively. These slopes are robust to exclusion of all values in the 10th and 90th percentiles of the distribution of HDRS values, indicating no undue leverage from outlying points. Substitution of these empirical estimates into Eq. (1) gives $z = -2.32$, $p = 0.02$.

The null hypothesis of no mediating effect is therefore rejected, and the alternative hypothesis upheld. Gauged by the criterion of Baron and Kenny (1986), the mediating role of responsiveness is apparently large since the regression coefficient of IQ on depression is reduced to statistical non-significance when fitted in a multiple regression of IQ on both responsiveness and depression ($\beta = -0.1$, $p = 0.44$).

Using the same methods we found no evidence that PND's association with infant temperament at 42 months of age (as measured by the Easy-Difficult

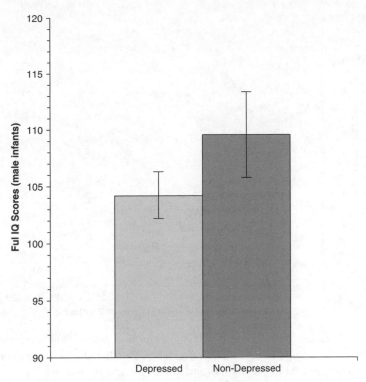

Figure 3   *Maternal depression and male IQ. Plotted values are group means (±S.E.). Columns show Full IQ scores of 42-month-old boys*

Table 4   *Cognitive/Language Profile scores of 42-month-old infants*

	Depressed (S.E.)	Non-depressed (S.E.)
Cognitive/Language Profile*	119.35 (1.48)	125.29 (2.06)
Cognitive	115.91 (1.76)	121.29 (2.26)
Language*	119.35 (1.61)	124.29 (1.73)
Verbal	126.87 (1.56)	129.94 (2.24)
Visual*	107.83 (1.44)	116.00 (2.56)
Logical relations	117.83 (2.06)	118.84 (2.58)
Basic skills*	104.22 (1.54)	109.58 (1.23)
Expressivity*	131.57 (2.48)	140.42 (2.58)
Receptivity*	137.04 (2.22)	145.42 (1.87)

*$p < 0.05$.

Scale) was mediated by maternal responsiveness ($z = -1.77$, ns). Finally, the effects of depression on Early Screening Profile scores were not found to be mediated via responsiveness at six months of age (Sobel test of Cognitive/Language Profile scores: $z = -0.7$, $p = 0.49$).

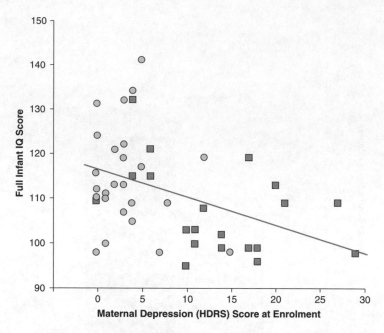

Figure 4   *Relationship of infant IQ with maternal depression. Plotted points represent depressed (■) and non-depressed (•) mother–infant dyads. Solid line is OLS regression line of depressed (■) and non-depressed (•) mothers*

In addition to using equation (1) for assessing the mediation hypothesis, the authors also compared the effects of both maternal depression and responsiveness in a regression analysis. When responsiveness was entered into a regression analysis together with depression, only responsiveness remained a significant predictor of infant IQ.

4. Discussion

As outlined in Section 1, there is strong evidence associating maternal mood disorder with problems in mother–infant interactions such as affective discordance, abrupt breaks in engagement and poor sensitivity to infants.

This study focused on testing an explicit mediation hypothesis linking the role of PND-impaired mother–infant interaction to negative child outcomes. Our results concur with this model and suggest that decreased levels of maternal responsiveness to and general stimulation of infants at an early age may exert a lasting effect on some, but not all, cognitive abilities. By 42 months of age, children from the depressed group performed more poorly on IQ tests, in particular on total IQ and on the performance subtests of arithmetic and geometric design. By contrast, differences between groups on the Cognitive Language Profile Scale including poorer expressive and receptive skills, reduced ability in conceptualization and poorer basic school skills did not seem to be mediated via responsiveness. Similarly, while infant temperament is associated with maternal depression, we find no compelling evidence of a mediating role for mother–infant responsiveness.

Worth noting is our finding that later cognitive problems were more pronounced in boys. This is consistent with some previous findings (e.g. Murray et al., 1992; Sharp et al., 1995). The mechanisms linking mother–infant interaction, gender, intellectual development and behaviour remain the subject of speculation (e.g. Tronick & Weinberg, 1997, suggest that boys are relatively more vulnerable). Close inspection of our data may provide a hint that levels of maternal responsiveness towards boys relative to girls could be very subtly different in depressed compared to non-depressed women, though not significantly so in this sample. However, this issue is likely to be a complex one, our study was not designed specifically to address it and our sample size is small. Also, the depressed group was a non-typical sample of women with PND, most of who are never diagnosed let alone admitted to a specialized inpatient facility. We must therefore refrain from speculation but suggest that this issue is worthy of further investigation.

Our data and that of others (e.g. Cicchetti et al., 2000) underline the clinical need for early intervention approaches to parent–child interaction in the management of PND, which at present are not incorporated in mainstream treatments. Both published data and intuitive considerations suggest that the connections between maternal depression and child cognitive and emotional development are complex, variable in time and reciprocal in nature. Clearly then, continued longitudinal studies will be essential in determining the mechanisms through which maternal depressive illness exerts lasting effects on the child. Studies designed to test explicit hypotheses concerning mediating and moderating mechanisms by which PND produces these effects will be of particular value. The data reported here suggest that mother–infant interactional behaviours, responsiveness among them, should be high on the list of such candidate mechanisms.

Finally, whatever the causative mechanisms, there is evidence that short-term interactional difficulties evinced by PND are associated with long-term consequences for the child. This indicates that following the results of Cicchetti et al. (2000) and Murray et al. (2003), further work into early intervention in mother–infant relationships should be a clear priority in PND research.

In the discussion, the authors argue that early maternal unresponsiveness, which stems from prenatal depression, has a direct effect on the IQ of children at 3.5 years. They also claim that, although the children of depressed mothers scored lower on tests of language and conceptual ability, this difference was not mediated by maternal responsiveness since the z score derived from formula (1) was less than 1 and not significant for the predicted pathway, maternal depression ⇒ maternal responsiveness ⇒ cognitive/language profile. On the face of it, this apparent difference in the mediation of infant WPPSI scores and scores and the cognitive/language profile seems puzzling since one might assume that the two scores would be measuring rather similar abilities; and the authors themselves do not offer any explanation for this discrepancy other than to note that 'decreased levels of maternal responsiveness ... may exert a lasting effect on some but not all cognitive abilities'. One useful way forward, and a technique that is advisable when several different measures have been gathered at the same time, is to examine the inter-correlation among measures. This would show, for example, the extent to which WPPSI scores were related to cognitive/language profile scores.

Acknowledgement

This research was supported by a grant from the Victorian Health Promotion Foundation.

Paper 3   Predictors of Theory of Mind understanding (Meins et al., 2002)

The next paper also describes a longitudinal study in which measures of maternal behaviour are used to predict children's ability some years later. Here mothers' speech to their infants at 6 months and a measure of infant attachment at 12 months are used to predict later performance in Theory of Mind (ToM) tasks. ToM is the ability to attribute mental states (thoughts and feelings) to other people and developmental psychologists use a number of standard tasks to assess ToM understanding. On average, children are able to succeed on standard ToM tasks somewhere between the ages of 3 and 4 years.

Previous research has suggested that children's social experience has an influence on the age at which they are able to pass standard ToM tasks. The general idea behind such claims (Cutting & Dunn, 1999) is that children who have greater opportunities to hear adults and older siblings discussing their thoughts and feelings are able to develop an understanding of the mental life of others at an earlier age. However, evidence of a link between children's social environment and their ability to succeed in ToM tasks does not necessarily imply a causal relationship since there could, in theory, be a common factor that these two measures share. The likelihood of a common factor increases if both measures are assessed at the same point in time. It is possible, for example, that children who are socially competent may have higher quality interactions with other people and also be better at solving ToM tasks while children who are less socially competent have lower quality interactions and are also less good at solving ToM tasks than their more socially competent peers.

In this paper, the authors use a longitudinal design in which they assess social interaction at 6 and 12 months. This is three years before most children will be able to pass ToM tasks and several months before they are able to use mental state language, that is words such as *think, remember* and *want*. As I noted in connection with Paper 2, the advantage of a longitudinal design is that it provides a powerful tool for the researcher to tease out patterns of cause and effect.

Child Development, 2002, 73, (6), 1715–1726

Maternal Mind-Mindedness and Attachment Security as Predictors of Theory of Mind Understanding

Elizabeth Meins, Charles Fernyhough, Rachel Wainwright, Mani Das Gupta, Emma Fradley, and Michelle Tuckey

Introduction

It is now more than a decade since researchers first turned their attention to social influences on the development of children's theory of mind (ToM). Since Dunn and colleagues (Dunn, Brown, Slomkowski, Tesla, & Youngblade, 1991) published their initial findings relating family environment to children's ToM abilities, there has been a steadily growing body of evidence suggesting that specific features of the early social environment are associated with precocity in children's understanding of mind. In their landmark study, Dunn et al. (1991) reported a relation between certain types of family interactions and children's subsequent ToM performance. They found that children were more likely to succeed on ToM tasks if their families had previously shown a tendency to discuss feelings and use causal state language, and if their mothers frequently attempted to control the behavior of older siblings. Subsequently, Perner, Ruffman, and Leekam (1994) reported that the mere presence of siblings had a facilitatory effect on ToM performance, although a reanalysis of these data suggested that this was true only for the presence of older siblings (Ruffman, Perner, Naito, Parkin, & Clements, 1998). Indeed, contact with older children and adults beyond the nuclear family appears to have a similar effect in aiding children's understanding of mind (Lewis, Freeman, Kyriakidou, Maridaki-Kassotaki, & Berridge, 1996). Recently, relations between global social factors and ToM performance have been reported. Children from families of higher socioeconomic status performed better on a range of ToM tasks than did peers from more disadvantaged backgrounds (Cole & Mitchell, 1998, 2000; Cutting & Dunn, 1999; Holmes, Black, & Miller, 1996), and mothers' educational attainment has been found to correlate positively with their children's ToM performance (Cutting & Dunn, 1999; Meins & Fernyhough, 1999). Despite this growing body of evidence, researchers have been somewhat cautious about making strong arguments for a causal role for any of these social factors in ToM development.

Such caution appears justified, because the mechanisms through which children's social environment might influence their ToM are, as yet, poorly understood. Dunn (1994) argued that the reason why certain types of social interaction (e.g., psychological discourse, sibling conflict management, joint play, shared jokes, and moral reasoning) related to ToM performance was because they provide contexts in which children are confronted with conflicting views on the world. In turn, such conflicts in perspective facilitate children's developing understanding that reality may be represented and misrepresented. Fernyhough (1996) presented a broadly Vygotskian account of how the internalization of dialog relating to perspectival conflict might underlie individual differences in ToM performance. In a different vein, Lewis et al. (1996) discussed an 'apprenticeship' model of ToM development, whereby children's interactions with older kin provide them with informal tutoring about the mind. Although these approaches make intuitive sense, they have thus far been unsuccessful in specifying precise mechanisms by which exposure to mental state language and perspectival conflict might lead to children being better able to understand the mental states of others.

One problem for such accounts has been the difficulty of establishing the direction of causation in these apparent environmental effects on ToM. Among the reasons for this difficulty is the fact that even longitudinal studies (e.g., Dunn et al., 1991) have assessed social interaction only during the months immediately preceding the ToM assessments. This is problematic because, at such an age, children have already acquired a considerable vocabulary of mental and emotional state words, and thus may themselves be the driving force behind conversations using psychological language. For example, Bretherton, McNew, and Beeghly-Smith (1981) reported that some children begin to use emotion words as young as 18 months of age; and by 28 months, children are capable of using a wide repertoire of psychological state language to comment on their own and other people's past, present, and future behavior (Bretherton & Beeghly, 1982). Consequently, the observed link between certain types of family environment or interaction and precocity in children's ToM performance may simply reflect children's own ability to use mental state language and engage others in psychological discourse.

To make stronger claims about the causal influence of social–interactional factors on ToM development, it is necessary to find evidence that supports a relation between ToM performance and individual differences in some aspect of social interaction present before children have begun to acquire mental state language. One such factor that has been found to relate to later ToM performance is infant–mother attachment security. Meins, Fernyhough, Russell, and Clark-Carter (1998) reported that children who had been securely attached to their mothers in infancy performed better than did their insecure counterparts on the unexpected transfer ToM task (Wimmer & Perner, 1983) at age 4. Such long-term longitudinal findings allow one to claim with greater confidence that this aspect of children's social interactions facilitates their understanding of mind independently of their own early mentalizing abilities.

> The unexpected transfer task, described later in the paper, is one of the standard ToM tasks. There are various versions of this task but, in essence, one character places something (usually chocolate) in one location and then leaves the scene. Next a second character moves the chocolate to a new location. Finally the unsuspecting first character returns to look for the chocolate and the child is asked to predict where that character will look. Children who succeed in this task realise that, although the location of the chocolate has changed, this first character does not know this and so will look in the original location.

However, there are still problems in making causal links between attachment security and children's later ToM performance, because it is not immediately obvious why a behaviorally based assessment of infant-mother attachment should be related to children's ToM performance 3 years later. Although attachment relationships ultimately become representational in the form of internal working models, Bowlby (1980) argued that these models are not stable or well established until 4 or 5 years of age. Consequently, no arguments for a direct link between infantile attachment security and ToM performance have been proposed. It may be that the observed security-related differences in ToM can be explained in terms of the other social factors found to influence children's understanding of mind. For example, it has been shown that, compared with their insecure-group counterparts, mothers of securely attached children are more sensitive tutors (e.g., continually using feedback from their child's performance to pitch instructions at an appropriate level) when collaborating with their children on a cognitive task (Meins, 1997a). Security-related differences in ToM performance could therefore be explained in terms of Lewis et al.'s (1996) apprenticeship model, with secure-group mothers proving to be more skilled and effective at providing their children with informal tutoring about the mind. Alternatively, secure-group mothers may be more likely to engage in the types of familial interaction shown by Dunn and colleagues (e.g., Dunn et al., 1991) to be related to superior ToM.

Meins et al. (1998) explained their findings somewhat differently, however, arguing that the reason for this link between attachment and ToM lies in security-related differences in mothers' mind-mindedness (Meins, 1997b); this is, the proclivity to treat one's infant as an individual with a mind, capable of intentional behavior. This explanation arose from Meins et al.'s (1998) finding that secure-group mothers were more likely than were their insecure-group counterparts to focus on their children's mentalistic attributes (rather than their physical appearance or behavioral tendencies) when given an open-ended invitation to describe their children. Moreover, children whose mothers had described them with reference to their mentalistic qualities showed higher ToM performance. Hoewever, as Meins et al. acknowledged, their study could not establish whether individual differences in maternal mind-mindedness lay behind security-related differences in children's ToM performance, because the mind-mindedness data were not collected until the children were 3 years of age. Thus, although they could give principled reasons why mind-mindedness should predate the formation of the attachment relationship, Meins et al.'s study could not test this hypothesis.

Subsequently, Meins, Fernyhough, Fradley, and Tuckey (2001) established that maternal mind-mindedness could be observed in infant–mother interactions during the first year of life. Mothers were classified as demonstrating mind-mindedness if they appropriately interpreted their infants' behaviour with verbal reference to its putative attendant mental states, such as thoughts, desires, intentions, and memories. This index of mothers' mind-minded comments turned out to be a better predictor of attachment security than did maternal sensitivity, which has traditionally been regarded to be the best indicator of subsequent attachment (see, e.g., Ainsworth, Bell, & Stayton, 1971, 1974).

Another previous paper by the authors (Meins, Fernyhough, Fradley & Tuckey, 2001) showed that individual variation in mothers' use of mental state language to their child – 'mind-mindedness' – was present even when infants were less than 1 year old and that this was related to attachment security. The previous findings are therefore an essential precursor of the methodology of this paper.

As well as replicating Meins et al.'s (1998) finding of greater mind-mindedness among secure-group mothers, Meins et al. (2001) provided support for the assumption that individual differences in maternal mind-mindedness pre-date the formation of the attachment relationship. This study also saw a refinement of the definition of maternal mind-mindedness. Rather than focusing on the mother's general proclivity to treat their infants as individuals with minds, Meins et al. (2001) argued that mind-mindedness at 6 months should be defined in terms of the mother's explicit use of mental state language to comment appropriately on her infant's mind.

Note that the Meins et al. (2001) paper established a working definition of mind-mindedness that is used here.

Meins et al.'s (2001) finding of a predictive link between maternal mind-mindedness and security of attachment is relevant to the issue of ToM development, for a number of reasons. First, it may help to explain security-related differences in ToM development, because early maternal mind-mindedness indexes a mother's capacity to represent appropriately the mental states of her infant, and thus 'communicate understanding of the child's intentional stance' (Fonagy & Target, 1997, p. 679). This representational component is also clearly an essential component of ToM, which requires children to represent the mental states of themselves and others. Thus, a focus on this representational component of the mother's activity would make it possible to avoid the paradox, noted above, of trying to explain individual differences in ToM in terms of purely behavioral measures of attachment security. Security of attachment may therefore not predict children's ToM independently of maternal mind-mindedness. Second, Meins et al.'s (2001) findings highlight the need to distinguish between general exposure to psychological state language and exposure to comments that are appropriate references to the infants' current mental state. If general exposure facilitates ToM, then one would predict that higher maternal use of all types of psychological language would relate to better performance on ToM tasks. Alternatively, it may be that only specific types of psychological state language relate to later ToM performance. For example, by commenting appropriately on their infants' ongoing mental states and processes, mothers are providing their infants with a representational reference (the linguistic comment) for their current experience. One could argue that this contingency and temporal contiguity between infants' behaviour and their mothers' mind-related comments would make the connection between behavior and its attendant mental states more transparent, allowing infants to integrate information on their behavior with this external linguistic perspective on their own mental states. According to this view, only exposure to mental state language that appropriately reflects the infants' mental states would facilitate ToM development. Investigating the relative contributions to subsequent ToM performance of early exposure to these different types of mental state language was a major objective of the present study.

The idea of using three different measures of mother–child interaction is to enable the authors to test a very specific hypothesis about social influences on the development of ToM. This is that mothers who use language to comment appropriately on their children's thoughts, feelings and intentions will promote the development of ToM. On this argument, the other two measures used in the study (mothers' general use of mental state language and security of infant attachment) will both be weaker predictors of later success in ToM tasks.

The general aim of the longitudinal study reported in this article was to investigate the relations between children's ToM development and two pre-existing social factors: early maternal mind-mindedness and infant–mother security of attachment. Our specific hypotheses were as follows: (a) mothers' use of mental state language to comment appropriately on their infants' minds at 6 months would be positively correlated with ToM performance at 45 and 48 months, (b) superior ToM performance at these ages would be observed in children who enjoyed a secure attachment relationship in infancy, and (c) mothers' use of appropriate mental state comments would be a better predictor of later ToM performance than would infant–mother attachment security. This study also set out to investigate how exposure to mental state language that does not appropriately reflect the infants' state of mind relates to children's subsequent ToM performance. Despite findings that general mental state language during the third and fourth years of life relates to superior ToM performance (e.g., Dunn et al., 1991), we hypothesized (d) that any such effect would be weaker than the effect for appropriate mental state comments. Thus, our final aim was to investigate the relative contributions of early exposure to these different types of mental state language to children's subsequent ToM.

Method

Participants

Participants were 57 children (28 girls, 29 boys) who were a subset of an original sample of 71 children who had been taking part with their mothers in a longitudinal study (Meins et al., 2001) since their first year of life. Participants were recruited through local health centers and baby clinics, with 60 per cent of mothers who were approached agreeing to take part (see Meins et al., 2001). The reduction in numbers between the original and present sample was due to 6 families moving away from the area, 5 mothers declining to continue because they were too busy, and 3 families being impossible to contact. Of the remaining 57 children, 54 were White, and 3 were of mixed race (2 children had a White mother and a Black father, 1 child had a White mother and an Asian father). As part of the earlier study, measures of maternal sensitivity and mind-mindedness were obtained at 6 months (M = 25, range = 23–28 weeks) and infant–mother attachment security was assessed using the Strange Situation procedure at 12 months (M = 53, range = 52–56 weeks). Children were followed up at 45 months (M = 45.8, range = 45–47 months) and 48 months (M = 48.3, range = 48–53 months) when their performance on age-appropriate ToM tasks was assessed.

Background Variables

Maternal education

Mothers' level of education was included as an independent variable to control for the possibility that maternal mind-mindedness may relate to the amount of time mothers have spent in the education system, and also because maternal educational level has been found to correlate positively with children's ToM performance (Cutting & Dunn, 1999; Meins & Fernyhough, 1999). Mothers were given a questionnaire in which they were asked to identify their highest educational qualification by choosing one of six categories. Each mother was awarded one of the following scores for educational level (North American equivalents to the British educational system are shown in parentheses): 0, no examinations; 1, CSEs (equivalent to high school up to age 16 for less academic students); 2, GCSEs or O-Levels (high school up to age 16 for more academic students); 3, A-Levels (high school up to age 18); 4, further qualification, not to degree level (e.g., nursing); 5, undergraduate degree; and 6, postgraduate qualification. Of the 57 mothers participating: 6 scored 0, 6 scored 1, 16 scored 2, 3 scored 3, 19 scored 4, 4 scored 5, and 3 scored 6.

Number of older siblings

Number of older siblings was included as an independent variable due to its reported relation with children's ToM performance (Lewis et al., 1996; Ruffman et al., 1998). Of the 57 participating children, 29 were first-born, 20 had one older sibling, 5 had two older siblings, 2 had three older siblings, and 1 child had four older siblings.

Assessment at Age 6 Months

Mothers were videotaped interacting with their 6-month-old infants in a 20-min free play session at the university's developmental research laboratory. Mothers were given no specific instructions on how to act during these sessions, other than being asked to play with their infants as they would do if they had a few spare minutes together at home. Mothers' behavior was coded for maternal mind-mindedness, and the play sessions were also coded for maternal sensitivity. This latter measure was included to control for the possibility that a more general measure of the quality of infant–mother interaction, rather than maternal mind-mindedness specifically, might predict children's subsequent ToM performance.

Like Paper 2, this study also uses free play as a context for assessing the quality of mother–infant interaction. All recordings were made in a standard setting. There is good evidence (Harris, 1992) that the essential quality of mother–infant interaction remains the same irrespective of whether observation takes place at home or, as in this case, in an observation laboratory. A purpose-built laboratory often affords better conditions for observation and videorecording than the home environment because it is usually quieter and better lit, and a standard set of toys or other items can be provided.

Maternal mind-mindedness

Every comment the mother made during the session was categorized. Following the criteria of Meins et al. (2001), a comment was defined as a discrete sound, single word, or sentence. For example, both of the following utterances would be scored as containing two comments: 'Ball. Ball.' and 'That's a nice ball. Do you like the ball?' These maternal comments were then categorized according to whether they included mental state language. We defined mental state language using Meins et al.'s (2001) category of mind-related comments: (a) comments on mental states, such as knowledge, thoughts, desires, and interests (e.g., 'You know what that is, it's a ball.'; 'I think that you think it's a drum.'); (b) comments on mental processes (e.g., 'Do you remember seeing a camel?'; 'Are you thinking?'); (c) references to the level of emotional engagement (e.g., comments about being bored, self-conscious, or excited); (d) comments on attempts to manipulate people's beliefs (e.g., 'You're joking.'; 'You're just teasing me.'); (e) the mother 'putting words into her infant's mouth' so that the mother's discourse took on the structure of a dialog between her infant and herself (e.g., 'He says, "I think I've got the hang of that now"', 'She says, "I'm not interested in him, I've already got one".')

Very clear details are provided of the way that maternal comments were coded, explaining both what counted as a comment and how the categories for coding were defined. Examples are provided of the various different ways that a mother might use mental state language in conversation with her child. The use of one category to distinguish different types of mental state language together with seven additional categories for other types of comment allowed all maternal language to be coded. This meets the expectation that coding categories should not only be mutually exclusive but also exhaustive.

Naturally, many of the comments made by mothers during the 20-min session did not contain mental state language. The coding scheme for mothers' comments included seven categories in addition to the category of explicit use of mental state language (these other categories were mother names object, mother describes object, mother imitates infant's vocalization, mother encourages infant to perform an action, mother gives positive feedback, mother directs attention, mother engages infant in standardized game routine). The videotapes were coded by a researcher who was blind to all other measures and to the study's hypotheses, and a randomly chosen fifth of the tapes was coded by a second blind researcher. Interrater agreement for assignment of maternal comments to the eight categories (the seven categories above and the mind-related comments category) was $k = .89$. Because the focus of the present study concerned the links between maternal mental state language and children's ToM performance, data on the other seven categories of maternal comments are not reported here. (Note that scores for none of these other categories were related to children's ToM performance.)

The researcher coding maternal language was not aware either of the experimental hypothesis or, equally importantly, of scores on other measures. Coding reliability was established through independent coding of a sample of videotapes by a second researcher. There was a high level of inter-rater agreement.

Next, we determined whose mental states mothers were commenting on. The vast majority of mothers' mental state comments referred to their infants' states of mind, and mothers only rarely commented on the mental states of people other than their infants. Only 6 mothers referred to another person's mental state, with a total of 11 comments in this category. Due to their rarity, these comments were excluded, and the analyses focused exclusively on mothers' mental state language that referred to their infants' mental states and processes.

The next stage of coding was to distinguish appropriate comments made by mothers on their infant's mental state from inappropriate comments. This distinction was key to the hypothesis being tested so it was essential that this coding was both valid and reliable. All coding involves some level of judgment by the coder but a judgment of this kind can be difficult to make unless there are very clear definitions of what constitutes an appropriate and an inappropriate comment. Here the coding uses three categories to distinguish appropriate from inappropriate comments. The criteria for appropriate utterances were: the mother comments on her child's psychological state and the rater agrees that the interpretation is correct; the mother links an ongoing activity to a similar event in the past or future; the mother suggests a way to proceed if there is a lull in activity. This gave three different categories, all of which were taken to be appropriate comments. There were three more categories which were, in effect, the mirror image of the appropriate categories: the mother made a comment about her child's psychological state that was not taken by the rater to be in accord with the child's actual state; the mother commented on a past or present event that did not relate to an ongoing event; the mother asked what the child wanted to do (rather than suggesting an activity) or commented that a child wanted to change an activity when he/she was already successfully engaged in an activity. There was also a final category of comment that was treated as inappropriate. This was when the mother made a comment that did not have a clear referent in the ongoing interaction.

These seven categories were designed to be both mutually exclusive and exhaustive. Maternal utterances that fell into one of the first three categories were coded as appropriate and those that fell into the latter four were coded as inappropriate. As before, one fifth of videotapes were coded independently by a second rater. There was higher inter-rater agreement on the appropriate/inappropriate coding.

The category of mothers' use of mental state comments referring to their infants' minds was subdivided to investigate the relative contribution to children's subsequent ToM performance of mothers' use of (a) mental state comments that were appropriate reflections of the infant's mental state, and (b) mental state comments that did not appropriately reflect the infant's mind. Each mind-related comment was coded dichotomously as appropriate or inappropriate using Meins et al.'s (2001) criteria for 'appropriate mind-related comments.' A comment was classified as an appropriate mind-related comment if (a) the independent coder agreed with the mother's reading of her infant's psychological state (e.g., if a mother commented that her infant wanted a particular toy, it would be an appropriate comment if the coder concurred that the infant's behavior was consistent with such a desire); (b) the comment linked the infant's current activity with similar events in the past or future, for example, 'Do you remember seeing a camel?' (while playing with a toy camel); (c) the comment served to clarify how to proceed if there was a lull in the interaction, for example, 'Do you want to look at the posters?' (after the infant had been gazing around the room, not focused on any object or activity, for 5 s). Criteria for 'inappropriate mind-related comments' were (a) the coder believed that the mother was misinterpreting her infant's psychological state (e.g., stating that the infant was bored with a toy when he/she was still actively engaged in playing with it); (b) the comment referred to a past or future event that had no obvious relation to the infant's current activity; (c) the mother asked what the infant wanted to do, or commented that the infant wanted or preferred a different object or activity, when the infant was already actively engaged in an activity or was showing a clear preference for a particular object; (d) the referent of the mother's comment was not clear (e.g., saying 'You like that' when the object or activity to which the comment referred was not obvious). The criteria for these two types of mind-related comments were exclusive and exhaustive. An independent, trained researcher, who was blind to all other measures and to the hypotheses of the study, coded mental state comments using the appropriate versus inappropriate criteria. A second trained researcher coded a randomly selected fifth of the infant–mother interactions. Interrater agreement was $k = .79$.

To control for maternal verbosity, scores for appropriate and inappropriate mind-related comments were computed as proportions of the total number of comments produced during the 20-min session. One might argue that these scores should be calculated as proportions of the number of mind-related comments, rather than total number of comments. We chose the latter method of calculating scores to present a truer picture of the frequency with which mothers made appropriate and inappropriate mind-related comments throughout the testing session. For example, if scores had been calculated as a proportional scores of 1 for appropriate and 0 for inappropriate mind-related comments would be awarded to a mother who made only one (appropriate) mind-related comment. We reasoned that this would not provide an accurate picture of such a mother's proclivity to engage in mind-minded discourse. That said, analyses using these alternative indices produced exactly the same pattern of results as those reported in the Results section.

The mean total number of comments produced during the session was 142.61 ($SD = 41.45$), for total number of appropriate mind-related comments $M = 13.83$ ($SD = 9.15$), and for total number of inappropriate mind-related comments $M = 2.07$ ($SD = 3.13$). With respect to the mean proportional scores for the whole sample, for appropriate mind-related comments $M = .10$ ($SD = .06$), and for inappropriate mind-related comments $M = .02$ ($SD = .02$). High scores for appropriate mind-related comments are indicative of greater maternal mind-mindedness.

In taking any measure of categories of maternal speech, a researcher has to decide whether to use number of utterances of each type or the proportion of each type. The advantage of the latter measure is that it takes account of the fact that some mothers say much more in a given time than others. The potential disadvantage is that proportions may mask real differences that are relevant to the study. For example, in this case, it could be that mothers who made frequent appropriate comments on their child's mental state had more influence on their child's development of psychological understanding than mothers who made few comments. Here the authors used the proportion of appropriate mental state comments in relation to total number of utterances. This measure does have the important advantage of quantifying appropriate mental state comments in relation to the total amount of speech. However, it is sometimes useful to consider both proportional data and actual numbers of responses to see if they lead to a similar conclusion.

Maternal sensitivity

Ainsworth et al.'s (1971) 9-point scale was used to assess how sensitive mothers were when interacting with their infants. This scale gives a global rating of mothers' sensitivity to their infants' cues, rather than coding specific types of maternal behaviour. Higher scores on this scale are indicative of more sensitive mothering. The videotaped play sessions were coded by a trained researcher, and a randomly chosen fifth of the tapes was coded by a second researcher. Both researchers were blind to all other measures and to the study's hypotheses. Interrater agreement was $k = .75$, with exact agreement for 79 per cent of the observations.

The maternal sensitivity measure is a well-established rating scale to assess how responsive mothers are to their infants. In cases where a new measure is used – in this case, maternal use of appropriate mental state language – it is useful to establish a relationship to an earlier and more widely measure.

Assessment of Attachment Security

Infant–mother attachment security was assessed using the Strange Situation procedure (Ainsworth & Wittig, 1969) when the children were 12 months of age. Of the 57 infants, 39 were classified as securely attached, with the remaining 18 falling into the three insecure categories (10 insecure–avoidant, 5 insecure–resistant, and 3 insecure–disorganized). With regard to the 14 children who were lost from the original sample, 10 were securely attached and the remainder were insecure–avoidant, suggesting that the balance of secure and insecure classifications among the lost participants was comparable with that in the sample as a whole. The Strange Situation tapes were coded by the first author, who has formal training in the Strange Situation coding procedure (Ainsworth, Blehar, Waters, & Wall, 1978), and a randomly chosen fifth of the tapes were coded for a second time by an independent trained rater. Interrater agreement was $k = .87$ using the ABCD categories, and $k = .85$ using a secure versus insecure distinction. The classification of the 1 child about whom the raters disagreed was resolved by discussion. Due to the low numbers of children in the separate insecure attachment categories, attachment security was treated as a dichotomous variable (secure/insecure) in the analyses.

> *Assessment of attachment security also makes use of a well-used and standardised measure. Within a sample of typically developing children, such as those who were recruited for this study, one would expect the majority to be classed as securely attached. This was the case here with over two-thirds of children falling into this category. The numbers falling into each of the three categories of insecure attachment would be expected to be small and so the decision to group these together into a superordinate category is sensible. As a general rule, it is a good idea to group categories together if few behaviours or few participants fall into them. Note, however, that it is much easier to group categories together after data collection than to break down a too-general category once it has been used. This latter process will inevitably involve recoding the data. So, if in doubt, use narrow categories in initial coding and amalgamate them later if necessary.*

Phase 1 Testing (Age 45 Months)

Children participated at home in two age-appropriate ToM tasks (appearance–reality and deceptive box), the presentation of which was counterbalanced.

> *Theory of Mind understanding was tested extensively in this study. In total, four different tasks were used, two at 45 months and two at 48 months. There are a number of issues to consider in assessing children's ability to pass ToM tasks. One is that different tasks place different cognitive demands on children – an issue that I discuss in more detail in Chapter 5 – and so it is wise to use a number of different tasks to get a clear picture of a child's understanding of ToM. Another, related, issue is that children can only pass or fail a ToM task and so the use of a single task would give every child a pass/fail score. This is not a discriminating measure and its use would make it more difficult to establish links between ToM understanding and maternal sensitivity. Using a total of four tasks – and an overall score – affords the opportunity of a larger range of scores especially since the appearance–reality task had four trials using different objects.*

The appearance–reality task

Children received a version of the task originally developed by Flavell, Flavell, and Green (1983). Children were given four trials, each using an object whose appearance was deceptive (a sponge that looked like a football, a torch that looked like a fish, a frog pencil sharpener, and a cat-shaped salt cellar). The experimenter (E) showed the object to the child, saying, 'When you look at this with your eyes right now, what does it look like?' After the child answered, E demonstrated what the object really was. The child was then asked two test questions: (a) 'What is this really and truly? and (b) 'When you look at it with your eyes right now, does it look like a [football] or does it look like a [sponge]'? The order of presentation of the four objects, and that of the 'look' versus 'really and truly' questions, was fully randomised and counterbalanced. Children received one mark if they answered both the reality and appearance questions correctly for each of the four objects, giving a score out of 4 for their overall performance on the appearance–reality task.

The deceptive box task

Children were given a version of the deceptive box task devised by Hogrefe, Wimmer, and Perner (1986). Each child was shown a tube of candies and asked what he or she thought was inside. The tube was then opened to show the child that it contained, not candies, but a pencil. The child was then asked, 'Can you remember what's inside here?' (memory control). A toy animal, Freddy the frog, was used as the naive other, and the child was asked, 'What does Freddy think is in the candies tube?' This task was scored dichotomously as pass/fail.

Phase 2 Testing (Age 48 Months)

The unexpected transfer task

At age 48 months, children were tested at home on two versions of the unexpected transfer task (Wimmer & Perner, 1983) to assess their understanding of how beliefs determine behaviour.

> *Given the number of ToM tasks that were used, spreading them over two sessions, three months apart, did not place too great a demand on the concentration of the children who were only aged four years at the final assessment session. Also, given that children's performance on such tasks may be inconsistent, the use of two separate sessions makes the overall assessment more reliable.*

The two versions used different toy animals and different colored boxes. In one story, participants were introduced to Charlie the Crocodile, and told that his favorite food was chocolate. A chocolate was placed into one of two small boxes – one red and the other blue. The child was told that Charlie was hiding his chocolate while he went for a swim. Charlie was removed from the scene, and a puppet, Cheeky Monkey, was introduced to the child. The experimenter announced that Cheeky Monkey was going to play a trick on Charlie. Cheeky Monkey then took the chocolate out of the box in which it had been hidden and placed it in the other box, closing both lids. The child was told that Charlie was about to return from his swim, and that he would want his chocolate. Two control questions were asked: 'Where was the chocolate in the beginning?' (memory control), and 'Where is the chocolate now?' (reality control). If a child answered either of these questions incorrectly, the story was briefly recapped and the two control questions repeated, but the child was not explicitly corrected. When correct answers had been given to both control questions, the test question was presented: 'Where will Charlie look for his chocolate?' The second version of this task was identical to the first, except that in this instance a different animal hid a toy in either a silver or gold box. For each of the two versions, children received a score of 1 if they passed, or 0 if they failed, giving an overall score between 0 and 2.

Receptive verbal intelligence

Children's receptive verbal intelligence was assessed using the British Picture Vocabulary Scale II (BPVS II; Dunn, Dunn, Whetton, & Burley, 1997) to control for the effects of verbal IQ on the other variables. The mean BPVS II score for the entire group was $M = 110.72$ ($SD = 12.02$).

> The use of a standardised vocabulary measure enabled the authors to consider the effects of children's language ability on their ToM performance. In most tests of cognitive ability, if not all, one would expect children who are intellectually more able to perform better than less able peers. In this case, previous research has also suggested that there are specific links between aspects of language ability and ToM performance so this is an additional reason for including the vocabulary test.

Composite ToM Measure

To provide a picture of children's overall ToM performance across the three tasks and the two testing ages, a composite ToM score was computed for each child. Previous studies using the same standard ToM tasks have found that performance across these tasks is highly correlated (e.g., Carlson & Moses, 2001; Hughes & Dunn, 1998; for studies employing similar composite measures, see Astington & Jenkins, 1999; Carlson & Moses, 2001; Cole & Mitchell, 2000; Cutting & Dunn, 1999; Dunn, Cutting, & Demetriou, 2000; Hughes & Dunn, 1998). To give equal weighting to each of the three tasks in our composite, scores for the individual tasks were scaled to give a maximum score of 2 for each task (cf. Hughes & Dunn, 1998). Scores for the appearance–reality task were divided by 2, and scores for the deceptive box were multiplied by 2. The maximum possible score for overall ToM performance was therefore 6. Composite scores ranged from 0 to 6, with a mean of 2.87 (SD = 1.86). Skewness for the composite measure was .10 with an SE of .32, z = .31, ns; and kurtosis was −1.07, z = 1.65, ns, leading us to assume that scores on our composite measure were normally distributed.

As already noted, the use of a composite ToM measure produced scores that ranged from 0 (failure in all tasks) to 6 (success in all tasks). Note that the distribution of scores was shown to be normal.

With respect to the reliability of the composite measure, all interitem (appearance–reality, deceptive box, and unexpected transfer scores) and item–total correlations were positive, and all were significant (rs between .30 and .80, df = 55), except for the correlation between appearance–reality and unexpected transfer task scores, r(55) = .13. Cronbach's a for the composite measure was .50, which is a modest level of reliability (Nunnally, 1967). Although this value is below that recommended by Nunnally (1978), there are several reasons for accepting it for the purposes of the present study. First, there is some disagreement about the need for strict adherence to a critical value of Cronbach's a, particularly when researchers are not making important decisions about the fates of individuals, and when complete homogeneity is not expected (Pedhazur & Schmelkin, 1991). Second, the reliability of our composite measure is in line with previous studies that have used similar composite ToM measures (Astington & Jenkins, 1999; Hughes & Dunn, 1998). Third, although the reliability of our measure is not as high as that reported in some studies (e.g., Cutting & Dunn, 1999), these studies have tended to use several versions of the same kind of task (e.g., false-belief prediction), in which higher reliability would be expected. In contrast, our aim was to give a picture of ToM performance across a range of tasks, which are nevertheless thought to tap a common underlying cognitive capacity (e.g., Perner, 1991).

There is considerable discussion of the validity of the composite ToM measure since it was not conventionally reliable using Cronbach's α to assess inter-item reliability. Cronbach's α is traditionally used to establish the overall reliability of a questionnaire or other assessments involving a number of different items. Unreliable items are systematically removed until α reaches at least 0.80. It is questionable whether such an approach is necessary here since the various ToM tasks are not intended to give an identical picture of ToM understanding. This is clearly indicated by the wide variation in the inter-task scores, which range from 0.13 to 0.80. For this reason, as well as for those given by the authors, the use of the composite measure seems fully justified.

Results

The next section of the paper describes the results. The authors began by looking at the inter-correlations of their various measures to see whether children's ToM scores were significantly positively correlated with the various measures of maternal responsiveness taken during the first year of life as well as the other variables – such as verbal IQ (vocabulary score), maternal education and number of siblings – which might be expected to affect the age at which children can pass tests of ToM. These same variables were then entered into a regression analysis to find out, more specifically, which variables were the best predictor of the composite ToM score.

Pairwise Correlations between Variables

Table 1 shows the correlation matrix for the relations between all of the independent variables and children's overall ToM scores. Children's ToM performance was positively correlated with their BPVS II scores, maternal educational level, mothers' appropriate mind-related comments, and maternal sensitivity. Thus, children performed better on the battery of ToM tasks if they had higher verbal IQs, and had mothers who were more highly educated, more sensitive with them at 6 months, and who commented appropriately on their mental states and processes at 6 months. Overall ToM performance was not related to mothers' inappropriate mind-related comments, attachment security, or the number of older siblings in the family.

Attachment security was positively correlated with mothers' appropriate mind-related comments, and negatively correlated with mothers' inappropriate mind-related comments. Children were therefore more likely to be

Table 1   Correlation matrix for independent and dependent variables

	BPVS	Mat Ed	Sibs	App	Inapp	MS	Sec	ToM
BPVS								
Mat Ed	.55****							
Sibs	−.16	−.20						
App	−.01	.16	−.13					
Inapp	.05	.03	.04	−.08				
MS	.16	.27	−.05	.39**	−.05			
Sec	−.10	−.07	−.06	.42***	−.54****	.14		
ToM	.37**	.29*	−.13	.34**	−.15	.32*	.16	

Note: BPVS = children's British Picture Vocabulary Scale II scores; Mat Ed = mothers' highest educational level; Sibs = number of older siblings in the family; App = mothers' proportional scores for appropriate mind-related comments; Inapp = mothers' proportional scores for number of inappropriated mind-related comments; MS = maternal sensitivity; Sec = attachment security; ToM = children's composite theory of mind scores.
*p < .05; **p < .01; ***p < .005; ****p < .001. All tests were two-tailed.

securely attached if their mothers commented appropriately on their mental states at 6 months, and refrained from using inappropriate mind-related comments. Maternal sensitivity was positively correlated with appropriate mind-related comments.

In this table, the critical line is the one at the bottom, showing the correlation coefficients for composite ToM scores and each of the other variables. Note that two correlations (vocabulary score and proportion of appropriate mental state comments) are highly significant (p < 0.01) and two more (maternal education and maternal sensitivity) are less significant (p < 0.05). From this, one would expect that the first two variables would turn out to be the best predictors of ToM scores in the regression analysis. However, it is important to carry out the regression analysis because the correlations merely show the independent relationship between each variable and ToM scores whereas multiple regression analysis directly compares the relative strength of each variable as a predictor.

More sensitive mothers were thus more likely to comment appropriately on their infants' mental states and processes. These findings on the relations between early maternal mind-mindedness, maternal sensitivity, and attachment security replicate Meins et al.'s (2001) findings in this subset of the original sample. Finally, children's BPVS II scores were positively correlated with maternal educational level, with children of more highly educated mothers obtaining higher verbal IQ scores.

Predictors of Overall Theory of Mind Performance

To establish which variables were independent predictors of overall ToM performance, a forward regression analysis was performed. Seven factors were entered into the regression: BPVS II score, maternal educational level, number of older siblings, maternal sensitivity, inappropriate mind-related comments, appropriate mind-related comments, and attachment security. The regression analysis showed that children's BPVS II scores were the best predictor of overall ToM performance ($R^2 = .16$, $T = 3.29$, $b = .41$, $p < .005$), followed by appropriate mind-related comments ($R^2 = .11$, $T = 2.80$, $b = .33$, $p < .01$). None of the other independent variables were significant predictors of composite ToM scores. Thus, children's BPVS II scores and mothers' appropriate mind-related comments were the only independent predictors of overall ToM performance, with children of higher verbal IQ and those whose mothers more frequently used appropriate mind-related comments at 6 months attaining higher scores on the composite ToM index.

Children's BPVS II scores and mothers' appropriate mind-related comments accounted for 16 per cent and 11 per cent of the variance in overall ToM performance, respectively.

Discussion

The results of the present longitudinal study provide broad support for our first hypothesis: that early maternal mind-mindedness, defined as the mother's proclivity to comment appropriately on her infant's mental states, predicts children's later ToM performance. Mothers' appropriate mind-related comments at 6 months accounted for 11 per cent of the variance in children's composite ToM scores. The regression analysis showed that the only other independent predictor of ToM performance was children's BPVS II scores, accounting for 16 per cent of the variance. This clear link between verbal IQ and ToM performance is in line with previous findings (e.g., Happé, 1995; Jenkins & Astington, 1996).

With respect to our second hypothesis, we found no relation between attachment security and children's ToM performance. The regression analysis showed that attachment security was not a predictor of ToM performance, and composite ToM scores and attachment security were not significantly correlated. We therefore failed to replicate previous findings of a link between security of attachment in infancy and children's ToM at age 4 (Meins et al., 1998). The results of the regression analysis thus supported our third hypothesis in showing that early maternal mind-mindedness is a better predictor of subsequent ToM performance than is infant–mother attachment security.

Our fourth aim was to investigate whether early exposure to mental state language that does not appropriately reflect the infant's mind facilitates subsequent ToM performance. Our results showed that early exposure to this type of general psychological state language was not related to ToM performance. The regression results thus provide support for our fourth hypothesis, showing that early exposure to appropriate mind-related comments is a better predictor of subsequent ToM performance than is exposure to mental state language that does not appropriately reflect the infant's state of mind.

Finally, some mention should be made of the relations between ToM performance and the other independent variables. With respect to family size, we found no relation between number of older siblings and ToM performance. Our findings thus add to a growing number of studies (Carlson & Moses, 2001; Cole & Mitchell, 1998, 2000; Cutting & Dunn, 1999; Meins & Fernyhough, 1999) that have failed to replicate findings of a facilitatory effect of siblings on children's ToM abilities (e.g., Perner et al., 1994; Ruffman et al., 1998). In line with previous findings (Cutting & Dunn, 1999; Meins & Fernyhough, 1999), the results of the present study showed that mothers' educational attainment was related to children's ToM performance, with children of more highly educated mothers attaining higher scores on the composite ToM measure. However, the regression analysis showed that maternal educational attainment was not an independent predictor of children's ToM. Maternal sensitivity at 6 months correlated positively with children's composite ToM scores, but, once again, the regression analysis showed that this variable was not an independent predictor of overall ToM performance.

In summary, the results of this study showed children's ToM performance to be significantly predicted by their mothers' tendency to comment appropriately on their mental states at 6 months. This relation between early maternal mind-mindedness and later ToM was independent of children's verbal ability, mothers' educational attainment, maternal sensitivity, and the number of older siblings in the family. Our data also show this relation to be independent of infant–mother attachment security. Finally, our findings suggest that only exposure to specific kinds of mental state language facilitates later ToM performance; namely, comments that are judged to be appropriate reflections of the infant's state of mind. Exposure to mental state language that is not matched to the infant's mind state was not found to correlate significantly with later ToM performance.

The findings of this study are therefore in line with a growing body of research that has demonstrated social influences on ToM development. With respect to their finding that children who had been securely attached in infancy went on to outperform their insecurely attached peers on a range of ToM tasks, Meins et al. (1998) suggested that one reason for this effect might be the greater proclivity of secure-group mothers to treat their children as individuals with minds. A later study (Meins et al., 2001) showed such individual differences in mind-mindedness to be present in the first year of life. The findings of the present study showed this measure of mind-mindedness to be a significant predictor of ToM performance more than 3 years later. However, contrary to previous findings, this study found no link between infantile attachment security and children's understanding of mind. Our results, therefore, support Meins et al.'s (1998) conclusion that the relation between attachment and ToM can be explained best in terms of individual differences in mothers' mind-mindedness.

Perhaps the most notable contribution of the present study is our identification of what is the earliest known social predictor of mentalizing development. Of particular importance is the fact that maternal mind-mindedness appears to have its effects independently of individual differences in children's own mentalizing abilities. As noted in the Introduction section, most previous longitudinal research in this area (e.g., Dunn et al., 1991) has only obtained measures of social environment and interaction at an age when children have already made considerable advances in mentalizing development, enabling them to talk competently about their own and other people's psychological states. In contrast, we found that children's ToM is predicted by maternal mind-mindedness at an age when children have not yet acquired any language, and are in the early stages of sensorimotor development. Moreover, the finding that neither maternal sensitivity nor infant–mother attachment security were independent predictors of children's subsequent ToM performance suggests that it is specifically early maternal mind-mindedness, rather than the general quality of infant–mother interaction, that influences the development of a representational theory of mind.

We should, however, hold off from making too strong a causal claim for the influence of mind-mindedness until additional research is performed to investigate its temporal continuity. Although our findings suggest that mind-minded comments may begin to influence children's developing ToM from the earliest months of life, we would equally expect exposure to such language to continue to play a role in the preschool years. Indeed, it may turn out that the importance of mind-mindedness lies not in any direct influence in the first year of life, but in its persistence into the preschool years, at which point it may begin to play its part in instructing children about how mental states underlie behavior. If, however, such continuities prove difficult to document, then we will need to establish precisely when the sensitive periods for exposure to appropriate mental state language might occur. One thing that seems certain is that the expression of mind-mindedness will change as the child matures. It is also important to bear in mind that genetically transmitted factors such as temperament might potentially explain the observed relation between mind-mindedness and children's ToM performance, and future research should attempt to investigate this possibility.

Given our suggestion of an influence of mind-minded language in mentalizing development, it is clearly essential to consider the possible contributions of the mind-minded comments of individuals other than the mother, and of comments made by the mother to other individuals, particularly siblings. One of the strengths of the studies of Dunn and colleagues is their ability to take a view of the entire family context, as well as children's interactions with peers (e.g., Brown, Donelan-McCall, & Dunn, 1996). Such studies are required to establish whether, for example, a mother's mind-mindedness with one infant carries over to her interactions with her other children. One would imagine that exposure to comments that reflect the mental processes of other individuals will also be important in nurturing the young child's understanding of mind. As Fonagy and colleagues (e.g., Fonagy & Target, 1997) have argued, caregivers' general tendency to explain people's behaviour with reference to their mental states (assessed by Fonagy's group from analysis of interview-derived recollections of attachment experiences) may be crucial in children's developing understanding of how beliefs and desires determine behaviour. However, the study reported here was unable to test the importance of mothers' reflections on others' mental states, because mothers commented so rarely on the mental states of people other than their infants. It is likely that our dyadic laboratory-based observation encouraged mothers to focus quite exclusively on their infants, rather than talk about their own mental states or those of absent others. We therefore acknowledge the need to investigate how mothers and other people use mind-minded discourse during daily caregiving activities and family routines in the home.

Despite these cautionary notes, it is possible to map out a developmental pathway to illustrate how early maternal mind-mindedness might influence children's later ToM development. Our specific proposal is as follows. We have shown that mothers routinely offer mentalistic comments on their infants' behavior even at 6 months of age. We suggest that exposure to such language from the earliest months of life provides children with an opportunity to integrate their own behaviour with an external comment that makes reference to the mental states underlying that behaviour. Such comments thus offer a scaffolding context within which infants can begin to make sense of their own behavior in terms of its underlying mental states. For example, one mother in the present study commented, 'You recognize this, don't you?' when her child immediately started playing with a toy that he had at home. Another mother asked her child, 'Are you thinking?' when she saw him sitting quietly, looking pensive. Repeated exposure to such comments about their activity (or lack of activity) with reference to their likely attendant mental states may ultimately help children to become aware of their own and other people's mental states and processes, and how they govern behavior. Indeed, some of the mind-minded comments observed in this study showed that mothers appear to expect their infants not only to understand what they are saying, but to respond with a clarification of precisely what they want or think. For example, after hearing her infant produce a particular vocalization, one mother said, 'That means you want something. What do you want?' Such instances may provide a further spur to children's making sense of behavior in terms of mental states. Such a view is in line with Harris's (1996; Harris & Leevers, 2000) suggestion that the apparent links between conversational language and mentalizing development can best be explained in terms of the opportunities such language provides for integrating subjective information on one's own mental state with an external linguistic comment.

Finally, the findings of the current study have clear implications for previous studies that have shown a link between exposure to general mental state language and ToM (e.g., Dunn et al., 1991). Why did this study find no such link with general mental state language, as indexed by our measure of inappropriate mind-related comments? One reason might lie in the age of the children participating in these different studies. Researchers such as Dunn et al. (1991) have focused their investigations on preschool-age children, whose mental states are arguably more transparent and readable than are those of 6-month-old infants. Indeed, young children are known to have problems in hiding their true feelings (e.g., Saarni, 1984). Consequently, mothers' comments on such children's mental states might be expected to be generally more accurate than would be the case with infants, and would thus be coded as appropriate mind-related comments according to the criteria described here. For example, without the ability accurately to read one's child's mental states, it would be impossible to produce the type of comment that Dunn et al. (1991) reported as relating to superior ToM performance (e.g., 'She didn't know I had promised it to you.'; 'He thought it was his turn.'). Rather than seeing our results as contradicting these earlier findings, we would instead suggest that our account is fully consistent with the work of Dunn and others relating to exposure to mental state language during the preschool years. Careful investigation of continuities and discontinuities in mind-mindedness and their relation with ToM would thus seem to be a priority for future research.

Acknowledgements

This study was supported by two grants from Staffordshire University and a grant from the Economic and Social Research Council (R000222355) awarded to the first two authors. The authors thank the mothers and children for their continued enthusiasm and commitment to the project, and

Bronia Hurst for assistance with coding. They also thank Robert Drewett for his statistical advice; and Sue Leekam, Ross Thompson, and three anonymous reviewers for their helpful comments on this article.

Addresses and affiliations

Corresponding author: Elizabeth Meins, Department of Psychology, University of Durham, Science Laboratories, South Road, Durham DH1 3LE, U.K; e-mail:elizabeth.meins@durham.ac.uk. Charles Fernyhough is also at the University of Durham; Rachel Wainwright, Mani Das Gupta, Emma Fradley, and Michelle Tuckley are at Staffordshire University, Stoke on Trent, U.K. At the time of this study, Elizabeth Meins and Charles Fernyhough were also at Staffordshire University.

Questionnaires

While observational data are invaluable for quantifying and evaluating behaviour involving young children, once children are older it is also possible to ask them directly about certain aspects of behaviour. In the next paper, the authors use a questionnaire to find out about the extent to which teenage girls and boys desire to be successful and how they feel about their success in relation to peers. These kinds of issues can only be investigated by asking participants about their feelings and attitudes either through interview or, as in this case, through a questionnaire.

There are a number of reasons why questionnaires rather than interviews are used for this kind of research. The most significant is that questionnaires are considerably more cost effective to administer since a group of participants can be tested on one occasion whereas interviews are usually conducted one-to-one. Another potential advantage is that completion of questionnaires is usually anonymous and so participants may feel less inhibited about revealing their true feelings or opinions than in conversation with another person.

As with observational coding, questionnaires have to be both reliable and valid. One fundamental aspect of reliability is that individual items in the questionnaire can be shown to be measuring the same variable, in cases where a single variable is being studied, or that groups of items within the same sub-scale are measuring the same variable. This kind of internal reliability is often assessed for a newly-developed questionnaire by calculating Cronbach's a which is, in essence, a coefficient of reliability. If Cronbach's a is at least 0.80, the questionnaire is considered internally reliable and all the questions are included. However, if Cronbach's a is less than 0.80, outlying items are removed or replaced and the value of Cronbach's a recalculated. This process continues until the desired value is attained. Another important aspect of reliability is that the general pattern of responses given to the questions should be the same when a questionnaire is completed for a second time by the same individual.

A questionnaire should also be valid. There are two kinds of validity. The first, face validity, means that a questionnaire produces similar findings to other well-established measures of the same phenomenon. The second, construct validity, is more difficult to establish since this means that a questionnaire is actually measuring what the authors claim.

There are particular issues in developing reliable and valid questionnaires for use with children. The participants in the next paper were 13- and 15-years-old so could deal with relatively complex questions. If questionnaires are used with younger children, it is important that the wording of questions is suitable for the age of children being assessed and the use of one or more pilot studies is essential.

In the next paper, the authors use a questionnaire to find out whether adolescent boys and girls differ in their reaction to doing better than their friends. The paper brings together previous findings from a number of different strands of research in order to arrive at the specific prediction for the study. This is that females, who tend to have a more egalitarian style of interaction than males, will feel more uncomfortable than males in dealing with situations where they achieve more highly than a female friend. Note that this research concentrates on same sex friendships in adolescence, a time when romantic interest in opposite gender peers increases. The authors note that 'even in adolescence and young adulthood, individuals form their identities through comparisons with others of the same sex' (p. 92) so for the issue they are examining, same sex peers are the most important. The focus on same sex peers also makes the study more straightforward because both males and females are likely to respond differently to same sex and opposite sex peers.

Paper 4   Sex differences in reactions to outperforming friends (Benenson & Schinazi, 2004)

British Journal of Developmental Psychology, 2004, 22, 317–333

Sex differences in reactions to outperforming same-sex friends

Joyce F. Benenson and Joy Schinazi

Self-evaluation is a process that relies heavily on comparing personal performance with the achievements of others. According to the Self-Evaluation

Maintenance Model (Tesser, 1988; Tesser, Millar, & Moore, 1988), the valence of an individual's self-evaluations in a specific domain depends on three factors: the individual's performance relative to another person, the individual's investment in the domain and the closeness of the bond between the individual and the person with whom the comparison is made. When the domain is important to the individual, and the individual is close to the person with whom the comparison occurs, relatively poor performance produces more negative self-evaluations in the domain. If the domain is important enough, this process can threaten the viability of the relationship.

Numerous studies have provided empirical evidence for this model (e.g. Guay, Boivin, & Hodges, 1999; Tesser, 1988; Tesser et al., 1988). Few studies, however, have focused on possible sex differences in the social-comparison process. This is surprising because by early childhood, children's interactions with peers universally are segregated by sex (for reviews, see Larson & Verma, 1999; Maccoby, 1988, 1998; Whiting & Edwards 1988). Although interest in other-sex peers increases during adolescence, studies have shown that even in adolescence and young adulthood, individuals form their identities through comparisons with others of the same sex (Meisel & Blumberg, 1990; Miller, 1984; Suls, Gaes, & Gastorf, 1979; for a review, see Larson & Verma, 1999). Given that, by adolescence, the majority of individuals' interactions have occurred and continue to occur within separate peer cultures, it is reasonable to postulate that fundamental differences in the ways the two sexes relate to their same-sex peers influence the processes and outcomes of social comparison.

Past research has shown that within their separate peer cultures, females and males differ in important ways in their interactions with their same-sex friends. One of the most prominent differences in the same-sex interactions of males versus females is males' hierarchical style of interaction versus females' more egalitarian style. This sex difference in style of interaction has been reported for young children (for reviews, see Maccoby, 1990, 1998; Omark, Strayer, & Freedman, 1980), children in middle childhood (e.g. Gilligan & Wiggins, 1988; Lever, 1978), adolescents (e.g. Douvan & Adelson, 1966; Karweit & Hansell, 1983; Savin-Williams, 1979, 1980) and adults (for a review, see Cross & Madson, 1997; also Rubin, 1985; Tannen, 1990). In discussing the empirical research on sex differences in children's styles of interactions, Maccoby concludes that 'the most interesting thing about all-boy and all-girl groups is the divergence in the interactive styles that develop in them. In male groups, there is more concern with issues of dominance' (Maccoby, 1990, p. 516). Males and females appear to differ dramatically to reactions to dominance or hierarchical relationships. Based on a detailed study of adolescents' friendships, Karweit and Hansell (1983) concluded that 'males more frequently choose up the status hierarchy than do females' (Karweit & Hansell, 1983, p. 127), yielding a vertical status hierarchy versus a horizontal or egalitarian friendship structure for females.

Evidence that females favour equality in their interactions can be found in several socio-linguistic studies, which consistently demonstrate that beginning in early childhood and continuing into adulthood, females use linguistic forms and engage in activities that highlight equality and downplay status differentials. For example, Sheldon's (1990, 1992) studies of conversations among same-sex triads of boys and girls demonstrated that as early as age three, girls were more egalitarian than boys in their speech styles, whereas boys' language was adversarial and controlling. The same-sex differences have been documented in middle childhood and adolescence across ethnic groups (Goodwin, 1990; Leaper, 1991; Leaper, Tenenbaum, & Schaffer, 1999) and in adulthood (Henley, 1995).

Given the more egalitarian nature of females' compared with males' relationships, an important question arises regarding sex differences in responses to unequal achievement in important domains. Because it is virtually impossible for two individuals continually to perform at the same level, the valence of self-evaluations and the resulting threat to the viability of a relationship would be expected to differ for the two sexes. Specifically, females would be expected to have more difficulty than males accepting differences in outcomes in domains of importance.

Based on a review of linguistic studies, Maltz and Borker (1983) explicitly concluded that 'a girl cannot assert social power or superiority' (Maltz & Borker, 1983, p. 205) in contrast to a boy who may show off continuously (see also Maccoby, 1990). In a year-long participant-observational study of children's play, Lever (1978) found that boys exuberantly competed to demonstrate their superior skill at various games and bragged at length about winning. Conversely, girls often preferred to disguise the winners or losers of games and to terminate games in which disputes arose as to who was performing better. Even more striking, in her own participant-observational study, Goodwin (1990) reported that a girl who appeared to behave in a superior fashion to her same-sex peers was ostracized totally by the other girls in her neighbourhood and school. In marked contrast, boys from the same sample engaged in persistent attempts to highlight achievement or status differences while still maintaining their relationships.

It is important to acknowledge that these studies did not assess more subtle forms of competition such as indirect, social or relational aggression (for reviews, see Crick, Casas, & Nelson, 2002; Underwood, 2003). Much research has shown that females' aggression is more likely to be subtle than overt. Nonetheless, the functions of this form of aggression are far from clear. For example, Owens, Shute, and Slee (2000) describe the exclusionary behaviour, indirect harassment, and non-verbal aggression that adolescent females direct towards other females in two schools in Australia. These researchers suggest that the functions of this type of aggression are to ensure inclusion, promote intimacy, and simply prevent boredom, but not to elevate one's status above all others. In fact, a female who appears superior, as in the study by Goodwin (1990), risks becoming the recipient of other females' aggression (Owens et al., 2000).

Several studies indicate that adolescent females may selectively direct both physical and more subtle forms of aggression to a new female who may be particularly attractive to adolescent males (Campbell, 1995; Owens et al., 2000). A new female automatically has a higher status than other females, because of males' greater attraction to novel versus familiar females. Attacking a new female either directly or indirectly both forces her to maintain a distance from her new peers and diminishes her status and attractiveness in the eyes of others.

The advantage of prior studies demonstrating that females dislike other females who outperform them is that they were conducted in naturalistic settings based on observations or in-depth interviews. None of them utilized standardized, quantitative measures, however. The next step therefore is to examine empirically whether females and males actually differ in their emotional reactions to their own superior performance to same-sex friends in important domains. The results would have important ramifications particularly if they demonstrated that females have more negative reactions than males to outperforming their same-sex friends.

Previous studies of outperforming same sex peers were carried out in naturalistic settings. This study uses a standardised questionnaire rather than observation or in-depth interview to provide a measure in which the responses of the different participants can be compared.

The goal of the first study was to compare the reactions of adolescent females and males to situations in which they imagined they had performed better than their same-sex friends. Adolescence was chosen, because it is an age when friendships become more important than ever, as the peer group replaces the family as the main source of social influence (Brofenbrenner, 1974; Richards, Crowe, Larson, & Swarr, 1998; Richards & Larson, 1989; for reviews, see Buhrmester, 1996; Buhrmester & Prager, 1995). The hypothesis was derived from linguistic and participant-observational research: girls were predicted to report more negative emotional responses than boys to the idea of performing better than their same-sex friends.

Study 1

Method

Participants

Ninety-nine students (48 males and 51 females) from grades 8 and 10 from the largest English-speaking high school in Montréal, Québec participated in the study. The grade 8 adolescents took classes in the junior high wing of the school, whereas the grade 10 adolescents' classes took place in the main part of the building. Students' ages averaged 13 years for grade 8 ($M = 13.77$, $SD = 0.65$ for females; $M = 13.71$, $SD = 0.62$ for males) and 15 years for grade 10 ($M = 15.63$, $SD = 0.60$ for females; $M = 15.59$, $SD = 0.58$ for males). Adolescents from grades 8 and 10 were selected to participate to determine whether sex differences would be heightened as adolescents left junior high school and entered high school where the focus on achievement and future roles becomes more apparent. Based on self-reports of their primary ethnic affiliation, 60 per cent of the adolescents considered themselves to come from White European backgrounds, 8 per cent African-Canadian, 7 per cent from Asian, 4 per cent Indian and 20 per cent from other ethnic backgrounds. The school reflected the ethnic diversity of the population of Montréal, Québec. Socio-economic status ranged from working class to lower-middle class.

> Note the specific reason for selecting participants from Grade 8 (age 13 years) and Grade 10 (15 years) to contrast pupils who were at junior high school with pupils at high school. The transition from one school to another around the age of 14 is common in many educational systems, but not all, so it is pertinent to question whether the school transfer itself is an important factor in influencing children's aspirations.

Procedure

One of three female researchers administered the questionnaire to each of the eight classes. The researcher first explained that she was interested in how adolescents felt about different aspects of their lives and that the questionnaire was not an evaluation of the participants. Participants were asked to be as honest as possible and were told that they could stop responding to the questions at any point. Students were informed also that their answers were confidential and anonymous. To ensure the independence of responses, participants were asked not to look at other students' responses, their desks were separated, and no talking was permitted during the administration of the questionnaire. Participants also were asked not to discuss the questionnaire with other students who had not yet responded to it. After completion of the questionnaire, participants were thanked for their help and were given the opportunity to ask the researcher any questions they had about the questionnaire.

All pupils in a class took part in the study so there were no exclusion issues and participants were told that they could stop responding to the questions at any point. The authors do not discuss the issue of informed consent. The British Psychological Society guidelines (see Chapter 2) are that the consent of parents or permission of teachers should be sought where a participant is under the age of 16 years.

The questionnaire was divided into three sections, each of which focused on four domains previously demonstrated to be important to adolescents: romantic relationships, close friendships, academics and athletics (Harter, 1990). In section 1, two questions in each of the four domains assessed students' desire to be successful in the domain, yielding a total of eight questions. In Section 2, four questions in each of the four domains assessed students' responses to an imagined situation in which they performed at a higher level than their same-sex friend yielding a total of 16 questions. Section 3 asked students to describe their current level of achievement in each of the four domains.

The overall structure of the questionnaire was developed from the widely used Self-Perception Profile for Adolescents (Harter, 1988), that asks for self-evaluations in eight domains. The questionnaire in this study uses the four domains in which success has been shown to be particularly important to adolescents in contributing to their overall feeling of self-worth. It asks questions about desire to be successful in these domains, actual success and reactions to doing better than a friend in each of the domains. Most responses are given on a 6-point rating scale that ranged from caring a great deal about something (6) to not caring at all (1). Note that the precise wording of the rating scale was varied according to the particular question being asked.

Part I: Desire to be successful

Two measures were used to assess the desire to be successful in each of the domains: caring about success and feelings concerning lack of success. For each of the four domains, participants were asked to report on a 6-point scale how much they care (1 = *Not at All* through 6 = *Care Extremely*) about being successful in the domain. For example, in the domain of academics, they were asked: 'How much do you care about getting good marks?' In the domain of friendship, participants were asked: 'How much do you care about having good friends?' Similarly, participants were asked to report on a 6-point scale how they feel (1 = *OK with It* through 6 = *Extremely Unhappy*) when they do not do well in each of the domains. For example, 'How do you feel when you don't get good marks?' 'How do you feel when you don't have good friends?'

Part 2: Responses to better outcomes within a friendship

In Part 2, participants were first asked to write down the initials of two good friends of the same sex. Two friends were used to allow participants to think about more than one friendship. Then, they were administered four measures that assessed their reactions to imagining that they had performed better than each of their same-sex friends within each of the four domains. The first three measures in each domain assessed on 6-point scales participants' emotional reactions to being more successful than their friends in each domain. The fourth measure asked participants to imagine each of their friends' emotional reactions if the participants were more successful in each domain and to circle phrases that best described what they believed each of their close friends' reactions would be to their greater success.

> Part 2 of the questionnaire is central to the study since it asks about positive and negative reactions to achieving greater success than a named friend. Note that participants were asked to complete this section of the questionnaire with respect to two named friends, identified only by initials. Before filling out the questionnaire, students were told that their answers would be 'confidential and anonymous'. In a study like this, it is very important that participants believe their answers will not be shown to anyone in the school: identifying good friends and how they and the participant might feel when one friend does better than the other is a highly sensitive issue, particularly for girls.

Caring about better outcomes Participants were asked to report on a 6-point scale (1 = *Not at All* through 6 = *Care Extremely*) how much they would care if they performed better than their friends in each of the domains. For example, 'How much would you care if you got good marks and your friend didn't?' 'How much would you care if you found new good friends and your friend didn't?'

Negative feelings about better outcomes Participants next were asked to report on a 6-point scale (1 = *OK with It* through 6 = *Extremely Unhappy*) how they would feel if they did better than their friends in each of the domains. For example, 'How would you feel if you got good marks and your friend didn't?' 'How would you feel if you found new good friends and your friend didn't?'

Time spent thinking about better outcomes Participants then were asked to report on a 6-point scale how much time they would spend thinking (1 = *No Time at All* through 6 = *Think All the Time*) about their doing better than their friends in each of the domains. In the domain of academics, they were asked: 'If you got good marks and your friend didn't, how much time would you spend thinking about it?' In the friendship domain, they were asked 'If you found new good friends and your friend didn't, how much time would you spend thinking about it?'

Beliefs about friends' attitudes regarding participants' better outcomes   For the fourth measure in each domain, participants were asked to circle any phrases that described how they thought their friends would feel towards them, given that the participants attained better outcomes than their friends. It was emphasized that participants should circle only those phrases that were relevant; if none were relevant, participants were told not to circle any of the phrases. The phrases were developed based on pilot interviews. Eight negative attributes (e.g. 'They would feel jealous of you', 'They would feel betrayed by you'), five neutral attributes (e.g. 'They would not feel bothered by the situation', 'They would feel this wouldn't change anything') and one positive adjective ('They would feel you try hard') were provided. Identical phrases were provided for each domain. Scores in each domain consisted of the number of negative phrases that participants circled.

This part of the questionnaire is described in detail as it was developed specifically for this study. The fourth section of Part 2 asks participants to circle phrases that describe how their friend might feel when the participant achieves more highly in each of the four domains. Note that the phases were ones that emerged in pilot interviews and so they are designed to capture the kind of things that participants might spontaneously report. Note also that participants were asked to circle only those phrases that were relevant and they were also explicitly told not to circle any phrases if none was relevant. This is an important feature of the instructions because participants may feel, unless told otherwise, that they have to choose at least one of the phrases.

Part 3: Actual success

For the third section, students were asked to report their actual level of achievement in each domain. They were asked whether they were romantically involved (1 = *No* or 2 = *Yes*), how they were performing in school (1 = *Below 40 per cent Average* through 7 = *90–100 per cent*), how they were performing athletically (1 = *Pretty Badly* through 7 = *Excellent*), and how many good friends they had at the time (1 = *1–2* through 4 = *More than 6*). Scales were based on students' responses to pilot testing indicating the number of points that best captured students' responses.

Results

The first part of the analysis establishes that male and female pupils care equally about success. This paves the way for the second set of analyses that directly test the experimental hypothesis.

Students' responses were collapsed across all four domains (romance, academics, athletics, and close friends), and the mean for the four domains together was used in the statistical analysis of each measure. This was done so that results could be generalized across domains. Further, initial analyses had shown that the sex differences were highly consistent across domain. Means are provided by domain in the tables.

Part I: Desire to be personally successful

Results were analysed with sex and grade as the independent variables, and the mean across the four domains for each of the two measures as the dependent variable in two separate analyses of variance (ANOVAs). Table 1 presents the means by domain for each measure to allow specific comparisons.

Table 1   *Desire to succeed in each domain*

| | Caring about success | | | | Negative reactions to lack of success | | | |
| | Females | | Males | | Females | | Males | |
Domain	M	SD	M	SD	M	SD	M	SD
Romance	3.96	1.00	4.02	1.49	2.80	1.28	2.54	1.56
Close friends	5.20	0.85	5.23	0.90	4.53	1.20	4.55	1.38
Academics	4.02	1.24	4.25	1.58	3.53	1.62	3.90	1.61
Athletics	4.74	1.61	4.85	1.22	3.90	1.58	3.98	1.73
All domains	4.48	0.64	4.59	0.80	3.69	0.89	3.76	1.02

Caring about success   Results yielded no significant sex or grade differences in how much participants cared about succeeding in the four domains, $F(1,95) = 0.59$, *ns* for sex and $F(1,95) = 1.97$, *ns* for grade. The Sex × Grade interaction also was not significant, $F(1,95) = 0.81$, *ns*.

Feelings about lack of success   Again, there were no significant sex or grade differences in participants' feelings about lack of success across domains, $F(1, 94) = 0.14$, *ns* for sex and $F(1, 94) = 0.01$, *ns* for grade. The Sex ´ Grade interaction also was not significant, $F(1, 95) = 0.54$, *ns*. Across all four domains, adolescents of both sexes indicated similar and high levels of wanting to be successful and not wanting to fail.

Part 2: Responses to better outcomes than same-sex friends

Results for the first three measures (caring about achieving better outcomes, negative feelings regarding achieving better outcomes and time spent thinking about achieving better outcomes) were analysed with sex and grade as the independent variables and the mean of scores in each of the four domains as the dependent variable in three analyses of variance (ANOVAs). For the fourth measure, number of negative phrases, an ANOVA was conducted with sex and grade as the independent variables and the mean number of negative phrases checked across all four domains as the dependent variable. Tables 2 and 3 display the means of responses in each domain. Results from three of the four measures confirmed the hypothesis that females would report feeling more negative than males if they performed better than their same-sex friends.

The results for the three rating scale measures are shown in Table 2. Remember that the rating scale ranged from not caring at all (1) to caring extremely (6). Only two of the mean scores were above 3 – female concern about doing better than friends academically and in athletics – and only one was below 2 – negative feelings of males to being more successful in forming a romantic attachment than a friend. Mean scores across domains lay between 2 and 3 in all cases, fairly close to the midpoint. Analysis of variance showed a gender difference in the predicted direction with females caring more and feeling less positive about doing better than their friends and listing more negative feelings that their friend might experience in such a case. None of the measures showed any effects of Grade, indicating that attitudes towards success were similar at 13 and 15 years.

Caring about better outcomes   Results indicated that females reported they would care significantly more than males if they attained better outcomes than their friends across all four domains, $F(1, 94) = 4.38$, $p < 0.05$. There were no significant main effects for grade, $F(1,94) = 1.10$, *ns*, and the Sex × Grade interaction also was not significant, $F(1,94) = 0.04$, *ns*.

Feelings about better outcomes   More specifically, females reported that they would feel significantly less happy than males if they attained better outcomes than their friends, $F(1, 94) = 4.62$, $p < 0.05$. There were no significant effects of grade, $F(1, 94) = 0.30$, *ns*, and no significant Sex × Grade interaction, $F(1, 94) = 0.47$, *ns*.

Time spent thinking about better outcomes   For the third measure, results showed no significant effects of sex, grade or Sex × Grade, $F(1, 94) = 1.67$, *ns* for sex; $F(1, 94) = 0.31$, *ns* for grade and $F(1, 94) = 0.82$, *ns* for the interaction, indicating that females did not differ from males in how much time they would spend thinking about attaining better outcomes than their friends.

Beliefs about friends' attitudes regarding participants' better outcomes   Based on the number of negative phrases circled, compared with males, females believed that their friends would have significantly more negative feelings towards them if they performed better than their friends, $F(1, 93) = 6.71$, $p < 0.05$. There were no significant effects of grade, $F(1,93) = 0.78$, *ns*, and the Sex ′ Grade interaction also was not significant, $F(1,94) = 0.04$, *ns*.

Part 3: Actual success

To examine whether level of achievement affected responses to performing better than friends, correlations were computed between participants' *reported* actual success in each of the four domains (whether they had a boyfriend/girlfriend, their number of friends, their marks in school and their degree of athletic success) and their scores on each of the four measures that assessed how much the participants would be affected by attaining better outcomes than their friends. None of the correlation coefficients were significant (all correlations below $r = 0.23$), indicating that actual success in a domain did not appear to influence participants' responses to imagining being more successful than their same-sex friends.

> There was no relationship between responses on each of the four measures of attitudes to doing better than a friend and self-reported achievement. Note, however, that there are no independent measures of achievement so it may not be actual success that was being measured.

Table 2 Responses to achieving better outcomes than friends

| Domain | Caring about doing better than friends | | | | Negative feelings in response to doing better than friends | | | | Time spent thinking about doing better than friends | | | |
| | Females | | Males | | Females | | Males | | Females | | Males | |
	M	SD	M	SD	M	SD	M	SD	M	SD	M	SD
Romance	2.45	1.20	2.19	1.12	2.22	1.29	1.83	1.18	2.20	0.98	2.06	0.87
Close friends	2.92	1.34	2.60	1.44	2.43	1.46	2.25	1.47	2.61	1.27	2.34	1.46
Academics	3.12	1.11	2.79	1.43	2.84	1.29	2.46	1.35	2.29	0.96	2.15	1.11
Athletics	3.02	1.22	2.54	1.38	2.61	1.25	2.02	1.16	2.14	1.17	1.85	0.87
All domains	2.88	0.88	2.52	0.79	2.52	0.92	2.13	0.88	2.31	0.78	2.10	0.82

Table 3 *Number of negative phrases chosen to describe friends' reactions towards the participants' better outcomes*

Domain	Females		Males	
	M	SD	M	SD
Romance	1.13	1.62	0.35	0.64
Close friends	1.98	1.97	1.21	2.00
Academics	0.76	1.57	0.32	0.56
Athletics	0.55	1.25	0.30	0.83
All domains	1.11	1.28	0.55	0.70

Study 2

Although the findings of the study provide clear support for the hypotheses that female adolescents have a less positive view of outperforming their friends than males, the authors went on to carry out a second study in which they investigated attitudes in older adolescents (aged 18 years). The second study also provided the opportunity for greater methodological rigour in the design. There were two important methodological advances. First, participants were asked to respond to questions about both hypothetical events (as in Study 1) and also to actual events. The idea behind this was that responses to events that had actually occurred might be different from responses to theoretical events. For example, reactions might be more or less extreme to an event that had actually occurred, such as getting better marks on a test.

The second methodological change was that participants were asked both about their reaction to doing better than a friend and achieving the same. The idea behind this was that males might be more reticent than females in admitting to negative emotions. If this was the case, the gender difference in Study 1 might have arisen from differences in reporting responses rather than a real difference in reaction to doing better than a friend. The opportunity to comment on both scenarios gave the opportunity to see whether females would show a greater difference in their reaction to similar and superior performance than males.

To examine whether the same results would be found in older adolescents as well as to enhance the validity and reliability of the results from the first study, a second study was undertaken. One of the limitations of the first study is that it does not address real events. Another limitation concerns the possibility of a negative responses bias on the part of females. In the latter instance, sex differences in responses may be an artefact of more general sex differences in the valence of emotional responses rather than specific to reactions to attaining better outcomes than friends. That is, females may be more likely than males to report experiencing negative emotions across a variety of social and non-social situations.

To address these limitations, in Study 2, participants were asked to respond to questions regarding both hypothetical and actual events. Further, participants were asked to respond to questions concerning their emotional responses to attaining both better outcomes and the same outcomes as a close same-sex friend. The domains of academics and romantic relationships were selected, because they are particularly important to older adolescents. The hypothesis was that, compared with males, females would have more negative reactions to performing better than their friends and more positive reactions to performing at the same level as their friends.

Method

Participants

Participants were 48 females (*M* = 18.75 years, *SD* = 1.68) and 49 males (*M* = 18.82 years, *SD* = 1.60) attending a junior college in Montréal, Québec. Students came from primarily White, middle class, English-speaking backgrounds. After graduation from high school in Québec, all students attend junior college for 2 years. For those students wishing to continue to university, marks received in junior college determine which university a student will attend. Thus, academic success is highly valued by this population.

Procedure

Groups of students were approached during their free time and asked to complete a brief questionnaire. The first page of the questionnaire asked each student to write the initials of his or her closest friend at the college, then to indicate on a 5-point scale ranging from (1) *Not Very Important* to (5) *Very Important* how important it is for the student to get good marks at the college and how important it is to find a steady boyfriend/girlfriend at the present time.

Then, each participant responded to 8 questions. Half of the questions addressed academic success, and the other half addressed romantic success. Within each of the two domains, participants were asked to respond to questions about two types of hypothetical outcomes and two types of actual outcomes. For both the hypothetical and actual outcomes, students responded to two questions: how they would feel if they were more successful than their close same-sex friend and how they would feel if they and their close same-sex friend were equally successful. Participants used the same scale to respond to each of the questions. The scale ranged from (1) *Quite Bad* to (5) *Quite Good*.

As examples, for the hypothetical events in the academic domain, participants were asked the following two questions: 'How would you honestly feel if at the end of the session you got better marks than your close friend did?' and 'How would you honestly feel if at the end of the session both you and your close friend got exactly the same marks?'

For the actual events in the academic domain, students were asked 'Has it ever happened to you that you got better marks than one of your good friends? If it did, how did you feel?' and 'Has it ever happened to you that both you and one of your good friends got almost exactly the same marks? If it did, how did you feel?' In the romantic domain, four analogous questions referred to participants' relative success compared with their friends in finding a girlfriend/boyfriend. All participants responded that all of the actual events actually had occurred to them.

Results

Because domain was not of interest, responses to the questions from the romantic and academic domains were averaged for the analyses. A t-test first was performed to ensure that there were no sex differences in the importance of the domains. The means for each domain were averaged and entered as the dependent variable with sex as the independent variable. There was no significant effect of sex, $t(95) = 0.44$, ns, indicating that males and females did not differ in the importance they attributed to the domains ($M = 3.30$, $SD = 0.87$ for females and $M = 3.38$, $SD = 0.83$ for males). The specific means for the importance of romance were 2.54 ($SD = 1.40$) for females and 2.82 ($SD = 1.24$) for males. The means for the importance of academics were 4.06 ($SD = 0.78$) for females and 3.94 ($SD = 1.07$) for males.

Two separate repeated-measures ANOVAs were then computed on responses to the hypothetical then actual questions averaged across the two domains with sex as the between-subjects variable and relative outcome (better performance than friend or same performance as friend) as the repeated factor. Significant interactions were followed up with Tukey's tests, $p < 0.05$. Means for each domain are displayed in the tables.

Table 4 presents the means for responses to the questions about the hypothetical events. There was no significant effect of sex, $F(1,95) = 0.43$, ns, but a significant effect of outcome, $F(1, 95) = 41.39$, $p < 0.001$, and a significant interaction between Sex and Outcome, $F(1,95) = 11.19$, $p < 0.01$. Unexpectedly, results showed that participants of both sexes reported that they would feel more positive when they and their same-sex friend achieved the same outcome ($M = 3.93$, $SD = 0.81$) as opposed to when they did better than their friend ($M = 3.32$, $SD = 0.74$). Follow-up Tukey's tests on the interaction between Sex ´ Outcome demonstrated that females reported more positive responses when they hypothesized attaining the same outcomes as their same-sex friend ($M = 4.13$, $SD = 0.81$) than when they imagined performing better than their friend ($M = 3.20$, $SD = 0.78$). Males did not differ in their responses to the two outcomes for same outcomes: ($M = 3.73$, $SD = 0.74$; for better outcomes: $M = 3.44$, $SD = 0.70$).

Table 4   Responses to better and equal outcomes for hypothetical situations

| Domain | Positive feelings about better outcomes | | | | Positive feelings about equal outcomes | | | |
| | Females | | Males | | Females | | Males | |
	M	SD	M	SD	M	SD	M	SD
Romance	2.88	0.87	3.14	0.93	4.06	0.91	3.88	1.01
Academics	3.52	0.97	3.73	0.86	4.21	0.92	3.59	0.86
All domains	3.20	0.78	3.44	0.70	4.13	0.81	3.73	0.74

Table 5 presents the means for responses to questions about the actual events (see Table 5). There was no significant effect of sex, $F = 0.52, ns$, but again a significant effect of outcome, $F(1,95) = 17.96$, $p < 0.001$, and a significant interaction between Sex and Outcome, $F(1,95) = 6.36$, $p < 0.05$. Results showed that, as before, participants of both sexes reported that they had felt more positive when they and their close same-sex friend achieved the same outcomes ($M = 3.71$, $SD = 0.77$) as opposed to when they had done better then their friend ($M = 3.36$, $SD = 0.64$). Tukey's tests on the interaction again showed that females reported more positive responses when they had attained the same outcomes as their friends ($M = 3.85$, $SD = 0.77$) as opposed to when they had performed better than their friends ($M = 3.29$, $SD = 0.70$). In contrast, males did not differ in the valence of their responses to the two outcomes (for the same outcomes: $M = 3.56$, $SD = 0.74$; for better outcomes: $M = 3.42$, $SD = 0.58$).

Although sex differences were not found in responses to performing better or the same as friends, difference scores in responses to the two outcomes

Table 5   *Responses to better and equal outcomes for actual situations*

| Domain | Positive feelings about better outcomes | | | | Positive feelings about equal outcomes | | | |
| | Females | | Males | | Females | | Males | |
	M	*SD*	*M*	*SD*	*M*	*SD*	*M*	*SD*
Romance	2.95	0.78	3.08	0.65	3.76	0.91	3.55	0.85
Academics	3.60	0.89	3.73	0.88	3.91	0.88	3.53	0.82
All domains	3.29	0.70	3.42	0.58	3.85	0.77	3.56	0.74

did demonstrate sex differences. Difference scores were computed for each participant between degree of positive affect reported in the condition in which the participant and good friend achieved the same outcomes and in the condition in which the participant did better than the friend. Difference scores were averaged across domains. Two-tailed t-tests comparing the difference scores for males and females on the hypothetical questions were significant: Females ($M = 0.94$, $SD = 1.09$) preferred the same over better outcomes significantly more than males did ($M = 0.30$, $SD = 0.78$), $t(95) = 3.34$, $p < 0.001$. Similarly, for the questions assessing actual events, females ($M = 0.56$, $SD = 0.90$) preferred the same over better outcomes significantly more than males did ($M = 0.14$, $SD = 0.74$), $t(95) = 2.52$, $p < 0.02$.

> In order to confirm the difference between males and females, there was one final statistical comparison in which the difference between ratings of the two types of outcomes was compared. This comparison showed that there was a greater difference in the ratings by females of the two outcomes than for males and so it reinforced the findings of the analysis of variance and post hoc comparisons.

General discussion

Results from both studies provided support for the hypothesis that females would report feeling more negative than males when they achieved better outcomes than their close same-sex friends. Further, results from Study 1 indicated that participants believed that their good friends would agree with their assessments: When asked what their good friends' attitudes would be if the participants were more successful than their friends, compared with males, females believed that their good friends would think more negatively of them.

These results were found across a number of domains that have been shown to be valued by both sexes in adolescence (Harter, 1990). Consistent with this, overall no sex differences were found in the present studies in the desire to achieve success in these domains. Further, there was no relation between actual performance in these domains and responses to questions about superior performance.

Importantly, at least by late adolescence, both females and males reported that they preferred to attain equal as opposed to better outcomes than their close same-sex friends. Tesser's model of the strain on relationships that results from unequal levels of performance thus was applicable to the relationships of both sexes (Tesser, 1998; Tesser et al., 1998). What needs to be added to the model, however, is that females are more sensitive than males to this strain.

Furthermore, a female may anticipate that another female would not make a good friend if the other female already had achieved more (Owens et al., 2000). Thus, females may reject other females even before they have formed a friendship with them. In contrast, males are more likely than females to be attracted to same-sex peers of higher status (Karweit & Hansell, 1983). Further research is necessary before the reasons that females react more negatively than males to other same-sex peers of higher status, whether friends or not friends, can be elucidated.

It is unlikely that the current findings were due to a greater negative response bias on the part of females versus males, because in Study 2, females reported more positive feelings than males in hypothetical and actual situations in which they and their friends were equally successful. Nevertheless, the findings are based on self-reports and therefore require replication with other methods. Numerous linguistic as well as participant-observational studies, however, provide evidence for the ecological validity of the results. Further, empirical studies on indirect aggression support the finding that females may be egalitarian at least partially because they are afraid of incurring other females' wrath if they attempt to outperform them (e.g. Owens et al., 2000).

The authors note that their findings are based on self-report data and, as such, would need to be confirmed by other measures. However, they point to the fact that there was support for their conclusions from studies looking at related issues such as differences in the language that males and females use in interacting with same sex friends. Consistency with findings from other studies, especially those using a somewhat different methodology, can provide important supporting evidence for the claims emerging from a single study.

These results have important implications for understanding the development of females' peer relationships. It is only relatively recently that empirical studies have focused on difficulties in females' relationships with one another (e.g.

Crick & Grotpeter, 1995; Lagerspetz, Bjorkqvist, & Peltonen, 1988; Underwood, 2003), whereas males' difficulties in relationships have received much attention (Crick et al., 2002). Most research on females' relationships has emphasized their strengths, particularly the intimacy and supportiveness that occur (e.g. Jordan, 1991; Rubin, 1985; Tannen, 1990; Taylor et al., 2000). The difficulties girls and women confront in their same-sex friendships deserve more careful analysis.

The results also contribute to an understanding of women's behaviour at work. The literature on business suggests that women face unique challenges in forming hierarchical relationships with other women. According to a recent report by several consultants for more than 100 of the top private corporations and public agencies in the USA including Fortune 500 companies, universities, professional associations and the army, individuals of both sexes across diverse professions reported that women are the first to attack a woman who gets promoted (Heim, Murphy, & Golant, 2001). Others have reported the same finding using rigorous empirical reviews (Eagly & Karau, 1991, 2002; Eagly, Makhijani, & Klonsky, 1992).

This may explain one of the most consistent findings in reviews of the literature on sex differences in managerial styles: Women behave more democratically than men (for reviews, see Eagly & Johnson, 1990; Hooijberg & DiTomaso, 1996; Klenke, 1994). To avoid eliciting the disapproval of subordinate females, female leaders may behave differently from male leaders, thus ensuring that outcomes are as identical as possible for all women involved, including the leaders (Heim et al., 2001). It is not always possible to implement this strategy, however, particularly when women are in leadership positions. Finally, it must be emphasized that women who get promoted also must contend with negative reactions from male subordinates, whereas men are more supported in their advancement by both other men and by women (Eagly & Karau, 2002).

What is crucial to interpreting the adult literature on leadership is the recognition that sex differences in responses to differential performance occur even in early childhood. Females and males develop with differing expectations for their same-sex peers. Females expect equality in their relationships, whereas males are more comfortable with hierarchies. Over the years of childhood and adolescence, these differences are likely to become accentuated.

Further research is needed to understand the reasons for sex differences in responses to unequal performance. One possible explanation is that females form more intimate relationships than males from early childhood onwards (for reviews, see Buhrmester & Prager, 1995; Cross & Madson, 1997; Gilligan & Wiggins, 1988). This intimacy may extend in adulthood to work relationships (Heim et al., 2001; Tannen, 1994) and even to imagining future friendships (Owens et al., 2000). As Tesser argues, the closer the bond, the more difficult it is for a relationship to absorb inequalities of performance in important domains (Tesser, 1988; Tesser et al., 1988). Loosening the closeness of bonds between women, in certain contexts, may alleviate some of the strain that results from unequal levels of performance and achievement. Concomitantly, strengthening the bonds between men may reduce acceptance of hierarchical relationships and produce more democratic decision-making.

The results of the current study have particular relevance for female adolescents. The strengths of females' friendships – the ability to share vulnerabilities and to receive empathic caring without being denigrated in a private relationship – are particularly important in adolescence when individuals of both sexes become more dependent on same-sex friends for identity formation (e.g. Buhrmester, 1996; Buhrmester & Prager, 1995; Richards & Larson, 1989; Richards et al., 1998). Adolescence also is a time, however, when individuals strive to begin to achieve success in public domains that will allow them financially to support families. In Western societies, women have joined the public work force in large numbers. One of the limitations of females' compared with males' relationships, therefore, may be greater psychological difficulty in integrating the maintenance of relationships with the desire to achieve personal success in domains that will result in financial payoffs and elevated status.

It is unknown whether females' greater negative reactions to unequal success within their friendships produce behavioural changes. The current research did not assess sex differences in willingness to compromise personal goals or friendships or, alternatively, to strive harder to attain personal goals or maintain friendships. It is plausible that, compared with males, females may not strive for personal goals as much as males when their same-sex friends are less successful than they are, or may not disclose their successes as much as males to friends, thereby compromising the honesty and self-esteem that females' friendships can provide. Rubin (1985) provides anecdotal evidence that successful adult women do not share their achievements with their same-sex friends unless they believe that their friends have experienced similar levels of success. At the same time, Heim et al. (2001) provide case histories of women forgoing professional success to maintain amicable collegial relationships at work. Empirical research is required to document whether individuals of each sex differ in their actual willingness to damage their own performance to maintain equality with their same-sex friends or coworkers.

Likewise, it remains unknown whether females are more likely than males to terminate same-sex friendships when levels of success become too disparate. Eder (1985) provides anecdotal examples of eighth-grade females who sacrificed their closest same-sex friendships when one member of the pair became either more or less popular. Newly popular females preferred to be friends with other popular females, as opposed to less popular females who were their former friends. Females who were once friends with newly popular girls preferred to find new friends who were at their own lower levels of popularity. Karweit and Hansell (1983) found that boys in contrast were much less likely than girls to sacrifice friendships when one individual became more successful than another. Empirical research is necessary to investigate whether these intriguing qualitative findings are valid across a number of samples.

Males who form less intimate relationships that often occur within a group may be less influenced by one friend's relative accomplishments. If a close friend who is a fellow group member became more successful in a domain, a male might feel that the status of his group, and therefore his own status, would be enhanced by his fellow group member's success. Further, there would be many other members of the group who were not as successful in the domain, so any one group member would not feel alone in his relative inferiority. Males' style of continually vying for relatively greater success with their friends has serious limitations, such as an unwillingness to express vulnerabilities or to elicit direct psychological support from their same-sex friends. Nevertheless, it is difficult to imagine that two friends will always attain identical levels of success, especially over an extended period of time. Thus, there may be some heretofore neglected benefits of males' friendships. Healthy development requires both striving to attain personal goals as well as developing close relationships (e.g. Blatt & Blass, 1996; Erikson, 1968). The process of balancing personal goals with relationships may require ensuring that close friends experience success in different domains, so that unequal levels of success in the same domain are less threatening to the friendship (Tesser, 1988). Alternatively, during periods in which levels of success in the same domain become too disparate, it may be necessary to decrease the intimacy of the friendship and utilize a more masculine style of relating.

Further research to elucidate both females' and males' responses to their own and others' superior performances in important domains will likely contribute to an understanding of human development. It is reasonable to postulate that individuals' responses to disparities in performance in important domains with same-sex friends will influence significantly their motivations both to continue the friendships and to perform well in a domain. The consequences of self-evaluations based on social comparison, therefore, deserve careful study to understand more completely how each sex balances relationships with personal achievements.

Acknowledgements

This research was supported by grants from the Le Fonds pour la Formation de Chercheurs et l' Aide à la Recherche du Québec and the Social Sciences and Humanities Research Council of Canada to the first author. The authors are grateful to Ms Sharron Falana and the teachers and students who participated in the project. Thanks also to Maya Cohen and Natasha Lekes for help with data collection and to the two anonymous reviewers for their thoughtful insights.

4

EXPERIMENTAL RESEARCH WITH
INFANTS AND TODDLERS

The next two chapters are concerned with experimental research in developmental psychology. The choice of experimental task is heavily dependent on the age of the children being studied so, in this chapter, I consider experimental research with children under the age of 2 years. Even within this relatively small age span, there is considerable variation in methodology. In essence, with young infants, who are unable to understand instructions or to produce spoken responses, experimenters have to rely on simple behaviours, such as sucking, leg kicking or looking, that are within the infant's repertoire. Even responses that involve object manipulation or pointing will not be within the competence of infants who are only a few months old. Alternatively, researchers can use physiological measures such as changes in heart rate or measures of neural activity in the brain.

Both behavioural and physiological measures are used to compare infants' responses to particular stimuli and events. However, although the measures themselves may appear relatively straightforward, there has been considerable controversy about how the results of experimental infancy studies should be interpreted. The argument centres round the kind of explanation that should be given for infant behaviour. Should, for example, responses be interpreted in terms of infants' ability to make relatively low-level perceptual distinctions or in terms of higher level abilities such as categorisation? Another point of controversy lies in the decision that authors have to make about whether they wish to claim that abilities present in very young infants are innate or learned. We discuss these issues of interpretation as we consider individual papers.

A small number of experimental techniques have become common in recent infancy research and these are the ones I focus on in this chapter. Paper 5 makes use of habituation (Sirois & Mareschal, 2002). The general idea behind habituation is that, if a stimulus is shown over a prolonged period, an infant's interest will gradually decline. Once habituation has occurred (as defined by a proportional drop in the level of response) a new stimulus is presented. If the new stimulus appears novel to the infant, dishabituation will occur and the rate of infant responding will increase.

As with a number of the other techniques that are described in this chapter, I have chosen to focus on the logic of the design rather than the detail of the technique. A detailed discussion of particular techniques is beyond the scope of this book and they are usually learned through specialist postgraduate training in a research laboratory.

The habituation/dishabituation paradigm

Paper 5   Infants' perceptions of four different languages (Christophe & Morton, 1998)

This paper uses non-nutritive sucking as a way of measuring infant behaviour. With visual stimuli, it is common to measure looking preferences (as in Papers 6 and 7) but, since there is nothing specific for babies to look at when stimuli involve language or tones (for example), sucking intensity is used to measure habituation and dishabituation. The overarching rationale is identical irrespective of whether the infant is responding by sucking or by looking. Following a habituation phase, novel stimuli are presented to see whether there is a significant increase in level of response, that is, whether infants show signs of dishabituation.

The researchers used a variant on the standard habituation/dishabituation method in which the amount of dishabituation to an experimental change is compared with that to a control change (Hesketh, Christophe & Dehaene-Lambertz, 1997). The amount of increased sucking during dishabituation has to be greater for the experimental change (in this case, from one language to another) than for the control change (in this case, from one speaker to another) in order for the authors to conclude that infants have been able to perceive the experimental change.

There was another important control in the design in that, across the three studies reported in the paper, three different foreign languages were compared with English, which is the language that the infants hear being spoken at home. Two of the languages were expected to be perceived by infants as differing from English (French and Japanese) and one (Dutch) was expected to be perceived as similar.

Developmental Science, 2002, 1(2), 215–219

REPORT

Is Dutch native English? Linguistic analysis by 2-month-olds

Anne Christophe[1] and John Morton[2]

[1]LSCP, CNRS-EHESS, Paris, France and MRC-CDU, London, UK, [2]MRC-CDU, London, UK

One of the most important tasks for a new-born infant is to learn its native language. The majority of babies grow up in a multi-lingual environment and must learn some characteristics of their mother tongue as early as possible so as to distinguish it from other languages. This is a particularly crucial ability, since infants could not possibly learn the syntax of a language (that is, discover the regularities shared by a number of sentences) if they worked on a database containing sentences from several different languages (Mehler et al., 1994).

It has been shown that newborns can discriminate between their mother tongue and a foreign language. Mehler, Jusczyk, Lambertz et al. (1998) found that 4-day-old French infants discriminate between French (their mother tongue) and Russian stimuli, showing a preference for their native language (see also Moon et al., 1993, for equivalent results with English and Spanish). In addition, newborns are able to discriminate between utterances in two foreign and unfamiliar languages (Mehler and Christophe, 1995; Nazzi, Bertoncini, and Mehler, 1998). Most of these studies have been replicated successfully using speech which has been low-pass filtered at 400 Hz. Under these conditions, prosodic features such as intonation and rhythm are preserved, whereas most phonemic information is missing. It is therefore probable that babies' ability to discriminate between languages is based on a representation of speech prosody. It is very likely that the infant's preference for their native language comes from their having learned its prosody in utero. However, we still do not know the precise nature of the prosodic representation that babies use to classify languages.

Babies of 2 months of age behave slightly differently from newborns. They still discriminate between their native language and other languages but they fail to show any recovery of interest when switched from one foreign language to another. Thus, Mehler et al. (1988) showed that while 2-month-old American babies were able to discriminate between English (their mother tongue) and Italian, they did not discriminate between French and Russian. A possible interpretation of this counter-intuitive result is that, while newborns still attempt to analyse in detail any speech sample they are exposed to, 2-month-old infants have sufficient knowledge of their mother tongue to be able to filter out any foreign language as being not relevant.

Hesketh, Christophe and Dehaene-Lambertz (1997) developed a variant of the contingent sucking response method which has the advantage that it can be used both with newborns and with 2-month-old infants and can be used with extended segments of speech. With this technique, 2-month-old English babies distinguished clearly between English and Japanese. It is this technique which we used to explore the infants' abilities further.

The Hesketh et al. variation (Hesketh et al., 1997) requires that an infant produces three high-amplitude sucks in order to trigger presentation of another sentence of a similar kind. So, for example, if an infant heard a Japanese sentence and produced three consecutive high amplitude sucks that were less than one second apart, this would trigger another Japanese sentence. So the more the infant sucks, the more sentences will be heard. The number of sentences of a given type that are triggered can then be used as a measure of infant responsiveness to each type of stimulus.

Method

The method for the Hesketh et al. experiment will first be briefly described (see Hesketh et al., 1997, for details). The other experiments to be reported used the same technique apart from changes in language. The stimuli consisted of 80 sentences, half in English, half in Japanese, between 15 and 21 syllables long. These were recorded by four female native English speakers and four female native Japanese speakers respectively. Speakers were native as to the aim of the experiment and were instructed to read as naturally as possible. Ten sentences from each speaker were selected and matched for syllabic length (17.8 syllables) and duration (3.1 seconds). Each infant underwent two changes in stimulation, one experimental (language) change, the other control (or speaker) change. The key measure was thedifference between these two changes.

Note that this study uses natural sentences of similar length, spoken by female native speakers. The reason for the choice of stimuli lies in the suggestion – made in the introduction to the paper – that young infants discriminate among languages on the basis of prosody. Prosody is the natural rhythm of a language and it incorporates such things as the length and type of syllables and the stress patterns within individual words and

> *sentences. Clearly, the typical prosodic pattern for a given language will be most evident in naturally spoken sentences. Furthermore, since prosody can be affected by sentence length, it is important that the sentences were of similar length. Also, had sentence length varied, infants might have paid attention to length rather than other features.*

Half the babies received the experimental change first and the control change second. In addition, the order of presentation of languages and of speakers was counterbalanced across subjects. This yielded eight conditions. In each of the three phases the baby heard sentences from two speakers with the idea of making speaker change mundane.

> *Note that two different speakers read the sentences that infants heard during habituation. The aim was to ensure that the infants would not regard a change in speaker as novel when the test phase began – since they had already had experience of this – and so changes in sucking in response to speaker change could serve as a control for responses to language change.*

Subjects were seated in a car seat placed in a soundproofed chamber and offered a standard (steam sterilised) pacifier. One experimenter, out of view of the baby and deaf to the stimuli, checked that the pacifier stayed in the baby's mouth throughout the experiment. A second experimenter monitored the experiment on the computer outside the chamber. The computer recorded the pressure of the infant's sucks via an analogue-digital card (NIDAQ), detected the sucking responses and delivered the sentences through a ProAudio 16 sound board according to the reinforcement schedule (see below). The computer also saved both the moment and amplitude of each suck as well as the stimuli triggered by the sucks. Hesketh et al. (1997) reported that the number of sentences triggered was a cleaner measure than the number of sucking responses. Only this measure will be reported here.

The experiment started with a short period without stimulation (about 30 secs) to settle the infants. The first phase of the experiment then began, during which infants heard sentences in either English or Japanese contingently upon their high-amplitude (HA) sucks. After a short 'shaping' phase, three HA sucks were required to trigger each sentence (such that there was less than one second between two consecutive sucks). There was an ISI of at least 600 ms between consecutive sentences. When reaching the end of an ISI period after presentation of one sentence, the program looked back to see if HA sucks had occurred recently: any sequence of three HA sucks such that the last one occurred within the last 600 ms was used to instantly trigger a new sentence.

This procedure ensured fluent presentation of sentences in case of sustained sucking activity. Within each phase of the experiment, the order of presentation of the sentences was quasi-random for each baby.

The habituation phase involved either English or Japanese. Once habituation had occurred, infants were then presented with either a speaker change or with a language change (that is English → Japanese or Japanese → English). Then they were presented with the change that they had not already received. Since babies can rapidly lose attention in studies like this, it is very important to control for the order of the two conditions. Note that, in test phases (as well as during habituation), two different speakers were used so that a change in speaker was not novel for the infants.

A switch in stimulation occurred after a predefined habituation criterion had been met. For two consecutive minutes the infant's HA sucking rate had to be less than 80 per cent of the maximum sucking rate from the beginning of the experiment. Each phase of the experiment lasted at least 5 full minutes. Sixteen babies aged between 6–12 weeks participated in the study, mean age 8 weeks 6 days. Subjects were randomly assigned to one of the eight conditions prior to testing.

The first phase of the experiment involved habituation. At the very beginning of the study the infants had to learn that sucking strongly on the dummy (high amplitude sucking) would control what they were listening to. Once this link had been established, stimulus presentation of either English or Japanese sentences was made contingent on sucking. Babies continued to hear sentences until their response level had dropped to a pre-determined criterion. In this study, the criterion was set at 80 per cent of the level of sucking at the beginning of the study for a two minute period. Since sucking rates fluctuate over time, it is important to determine the length of time over which the reduced level of sucking is measured. The time taken to reach this criterion of 80 per cent sucking over two minutes would have varied from infant to infant since there are typically quite large individual differences in the time taken to habituate.

To assess the effect of the experimental manipulation, two kinds of analyses were performed on the data: ANOVAs and non-parametric tests. For each baby we counted the number of sentences triggered during the two minutes before and after the experimental (language) switch. The difference between these two values gives us a measure of dishabituation to the language shift. The equivalent measure was computed for the control (speaker) switch. The difference between these two dishabituation scores represents a discrimination index for each baby: whenever this value is positive, the baby reacted more to the language change than to the speaker change. These values are shown in Figure 1 (left hand column).

A Wilcoxon signed ranks test showed that the median of the discrimination index for the number of sentences triggered was significantly above zero ($Z = 3.4$, $p < 0.001$). In the ANOVAs, the dependent measure was the dishabituation scores for the Experimental and Control switches. There was one within-subject factor (Experimental vs Control switch) and two between subject counterbalancing factors, Order (experimental switch first, versus control switch first), and Language (English first vs Japanese first). There was a main effect of the Experimental factor ($F(1,12) = 11.6$, $p < 0.01$), no significant effect of any of the counterbalancing factors, and no interactions between the Experimental and counterbalancing factors.

Discrimination of two foreign languages: French vs Japanese

Previous experiments using other techniques have indicated that 2-month-old infants discriminated their native tongue from other languages, but that they failed to distinguish between pairs of unfamiliar languages.

Our next experiment, then, involved testing English babies on French and Japanese. These languages are very different from each other as well as from English; for instance, French has fixed word stress, and rather simple syllabic structure through resyllabification; Japanese exhibits pitch accent, is left-recursive (while both French and English are right-recursive), and prohibits consonant clusters (Dupoux et al., submitted). Sixteen babies took part in this experiment, mean age 9 weeks, 5 days.

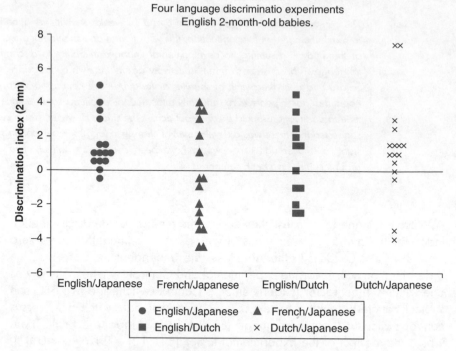

Four language discriminatio experiments
English 2-month-old babies.

Figure 1   *Results of four language discrimination experiments using the modified non-nutritive sucking method (Hesketh et al., in press) where sentences are presented contingently upon sucking responses and each baby is submitted to two shifts of stimulation, one experimental (language change) and one control (speaker change). A discrimination index is computed for each baby: it represents the difference between the increase in the number of sentences triggered for the language change and the increase for the speaker (or control) change. Whenever this value is positive, the baby showed more interest in the language change than in the speaker change. Increases in the number of sentences triggered are computed using two minutes before and after each shift of stimulation.*

similar) but the majority had scores that were greater than 1, indicating greater response to the language change than to the speaker change. This pattern was reflected in the outcome of the inferential statistics. These showed that the relative number of sentences triggered was above zero; and that there was a main effect of type of change. There were no other significant effects, showing that the infants' responses were not affected by which language they had heard during the habituation phase or by any other of the counterbalanced variables. Note, however, that in spite of group effects, there was considerable individual variation among the scores. Such variation is often not reported in detail but, for developmental psychology research, it is important to show whether effects are homogeneous or, as here, variable from participant to participant. The presentation of individual scores allows the reader to gauge the extent of individual variation.

The distribution of the discrimination index can be seen in the second column of figure 1. The infants gave no indication of being more interested in language change than in speaker change (Wilcoxon, $Z < 1$; ANOVA: $F(1,12) < 1$). This result is significantly different from the results of the experiment with English and Japanese. In an ANOVA contrasting the distribution of discrimination indices in these experiments, $F(1, 28) = 8.32$, $(p < 0.01)$.

> The infants in this study were growing up in an English-speaking community and so English would have been familiar and Japanese unfamiliar. In the second study, the factor of familiarity is distinguished from that of difference by presenting two unfamiliar but different languages. As the authors have explained, at the level of prosody, French and Japanese are very different. Japanese has an open syllable structure in which the great majority of syllables end in a vowel. Japanese also does not use consonant clusters which means that most syllables are of the form consonant–vowel (as is typified by the word Sudoku which has recently come into English). French has a more complex syllable structure which allows consonant clusters although it does have fixed word stress. These differences mean that, at the prosodic level, it should be relatively easy to tell the two languages apart.

> The results of the second study are shown in column 2 of Figure 1 where it can be seen that the pattern of results looks very different from the first study. Now scores are spread evenly from +4 to -4, indicating the some infants responded more to a change in speaker and some to a change in language. Overall, there was no main effect of type of change.

The lack of interest shown by 2-month-olds in the differences between foreign languages is in line with previous work. Paired with Nazzi et al.'s (1998) confirmation that newborn infants can discriminate between sentences belonging to two foreign languages (with the same experimental technique as here), this result confirms the developmental trend already described. Our best interpretation is that 2-month-old infants have enough knowledge of the properties of their native language to be able to filter out foreign input as being irrelevant to their language learning. In that case, both French and Japanese would simply be classified as 'foreign' and would not be analysed to a sufficient depth to allow the differences to be detected.

The results of the first two experiments immediately pose a new question: how specified is the 2-month-olds' representation of their mother-tongue? What do they consider native, and what do they filter out as being foreign? To answer this question, we picked a language which shares with English a number of prosodic properties. Dutch, like English, has vowel reduction, complex syllabic structure, and the same sort of word stress as English. These factors lead to both

English and Dutch as being heard as stress-timed (Cutler et al., 1997). In fact, Dutch and English have already been shown to be rather similar to babies' ears: Nazzi et al. (1998) demonstrated that French newborns do not distinguish between Dutch and English filtered sentences.

Discrimination of two stress-timed languages: English vs Dutch

There is an interesting developmental pattern here in that previous studies, using both the same and different paradigms, have found that newborn infants respond differently to sentences from two different languages. The suggestion here is that slightly older infants, who have greater familiarity with the prosody of the language of their speech community, do not attend in detail to unfamiliar languages and so are no more sensitive to changes in speaker than in language when neither language is familiar. This suggestion paves the way for a third experiment in which a native language (English) is contrasted with a 'foreign' language with similar prosody (Dutch).

There are two main possibilities for this experiment. On the one hand, it is possible that English 2-month-olds would behave exactly like the French newborns, and confuse the two languages. On the other hand, they may be able to discriminate Dutch from English, thanks to their exposure to English. Unlike Nazzi et al. (1998), we decided to use unfiltered sentences, as in our previous experiments. This means that, as Dutch and English differ widely in their phonemic inventories and phonotactics, being very distinct for adult listeners, these factors could give the infants additional cues for making the discrimination. Sixteen babies participated in the study, mean age 10 weeks 1 day.

The data are shown in the third column of figure 1. The group showed some interest in the shifts between Dutch and English but the relative increase in sucking rate was only marginally significant (ANOVA: $F (1,12) = 4.17$, $p = 0.064$; Wilcoxon, $Z = 1.85$, $p = 0.065$). The distribution of the discrimination index scores for English/Dutch was not significantly different from that for English/Japanese (ANOVA $F (1,28) < 1$, $p = 0.10$) and was marginally different from that for French/Japanese ($F (1,28) = 3.97$, $p < 0.06$).

The results of this third study showed a pattern that was somewhere in between that of the first two studies. A majority of participants had positive scores on the discrimination index but six did not. The lack of a consistent preference for a language change was borne out by the finding that the discrimination index scores were only marginally different from those in the French/Japanese study. Note, however, that there was a wide spread of scores, suggesting that some infants were responding to the language change while others were not.

Is Dutch native English? Dutch vs Japanese

> *This pattern of individual variation was repeated in the final study in which infants were presented with sentences from Dutch and Japanese. Overall results were marginally different from that for the French/Japanese discrimination but not for English/Japanese or English/Dutch.*

The previous experiment indicated that some babies of 2 months find it hard to discriminate between English and Dutch sentences. This cannot be attributed to a lack of interest of infants, since their mother tongue is present in the experiment. Instead, this result indicates that at least some of the infants confuse sentences from the two languages. In addition, it is possible that we tapped in a transition period where babies start paying attention to cues that distinguish Dutch from English (which might be phonemic). Taken to its limit, this result implies that our babies, or at least some of them, consider Dutch sentences as belonging to their native language. If this is truly the case, we predict that these infants should discriminate between Dutch (assimilated to native) and Japanese. This is what we tested in the next experiment. Sixteen babies, mean age 9 weeks 4 days, participated in the study.

The distribution of discrimination index scores is shown in the fourth column of figure 1. A majority of the infants were more interested by the language change than by the speaker change. Just like in the previous experiment, we observed marginally significant discrimination (F (1,12) = 3.4, p = 0.09, Z = 1.9, p = 0.054). The distribution of the discrimination index scores for this experiment was not significantly different from English/Japanese (F (1, 28) < 1), was marginally different from French/Japanese (F(1, 28) = 3.89, p = 0.06), and was not different from English/Dutch (F < 1). Inspection of Figure 1 shows that there is a wide distribution of data, suggesting that the group is not homogeneous. In other words, some infants have specified native sufficiently to exclude Dutch, whereas the rest have not.

Discussion

Using the modified contingent sucking response we have shown that English 2-month-olds discriminate English from Japanese but not French from Japanese. Given that this habituation-dishabituation technique measures infants' interest in changes in auditory stimulation, it allows us to evaluate their spontaneous partitioning of perceptual space into categories. In the present case, the results suggest that babies form two major categories, one for English, which could be termed 'native' or 'mother tongue', and one, with French and Japanese, of 'foreign languages'.

In the last 2 experiments of this paper, we studied English infants' perception of Dutch, a language that is prosodically very similar to English. We contrasted Dutch to English and to Japanese. If English babies treat Dutch as native, they should not be able to discriminate between English and Dutch, but should readily distinguish Dutch from Japanese; in contrast, if they have already set up their *native* category such that Dutch is excluded, they should distinguish between Dutch and English but ignore the difference between Dutch and Japanese, both of which would be in the category *foreign*. Both experiments gave marginally significant results, indicating that some English babies consider Dutch as native but others do not. The former would distinguish Dutch from Japanese but not from English; the latter group would distinguish Dutch from English but not from Japanese. If we tested babies in both conditions, we predict that whenever one condition works the other would not. What factors may account for this individual variation? The most obvious candidate is age. At one month, all infants might regard Dutch as native, whereas by four months they might all have excluded it. Further, we would expect early exposure to different languages to affect the speed of setting up a tight specification of native but it is unlikely to be a factor in our experiments since we selected the babies to come from monolingual English households.

Eventually we will need to distinguish between environments where second languages are addressed to the infant from those where second languages are present but not directly addressed. The second case might accelerate the definition of native whereas the first case, true bilingualism, might lead to confusion. Recent experiments by Bosch and Sebastian (1997) showed that by four months of age, bilingual Spanish/Catalan babies already behaved differently from monolingual babies (either Spanish or Catalan). Monolingual babies oriented faster to their mother tongue than to English. In contrast, bilinguals orient to Spanish or to Catalan significantly more slowly than to English. Is this because of confusion? Apparently not, since in more recent and still unpublished work, these authors showed that, although Spanish and Catalan are close, both monolingual and bilingual 4-month-olds can discriminate between them. Of course the gap between these 4-month-olds and our 2-month-olds is enormous and it could be that at 2 months bilingual babies are confused. At any rate, it has become clear that, from birth, infants work hard at learning what language is native.

One of the key points raised in the discussion is that some of the infants appeared to be treating Dutch as though it were their native language while others were not. The authors suggest that age may play an important part in performance in the studies. However, they do not look at age factors within their own data which might have provided some support for their argument. If there is a developmental story to be told here, a longitudinal study beginning at birth and spanning the first few months of life could show whether the authors' explanation is correct that a native language is treated differently from a foreign language as babies gain experience.

Acknowledgements

The work reported in this paper was assisted by a grant from the Human Frontiers Science Programme, the Human Capital and Mobility Programme, and the European Science Foundation. We especially want to thank Sarah Hesketh, Jon Bartrip and Sarah Minister for their help in recruiting and testing subjects.

Intermodal preferential looking

The next paper uses preferential looking to investigate young children's ability to tell the difference between an accurate pronunciation of a word and a slight mispronunciation. Unlike the previous study, there was no need for a familiarisation phase because the words chosen are already familiar to the children.

Paper 6 Young children's ability to detect mispronunciations of words (Bailey & Plunkett, 2002)

Cognitive Development, 2002, 17, 1265–1282

Phonological specificity in early words

Todd M. Bailey, Kim Plunkett

Department of Experimental Psychology, University of Oxford, Oxford, UK

1. Introduction

> *The authors begin by citing evidence to show that young children appear to have difficulty in hearing the difference between two similar words – or between a word and a mispronunciation of that word. The question they address in this paper is why young children show such confusions.*

In contrast to adults, children are relatively poor at distinguishing between minimally different words (Gerken, Murphy, & Aslin, 1995). Even though children can discriminate the phonological contrasts of their native language by the age of 2 months (Kuhl, 1987), they fail to exercise this ability consistently in distinguishing between different words. In particular, children have more difficulty distinguishing two syllables when they are used as words to refer to objects than when the same syllables are used nonreferentially (Stager & Werker, 1997). Stager and Werker found that 14-month-olds failed to discriminate the minimal pair 'bih' and 'dih' when the syllables accompanied images to which they ostensively referred. In contrast, children succeeded at the discrimination task when the syllables accompanied abstract checkerboard patterns which presumably were not interpreted as potential referential targets. Older children also have a limited ability to make fine phonetic distinctions in identifying words (Barton, 1980; Walley, 1987). Eilers and Oller (1976) taught 2-year-olds to refer to a novel toy with a name (e.g., 'gar') which was similar to a real word (e.g., 'car'). When told whether a piece of candy was hidden under the 'gar' or the 'car,' children went to the wrong location between 10 and 60% of the time, depending on the particular pair of syllables involved.

A natural explanation for the relatively poor word discrimination ability of children is that early lexical representations may contain only partial phonological specifications for words, and that discrimination ability approaches adult levels only when lexical specificity increases. Two accounts have been offered to explain the increase in the specificity of phonological representations. One is that as children grow older their vocabulary increases and they need, therefore, to specify words in more detail to tell them apart from an increasing number of other words (Charles-Luce & Luce, 1990; Jusczyk, 1986; Metsala, 1999; Stager & Werker, 1997). The other is that the phonological specifications for individual words become more detailed as children become more familiar with those words (Barton, 1976, 1980; Metsala, 1999).

Two contrasting theories are considered. The first is that the phonological detail that young children store about an individual word becomes more specific with age, as they are required to make distinctions among an increasing number of words that are very similar to one another. This means that older children, who know more words, will be able to make finer discriminations than younger children; and furthermore, words that are very similar to a lot of other words will have a more detailed phonological representation. The second possibility is that it is not age per se, or the number of words a child knows, that is important but the familiarity of the words. On this account, the phonological information about familiar words should be better than for less familiar words.

The first of these explanations is a developmental one because the amount of specification would depend on the size of the child's vocabulary, which changes with age. Charles-Luce and Luce (1990, 1995) examined the vocabularies of 5-,7-year-olds and adults, and confirmed that words in a child's lexicon have fewer phonologically similar neighbors than those in the adult lexicon. They suggested that since children's words are more discriminable, children may employ less detailed representations, or may not organize the details used for word recognition to the same extent that adults do. Similarly, Jusczyk (1993) argued that the most efficient representation for a word would have just enough detail to achieve successful recognition. Therefore, he argued, the amount of detail in the mental lexicon should increase with vocabulary size. Moreover, the efficiency argument suggests that the amount of detail should be greatest for words in dense neighborhoods, in order to maintain distinctions among a tight cluster of similar-sounding words. Metsala (1999) also argued that children's lexical representations change as a function of vocabulary size and neighborhood density.

The developmental route to increasing phonological specificity predicts that young children in the early stages of vocabulary growth will generally be very poor at distinguishing accurate pronunciations of words from slight mispronunciations, that is, from minimally different nonwords. Children's ability to make such distinctions should increase gradually as they get older and acquire more words. In addition, this hypothesis predicts that the ability to distinguish accurate from inaccurate pronunciations should be correlated with children's vocabulary size. Finally, if lexical specificity is determined word by word depending on the local neighborhood density (i.e., the number of other words in the lexicon which are similar to a particular word), then the ability to distinguish accurate from inaccurate pronunciations should be correlated with the neighborhood density for individual words.

The second explanation is not developmental in the sense that the changes are linked to familiarity with particular words and not to age. Barton (1976) found that the ability of children from 2 to 3 years of age to distinguish minimally different words increased with word familiarity. Metsala (1999) argued that words entering the lexicon earlier achieve more adult-like representations before words learned at a later age, either due to familiarity (i.e., frequency of exposure) or to age-of-acquisition effects. Whereas the developmental hypothesis predicts age differences, the familiarity hypothesis predicts that younger children should have just as well specified phonological representations of words familiar to them as older children do – the only difference between younger and older children should be in the number of familiar words in their vocabulary. The familiarity hypothesis predicts that very young children and older children will both have difficulty making fine phonological distinctions for recently learned words, but will be able to make finer distinctions for more familiar words learned at a very young age.

A recent study by Werker, Fennell, Corcoran, and Stager (2002) offers evidence in support of the developmental hypothesis. They tested toddlers aged 14, 17, and 20 months in a word-learning task. After learning to associate similar pseudo-words ('bih,' 'dhh') to different pictures, children were tested either with the same word-picture pairs, or with reversed pairings. In the reverse condition, children in the two older groups detected the mismatch between word and picture (as revealed by release from habituation), while children in the youngest group did not. Vocabulary size was related to children's ability to detect mismatches in the 17-month-old group but not in the 20-month-old group. Werker et al.'s results indicate that by 17 months of age, but not 14 months, children can represent newly-learned words with enough detail to distinguish slight differences in an on-line habituation task. Werker et al. suggest a developmental interpretation of their findings whereby young language users reach a threshold vocabulary size around 17 month of age that triggers the encoding of phonological detail.

The authors describe a study by Werker and colleagues that found a significant effect of age and vocabulary in a study in which toddlers of 14, 17 and 20 months were compared on a word-learning task. (Older children and those with larger vocabularies did better.) They go on to describe a study by Swingley and Aslin where there was no effect of age or vocabulary size. Note that both studies used measures of looking time but, as the authors go on to point out, there was an important difference in their methodology.

In another study, Swingley and Aslin (2000) investigated the effects of age and vocabulary size on the phonological detail associated with familiar words. They examined the looking behavior of toddlers, aged 18–24 months, when asked to direct their gaze toward one of two pictures whose name was either pronounced accurately (e.g., 'dog') or mispronounced slightly ('tog'). On average, children looked at the target picture more when its name was pronounced correctly than when it was mispronounced. The size of the pronunciation effect was not correlated with either age or vocabulary size. In a later study, Swingley and Aslin (in press) obtained similar results for 14-month-olds. Thus, Swingley and Aslin's results do not support a developmental hypothesis. Indeed, they conclude that in contrast to the findings of Werker and her colleagues, their findings support a continuity hypothesis in which 'infants' learning of phonetic categories over the course of the first year is indeed relevant for the representation of infants' first words.' Insofar as Swingley and Aslin (2000, in press) found no differences in the phonological detail associated with familiar words from 14 to 24 months of age, their results are also consistent with the familiarity hypothesis.

Werker et al. used habituation followed by dishabituation (as in Paper 5) and pseudo-words while Swingley and Aslin used inter-modal preferential looking and real words. Habituation relies on repeated presentation of a stimulus which is not familiar at the start of the session (as in Paper 5). This means that what is being measured is learning during the familiarisation period, as indicated by decreased looking time. Then a new stimulus is presented to see if it stimulates an increase in looking, the assumption being that increased looking indicates that the new stimulus is seen as different from the first stimulus. Inter-modal preferential looking does not involve a prior learning phase but, instead, endeavours to find out what infants and toddlers already know. This is why the Swingley and Aslin study used real words that were already familiar to the children they were testing.

Although the studies of Werker et al. (2002) and Swingley and Aslin (2000, in press) appear to yield conflicting results at least as far as the 14-month-olds are concerned, it is important to note that these two research groups used quite different experimental methods; an habituation switch task and an inter-modal preferential looking task, respectively. Furthermore, Swingley and Aslin used words that are familiar to the children in their study whilst Werker et al. used novel pseudo-words. Either or both of these factors may have conspired to produce the differing pattern of results. On one issue though, both Werker et al. and Swingley and Aslin seem to be agreed: by 20 months of age, young children can detect slight mispronunciations of words, be they novel or familiar. Taken together, these findings seem to undermine the familiarity hypothesis. However, this conclusion may be premature given the plethora of findings discussed earlier that much older children are relatively poor at distinguishing between minimally different words (Barton, 1976, 1980; Eilers and Oller, 1976; Gerken et al., 1995; Metsala, 1999; Walley, 1987). We therefore set out to test the familiarity hypothesis directly, as well as to see whether the null developmental effects reported by Swingley and Aslin replicate even when age is manipulated experimentally.

In an effort to distinguish between the developmental hypothesis and the familiarity hypothesis, we tested the effects of word familiarity on the ability of 18- and 24-month-olds to distinguish words from minimally different nonwords. We focused on these age groups because lexical development makes dramatic advances during this period (Fenson et al., 1994; Goldfield & Reznick, 1990; Hamilton, Plunkett, & Schafer, 2000). Rapid changes in vocabulary offer an excellent opportunity to observe the effects of familiarity, vocabulary size, and neighborhood density on the specificity of phonological representations. Like Swingley and Aslin (2000), we used an inter-modal preferential looking task (Golinkoff, Hirsh-Pasek, Cauley, & Gordon, 1987) to test children's ability to match a spoken word (e.g.,

'Look! Frog!') with the picture it names, as distinguished from a distracter picture (e.g., a goose) presented alongside the target (cf. Reznick, 1990; Schafer & Plunkett, 1998; Thomas, Campos, Shucard, Ransay, & Shucard, 1981). In this task, children generally look back and forth between the two pictures, but if they recognize the spoken word children tend to gaze longer at the target picture than at the distracter. In our study, the name of the target was sometimes pronounced accurately and was sometimes mispronounced (e.g., 'Look! Prog!'). Any deviation in the amount of target looking for inaccurate pronunciations compared to accurate ones would indicate that the inaccurate pronunciations are not being misperceived as perfectly good pronunciations. Thus, changes in target looking offer a measure of children's sensitivity to mispronunciations of the target words.

In this study both age and familiarity were varied and the level of mispronunciation was also carefully controlled by using mispronunciations that differed from the correct pronunciation by either one or two phonological features.

In addition to accurate (OK) pronunciations, we included two levels of mispronunciation (1-Off and 2-Off) in which the initial consonant of the target word was mispronounced by one or two phonological features, respectively (e.g., 'prog' or 'krog' for the target 'frog'). We predicted that the preference to look at targets in response to accurate pronunciations would be reduced or eliminated by mispronunciations. We also anticipated that children would be more sensitive to 2-Off mispronunciations than to 1-Offs, so we expected less target looking for 2-Offs than for either OK or 1-Off pronunciations.

We assessed the effects of word familiarity by contrasting recently learned words with more familiar words. Averaged across children, word familiarity is confounded with developmental factors, including age and size of vocabulary. However, these variables can be teased apart by taking account of each child's vocabulary development. We therefore identified different test words for each child in order to compare older and younger children's recognition of words that they had learned recently with words that they learned much earlier and had therefore known for some time. The developmental hypothesis predicts that older children should be more sensitive than younger children to mispronunciations, so that the reduction in target looking for inaccurate compared to accurate pronunciations should be greater for older children than for younger children. It also predicts a positive correlation between children's vocabulary size and their sensitivity to mispronunciations, and likewise a correlation between words' neighborhood densities and children's sensitivity to mispronunciation of those words. This hypothesis does not predict a difference between recently learned words and more familiar words. In contrast, the familiarity hypothesis does not predict a difference between older and younger children. It also does not predict that either vocabulary size or neighborhood density should be correlated with sensitivity to mispronunciations. It does predict that older and younger children should all be more sensitive to mispronunciations of words which were learned much earlier, and less sensitive to mispronunciations of words which were learned recently. Therefore, if the familiarity hypothesis is true, we would expect the difference in target looking for inaccurate compared to accurate pronunciations to be greater for early words than for recently learned words.

> *Unlike previous studies, the words used in this study were individually chosen for each child based on their vocabulary knowledge. This allowed a very precise comparison between words that children had learned recently and words that had been learned a few months earlier. Vocabulary data for each child also allowed the authors to take account of age and vocabulary knowledge as two separate factors. In general, the older children are, the more words they know. However, especially in the first two years of life, there is considerable individual variation in the rate at which children acquire new words.*

2. Experiment

2.1. Method

2.1.1. Experimental design

> *The essence of the inter-modal preferential looking, which was specifically designed for experimental research on young children's language comprehension, is that an auditory stimulus (in this case a word) is presented via a loudspeaker located in the middle of two video screens, one of which shows a target item and the other a carefully matched item. At the start of each trial the toddler can see both screens and the amount of looking to each is recorded. Then, after a specified time, the target word is played through the loud speaker and looking times are recorded. The critical comparison is between looking time to each screen before the word presented and looking time to each screen after the word is presented. In theory, before they hear a word, toddlers should look at each screen for a similar amount of time, providing that the two stimuli are equally unfamiliar and equally attractive. Then, after hearing a word, infants should show more looking to the screen that matches the word.*

Children sat on their caregiver's lap, looking at pairs of images and listening to an auditory stimulus naming one of the images with either an accurate or inaccurate pronunciation. Looking behavior was monitored to assess the extent to which infants preferred the named target image to the distracter.

We identified familiar words specific to each child, including four words which were understood from an early age, and four words which were learned relatively recently. Across children, 30 different words were tested, so results should reflect general characteristics of the lexicon, and not just potentially idiosyncratic features of one or two words (cf.Gerken et al., 1995; Swingley, Pinto, & Fernald, 1999; Werker et al., 2002).

Each child heard three pronunciations of her eight test words (e.g., 'bib,' 'gib,' and 'kib'). In addition to an accurate (OK) pronunciation, there were two mispronunciations (1-Off and 2-Off), with one and two major class feature changes, respectively, to the onset consonant. Each feature change altered the place of articulation, the manner of articulation, or the voicing of the initial consonant. By comparing nonwords to real words, the present study investigates the degree of phonological detail already present in the child's lexicon (also see Gerken et al., 1995). In this respect this study differs from studies which teach children new words and thereby confound new phonological details and prior lexical knowledge (Edwards, 1974; Eilers & Oller, 1976; Garnica, 1973; Shvachkin, 1973; Stager & Werker, 1997).

For each target word, there were two mispronunciations in which the initial consonant differed from the original. In one mispronunciation, the change involved only one phonetic feature while, for the other, the initial consonant differed by two features from the original.

2.1.2. Participants

Forty-eight children participated in the study. Half the children were about 18 months of age (range 17.8–19.1, M = 18.5, Median = 18.5; 15 boys, 9 girls), and half were about 24 months of age (range 23.5–28.2, M = 24.9, Median = 24.8; 13 boys, 11 girls). Participants had no known hearing or visual impairments, and came from monolingual English-speaking families.

2.1.3. Stimuli

Stimuli were based on 30 monosyllabic concrete nouns. These are listed in Table 1, along with the number of children who heard each mispronunciation. These words were a subset of nouns included on the Oxford Communicative Development Inventory (OCDI; Hamilton et al., 2000). Visual stimuli were computer images created from photographs, with one image depicting each word.

Note that only nouns were tested as the experimental procedure involved the presentation of pictures that depicted the target word. Such depiction is most straightforward in the case of nouns since verbs and prepositions, which may also appear in a child's early vocabulary, are hard to depict in an unambiguous way in a simple picture. Note also that the words used were all one syllable in length and so similar for all children (given that the actual words used varied from child to child).

Auditory stimuli were recordings of a female voice saying each word, spliced into the carrier phrase 'Look! — !' Pronunciations for each word were chosen in triples (e.g., 'bath,' 'dath,' 'nath'), including the citation form, a 1-feature mispronunciation and a 2-feature mispronunciation. As many different triples as possible were identified for each word. Each 1-feature mispronunciation was derived by changing one major class feature (voicing, or place or manner of articulation) in the initial consonant of the word, and each 2-feature mispronunciation was derived from the corresponding 1-feature mispronunciation by changing an additional, different feature. For example, the word 'bib' could be mispronounced as 'gib' by changing the onset's place of articulation. A further alteration, this time affecting voicing, could produce 'kib' from 'gib.' This process ensured that the 2-feature mispronunciations were phonologically and perceptually further than the 1-feature mispronunciations from the citation form. Previous studies of misperceptions which have manipulated the number of featural changes (e.g., Gerken et al., 1995) have not controlled features to this extent, and it is possible that effects attributed to changing two features rather than one in these studies are really due to differences in the types of features changed rather than their number (cf. Edwards, 1974; Garnica, 1973; Shvachkin, 1973).

Potential mispronunciations were checked against common English words (those with a frequency count of at least 25 in the CELEX database; cf. online http://www.kun.nl/celex/), and against less common words which might nevertheless be familiar to a 2-year-old. Mispronunciations were avoided if they were at most one onset feature different from any such word. Words were spoken with an enthusiastic, infant-directed melody, and recorded digitally at a sampling rate of 22.05 kHz.

> Note that the authors were careful to ensure that none of the mispronunciations was similar to another real word. They also carefully controlled the kind of features that were used to create the mispronunciations.

2.1.4. Procedure

In the week prior to the testing of each child, parents completed the OCDI, identifying words their child understood. These reports were used along with an earlier OCDI for the child, obtained when the child was 12–15 months old, and in consultation with the parents to identify the four words (from the set of 30) that the child understood earliest, and the four words that the child learned most recently. A pronunciation triplet was chosen at random for each of these eight words.

Table 1 *Stimuli and number of participants by age and word recency of acquisition*[a]

OK	1-Off	2-Off	Feats	E18	R18	E24	R24
bath	dath	lath	pm	5		3	
bath	dath	nath	pm			4	
bath	dath	rath	pm			2	
bath	dath	zath	pm			2	
bath	rath	zath	pm	8		2	1
bib	gib	kib	pv	2	2	5	
bib	pib	kib	pv	2		1	
bib	pib	tib	pv	2		1	
bib	vib	dhib	pm		1		
bike	pike	kike	pv	2	9	2	2
bird	dird	lird	pm	3	1		
bird	dird	rird	pm	2	1		
bird	dird	zird	pm			2	
bird	mird	nird	pm	3	3	4	1
boot	goot	coot	pv	2	5	5	2
brush	drush	trush	pv	1	1	1	1
brush	prush	frush	mv			1	3
brush	prush	trush	pv	1	2		
bus	muss	nuss	pm		6	5	3
coat	toat	soat	pm	3		2	3
cup	gup	dup	pv	6	5		
dog	tog	kog	pv	13	1	1	
doll	zoll	soll	mv	1	5	3	4
face	thace	dhace	pv		5	1	4
fish	shish	chish	pm		1		
fish	sish	zish	pv	2	4	4	
fish	thish	dhish	pv		1	1	
fish	vish	zish	pv	1		1	
frog	prog	brog	mv				1
frog	prog	trog	pm	1	6	1	4
girl	dirl	nirl	pm				7
girl	dirl	rirl	pm				1
girl	dirl	zirl	pm		1		2
goose	koose	toose	pv		2		5
juice	chuise	shuice	mv	4	1	8	2
leg	zeg	seg	mv		3	2	4
milk	bilk	pilk	mv			2	
milk	nilk	dilk	pm			2	
milk	nilk	rilk	pm	4	1	4	
milk	nilk	zilk	pm	1		1	
milk	vilk	dhilk	pm	1		2	
milk	vilk	zilk	pm	4		1	
mouse	nouse	rouse	pm				1
mouse	nouse	zouse	pm			1	
mouse	vouse	dhouse	pm	1			
mouse	vouse	zouse	pm				2
mouth	bouth	douth	pm			1	
mouth	nouth	louth	pm	2	1	1	
mouth	nouth	routh	pm		1		1
mouth	vouth	dhouth	pm		1	1	
plane	blane	glane	pv		1		

Table 1   (Continued)

OK	1-Off	2-Off	Feats	E18	R18	E24	R24
plane	klane	glane	pv	3	4	2	1
plate	blate	glate	pv	1			1
plate	klate	glate	pv		1		2
sheep	theep	dheep	pv	3	1		
shirt	chirt	jirt	mv				10
shorts	chorts	jorts	mv		1	1	7
sink	zinc	dhink	pv				3
slide	flide	plide	pm		5	2	3
swing	twing	kwing	pm		2	5	1
watch	votch	dhotch	pm	2	5		5

ᵃ Columns show pronunciation triplets, features mispronounced in the 2-Off form (p: place, m: manner, v: voicing), number of 18-month-olds for whom the word was early (E18) and recent (R18), number of 24-month-olds for whom the word was early (E24) and recent (R24). Bilabial phonemes, /b/,/p/,/m/, and labio-dental phonemes, /v/ and /f/, were all treated as having the same place of articulation. Note on transcription: 'th' and 'sh' represent voiceless dental and palatal fricatives, respectively, 'dh' and 'zh' are corresponding voiced fricatives. Post-vocalic 'r' (e.g., in 'bird') is not pronounced in the British pronunciations used in this study.

> *Data on the language ability of each child was collected using a standardised measure of vocabulary in which parents are asked to indicate which words their children understood. This kind of measure has been shown to be reliable and to produce data that are similar to data from both parental diary records and experimental testing of vocabulary (Harris & Chasin, 1999).*

Children were tested using a preferential looking procedure (for details, see Schafer & Plunkett, 1998). On each trial, the child saw pictures of two objects and heard 'Look! X!' ostensibly directing the child's attention to one of the two images. The images were displayed for 5.5 s, and the auditory stimulus was timed to have the onset of the target word mid-way through the trial. Miniature cameras directly above the images recorded a split-screen twin image of the infant during the session.

> *The pictures on the two screens were displayed for a total of 5.5 seconds on each trial and looking towards each screen was recorded using a video camera. Half way through each trial, the toddler heard a female voice saying the target word, preceded by 'Look!' to gain attention. There were 12 trials presented one after another in a block and then, after a pause, there were another 12 trials. Given that each trial is only 5.5 seconds long, the total time that toddlers have to look at the stimuli is just over a minute (with a brief pause in between each trial).*

There were two warm-up trials involving the words 'ball' and 'shoe,' accurately pronounced. These words are often among the earliest learned (Hamilton et al., 2000). Following the warm-up trials, there were two blocks of 12 test trials. The first block included two early words and two recent words, with three pronunciations (accurate, 1-Off and 2-Off) for each word. The second block included the other four words. Images were paired up by recency of word acquisition, so images for the referents of early words always occurred together, and images for recent words occurred together. Each image appeared equally often as a potential target and distracter, always paired with the same second image, and targets appeared equally often on the left and right sides. The order of trials within each block was randomized.

We scored each child's looking behavior from the video recordings by measuring the lengths of individual gazes throughout each trial as described in Schafer and Plunkett (1998). The onset of the target word divided the trial into pre-target and post-target phases, and separate scores were computed for each phase. In order to partially factor out the minimum reaction times of both child and scorer, the shift from pre- to post-target phases was placed 400 ms after the onset of the target (see Swingley et al., 1999).

Looking time to each stimulus before the word was presented was compared with looking time after the word. Note that, in order to allow time for the toddler to react to the word, the post-word period was counted as starting 400 milliseconds after the beginning of the word.

2.2. Results

On the OCDI vocabulary assessments, 24-month-olds were reported to know 70 per cent more words ($M = 340$, $S.D. = 47$, $n = 17$) than were the 18-month-olds ($M = 201$, $S.D. = 62$, $n = 23$), $t(38) = 7.8$, $p < .001$.

The main data for this study is derived from the lengths of children's gazes at target and distracter images, before and after the target is named by the auditory stimulus (i.e., pre- and post-target). Although each trial began only when the child's attention was focused on the visual display, children's attention nevertheless sometimes wandered during a trial, as indicated by little or no looking at the visual stimuli. Trials were included in the analysis only if the participant was looking at the stimuli for at least 1.5s in both the pre- and post-target phases of the trial. This criterion excluded about 8 per cent of all trials.

Note that toddlers had to be looking for a minimum time at the stimuli in order for data to be included in the analysis. This criterion excluded 8 per cent of the data which shows that, even when infants are required to look at stimuli for a relatively short time, their attention can still wander.

Table 2 *Longest look at target minus longest look at distracter (ms)[a]*

Recency	Pre-target			Post-target		
	OK	**1-Off**	**2-Off**	**OK**	**1-Off**	**2-Off**
Age: 18 months						
Early	11	8	139	523	276	79
Recent	−86	85	154	624	253	560
Age: 24 months						
Early	−212	77	−23	711	351	195
Recent	−183	−129	14	440	384	344

[a]S.E. = 80, based on pooled variance from repeated measures ANOVA.

The main question for this study was whether children recognized words just as easily when they were mispronounced as when they were pronounced accurately. Did children look at images which were named more than they looked at distracter images, and was the amount of target looking affected by pronunciation accuracy? The dependent variable for the preferential looking task was the longest look difference (LLD) between the duration of the longest look at the target image and the longest look at the distracter.[1] Table 2 summarizes the LLD scores. On average, children were equally interested in both images before one of them was named. This is shown by the pre-target phase scores, which were generally close to zero. In contrast, scores for the post-target phase were positive. This indicates that children looked at target images more than distracters once the targets were named. Post-target changes in looking relative to the pre-target phases are shown in Fig. 1. Each triplet of bars represents the change in target looking for OK, 1-Off, and 2-Off pronunciations, respectively. These post-target changes indicate the extent to which children perceived the auditory stimulus for a given trial as a name for the target image.

> Analysis was based on the longest single look to the target minus the longest look to the distractor in both the pre-word and post-word phases. The footnote explains that this measure is more sensitive than total looking time in each part of the trial although, as you might expect, the two measures are highly correlated. Before children hear the word, their looks to the two screens are of similar duration but, after they hear the word, they spend longer looking at the target picture.

An omnibus repeated measures analysis of variance (ANOVA) included the factors age, recency of acquisition, pronunciation accuracy, and trial phase.[2] The main effect of trial phase was significant [$F(1,46) = 65$, $P < .001$], as was the interaction between trial phase and pronunciation accuracy [$F_{(2,92)} = 10$, $P < .001$]. No other effects approached significance in this overall ANOVA, Ps > .10. In Fisher–Hayter pairwise comparisons, the effect of trial phase (i.e., the increase in target looking after the target was named) was significantly greater for OK pronunciations ($M = 692$ ms, $S.E = 83$) than for either 1-Offs ($M = 305$ms, $S.E = 82$) or 2-Offs ($M = 223$ms, $S.E =81$), $P < .05$. The difference between 1-Off and 2-Off pronunciations was not significant. These results reflect a general tendency for subjects to look at the target image after it was named, particularly if named by an accurate pronunciation. Moreover, children clearly distinguished between accurate and inaccurate pronunciations.

> *The ANOVA, in which all variables were entered, showed that there was only one significant main effect of trial phase (pre-word versus post-word) and one interaction (with pronunciation). This is what would be expected if looking had been affected by the presentation of the word and if pronunciation was having an effect after, but not before, the word was presented. Pairwise comparisons showed that, when a word was pronounced correctly, toddlers looked at the screen showing a picture of the target significantly longer than they looked at the other screen. However, in the case of both types of mispronunciation, the differences in looking pre- and post-word were considerably less.*

Additional planned comparisons examined the simple effects and interactions of primary interest, using the Holm multistage procedure to control the Type I error rate for each family of comparisons (alpha = .05).[3] The first set of comparisons tested whether children recognized target words at each level of age, recency, and pronunciation accuracy. Did the amount of target looking increase in response to the auditory stimuli? We expected children to recognize words when they were pronounced accurately, and possibly to also recognize them when they were mispronounced by one or two features. Consequently, we predicted that OK pronunciations would produce increases in target looking in the post-target phase compared to the pre-target phase, and that 1-Offs and 2-Offs would produce similar, but smaller, effects. Significant effects (using the Holm procedure) of target phase are summarized in Table 3. In response to OK pronunciations, target looking increased significantly for both age groups, and for both early and recent words. In response to 1-Off pronunciations, target looking increased only for 24-month-olds' recent words. In response to 2-Off pronunciations, target looking increased only for 18-month-olds' recent words.

> *Table 3 shows which comparisons of pre-word and post-word looking times were significant. For both the younger and older children, early and recently acquired words produced a significant increase in looking to the target after presentation of the word. For mispronounced words there were no changes in looking.*

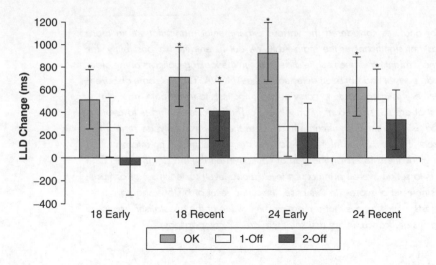

Figure 1   Post-target change in LLD, as a functions of age, recency of acquisition, and pronunciation accuracy. Error bars show 90% CI. (*) P <.05

Table 3   Summary of tests of post-target changes in LLD

	OK		1-Off		2-Off	
Age (months)	Early	Recent	Early	Recent	Early	Recent
18	*	*				*
24	*	*		*		

*Significant in Holm multistage procedure, alpha < .05 for the whole family, 1-tailed.

The second set of comparisons tested whether children distinguished mispronunciations from accurate ones at each level of age and recency. Did children look at target images just as much when their names were mispronounced as when they were pronounced properly, or did mispronunciations reduce the amount of target looking? If children distinguished mispronunciations from the real target words, then post-target change scores should be greatest for OK pronunciations, smaller for 1-Off pronunciations, and smallest for 2-Off pronunciations. If children confuse mispronunciations for accurate ones, post-target change scores should be the same across all levels of pronunciation accuracy. One-way ANOVAs at each level of age and recency identified a significant effect of pronunciation accuracy only for 24-month-olds' early words, $F(2,183) = 6.6.$[4] For these words, Fisher-Hayter pairwise comparisons showed that the amount of target looking was significantly greater for OK pronunciations than for either 1- or 2-Off pronunciations. The amount of target looking for 1-Off pronunciations did not differ from 2-Offs.

A second set of analyses considered the various experimental manipulations in more detail. Age was not significant in the main ANOVA but it remained a possibility, for example, that there might have been subtle differences in the looking patterns of the older and younger toddlers that had not been detected by the ANOVA. There is some disagreement about whether it is appropriate to carry out post hoc tests to investigate main effects or interactions that are not significant in an ANOVA. The important thing is to avoid a Type 1 error, that is, to claim a significant effect where there is, in reality, no real difference between sets of scores. Since inferential statistics are, by definition, an interpretation of the data the guideline is to err on the side of caution in attributing significance. One way to do this is to set an overall significance level (alpha level) for each set of comparisons within a single set of scores. In this case, the alpha level of 0.05 is shared across each family of tests, which means that a more extreme value of the test statistic has to be obtained to reach significance. In the first set, there are 12 comparisons.

The third and fourth sets of comparisons tested simple effects of recency and age on children's sensitivity to mispronunciations. Was the reduction in target looking for mispronunciations compared to accurate pronunciations affected by recency of acquisition or by children's age? Sensitivity scores for each trial measured the decrease in target looking for 1-Off and 2-Off pronunciations compared to OK pronunciations. These mispronunciation sensitivity scores are shown in Fig. 2. If lexical specificity increases as a function of word familiarity, then early words should show greater decrements than recent words. Similarly, if lexical specificity increases as a function of age, then 24-month-olds should show greater decrements than 18-month-olds. However, there was no significant effect of recency on the sensitivity of either age group to either 1- or 2-Off pronunciations (using the Holm procedure). Neither was there a significant effect of age on sensitivity to 1- or 2-Off pronunciations of either early or recent words.

The final analyses consider the relation between looking times and vocabulary knowledge in the light of a number of alternative hypotheses. There was no relationship between vocabulary size and children's responses to mispronounced words, suggesting that the ability to discriminate correct from incorrect pronunciations was not related to the number of words that children know.

The developmental hypothesis, that lexical specificity is driven by the need to distinguish among different words in the lexicon, makes the further prediction that, across all ages, children who know more words will be more sensitive to mispronunciations than children who know fewer words. If this is correct, there should be a negative correlation between children's vocabulary sizes, as measured by the OCDI, and their sensitivity scores for 1-Off and 2-Off pronunciations. These correlations were not observed in our data, Pearson's rs = .063 and −.066 for 1-Off and 2-Off pronunciations,

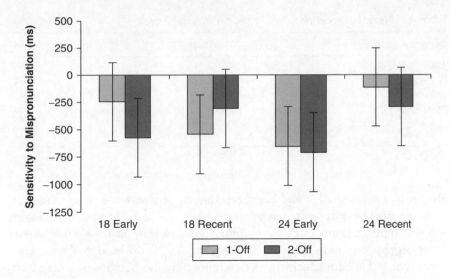

Figure 2 *Sensitivity to mispronunciations (decrease in target looking for mispronunciations compared to accurate pronunciations), as a function of age and recency of acquisition. Error bars show 90 per cent CL*

respectively, $n = 40$, one-tailed $Ps > .34$. In both cases the correlation coefficients are very small, and the trend for 1-Off pronunciations is in the opposite direction to that predicted.

An alternative version of the developmental hypothesis is that lexical specificity is determined word by word depending on the number of words in the lexicon which are similar to a particular word. According to this version, sensitivity to mispronunciations should be correlated with neighborhood density regardless of a child's age or vocabulary size. We tested this prediction in two analyses which make different assumptions about between-participant differences in sensitivity. The independent predictor variable in all analyses was neighborhood density, based on each child's OCDI.[5] The neighborhood density score for each test word counted the number of words the child knew which were no more than one phoneme different from the accurate pronunciation of the test word (including the test word itself). The number of words in the neighborhood of test words is summarized in Table 4.

> There was also no relationship between looking times and the number of similar-sounding words that children knew. Thus the study did not support the hypothesis that the specificity with which children coded the phonology of a word was affected by, so-called, neighbourhood density effects.

Table 4   *Neighborhood density of children's target words*

Recency	Mean	S.D.
Age: 18 months		
Early	1.84	0.39
Recent	1.79	0.45
Age: 24 months		
Early	2.24	0.67
Recent	1.73	0.47

The first analysis of neighborhood density assumed that differences between participants were due substantially to nuisance factors, and tested the within-participants effect of neighborhood density in a repeated measures regression model (see Lorch & Myers, 1990 on repeated measures regression). If lexical specificity is determined by the number of words in a word's phonological neighborhood, then the regression coefficients for neighborhood density should be negative. In fact, the standardized neighborhood density regression coefficients did not differ from zero, $bs = .037$ and .016 for 1-Off and 2-Off sensitivity, respectively. These coefficients represent trends in the opposite direction to that predicted by the neighborhood density hypothesis. Neither trend is significant, $Fs < 1$ for both.

The second analysis of neighborhood density assumed that differences in sensitivity between participants were due primarily to differences in the average numbers of neighbors for their target words. This analysis treated the different target words for each child as independent measures, and tested for a correlation between neighborhood density and sensitivity to mispronunciations across all 228 trials for which data were available. If lexical specificity is determined by the number of words in a word's phonological neighborhood, there should be a negative correlation between neighborhood density and sensitivity scores. The independence assumption may or may not be justified. If the assumption is correct, then this analysis would have greater power than the repeated measures analysis above to detect a relationship between neighborhood density and sensitivity to mispronunciations. In other words, this analysis gives any such effect the greatest opportunity to reveal itself in our data. On the other hand, if the assumption is incorrect, this analysis could inflate any spurious trend and produce a false significant result. Therefore, a significant result would have to be interpreted with caution. Our data revealed no correlation between neighborhood density and sensitivity to mispronunciation, Pearson's $rs = .069$ and $-.018$ for 1-Off and 2-Off sensitivity, respectively, $n = 228$, one-tailed $Ps > .39$ for both. Neither correlation coefficient differs significantly from zero, and that for 1-Off sensitivity is in the opposite direction to that predicted.

2.3. Discussion

> The authors discuss two possible interpretations of their results. The first is that young children are able to recognise a mispronunciation as a real word. This claim is based on evidence that, even though children showed a large and consistent change in looking to correctly pronounced words, they also showed some change in looking to mispronounced words. However, an alternative explanation is that the children ho ~~~~~ partly specified information about the sound of a word and so, in some cases ~~~~~ le to detect mispronunciations while in other cases they were not. Averar~~ would give an intermediate pattern of looking for the mispronour~ greater than in the pre-word part of a trial but less than for corre~ The results of the present study do not allow these two explan~ although it is clear that the ability to detect mispronunciatior~ size or age or to how recently a word has entered a chilc~

Even slightly inaccurate pronunciations of words interfered with identification of the referent by 18–24-month-olds in the preferential looking task. Children looked at the target image less when its name was mispronounced than when it was pronounced properly. This finding confirms the conclusion of Swingley and Aslin (2000) that the lexical representations of very young children have enough phonological detail to allow detection of single-feature word onset mismatches between auditory stimuli and lexical entries. The present study amplifies Swingley and Aslin's findings in showing sensitivity to mispronunciations of recently learned as well as more familiar words for each child, across a wide range of words and covering a wide variety of initial consonants mispronounced in various ways.

Although the children in our study distinguished inaccurate from accurate pronunciations, they nevertheless looked at the target image more than the distracter even when the name was mispronounced. They associated inaccurate pronunciations with the intended target images to some extent. A similar pattern was observed by Swingley and Aslin (2000), who also found that mispronunciations elicited intermediate levels of target looking. This general pattern of results can be explained in terms of partial activation produced by phonological similarity computed with respect to fully specified lexical entries, as Swingley and Aslin argue. Children may detect mispronunciations as such (perhaps implicitly), but still be able to recognize the intended target words. In the same way, an adult might interpret 'bomato' as a failed attempt to say 'tomato,' especially when seeing a picture of one. For adults, such a mispronunciation can activate the target lexical entry and prime subsequent recognition of semantic associates of the mispronounced word (Connine, Blasko, & Titone, 1993; Marslen-Wilson, Moss, & van Halen, 1996).

However, a second explanation for the results cannot be ruled out. It could be that children's lexical entries are only partly specified, and that some mispronunciations are distinguished from accurate ones while others are not. Averaged across trials and across children, responses to partially specified lexical entries would produce the overall pattern of results observed in the present study and in that of Swingley and Aslin (2000). Although the results of both studies clearly establish that young children have at least a certain amount of phonological detail in their mental lexicons, it is not clear whether the specificity in children's lexical entries approaches adult levels. Indeed, the findings of studies with much older children indicate that they are still relatively poor at distinguishing between minimally different words (Barton, 1976, 1980; Eilers & Oller, 1976; Gerken et al., 1995; Metsala, 1999; Walley, 1987). In addition, the present study (and the greatest number of stimuli in Swingley & Aslin) involved only onset mispronunciations. In principle, children could have identified the intended target by focusing on syllable rimes. An important question for the future is whether mispronunciations of final consonants or phonemes in other syllable positions would also produce intermediate levels of target looking.

Despite our effort to test children on some of their earliest words as well as some of their most recently learned ones, we did not observe any clear effect of word familiarity on children's sensitivity to mispronunciations. Although naming effects were observed for mispronounciations of recently learned words and not mispronunciations of early learned words (see Table 3), no overall effects of word familiarity (recency) were statistically significant. Our study thus fails to confirm the hypothesis that the degree of familiarity with individual words is an important factor in the level of phonological detail available for discriminating them from similar words (cf. Barton, 1976, 1980). If familiarity does play a role in phonological specificity, perhaps its effects are confined to a child's first few experiences with particular words, at levels of familiarity even below the recently learned words that we tested. Alternatively, familiarity effects may emerge too gradually to be detected over the range examined in the present study. In that case, they may be observable only in older children whose vocabularies span a wider range of familiarity levels.

If increases in lexical specificity occur as a result of the need to distinguish words in a growing vocabulary, then older children should be more sensitive than younger children to mispronunciations, and sensitivity should be correlated with both vocabulary size and neighborhood density. None of these effects was found in the present study, where age was manipulated as an experimental factor. Swingley and Aslin also reported no correlation between sensitivity and vocabulary size, though they did not manipulate age experimentally. The absence of an age effect in the current study therefore strengthens the finding of their study that sensitivity to mispronunciations was uncorrelated with age. It should be noted that Swingley and Aslin assessed production vocabulary, whereas we used a measure of comprehension vocabulary. As Swingley and Aslin point out, comprehension vocabulary is arguably more relevant than production vocabulary to the proposal that specificity is determined by the need to discriminate similar words. Combined with the results of Swingley and Aslin, the present study suggests that vocabulary size has little, if any effect, no matter how it is measured. The present study also found no relationship between the neighborhood density of individual words and children's sensitivity to mispronunciations of those words. We conclude that if there is any tendency for words to have more or less detailed representations depending on the number of similar words from which they must be distinguished (e.g., Jusczyk, Luce, & Charles-Luce, 1993), this tendency is not prominent over the range of vocabulary development occurring from 18 to 24 months of age. Of course, the vocabulary of adults is several orders of magnitude greater than that of the children we tested. An overall age or vocabulary effect could operate at a later age or gradually over a broader age range than the 18–24-month-olds participating in the current study. This is an important question for future research.

Our results, together with those of Werker et al. (2002) and Swingley and Aslin (2000) would seem to suggest that earlier research has underestimated the amount of phonological detail associated with words used by older children. If children during the second half of the second year of life can detect slight mispronunciations of words, then presumably older children can too. However, we would advocate caution in concluding that 1-year-olds have the same level of phonological specification available to them as adults. Above chance responding in an inter-modal preferential looking task or in an habituation switch task is indicative of some detail in young children's phonological representations but not necessarily of full phonological specification. On this interpretation, experiments with older children demonstrating phonological underspecification may be entirely consistent with the results of experiments with 1-year-olds. This leaves open the question of how long-term phonological representations are accessed in the developing mental lexicon, and how they eventually come to be fully specified.

Acknowledgments

This work was supported by a grant from the Biotechnology and Biological Sciences Research Council, UK to the second author. The authors are grateful to Daniel Swingley for valuable contributions in the early stages of this work, to Linda Irving Bell for pronouncing and mispronouncing our stimuli and to anonymous reviewers for helpful suggestions.

Notes

1 The LLD measure is highly correlated with the proportion of target looking more commonly reported (e.g., Golinkoff et al., 1987; Meints, Plunkett, & Harris, 1999; Meints, Plunkett, Harris, & Diminock, 2002; Schafer & Plunkett, 1998; Swingley et al., 1999). In our experience LLD provides a small, but consistent, improvement in sensitivity to differences in target looking. The results of preliminary analyses of proportion looking times for the present study were consistent with this conclusion. Preliminary analyses were also performed on latencies of the first gaze shift following the onset of the target word. These analyses yield similar patterns of results to those revealed by the analysis of LLD scores.
2 Because we tested each child on different words, items analyses are neither necessary nor appropriate for our data; see Raaijmakers, Schrijnemakers, & Gremmen (1999).
3 Several reviewers suggested collapsing the data across age, recency, or levels of mispronunciation. The overall conclusions are not changed by any such maneuver.
4 Using the Holm procedure to control family-wise error rate, alpha = .05 for the whole set of comparisons. In less conservative simple ANOVAs with alpha = .05 per comparison, the effect of pronunciation accuracy was significant for 18-month-olds' early and recent words, $Fs(2,183) = 3.5$ and 3.2, respectively, $Ps = .032$ and $.045$. The effect was not significant for 24-month-olds' recent words, $F < 1$
5 At the time of this *post hoc* analysis, the raw OCDI data for some children were unavailable. The analysis was conducted on the available data for 23, 18-month-olds and 11, 24-month-olds.

Visual fixations to targets

In the final paper in this chapter we consider a study of factors that affect infants' ability to look at the same thing as somebody else. This study is rather different from the other infant studies considered so far because, although it involves the assessment of looking behaviour, here the looking is to objects set out across a room. The study is concerned with how adults direct the visual attention of infants and toddlers to objects both behind and in front of them.

Previous research has established that infants show developing abilities to follow the line of regard of another person towards a target. A number of factors have been identified as making this task more or less difficult, including the way that an adult seeks to draw attention to the target (by looking, pointing or verbalising), the location of the target (behind or in front of the infant) and the distinctiveness of the target. The aim of this paper is to look at the interaction of all of these factors.

Paper 7   Joint visual attention in mothers and infants
(Deak, Flom & Pick, 2000)

The specific hypothesis being examined in this paper is that infants, who are younger than 1 year old, have limited ability to locate a specific target because, although they turn in the general direction indicated by an adult, they are likely to fixate on the first object they encounter. This means that objects that are to the side of the infant are often missed and targets that are actually behind the infant are very unlikely to be fixated. According to George Butterworth (Butterworth, 2001), the explanation for this is that, before the age of 1 year, infants' attention is captured by the first object they encounter when turning to follow the adult's direction of regard. A few months later, infants are able to extrapolate from the adult line of regard to locate the correct object, while ignoring other objects that may be closer or more attractive. However, their ability to locate an object is still bounded by what they can see and so they will still fail to locate an object that is behind them. According to Butterworth, the final stage of following the adult's line of regard does not occur until infants are 18 months of age when they are able to fully represent the space all around them.

Butterworth's view of the developing ability of infants to locate objects that are being looked at by someone else (that is, to share visual attention) is essentially maturational, being explained by the developing cognitive abilities of the infant to represent the world. The authors of this paper propose an alternative to Butterworth's explanation. This is that it is not infants' representation of the world that changes but, rather, their sensitivity to fine-grained perceptual information about an adult's line of regard. Thus, if there are stronger perceptual cues to the identity of the adult's regard, then even young infants should be able to locate a target correctly.

Developmental Psychology, 2000, Vol 36 (4), 511–523

Effects of Gesture and Target on 12- and 18-Month-Olds' Joint Visual Attention to Objects in Front of or Behind Them

Gedeon O. Deák

Vanderbilt University

Ross A. Flom and Anne D. Pick

University of Minnesota, Twin Cities Campus

By the end of their first year, infants are sensitive to information specifying where others are looking. Scaife and Bruner (1975) first documented infants' tendency to turn to follow an adult's gaze. Gaze-following is a critical component of joint visual attention, defined as looking toward the object of another person's attention because it is the object of their attention. Joint visual attention is a particularly important social event because it is thought to be the earliest manifestaion of intersubjectivity, that is, the ability to infer others' mental states (Baron-Cöhen, 1995; Tomasello, 1995; Trevarthen & Hubley, 1978). It also seems to facilitate language development. Toddlers' vocabulary is predicted by the frequency of mothers' and infants' joint visual attention (Tomasello & Todd, 1983). It is also predicted by infants' responsiveness to pointing (Harris, Barlow-Brown, & Chasin, 1995; Smith, Adamson, & Bakeman, 1988). In addition, failure to respond to others' gaze predicts childhood autism, which is typified by severe language deficits (Loveland & Landry, 1986; Mundy, Sigman, & Kassari, 1990). Finally, infants use a speaker's gaze to infer which of several objects is the referent of a novel word (see Baldwin, 1995).

Because joint visual attention has implications for early social and language development, it is important to understand how adults' actions elicit joint attention with infants. Infants are sensitive to changes in the orientation of an adult's head and eyes and to movement of the head, particularly motion contingent on the child's actions (Corkum & Moore, 1995; Hains & Muir, 1996; Johnson, Slaughter, & Carey, 1998). Between 9 and 15 months of age, infants follow at least two attention-specifying gestures: (a) turning the head to gaze at an object and (b) pointing (with outstretched arm) at an object (Butterworth & Cochran, 1980; Butterworth & Grover, 1988; Butterworth & Jarrett, 1991; Collis, 1977; Morissette, Ricard, & Gouin Décarie, 1995; Murphy & Messer, 1977). Butterworth and Cochran (1980), for example, found that 12-month-olds often followed their mother's gaze to the correct quadrant of the room. Similarly, Morissette et al. (1995) found that 12-month-olds accurately followed an adult's gaze and pointing to one of four locations.

Despite this evidence, 12-month-olds' ability to follow another's gaze appears limited. Butterworth and colleagues (1991b; Butterworth & Cochran, 1980; Butterworth & Jarrett, 1991) found that infants younger than 12 months turn in the direction of an adult's gesture, but they fixate on the first object along the scan path even if it is not the target object. The researchers also found that infants establish joint visual attention to objects within their visual field before they do so for objects outside their visual field (i.e., behind them). The ability to ignore objects in front of them and to follow an adult's gaze to targets behind them emerges between 12 and 18 months of age.

Butterworth (1991b) attributed these changes to infants developing joint visual attention mechanisms. The earliest, ecological mechanism is largely driven by interesting or attractive objects in the environment. An adult looking toward an object compels infants to turn in the appropriate direction until they see an interesting object (whether or not it is the object of the adult's attention). There is no attempt, however, to coordinate attention with the adult. At around 12 months of age, a new geometric mechanism emerges. Now infants can extrapolate an imagined line from the adult's direction of gaze (or point) to an object. Infants will follow a gesture to the target even if another object is closer to their midline – but only if the target is within their visual field. They will not follow a gesture to look at targets behind them, presumably because they can form only non-Euclidean or egocentric spatial representations. That is, they cannot represent their environment as a plane, some region of which is visible from their vantage, and other regions of which might be visible to another person. This Euclidean representation must await the emergence of a representational mechanism at around 18 months of age. Thereafter infants can infer that things occupy space currently out of view and that other people can see objects that the infant cannot see. Other researchers also believe that by 18 to 24 months, infants can make inferences about other people's unobservable mental states, including attention (Baron-Cohen, 1995; Dunham & Dunham, 1995; Repacholi & Gopnik, 1997; Tomasello, 1995; Wellman, 1993).

Butterworth and colleagues (Butterworth & Cochran, 1980; Butterworth & Jarrett, 1991) have reported evidence consistent with this theory, but there are other possible accounts of the development of joint visual attention. These deserve serious consideration because Butterworth's theory, in which two qualitatively different mechanisms are acquired during infancy, is not optimally parsimonious. One alternative, explicated by Moore and Corkum (1994), is that joint visual attention is learned. It follows months of reciprocal social interactions between infants and caregivers in which changes in facial expression and gestures play an important role. Joint attention might emerge from learning to turn in the direction of the caregiver's gaze, because doing so is more likely to result in an interesting sight. Thus, social learning drives joint attention, though learning is constrained by certain causal and social sensitivities (Corkum & Moore, 1998; Moore & Corkum, 1994). Such a learning mechanism could also explain progressive improvement in accuracy of joint attention. For example, early in conditioning, following gaze to the correct side (i.e., the infant's left or right) might be reinforced because fixating on any interesting object is sufficiently interesting. But over time, infants could learn to follow gaze to the precise object of the caregiver's attention, even if it is initially out of sight, because finding the true object of attention prolongs enjoyable social interaction with the caregiver. Although the studies reported here do not directly test a conditioning account of joint visual attention, such an account is more parsimonious than Butterworth's theory. If behavioural evidence is inconsistent with Butterworth's account, a conditioning account will remain credible.

We hypothesized that the critical findings for Butterworth's account – specifically, failure of 9–12-month-olds to follow gaze to targets behind them – might instead be explained by perceptual factors. Younger infants sometimes might fail to detect changes, especially small changes, in adults' gaze direction. More elaborate or expansive gestures, such as pointing at an object or talking about it while looking at it, might elicit joint attention more reliably from 12-month-olds. We investigated this hypothesis in Experiment 1.

If younger infants are unlikely to detect small changes in gaze direction, the standard laboratory procedure for testing joint visual attention might prevent infants from following another's gaze to objects outside their visual field. When infant and adult face each other straight on (i.e., the typical procedure), the adult makes only a small head turn to look at an object behind the baby but makes a large head turn to look at an object in front of the baby. This confound is depicted in Figure 1. Infants, especially younger infants, might be more likely to notice and follow larger head turns. We tested this hypothesis in Experiment 2 by rotating the mother so that the magnitude of her head turn was independent of the location of objects relative to the infant. That is, the mother turned her head the same radial distance whether the target was in front of or behind the infant.

We also hypothesized that the nature of the target objects affects whether young infants engage in joint visual attention with an adult. In many studies (e.g., Butterworth & Jarrett, 1991; Morissette et al., 1995), potential target objects are identical and often quite simple (e.g., yellow squares). Infants might expect adults to direct their attention to items that are distinctive and moderately complex. If objects are distinctive and complex (i.e., interesting), infants might look at the specific object an adult is attending to, even if it is outside of their visual field. In contrast, if objects are identical and simple, infants might quickly stop responding to adults' gestures.

In this study we investigated the effects of three factors on joint visual attention in 12- and 18-month-olds. These factors were the type of attention-directing gesture, the magnitude of the gesture (i.e., large vs. small head turns), and the distinctiveness of the target objects.

Experiment 1

In Experiment 1 there were two independent variables, type of gesture used to direct the infant's attention (looking, looking + pointing, looking + pointing + talking) and the distinctiveness of the target that is presented. Both factors have been studied in previous research but this study brings them together. Looking at two independent variables allows an experimenter to study how the variables interact with each other.

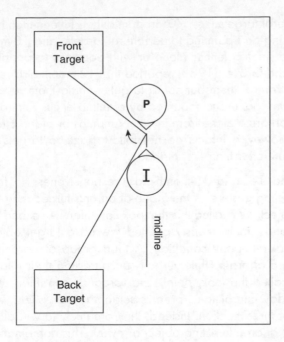

Figure 1 *Schematic diagram of typical joint attention paradigm with infant (I) and parent (P). Note that parent produces a small head turn to gaze at target behind infant (back target) but a large head turn to gaze at target in front of infant*

In the first experiment, we explored the relative effectiveness of different gestures and different kinds of objects in promoting joint visual attention. Parents were instructed to produce one of three gestures toward a specified object. The objects were either identical or distinctive. The designated target object was located in different regions of the infant's visual field (i.e., front, periphery, or back). Twelve- and 18-month-olds were recruited in order to test the hypothesis that the ability to follow an adult's gesture to targets outside the visual field emerges between 12 and 18 months of age.

Gesture type

Head-eye orientation indicates the locus of a person's attention, as does the direction of a point. Gaze and pointing are not, however, equivalent. When Butterworth and Grover (1988) and Morissette et al. (1995) compared infants' responses to adults' gaze orientation alone versus to adults' gazing and pointing, infants older than 9 months more often followed adults' gazing and pointing. Even when pointing accompanies gaze, however, infants' responsiveness depends on target location (i.e., front, periphery, or back). Morissette et al. (1995) found that 12-month-olds reliably followed gazing and pointing to front targets (i.e., 20° from midline) but not to peripheral targets (i.e., 70° from midline). Fifteen-month-olds reliably followed gazing and pointing to peripheral targets, and 18-month-olds reliably followed gazing (either alone or with pointing) to peripheral targets. Butterworth and Grover (1988) reported that 12-month-olds reliably looked at targets in front of them but not at targets behind them, even if the adult pointed. In sum, gaze accompanied by pointing elicits joint attention more effectively than gaze alone from infants 9 months or older. Even with pointing added, however, infants do not follow gaze to targets outside their visual field until after their first birthday.

We compared 12- and 18-month-olds' responsiveness to three different attention-directing gestures. One group of parents turned their head to gaze at a target object. We called this the *look* condition. A second group of parents gazed and simultaneously pointed toward a target object. This was called the *look-and-point* condition. A third group of parents gazed and pointed toward a target while verbally encouraging their infants to look at it. This was called the *look, point, and verbalize* condition. We presumed that in everyday interactions, parents seldom remain silent while trying to direct their infant's attention. Instead, they are likely to verbally exhort their infant to look at an interesting object or event. This combination of actions is therefore believed to be representative of everyday parental bids for infant attention. The effect of parents' verbalizations on joint visual attention has not previously been explored.

A secondary question was whether children respond more readily to some attention-directing gestures than to others. That is, gestures that more reliably elicit joint attention might also elicit it more rapidly. We tested whether more elaborate attention-directing gestures elicit a higher percentage of hits (i.e., looks at target) within a few seconds of the onset of the parent's gesture.

Target Type

Half of the infants in every group saw identical blue squares at each target location on every trial. The other half saw multicolored, irregularly shaped objects with gaudy decorations attached. Because each object in the latter set was unique, the targets necessarily differed across location and trial. We speculated that in previous investigations, 9–12-month-olds followed adults' gaze in the correct direction but fixated at the first object along the scan path because all objects were identical. If all objects are identical, there is little motivation to search for and identify a particular item. The parent's gesture loses its validity, in a sense. Even in older infants, the added effort required to turn around to follow another's gaze might have exceeded their motivation to look at simple, identical targets. In general, the presence of distinctive objects may help sustain infants' interest in the joint attention task. For these reasons, half of the infants saw distinctive objects, and half saw identical objects. We expected the former to follow parents' gestures more reliably. We also predicted that the frequency of gaze-following would decrease across trials more for infants who saw identical targets than for infants who saw distinctive targets.

> *The two types of target were chosen so that one – blue squares – was inherently less attractive than the other because it was less visually complex. All else being equal, an infant will spend longer looking at a more complex stimulus. Note that the types of target differ not only in visual complexity but also in novelty. The blue squares are identical to one another and are used across trials while each of the multicoloured stimuli is unique.*

Method

Participants

One hundred and twenty infants and parents participated. Sixty 12-month-olds (30 girls, 30 boys; mean age = 12 months 7 days, range = 11 months 18 days to 13 months 4 days) and sixty 18-month-olds (30 girls, 30 boys; mean age = 18 months 7 days, range = 17 months 15 days to 19 months) were included in the analyses. Twelve additional infants were excluded due either to experimenter error ($n = 4$) or fussiness ($n = 8$). Infants were recruited from a database maintained at the University of Minnesota and were primarily Caucasian and middle class. Parents were initially contacted by telephone.

> *Note the large number of participants used, with 60 in each age group. The complex nature of the design, in which there were six different sub-groups, required this large number since there were only ten infants in each condition. Participants appear to have come from similar backgrounds but there is no attempt here to look for individual variation in infants' ability. This is typical of studies of infant perception, where the implicit assumption is that development will be similar across a sample of infants of the same age. The assumption in studies of language development tends to be that infants and toddlers of the same age will differ in their ability.*

Apparatus and objects

To eliminate any interesting visual stimuli other than the target objects, we conducted the experiment in a room in which white sheets were hung from ceiling to floor around the perimeter. The space within the sheets measured 4.4×3.2 m. The infant was seated in a booster chair in the center of the room. The parent's chair faced the infant seat. The seats were situated so that the infants' and parents' eyes were at the same height.

One set of objects included 4 identical squares (15 cm × 15 cm) covered with blue construction paper. The other set included 14 irregular polygons, similar in size to the squares, covered with multicolored construction paper and decorated with various colorful, shiny items. Each object in the latter set had a unique shape, color scheme, and decorations. Objects were mounted on four movable, white stanchions placed in front of the sheets and were turned so that each target faced the infant. A video camera mounted on the ceiling directly above the infant's head recorded a bird's-eye view of the infant. The objects were not visible on videotape. A digital stopwatch was electronically printed on the videotape for coding purposes. A hand-held stopwatch was used during the session to monitor trial length.

Design

Twelve- and 18-month-olds were quasi-randomly assigned to 12 groups, with the constraint that each group included approximately equal numbers of girls and boys. Each of 6 groups within each age received one of three parental gestures (look; look and point; or look, point, and verbalize) and one of two types of objects (identical or distinctive).

Object location was varied within-subjects. Ten locations were paired, one on each side of the room, in five "latitudes" ranging from the front to the back of the infant. The configuration is represented in Figure 2. Note that Locations 1 and 2 were in front of the infant, that is, close to the infant's midline and within his or her midline visual field. Location 3 was in the infant's periphery (75° from midline), and Locations 4 and 5 were behind the infant, outside her or his visual field.

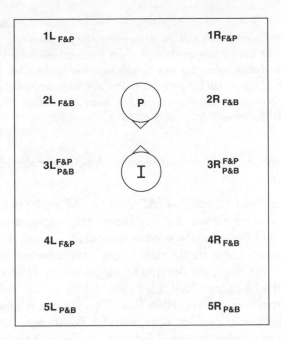

Figure 2   *Schematic diagram of room showing location of infant, parent, and targets in Experiment 1. P = parent, I = infant; F&P = front and periphery configuration; F&B = front and back configuration; P&B = periphery and back configuration. Distance from infant's midline, and side of the room, are specified by location codes (e.g., 2L)*

An object was placed at 4 of the 10 target locations in every trial. Three trial configurations were used (similar to those used by Butterworth & Jarrett, 1991). In front-and-periphery (F&P) trials, objects were at Locations 1 and 3. In front-and-back (F&B) trials, objects were at Locations 2 and 4. In periphery-and-back (P&B) trials, objects were at Locations 3 and 5. In each configuration, the four objects were in two parallel right-left target pairs. One object (either front or peripheral) was therefore seen first if the infant turned from midline to scan in either direction.

Peripheral objects were present in two configurations: F&P and P&B. In the former they were the second object seen when scanning from midline; in the latter they were the first object seen. Varying the location of objects accompanying the peripheral target allowed us to test Butterworth's (1991b) finding that 12–18-month-olds fixate on the first object along the path they are scanning when the target is far from the infant's midline.

> There were ten possible locations for targets and, on each trial, stimuli were placed in four locations, with two targets on the right and two in the mirror image position on the left. Targets were either at the front, the side or behind the infant. On every trial, it was

In all configurations, the first and second objects on one side were separated by 60°.

All infants completed 12 trials; 4 F&P trials, 4 F&B trials, and 4 P&B trials. On each trial one object was the designated target toward which the parent gestured, and the other three were distractors. Across 4 trials within a given configuration, the designated target was at each location once. Across all 12 trials, then, the designated target was at each location once, except twice it was at Locations 3 left and right (i.e., for F&P and P&B trials). Every infant within a condition ($n = 10$) received a different random order of configurations and locations, with the constraints that each parent gestured toward a different target location on the first trial and no more than 2 successive trials were in the same configuration.

Procedure

The purpose of the experiment and the procedure were explained to the parent upon arrival at the laboratory.[1] The parent was instructed to use a particular gesture to direct her infant's attention.[2] Parents in the *look* condition were instructed to turn their heads and look directly at the target object, without gesturing or speaking. Parents in the *look-and-point* condition were instructed to turn their heads to look at the target object and to point to it without speaking. Parents in the *look, point, and verbalize* condition were instructed to turn their heads to look at the target, point to it, and verbally encourage their child to look at it. Parents in this group were asked to say whatever they would normally say to redirect their child's attention. Parents were instructed to play with and distract their child between trials but not to touch the child once a trial began (in pilot testing, parents sometimes touched their children to encourage them to look at the target). Parents who did not follow the instructions (e.g., who talked to their infant during trials, unless in the look, point, and verbalize condition) were replaced. Before each trial, the experimenter told the parent which location contained the upcoming target. The parent then called the infant until she or he looked at the parent. The experimenter then signaled the parent to begin the trial, whereupon the parent gestured toward the designated target. The experimenter did not give the signal until he or she saw that the infant was looking at the parent. Each trial lasted 15 s from when the parent first turned toward the target.

> At the beginning of each trial, the infant is looking at the parent. This is important because it ensures that, at the start of each trial, the infant is in a position to observe the adult's change in attention. Trials lasted for 15 seconds and the infant's looking was recorded for each trial.

Coding

A coder recorded the direction of every visual fixation by every infant. A fixation was defined absence of head movement (i.e., scanning or turning) for at least 0.5 s.[3] The radial orientation (i.e., direction) of the infant's head during a fixation was measured by an acrylic disc, marked with 35 radial lines separated by 10°, mounted on the video monitor. The center of the disc was placed over the center of the infant's head and adjusted so that the child's midline was at 0°. Head orientation was then measured for every fixation within 15 s of the onset of the parent's gesture. Any fixation within 25° of the designated target was coded a 'hit.' These fixations were an average of 13° (*SD* = 7°) from the actual target location. We do not know how much of this deviation reflects measurement error, but because there were no objects visible to the infant other than the target and the three distractors, and the closest distractor was 60° from the target, the 25° criterion seems reasonable. For an unbiased test of infants' to follow gestures to the designated target, any fixation within 25° criterion seems reasonable. For an unbiased test of infants' propensity to follow gestures to the designated target, any fixation within 25° of any of the three distractor objects was coded a 'miss'. Coders were blind to target type (i.e., identical or distinctive) and to the exact locations of the objects.

> The coding of fixations was done very precisely, using an overlay on the monitor that indicated degrees of head turn. Note that there is a precise definition of what constitutes a fixation and a 'hit'. Looks of less than 500 milliseconds were not counted as fixations; and any fixation that was within 25 degrees of the target was counted as a 'hit' while fixations that were within 25 degrees to a non-target were counted as a 'miss'. The use of 25 degrees is appropriate since the closest distance between two targets on a trial was 60 degrees.

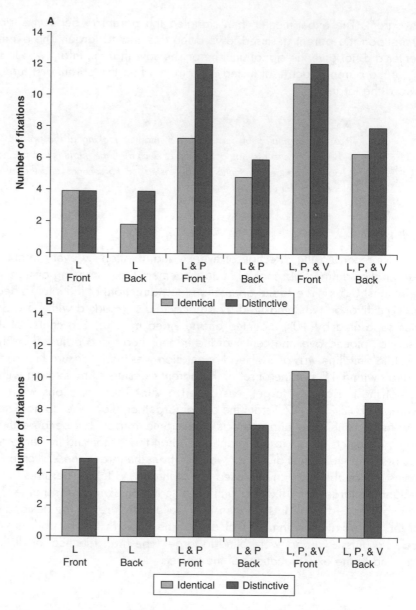

Figure 3   *Mean number of fixations on front and back targets, by gesture combination and target type in Experiment 1. A: 12-month-olds, B: 18-month-olds, L = look condition: L & P = look-and-point condition: L, P, & V = look, point, and verbalize condition*

A second coder, naive to the hypotheses of the study, independently recoded 36 randomly selected infants (twenty 12-month-olds and sixteen 18-month-olds; 30 per cent of the sample). Interrater agreement for hits and misses was assessed by kappas (Cohen, 1960), which adjust for base rates and thus are more conservative than simple agreement. The mean kappas were .80 for 12-month-olds and .76 for 18-month-olds; this exceeds the criterion for good agreement using kappas.

The reliability of coding was calculated from an independent recoding of 30 per cent of the sample. The agreement was close to 80 per cent on a conservative test of agreement. This may seem low since it might appear that the measure of looking is very objective. However, it is not always easy to tell where an infant is looking, especially when the video shot is from above. The assumption is that the infant is looking straight ahead but, especially with a head turn to the side, the eyes may be looking to the right or left of the midline. More accurate information about where someone is looking can be gained by using an eye tracker but, until recently, such devices were not suitable for use with young children. The new generation of eye trackers, which use beams of infrared light, is now enabling very accurate data to be collected on the direction and duration of infants' gaze.

Results

The main dependent variable was the frequency of visual fixations of designated targets during test trials.[4] The total number of hits across all 12 trials is shown in Figure 3A (12-month-olds) and 3B (18-month-olds). Because the literature suggests that 9–18-month-olds follow adults' gestures more often to targets within their visual field than to targets outside their visual field, total hits were divided into 'front' and 'back' hits. Front hits were the number of correct hits in all trials in which the designated target was at Locations 1 or 2, or 3 F&P. Back hits were the number of hits when the target was at Locations 4 or 5, or 3 P&B. Location 3 was considered a front target if the ipsilateral distractor was behind the infant (P&B trials) and a back target if the distractor was in front of the infant (F&P trials). This is consistent with findings that infants are less likely to follow gaze to a peripheral target if the distractor is in front of the target than if the distractor is behind the target (Butterworth & Jarrett, 1991). In other words, peripheral targets are treated by infants more like back targets in an F&P configuration and more like front targets in a P&B configuration. This justifies the designation of Location 3 as either front or back, but note that the results below are similar if Location 3 trials are excluded from the analyses.

In order to analyse the results, hits were divided according to target location, in front or behind the infant. This raised the question of how to classify fixations on targets that were to the side of the infant. The solution was to count a target to the side as being 'in front' when the distractor on the same side was behind the infant and as 'behind' when the distractor was in front of the infant. Figure 3 presents the mean number of fixations across all six conditions of the study. It is clear from the results that looking alone produced fewer fixations to targets compared with trials involving pointing and vocalisation. It is also clear that, in general, distinctive targets elicited more fixations than identical targets and targets to the front more than targets that were behind the infant.

Total front and back hits for each infant were entered into a multivariate analysis of variance (MANOVA), with age (12- vs. 18-month-olds), gesture (look vs. look-and-point vs. look, point, and verbalize), target (identical vs. distinctive), and gender as between-subjects variables.

Although 18-month-olds fixated somewhat more than 12-month-olds on correct target objects (Ms = 14.3 vs. 13.3, SDs = 7.3 and 7.5), the multivariate age effect was not significant, $F(2,95)$ = 1.9 (Hotelling's T^2 is reported for all multivariate tests). Univariate tests showed that the age effect was not reliable for either front or back hits. The data therefore do not confirm that 12-month-olds are less able than 18-month-olds to follow gestures outside their visual field.

The two conditions involving pointing produced more fixations to the target than looking alone for both front and back targets. However, verbalisation did not increase accuracy. One issue here is that the nature of the targets was such that mothers would have been unlikely to use a specific name. They were instructed to use language to direct their infant's attention but, given the nature of the targets, it is unlikely that they would have been able to say more than 'Look at that one' or 'Look at the shiny one'. Naming could well have improved accuracy as the studies using inter-modal preferential looking indicate (see Paper 6).

Infants' hit frequency differed significantly across gesture conditions, $F(4,188)$ = 24.4, $p < .001$. Infants whose parents only looked at targets produced a mean of 7.4 hits (SD = 4.3); infants whose parents looked and pointed produced a mean of 15.9 hits (SD = 7.1); and infants whose parents looked, pointed, and verbalized produced a mean of 18.2 hits (SD = 5.5).

Post hoc comparisons revealed that infants produced more hits in the look-and-point condition than in the look condition ($p < .05$ by two-tailed Scheffé tests). The difference between the look, point, and verbalize condition and the look-and-point condition, however, was not significant. Thus, pointing significantly added to the efficacy of the looking gesture, but parental verbalizations did not reliably increase joint attention above and beyond looking and pointing. It is important to note that the effect of parental gesture was significant for back and front hits, $F(2,96)$ = 10.6 and 48.4, respectively, ps < .001. This suggests that infants follow gestures to targets behind them more frequently if the gestures are more elaborate and therefore, perhaps, more noticeable.

> Infants were more likely to correctly identify a distinctive target than an identical target for both front and back locations but, as becomes clear, there was an interaction between gesture and type of target for front targets. Such higher order interactions make main effects difficult to interpret. Further exploration of the effect of target type is reported in the next paragraph which suggests that infants lost interest in the identical targets over time.

Target type also influenced infants' his frequency, $F(2,95)$ = 5.2, p < .01. Infants followed gestures a mean of 12.5 times (SD = 7.7) to identical targets and 15.2 times (SD = 6.8) to distinctive targets. Univariate tests showed that this effect was significant for front targets, $F(1,96)$ = 9.3, p < .005, as well as for back targets, $F(1,96)$ = 3.9, p = .05. This suggests that infants more often follow gestures to distinctive, complex targets than to repetitive, simple targets. Perhaps infants habituate to gestures that terminate in boring targets. We tested this hypothesis separately (see below).

Although girls followed parents' gestures more often (M = 15.1, SD = 8.1) than boys (M = 12.6, SD = 6.4), the gender effect did not achieve statistical significance, $F(2,95)$ = 2.2. Sex differences in joint attention are not predicted by any previous findings.

The MANOVA revealed only one significant interaction: Gesture × Target Type, $F(4,188)$ = 2.9, p < .03. The interaction was reliable for front targets only, $F(2,96)$ = 4.7, p < .02. The advantage of distinctive over identical targets was greater in the look-and-point condition than in the other gesture conditions.

To test the hypothesis that infants more rapidly habituate to nondistinctive targets than to repetitive, identical targets, we examined the difference between total number of hits in the first six trials and in the last six trials. If rate of habituation differs for identical and distinctive targets, the difference between the first six and last six trials should be larger for identical targets. Difference scores were entered into an analysis of variance (ANOVA), with age (12- vs. 18-months), gesture (look vs. look and point vs. look, point, and verbalize), and target type (identical vs. distinctive) as between-subjects variables. Total number of hits was covaried to control for individual differences in overall responsiveness. The analysis showed no significant effects except a main effect of target type, $F(1,107)$ = 5.2, p < .03. Infants' gesture-following declined more across trials when targets were identical than when they were distinctive.

To test how rapidly 12- and 18-month-olds responded to different gestures, we compared, by gesture condition and infant age, the percentage of hits that occurred within 5 s of the onset of the parent's gesture. This provides some indication of how rapidly infants responded to different gestures. Overall, 49 per cent of infants' hits occurred within 5 s of gesture onset (the remainder occurred within the subsequent 10 s). An ANOVA revealed that the percentage differed marginally by age, $F(1,114) = 3.6$, $p < .06$, and significantly by gesture, $F(1,114) = 4.2$, $p < .02$. Older infants more than younger infants tended to look at the target during the first 5 s more than looking alone. Mean percentages (and standard deviations) are shown in Table 1.

Speed of responding to a target can also vary, as well as accuracy, and so fixations that occurred within 5 seconds were subjected to further analysis. This accounted for about half of the total fixations although the authors do not give any rationale for their choice of 5 seconds as a cut off. Normally such decisions are made on the basis of looking at the distribution of all response times.

To assess individual infants' consistency in establishing joint attention, we counted the number of trials (out of 12) in which an infant looked at the target at least once. Trials in which the infant looked at the three distractor objects more often than the target were not counted. The overall mean was 7.0 trials ($SD = 2.7$). Six infants (all of them 12-month-olds) looked at the target more than at the distractors on only 0–2 trials, and 24 infants (16 of them 18-month-olds) did so on 10–12 trials. Sixty-one percent of the sample (thirty-four 12-month-olds and thirty-nine 18 month-olds) looked at the target more than at the distractors on most trials (at least 7 out of 12). Most infants, them, responded to adults' gestures on most trials.

The data allowed a test of Butterworth's (1991b) claim that 12-month-olds' visual attention is captured by the first object seen as they scan in the direction of an adult's gaze. The number of hits when the target was at Location 3 during P&B trials (i.e., peripheral target was the first object in the scan path) was compared with the number during F&P trials (i.e., peripheral target was second). If infants tend to fixate the first object on the scan path, they should produce fewer hits to peripheral targets when the distractor is in front than when it is in back. The difference for each child between Location 3 hits in F&P trials and in P&B trials was entered into an ANOVA, with age and target type as between-subjects variables. There were no significant effects, and the mean difference across all children was not significantly different from zero ($M = 0.06$, $SD = 2.1$, $t(119) < 1$. There is no evidence, then, that 12- and 18-month-olds looked less often at peripheral targets when the distractor was close to midline.

Table 1 *Mean percentages (and standard deviations) of hits produced within 5 seconds of the parent's gesture, by age and gesture condition: experiment 1*

Age of infant (in months)	Look		Look and Point		Look, point, and verbalize	
	M	**SD**	**M**	**SD**	**M**	**SD**
12	33.1	29.1	57.1	20.5	46.5	11.3
18	54.4	31.6	59.9	18.1	50.6	13.2

The data from the present study were compared with those of Butterworth (1991) to see whether the younger infants were likely to fixate on the first stimulus they encountered as they turned to follow the mother's line of regard. This involved analysis of responses to trials involving a stimulus placed at position 3, to the side of the infant. Depending on the position of the other stimuli, targets at this position would either be first or second on the infant's scan path, assuming that they turned to the side that their mother was indicating. Comparisons indicated that there was no effect of position on the scan path although the only data that were analysed were 'hits'.

The findings thus far generally do not confirm Butterworth's (1991b,1995) theory that 12-month-olds cannot follow gaze to targets outside their visual field. These results might, however, reflect a statistical artifact. Some conditions might elicit overall higher base rates of scanning the room and looking at different objects. This would elevate the number of hits to the designated target as well as to distractor objects. The apparent increase in joint visual attention would in fact be an artifact of increased looking activity. To rule out this possibility, we conducted analyses taking into account base rates of looking at all objects. Difference scores were calculated by subtracting the average number of fixations of the three distractor objects in every trial from the number of looks to the target object. A difference score of zero would mean that infants looked on average at any given distractor as often as they looked at the target object. This would suggest that parents' gestures did not guide infants' looking. Positive scores would suggest that infants looked more often at the designated target than at any given distractor. This is a more controlled assessment of the incidence of joint visual attention.

The final analysis took account of total number of fixations, since the chances of both 'hits' and 'misses' would be increased for an infant who had a large number of fixations. This kind of technique – in which positive responses are offset against negative responses – is common in studies where individuals are likely to show individual differences in rates of, and preferences for, particular kinds of response. Using the difference between fixations to the target and average fixations to the three detractors, looking to targets both behind and in front of the infant remained significantly greater than to non-targets.

Difference scores for the six trials in which the target was in front of the infant were significantly greater than zero ($M = 7.2$, $SD = 4.3$), $t(119) = 18.0$, $p < .001$. Difference scores for the six trials in which the target was behind the infant were also greater than zero ($M = 4.0$, $SD = 4.2$), $t(119) = 10.4$, $p < .001$. This suggests that infants followed gestures to targets outside of their visual field. Perhaps only 18-month-olds contributed to this effect. This was not the case, however 12-month-olds' difference scores for back targets exceeded zero ($M = 3.1$, $SD = 3.4$), $t(59) = 7.0$, $p < .001$. Their differences scores for front targets also significantly exceeded zero ($M = 7.7$, $SD = 4.7$), $t(59) = 11.9$, $p < .001$. Even among 12-month-olds whose parents only looked at the target, back target difference scores exceeded zero ($M = 1.6$, $SD = 2.7$), $t(19) = 2.7$, $p < .02$. This is the first demonstration that 12-month-olds reliably follow an adult's gaze to targets outside their visual field, even when there are distractor objects in front of the infant.[5]

Discussion

These findings have several implications for previous findings and current hypotheses about infant joint attention. Similar to earlier findings (e.g., Butterworth & Grover, 1988) demonstrating that some gesture combinations are more effective than others at guiding infants' attention, the results of Experiment 1 reveal that pointing and looking at a target are more compelling than looking alone. Why is pointing so effective? Perhaps infants have learned that pointing is an intentional request to recruit and direct another person's attention, whereas gaze if not necessarily intended to direct attention, and therefore does not always mandate a shift of attention. Another possibility is that pointing is a better geometric cue than head orientation of a person's head, an outstretched arm provides a longer, more precise segment of the vector. Finally, pointing might be more effective because raising and outstretching one's arm is more noticeable than simply rotating one's head, particularly if the radial magnitude of the head turn is small. We tested this last possibility in Experiment 2.

The gesture effect raises ancillary questions. For example, the effects of looking and pointing might be cumulative. Perhaps looking and pointing toward a target provide a critical mass of redundant information about the location of the object of attention. Future studies that independently vary looking and pointing could address this possibility. A related question is whether looking and pointing together imposed a ceiling effect, Verbally exhorting infants to look at the target did not significantly increase the frequency of joint visual attention above looking and pointing. It is unlikely, however, that parental utterances have no effect on joint attention. More likely, pointing was so effective that it masked the effects of verbalizations. Further research on the effects of parental verbalizations on infant attention will be needed to resolve this issue.

Infants more often followed an adult's gesture to distinctive and relatively complex target objects than to identical and simple objects. Infants might have been less motivated to follow adults' gestures if, after a few trials, they came to expect gestures to indicate repetitive, boring objects. This is supported by the finding that target type alone contributed significant variance to the difference between hits in the first and second half of the session (when total hits were covaried). More generally, the target type effect exemplifies the triadic nature of joint attention: Another person's gesture mediates the infant's allocation of attention to an array of objects and events within a perceptually shared (or shareable) environment. Not all objects and events are equally worthy of joint attention. There is evidence, for example, that infants follow gestures to moving objects more than to static objects (Butterworth, 1991a). Some objects are more interesting to look at than others, and it might be possible to specify the stimulus variables that mediate these differences. Yet not everything that interests adults (e.g., stock reports, rare coins) interests babies. Part of the 'economics' of joint attention involves knowledge of what kinds of things are likely to interest another person. If an adult often calls attention to uninteresting things, a baby should learn to ignore that person's gestures as invalid. The target-type effects imply that infants rapidly adapt to the validity of an adult's attention-specifying gestures and habituate to gestures that do not 'pay off' in interesting sights.

To maximize the possibility of finding a target-type effect, we conflated complexity and distinctiveness. That is, distinctive targets were also more complex, and therefore we do not know how each variable contributed to the effect. Future studies are needed to determine how these variables affect infants' persistence in following adults' gestures. Moreover, only two levels of distinctiveness and complexity were tested, yet both variables are multidimensional and difficult to define. Future research should establish how different aspects or degrees of distinctiveness and complexity influence joint visual attention. An informative starting point would be provided by naturalistic studies of the kinds of objects and events that infants and adults spontaneously call to one another's attention.

There is an alternative explanation of the target-type effect. Perhaps parents gesture more emphatically or effectively toward some targets than others. Parents might gesture more emphatically toward interesting targets because such targets are worth pointing out or toward boring targets to overcome the target's shortcomings. By this account, the target-type effect might be conflated with an unintended gesture effect. This suggests a more general question: Did the manner in which parents executed a gesture influence the probability that the child would follow it? If so, an adult observer should be able to predict whether the target object was interesting on the basis of the gesture's efficacy. In addition, an observer's estimate of the efficacy of the gesture should predict the incidence of joint attention. To test these hypotheses, a coder with extensive experience observing and testing infants coded videotapes of parents in the look-and-point condition. The coder rated, on a 5-point Likert scale, the effectiveness and enthusiasm of the parent's gesture in every trial. The coder was blind to the target type and to the infant's response. After coding all 12 trials for an infant, the coder inferred whether the targets had been 'interesting' or 'boring.' The gesture efficacy across 12 trials was averaged for each parent. The difference of the means for parents who gestured at identical targets (M = 2.4) versus distinctive targets (M = 2.6) did not reach conventional levels of significance, t (34) = 1.7, $p < .11$. We cannot conclude that parents systematically gestured more effectively or emphatically toward distinctive targets. Moreover, parents' mean gesture efficacy was unrelated to how often infants looked at target objects ($r = .09$). Finally, the coder was correct only 55 per cent of the time about the target type, which does not differ from chance. These findings, although limited, reveal no evidence that parents' production of a given gesture differed as a function of target type.

In the current findings, as in Butterworth and Jarrett's (1991) study, 12-month-olds followed gestures more often to targets in front of them than to targets behind them. The current results nonetheless fail to confirm Butterworth's (1991b) developmental theory. Butterworth's theory suggests that between 12 and 18 months of age, infants develop the ability to represent the environment as a Euclidean space in which different people can look at different locations, not all of which are visible to all viewers. Twelve-month-old infants will not follow another person's gaze to unseen locations even if there are no distractors in view. By 18 months, infants follow another's gaze to unseen locations unless there is competition from visible distractors. During and after this period there is a decoupling of joint visual attention from the visibility of different locations. In contrast to this picture, 12-moth-olds followed gestures to targets behind them, even when there were competing objects in the visual field. Also, the differences between 12- and 18-month-olds were small and not significant. Perhaps these differences, as reported in previous studies (e.g., Butterworth & Jarrett, 1991), are apparent only when adult gestures and visual targets are subtle and not compelling. Providing more informative gestures and more distinctive targets increased both 12- and 18-month-olds' tendency to follow gestures to targets out of view. This suggests that deficits in spatial representation (i.e., a non-Euclidean schema) do not explain why infants more reliably follow gestures to front targets. Rather, we must consider how and why specific combinations of gestures compel infants to look at a particular location inside or outside their current visual field. This apparently depends partly on how compelling the gesture is and whether it is likely to terminate in a distinctive, interesting target.

Experiment 2

Having shown that there did not appear to be a developmental progression from a geometric to a Euclidian representation of space, as proposed by Butterworth, the authors go on to pursue an alternative explanation for why infants respond more readily when an adult indicates a target in front of the infant than a target located behind. This hinges on considering how good an indicator of location a particular gesture is. Interestingly, this is similar to the explanation given by Butterworth for the advantage of pointing over gaze as an indication of location since he argues, following the principle of levers, that a short lever (the nose) gives a much less precise indication of direction of regard than the longer lever formed by the outstretched arm and pointing index finger (Butterworth & Itakura, 2000).

The purpose of Experiment 2 was to explore why young infants more readily follow adults' gestures to locations within their current visual field than to locations outside their visual field. In regard to objects behind them, infants more often followed looking and pointing than looking alone. To understand this finding, consider again the spatial arrangement in Figure 1. When the infant and parent face each other (as in Butterworth & Cochran, 1980; Butterworth & Jarrett, 1991, and Experiment 1 of the present study), the distance that the parent's head rotates from the infant to the target depends on the target location. Targets behind the infant are close to the parent's midline, whereas those in front of the infant are in the parent's periphery or behind the parent. To look at an object behind the infant (e.g., Location 5), the parent produces a small head turn. To look at an object in front of the infant (e.g., Location 1), the parent produces a large head turn. Infants might detect a larger movement more readily than a smaller movement.

To investigate this possibility, we changed the spatial arrangement of the infant and parent in relation to the objects. The new configuration is depicted in Figure 4. Infants were situated as in Experiment 1, but parents were rotated 90° (to the infant's left or right). In this configuration, in order to look at one front and one back target (Locations F/S and B/S in Figure 4), the parent must produce relatively small but equal-sized head turns. To look at the other front and back target (Locations F/L and B/L in Figure 4), the parent must produce relatively larger but nonetheless equal-sized head turns.

In order to examine the possibility that infants find it easier to detect and respond to large movements of the head and arm, the seating of the adult in relation to the infant was altered to remove the confounding of target location and amount of movement required to look at or point at the target. Targets remain either behind or in front of the infant but, since they were located to either side of the adult, the amount of movement required to indicate location was now the same for the two targets to the infant's right (one in front and one behind) and the same for the two targets located to the infant's left (again, one in front and one behind). This change in the procedure enabled the experimenters to disentangle the front-back location of the target from the amount of movement required for a head turn or point to the target.

If 12-month-olds follow gestures to front targets more than to back targets because their spatial representations are egocentric, gesture magnitude should not mediate joint visual attention. If the front target advantage is an effect of gesture magnitude, however, infants should follow large gestures (i.e., toward/L locations) more than small gestures (i.e., toward/S locations) whether the target is within or outside their visual field.

Two gesture conditions were included: look and look and point. The latter was included because the effect of head-turn magnitude might be reduced when pointing is added. Pointing is a relatively noticeable body motion, and it provides redundant spatial information. Both 12-month-olds and 18-month-olds participated.

Method

Participants

Forth-eight infants and their parent participated in Experiment 2. Twenty-four 12-month-olds (12 girls, 12 boys, mean age = 12 months 1 day, range = 11 months 3 days to 12 months 2 days) and twenty-four 18-month-olds (12 girls, 12 boys: mean age = 18 months 3 days, range = 17 months 18 days to 18 months 13 days) were included in the final analyses. Infants were recruited as in Experiment 1.

Materials

The apparatus and distinctive objects of Experiment 1 were used.

Design

Infants (12- and 18-month-olds) were quasi-randomly assigned to one of two gesture conditions (look or look and point), with the constraint of equal numbers of boys and girls in each group.

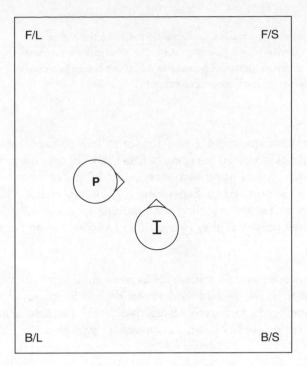

Figure 4   *Schematic diagram of room, showing location of infant, parent, and targets in Experiment 2. P = parent; I = infant; F = front target; B = back target; S = target brought into view by a small gaze shift; L = target brought into view by a large gaze shift (e.g., F/S is the target in front of the infant that the parent looks at by producing a small head turn)*

Target object locations were symmetrically paired. Two objects were on the infant's left, and two were on the right. Object pairs were separated by 60°. One pair was in front of the infant, and the other was behind. This configuration was used on every trial. Every infant completed 3 trials with each of four target locations, for a total of 12 trials. Trials were in blocks of four, with target location counterbalanced. Target location order was randomized within blocks. Parents were seated to one side of the infant, rotated 90° so that their midline gaze direction was perpendicular to the infant's gaze direction. The side the parent faced (left or right) was counterbalanced. From either side, parents made a small head turn to look at one target in front of the infant (F/S) and one target behind the infant (B/S). Likewise, parents made a large head turn to look at another front target (F/L) and another back target (B/L). Parents began each gesture facing midline rather than looking at the infant. A different distinctive object was the target in each trial.

The overall design of Experiment 2 is simpler than Experiment 1 since the critical comparisons are between target locations and type of gesture. The third gesture condition (involving vocalisation) was dropped, presumably because it had not been significantly different from the looking + pointing condition in Experiment 1.

Procedure

The protocol for Experiment 2 was similar to that of Experiment 1 except that (a) locations remained the same across trials, (b) only distinctive objects were used, (c) parents never verbalized, and (d) parents were seated perpendicular to infants. As in Experiment 1, parents verbally elicited their infant's attention before executing each gesture. Consequently, infants were looking at their parent, slightly to one side of midline, when the trial began.

Coding

The coding procedure and criteria for Experiment 2 were identical to those of Experiment 1. A second coder recoded videotapes of 15 infants (eight 12-month-olds and seven 18-month-olds; 31 per cent of the sample). The overall kappa was .91, which is excellent agreement.

Results

Infants' total number of fixations on target objects were first analyzed for the effects of infant's gender and parents' seating side (right vs. left). Boys made slightly more hits than girls ($Ms = 11.9$ and 9.7, respectively), but the difference was not significant, $t(46) = 1.4$, $p > .15$. The effect of the parent's seating side was also nonsignificant, $r(46) = 0$. These variables therefore were excluded from subsequent analyses.

Infants' total number of fixations on target objects, in all 12 trials, were entered into a 2×2 ANOVA, with age (12- vs. 18-month-olds) and gesture (look vs. look and point) as between-subjects variables. The main effect of age was significant, $F(1,44) = 6.6$, $p < .02$ Twelve- and 18-month-olds produced a mean of 9.1 ($SD = 5.0$) and 12.5 ($SD = 5.3$) total looks, respectively. The gesture effect also was significant, $F(1,44) = 14.8$, $p < .001$. Infants in the look condition produced a mean of 8.2 ($SD = 3.7$) total hits versus a mean of 13.3 ($SD = 5.6$) in the look-and-point condition. The interaction was not significant, $F(1,44) < 1$.

The main analysis was carried out on the number of fixations to target objects on each trial. There was a significant effect of both age and gesture type, with the older infants making more fixations to the target than the younger infants and the looking + pointing producing more fixations than looking alone. Since the interaction was not significant, this means that both older and younger infants responded similarly to the two types of gesture.

The critical questions involve effects of target object location (front vs. back) and parent's gesture magnitude. Regarding target location, mean total hits to front targets (locations F/S & F/L) and back targets (B/S and B/L), by age and gesture, are shown in Figure 5. Difference scores were calculated for every trial by subtracting the average number of hits to the three distractor objects from the number of hits to the target object. As in Experiment 1, this controls for possible between-group differences in base rates of scanning the room.[6]

> *The second set of analyses again used difference scores to control for individual differences in the total number of fixations. Older and younger infants responded differently to targets located to front and back, with the 12-month-olds being less likely to fixate on targets located behind them than 18-month-olds but showing similar fixation patterns for targets located to the front.*

Differences were summed for front and back target trials and were compared by MANOVA. The effect of age was significant, $F(2,43) = 5.8$, $p < .01$. One-way analyses revealed that 12-month-olds followed gestures to back targets less frequently than 18-month-olds, $F(1,44) = 11,7$, $p < .001$. This is consistent with results reported by Butterworth and Cochran (1980) and Butterworth and Jarrett (1991). The age difference was not significant for front targets, $F(1,44) = 2.0$. As in Experiment 1, a separate analysis showed that 12-month-olds looked more often at back targets than at the distractor objects (M = 1.4, SD = 2.5), $t(23) = 2.6$, $p < .02$, even though two distractors were within the infant's visual field.

The effect of gesture was significant, $F(2,43) = 12.3$, $p < .001$. The advantage of pointing was significant for front targets, $F(1,44) = 24.9$, $p < .001$, and marginally significant for back targets, $F(1,44) = 3.9$, $p < .06$. This replicated the results of Experiment 1 and was consistent with the argument that infants in previous studies did not look behind them because gaze alone is less noticeable than gaze combined with pointing. The interaction of age and gesture was not significant.

> *Pointing again increased the likelihood of an infant fixating on a target although the effect of gesture was only marginally significant for targets behind the infant. The data in Figure 5 show that the younger infants produced only a small number of fixations to targets behind them in both gesture conditions. The data here – and in the analysis – are conflated across right and left positions and therefore include both cases where the target was behind the adult (requiring a large indicative movement) and cases where it was in front (requiring a small indicative movement). It is therefore hard to interpret these results.*

The second question was whether infants respond to large head turns more often than to small head turns. The total number of target hits on trials in which parents made small head turns ($M = 4.5$, $SD = 2.9$) was compared with the total number on trials in which parents made large head turns ($M = 6.3$, $SD = 3.3$). These were entered into a repeated-measures ANOVA, with age and gesture type as between-subjects variables. There was a significant within-subjects effect of gesture magnitude, $F(1,44) = 14.5$, $p < .001$. There was no interaction either with age or gesture type. Thus, regardless of infants' age and whether or not parents pointed, the magnitude of the parent's head turn from midline to target influenced whether, and how often, infants followed the gesture.

The final analysis examined how the size of adult movement affected infants' detection of targets. The authors compared the number of 'hits' following a small head (and arm) movement with the number following a big movement. The effect of size of movement was significant and there was no interaction with either age or gesture type. Thus, infants were more likely to correctly locate a target when it was indicated by a big movement than a small movement. Since the magnitude of the head turn and the amount of movement required to produce the point are closely related, it is not surprising that there is no interaction with type of gesture.

This effect may be better understood by examining Figure 6, which shows 12- and 18-month-olds mean hits toward each target location (F/S, F/L, B/S, and B/L). Clearly, infants responded least often to small gestures toward targets behind them. Follow-up ANOVAs on total hits at each location, with age as a between-subjects variable, showed that the age difference was relilable at the F/S target location, $F(1,46) = 4.4$, $p < .05$, and the B/L location, $F(1,46) = 7.6$, $p < .01$.

The authors do not explicitly test the hypothesis of interaction between location (front and back) and the amount of movement required although they do note that both groups of infants showed the smallest number of hits to targets that were located behind them and indicated by a small movement of the adult's head (and arm). They note that there is no age difference for targets of this B/S type or for F/L targets. Arguably, these are respectively the most difficult and easiest targets to detect. For the two intermediate targets, B/L and F/S, older infants were more accurate than younger infants.

Discussion

The general conclusion drawn by the authors from Experiment 2 is that younger infants (aged 12 months) are less responsive to small changes in the direction of gaze than older infants (aged 18 months). They suggest that the particular difficulty of the B/S

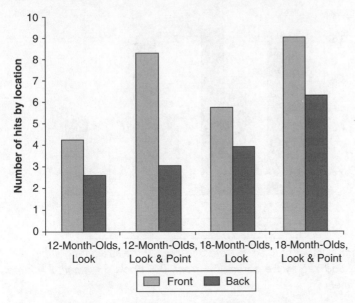

Figure 5   *Mean number of correct looks toward front and back targets, by age and gesture combination: Experiment 2*

condition stems from the fact the infants may have been confused about whether their mother was pointing to or looking at them or a target since the infant and the B/S target were in line with one another. This is certainly a possibility but it could also be that targets behind the infant are more difficult than targets in front and that a small movement is more difficult to follow than a large movement. Whatever the explanation, however, it is clear that it is not the case that infants cannot locate objects located behind them but, rather, that they find it more difficult.

The results of Experiment 2 inform our interpretation of Experiment 1. Unlike in Experiment 1, 18-month-olds established joint attention significantly more often than 12-month-olds. Because half of adults' gaze shifts were small in Experiment 2, compared with only one fifth in Experiment 1, the discrepancy suggests that 12-month-olds are less likely than 18-month-olds to respond to small shifts in adults' gaze, perhaps because small shifts are hard to detect. Also consistent with this possibility is the finding that 18-month-olds more often followed gaze to back targets, but there was no age difference in following gaze to front targets. This and previous findings (Butterworth & Jarrett, 1991) support the hypothesis that 12- and 18-month-olds differ in responsiveness to small deviations in gaze directions.

The hypothesis is most strongly supported by a significant effect of gesture magnitude, independent of target location. When parents rotated their head further to look at a target object, infants more often followed gaze.

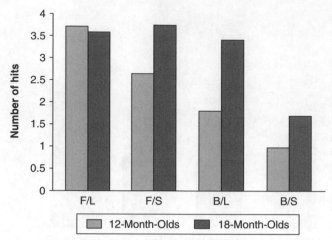

Figure 6   *Mean number of looks to front and back targets requiring either a small or large head turn by the parent (F = front, B = back, S = small, L = large), by age: Experiment 2*

Previous studies did not reveal this effect because the radial distance, or magnitude, of parents' head turns was conflated with target location. Rotating the parent 90° from the infant's midline separates these variables and reveals that infants are more responsive to large head turns, presumably because these turns are more readily detected.

Separate analyses of each target location showed a subtle manifestation of this effect. A reliable age difference was found for the B/S target location. Figure 4 suggests a speculative account of this effect. In these trials, the infant's head is very close to the line of gaze between the parent and the B/S target, so it is difficult to discern whether the parent is looking at the target or the infant. Infants might have believed that their parent was looking at them. In this case, turning around would interrupt what the infant perceives as a face-to-face interaction initiated by parental gaze. Such interactions are compelling or rewarding to infants, so there is actually a disincentive to turn to look at the B/S target. Thus, the B/S disadvantage might stem from 12-month-olds' inability to discriminate whether a parent is looking at them or at an object a few degrees off center. Presumably, 18-month-olds are better able to differentiate small deviations in gaze direction and therefore show a smaller B/S disadvantage. This implies that the target location effect (i.e., following gaze less often to back targets) rests on the infant's ability to discriminate small changes in adults' gaze direction. Although this tentative explanation goes beyond the current data, it is consistent with other reports (Butterworth & Jarrett, 1991; Morissette et al., 1995).

Experiment 2 also provides strong evidence for a target location effect. The analysis of difference scores for back targets in Experiment 2 controls for both gesture magnitude and base rates of scanning for objects. It is therefore the first unconfounded demonstration that 12-month-olds, compared with 18-month-olds, follow adults' gestures less often to back targets.

In spite of the observed effects of target location and gesture magnitude, when parents gestured toward back targets, 12-month-olds looked significantly more at those objects than at distractor objects. This replicates the critical finding in Experiment 1 that 12-month-olds follow parents' gestures to targets outside their visual field.

Finally, the advantage of looking and pointing over gaze alone in recruiting infants' attention was replicated. This advantage for targets behind the infant was also replicated. This is consistent with the argument that pointing is effective because it is more readily noticed or detected than a simple head turn.

General discussion

What is the significance of the finding that 12-month-olds can follow an adult's gaze to targets outside their visual field? Broadly, the findings refute theories that 12-month-olds are categorically limited to egocentric and non-Euclidean spatial representations. More specifically, they refute the hypothesis that 12-month-olds neglect targets outside their current visual field. This fits earlier evidence that 8- and 9-month-olds sometimes form nonegocentric spatial representations. For example, Presson and Ihrig (1982) found that most 9-month-olds, after learning to turn toward a specific location, continue to turn toward that location after being rotated 180° if a landmark (their mother) remains in the same place. Thus, infants sometimes represent an 'absolute' location even if they are moved, suggesting that they can form nonegocentric spatial representations. The current evidence broadens this conclusion. Twelve-month-olds sometimes locate objects that are out of sight by responding to a social-spatial cue-namely, the direction of an adult's gaze.

How do these results inform theories of joint attention? Butterworth (1991b) proposed that a geometric mechanism, which allows infants to extrapolate imaginary lines of gaze and thereby follow gaze to peripheral targets, emerges by 12 months. A representational mechanism, which allows infants to ignore frontal distractors and follow gaze to targets outside of view, emerges by 18 months. One interpretation of the current data is that this timetable is accelerated, with a representational mechanism coming online by 12 months.

An alternative, parsimonious explanation is that infants acquire the tendency to respond to adults' attention-specifying gestures (e.g., direction of gaze) through gradual learning processes. There is ample evidence that infants learn cotingent responses in face-to-face interactions (e.g., Dunham & Dunham, 1995; Hains & Muir, 1996). Infants younger than 12 months can, for example, be conditioned to follow an adult's gaze (Corkum & Moore, 1998). Infants ostensibly are rewarded in everyday situations for following an adult's gaze or point, because doing so brings interesting events or objects into view. Nine- to 12-month-olds might initially look in the general direction of an adult's head turn or point. Over the next 6–9 months, infants learn more precisely to discern the location of the target object or event. Later still, this faculty will be integrated with the emerging ability to make inferences about other people's attentive states. Between 9 and 18 months, the growing ability to detect small changes and discrepancies in adult gaze direction can account for a 12-month-old's relative insensitivity to parental gaze toward objects behind the child – or, more precisely, to objects that lie close to the line of gaze from parent to child. Note that although infants are minimally sensitive to whether an adult is making eye contact or looking a few degrees away (Symons, Hains,& Muir, 1998), discrimination is unreliable. Inconsistent response to small gaze shifts might account for the infrequency with which 12-month-olds, compared with 18-month-olds, followed gestures to Location B/S in Experiment 2. This implies perceptual learning about gaze information during the second year.

If infants learn through conditioning to respond to changes in a caregiver's gaze direction, cluttered visual environments (i.e., rooms with many interesting objects) might provide reinforcement for turning only part of the way toward the correct target, because interesting distractor objects will cross their visual field before the precise target of adult attention does. This can account for the phenomenon reported by Butterworth and Jarrett (1991). Nevertheless, our evidence suggests that by their first birthday, infants have learned to ignore objects within their visual field and to follow adults' gaze, with or without pointing, to target objects outside their visual field. This account makes no commitment as to how other aspects of joint attention (e.g., attentiveness to adults' faces, conceptual inferences about others' mental states) are acquired. The point is that available data on developmental improvement in the precision and reliability of gaze-following are not inconsistent with an account based on conditioning and perceptual learning.

The authors make a number of suggestions about why locating an object behind is difficult for young infants. Clearly, looking for a target that is outside the visual field at the beginning of the search is more demanding of memory and co-ordination than searching for an object that is within the visual field. It may prove difficult to disentangle these various factors that, in the real world, go together. Furthermore, it could be argued that the best way to attract attention to an object outside the visual field is through the use of sound. Right from birth, infants will orient to a sound; and the ability to locate the origin of a sound increases in accuracy in the first year of life (Fernald, 2001). So it could well be that looking or pointing are not the most ecologically valid ways of drawing attention to something that is behind somebody; and that language may play an important part. After all, in a traditional English pantomime, when a villain is visible to the audience but not to an actor, the audience traditionally shouts out 'It's behind you!'.

Why did our results show that 12-month-olds can search for objects behind them, when other investigations (e.g., Butterworth & Jarrett, 1991) have not? One reason is that half of the infants in Experiment 1 and all of the infants in Experiment 2 saw interesting and unique objects. Distinctive, complex targets might compel more consistent and frequent joint visual attention than identical, simple targets. In many studies of joint visual attention, infants have followed adults' gestures to repetitive, uninteresting objects. Infants might quickly tire of following an adult's gaze to identical pegs (Morissette et al., 1995) or yellow squares (Butterworth & Jarrett, 1991). This is implied by the greater split-half decline in joint attention to identical targets than to distinctive targets (Experiment 1). In the former condition, apparently, infants learned that the parent's attention-specifying gestures were not valid and habituated to the gestures. In normal circumstances, parents' attentive gestures terminate in objects or events that are interesting to babies. Previous laboratory studies of infant joint attention might have underestimated the frequency or persistence of infants' gaze-following by asking infants to follow invalid gestures to boring targets.

The second reason, as previously discussed, is that during face-to-face interactions, infants might not notice small shifts in an adult's gaze. There is a complication here: If the infant turns around to search for the target of a parent's gesture, both the gesture and parent are taken out of view. The social signal is rendered unavailable. Now the infant cannot directly extrapolate a vector to the target because the information that specifies the vector – the parent's head and/or hand direction – is out of view. The infant must rely on a representation of the position of the adult's head and/or hand (this is similar to Buttterworth & Grover's, 1988, geometrical mechanism). This memory requirement apparently makes it more difficult to locate the correct target.

There is yet another possible reason why infants less frequently follow gaze to back targets. In comparison to scanning the front visual field, turning around to search behind oneself requires a relatively extensive, deliberate sequence of actions. Infants (not to mention adults) might need to be more motivated to turn around to search for a target. This level of motivation might require both a compelling gesture and the expectation of an interesting target. If these conditions are necessary, previous studies of joint visual attention might not have motivated infants to turn around. Infants' motivational requirements, as well as their ability to detect adults' gestures, might explain the relative infrequency of joint visual attention to back targets. Future studies that manipulate reinforcement contingencies for joint visual attention should address this hypothesis.

The current findings expand our knowledge of the complexity of infants' joint visual attention between 12 and 18 months of age. To predict whether an infant will follow an adult's gesture, we must take into account the nature and complexity of the visual targets, infants' expectations about adult gestures, and the relative spatial arrangement of the infant, adult, and target. From an early age, infants are sensitive to ecological and geometric information, capable of representing space outside of view, prone to form social expectations, and inbued with the affective and motivational propensity to engage in face-to-face communication with adults. Together, these skills permit the development of a complex system for responding to social information about a shared environment.

Notes

1 During initial telephone contact we asked any primary caregiver to accompany the infant. All but 2 infants were brought by their mother.
2 Although using parents to deliver gestures probably introduced some error variance due to individual differences in parents' manner of gesturing, this procedure was chosen for several reasons. First, it minimized negative affective responses from infants caused by interactions with strange adults. Second, because dyads were randomly assigned to conditions, it is likely that any individual differences were reasonably well distributed. Third, greater error variance would tend to increase Type II error, however, the critical hypotheses examined here all stipulate rejection of the null hypothesis; thus, it is increases in Type I error that would have been of concern.
3 Given that adults' fixations are as short as 200 ms and that young infant's visual scanning and processing are somewhat slower than adults', 500 ms seemed a reasonable, if slightly conservative, criterion for fixations in 12-18-month-olds.
4 This measure is highly correlated with total looking time ($r = .77$; Flom, Burmeister, & Pick, 1998).
5 Because mean difference scores in some conditions were positively skewed, we conducted another analysis of the log of each infant's difference score plus 10. This provides a more normally distributed sample in which scores greater than 1.0 indicate more fixations on the target than on any given distractor. This more conservative test yields similar results. For example, 12-month-olds in the look condition produced difference logs greater than 1, $t(19) = 2.6$, $p < .02$.
6 Note that the same pattern of findings is obtained if simple number of hits, rather than difference scores, is analyzed.

5

EXPERIMENTAL STUDIES OF OLDER CHILDREN

Once children become capable of using and understanding language, researchers often turn to experimental tasks that involve verbal instructions and, often, verbal responses. The use of language-based tasks offers a much wider range of experimental techniques than the non-linguistic tasks that are used in infancy research. However, there are potential problems with the use of language because it is essential to be sure both that children fully understand what they are required to do in a study and that their own use of language does not obscure their responses.

In both the case of instructions and of children's responses, subtle differences may exist between adult and child use and understanding of language. For example, studies may use words like 'real', 'really', 'same' and 'different' which are understood somewhat differently by older and younger children. Young children use the word 'real' to mean 'authentic' and so they talk about 'The real Father Christmas' and 'The real Darth Vader' whereas older children (from the age of 4 years onwards) also begin to use 'real' to refer to the notion of existence (Bunce & Harris, submitted). This means that questions about whether something is real or not will be interpreted differently according to the age of the child. Similar developmental changes in the understanding of the word 'same' have also been documented (Karmiloff-Smith, 1979).

Children's own use of language can also, sometimes, be misleading. A common problem is that younger children, with less sophisticated language skills, may find it difficult to provide a coherent explanation for a belief or behaviour. In such cases, it is often difficult to know whether there is a problem with their level of understanding or with their ability to put their understanding into words. For this reason, researchers often look for related changes in the kinds of non-verbal and verbal responses that children give.

Cross sectional studies

As I noted in Chapter 2, the majority of studies in developmental psychology involve cross sectional designs in which the performance of children of different ages is compared over the experimental tasks. We begin the chapter with two such studies that illustrate what can be learned about differences in the abilities of older and younger children. In both cases, the age range chosen for the participants is determined by the point in development where change is expected to occur.

Paper 8   Children's understanding of other people's emotions (Bradmetz & Schneider, 1999)

In this paper, the authors investigate children's understanding of other people's belief-based fears. This can be seen as an extension of research into Theory of Mind (ToM) understanding (see Paper 3). The difference is that standard ToM tasks ask what another character will *think* as a result of what they know (and don't know) whereas this paper is concerned with what another character will *feel* as a result of what they know.

Belief-based emotion attribution was first studied by Paul Harris and colleagues (Harris, Johnson, Hutton, Andrews & Cooke, 1989) who developed tasks such as *Mickey the Monkey* to investigate children's understanding. In the task, a mischievous toy called Mickey plays tricks on other animals. In one trick, he secretly replaces a nice drink with an unpleasant liquid. Children are asked how the toy who is the butt of the joke – and does not know what Mickey has done – will feel on first seeing the container and how he will feel after seeing the real contents.

Harris et al. (1989) found that most 4-year-old children could not correctly predict the initial emotion but 6-year-olds were able to do so and could also explain why the toy would initially feel a positive emotion at the prospect of a nice drink. This is rather later than successful performance in a traditional ToM task such as the Sally-Ann task (Baron-Cohen, Leslie & Frith, 1985). In this task, a girl doll (Sally) hides a marble and then goes for a walk. A second doll (Ann) then moves the marble while Sally is still away and so cannot see what has happened. The children are asked where Sally will look for the marble. This is a question about an action based on a belief. Paper 8 uses a familiar fairy tale, *Little Red Riding Hood*, to explore children's understanding of emotion based on a belief.

British Journal of Developmental Psychology, 1999, 17; 501–14

Is Little Red Riding Hood afraid of her grand-mother? Cognitive vs. emotional response to a false belief

Joël Bradmetz and Roland Schneider

University of Franche-Comté, Besançon, France

The topic of this study is the achievement of rationality and consistency of thought in the young child from 4 to 7 years of age. It echoes Piaget's pre-occupations and tries to improve the description of cognitive development from the stage of reflection (i.e. awareness of some mental states; secondary intention according to Brentano, 1874) at 4 years of age, to the stage of reason described by Piaget in terms of the concrete operational stage. In order to demonstrate both the generality and the robustness of the child's cognitive inconsistency during this period, a well-studied domain in contemporary child psychology was chosen: the acquisition of a theory of mind. The aim was to demonstrate that, despite the so-called conceptual revolution taking place at 4 years of age, a consistently logical appreciation of false belief is not achieved before 7 or 8 years of age, because of its computational complexity and the mental load that it imposes. Success on the standard task (Wimmer & Perner, 1983) does not directly entail that a genuine concept of belief underlies the accurate predictions, nor that all the deductive consequences of a given belief can be calculated.

> The authors argue that children can pass a traditional ToM task without fully understanding all the consequences of someone having a particular belief. Such consequences entail not only understanding how someone will act but also how they will feel, what they might say or, even, how they might act in the future. They also note that, in standard ToM tasks, in which children are asked to predict someone's behaviour, there may be external cues that guide children to the correct decision whereas such cues are not available to explain what someone might say or feel.

Several findings indicate the gradual acquisition of false belief attribution in young children. Clements & Perner (1994) showed an implicit understanding of false belief earlier than on the standard task (Wimmer & Perner, 1983); Mitchell (1994) argued that, because of the realist bias, various external indices of the mental state (e.g. the posting procedure in the Smarties task) help to reduce the age of success on the task. On the other hand, a task in which child is asked to predict what a protagonist will say about the contents of a box that has been modified during his or her absence (Hogrefe, Wimmer & Perner, 1986) is more difficult than the standard task of Wimmer & Perner (Bradmetz, 1998).

It is likely that from 4 to 7 years of age, each peripheral module has its own resources for computing a false belief and that these various modules are only partially integrated into a single coherent system by means of operational structures and consciousness. This effect is evident in the examples cited above concerning the constitution of a single belief (the *ontological* aspect): implicit (visual) belief seems easier than embodied belief (posting procedure) which is easier than procedural belief ('Where will Maxi look for his chocolate?') which is itself easier than declarative belief (what will a protagonist say about the content of the box modified in his or her absence?). It is argued that developmental difficulties also appear in the *epistemological* aspect, i.e. coordination of various modular assessments of a false belief as long as the explicit coordination structure in not in place.

Following philosophical usage, the structure which eliminates contradiction and implies the logical integration and coordination of the various points of view of the other is called 'third-person', and the intermediate structure which is based only on perspective separation and opposition *via* one modular evaluation is called 'second-person'. During the intermediate period, children understand that their beliefs can differ from those of another person, but it is not yet an amodal or intermodal concept of belief; rather, it is tied to particular modules. Data from the different peripheral systems are not yet easily commensurable with one another and the characteristic of this period is an instability of response and systematic *décalages* between, for example, the cognitive and emotional assessment of a false belief which is the focus of this study. In other words, the child who interacts on the basis of a second-person structure interacts with a partial person and a partial mind. (There is an analogy with the partial and total object of the psychoanalytic theory.)

The argument here is that there is a developmental progression from being able to understand – in a given situation – that the beliefs of one person may not be the same as those of another to understanding this idea in the abstract, as applicable to any situation involving beliefs and their consequences.

Piagetian studies have illustrated this type of developmental progression in the preoperational stage. Children understand *pre-concepts* around 4–5 years of age (Bradmetz, 1996), but integrate them into a coherent and closed structure only around 7 or 8 years of age. For example, when asked: 'Which is the longer of these two sticks?' they are able to compare two sticks of different lengths around 4 years of age, revealing an understanding of what is the length of an object, but they will not be able to transform this pre-concept into a concept (i.e. conservation and invariance of length) until 7 or 8 years of age.

The authors draw an analogy with Piaget's idea of the developmental progression from pre-operational thought to thought involving wider-ranging concepts that appears during the stage of concrete operations. The paper uses this framework, together with philosophical work on the nature of belief and desire, to provide a wider context for the research. This framework is reflected in the general discussion of the findings.

To investigate the dissociation between the assertion of a false belief and the negation of one of its logical consequences, it was decided to contrast two assessments of a situation: a cognitive and an emotional assessment. If the child has developed a mentalistic theory of mind, he or she should understand that emotion is founded on the doxastic attitudes of an agent and not on the actual state of affairs when these conflict. This was demonstrated by Harris, Johnson, Hutton, Andrews & Cooke (1989) in a set of experiments in which children had to assess the emotional state of a protagonist who had been deceived by a joker. The experimental design consisted in questioning the child about the emotions of the protagonist (happiness about a desired food or drink and sadness about a disliked food or drink), first when he falsely believes he knows the contents of a box (that has been modified without his knowledge) and, second, after he has discovered the real contents of the box and the deception. The child is also questioned about the reason for which the protagonist is happy (sad) at first and then sad (happy). The authors demonstrated an increasing age-linked justification of emotion based on the belief of the protagonists and not on the actual state of affairs, but noted difficulties even up to 6 years of age. These results are important and confirm the relevance of the belief-desire psychology framework. Within this framework, however, they are not counter-intuitive because the authors did not try to contrast various evaluations of a false belief situation: they did not ask the child where the protagonist would look for the desired food or drink before or after questioning him about his emotional state. Ruffman & Keenan (1996) conducted a series of experiments to assess the appearance of a belief-based concept of surprise in the child. They discovered a lag between the understanding of a false belief and the mastery of surprise, because it is not until 7 years of age that children reach the latter. In earlier phases, surprise is understood in terms of desire (3–4 years) and ignorance (5–6 years).

The goal of the present study is different because it does not examine the development of the link between a specific emotion and its cognitive basis, but the extent to which an understanding of false belief permeates the entire conceptual organization and modifies or inhibits basic emotion attributions that are acquired early by children. In other words, in demonstrating the difficulty with which a belief-based rationality (as measured by the success on the Maxi task) is employed to moderate autonomous judgments of emotion, the incompleteness and inconsistencies of the underlying concept of belief are also demonstrated. Although the relevance of mentalistic belief–desire–emotion psychology is not disputed, its acquisition should be progressive and monitored by parallel and modular processes. This can be demonstrated by revealing contradictions in the child's reasoning during an intermediate period between 4–5 and 7–8 years of age. From this point of view, the crucial fact is not the increasing mastery of emotion attributions with age, but the expected contradictions or fluctuations between various false belief judgments and the inability to overcome them before sufficient computing capacities and conceptual organization become available.

The aim of this study was to examine the coherence of children's reasoning about the beliefs of another person and the consequences of these beliefs. The assumption is that younger children, while understanding something about the beliefs of others and the consequences of holding a particular belief, will not adopt a coherent and internally consistent view. In other words, there will be contradictions in the various views that younger children hold about how someone will feel, think and act, whereas older children will show evidence of a coherent view in which feelings, thought and action are internally consistent. Specifically, it was predicted that younger children will be able to predict what someone will think while not understanding how that person feels. They will thus hold inconsistent views on likely thoughts and feelings whereas, in older children, there will be an internal coherence to the two types of view.

This hypothesis of a systematic *décalage* between cognitive and emotional evaluation is explained by the absence of a third-person structure that overcomes contradiction. It is also based on the fact that, despite its cognitive basis, an emotional response has a vividness which renders it less penetrable and modifiable than a cognitive response. If it is first supported by the actual state of affairs it is assumed that it will be more difficult to modify or inhibit than a more neutral response. In each of the following experiments a protagonist has a false belief, as in the classical tasks. The real state of affairs should lead the child to attribute to the protagonist a belief (B) and an emotion (E) whereas the state of affairs believed by the protagonist implies attributing to him a belief (B$^+$) and an emotion (E$^+$). The youngest children were expected to give B and E responses and the oldest were expected to give B$^+$ and E$^+$ responses. The hypothesis tested here is that the pattern B$^+$E will be observed during a long developmental period whereas the pattern BE$^+$ will never be observed. From a functional point of view, this assumption is founded on a modular-like conception of the mind which supposes that the child is able to act before understanding and that implicit knowledge comes before explicit knowledge, i.e. that each system which computes a particular type of response is not, at first, linked to the other systems.

The specific prediction is that children who are in the process of developing a coherent view of belief and its consequences will correctly predict the thoughts but not the beliefs of another person, but that no children will show the reverse pattern.

Experiment 1

Method

Participants

A total of 53 participants, 27 girls and 26 boys, took part in the experiment (mean age = 59.8 months, SD = 11 months). All the children came from a French kindergarten.

Procedure

During the week preceding the experiment, the teachers told children the story of Little Red Riding Hood several times, until they all knew its main episodes. The following week, the experimenter interviewed each child individually. He told the child the story again up to the moment when Little Red Riding Hood enters the grandmother's house. Then the experimenter asked the child three questions: (1)'When Little Red Riding Hood goes into grandmother's house, does she think the wolf is in the bed or does she think the grandmother is in the bed?' (order counterbalanced across the sample); (2) 'When Little Red Riding Hood goes into grandmother's house does she feel afraid?' and (3) 'Why?'.

Results

Table 1 shows the number of children in each age group giving three different response patterns. All the children who answered both questions correctly (i.e. that Little Red Riding Hood believed the grandmother was in the bed, and was not afraid – final row of Table 1) also provided good justifications: 'Because she believed the grandmother was in the bed, she was

Table 1   *Number of children in each age group giving three different response patterns*

Belief	Emotion	3 years	4 years	5 years	6 years	Total
Wolf	Afraid	5	6	4	0	15
Grandmother	Afraid	3	9	9	3	24
Grandmother	Not afraid	0	1	9	4	14

not afraid of her grandmother!' 'Because she believed there was nobody else in the house!', 'Because she didn't know the wolf was in the bed!', etc. Children who said that Little Red Riding Hood believed the grandmother was in the bed, and was afraid, mostly justified their answers by invoking the wolf: 'Because it is a wolf!' 'Because the wolf wants to eat her!', 'Because the wolf is dressed like the grandmother'; sometimes they mentioned a likely outcome: 'Because, afterwards, the wolf will eat her!' or 'Because the wolf had eaten her! (3;4)'. Four 3-year-olds did not justify Little Red Riding Hood's fear. There were also three children intrigued by the situation and the disguise of the wolf: 'She feels a little frightened because she can see the ears and the teeth (5;11)',.'Because she can hear strange breathing (4;10)', 'Because his skin is not pink enough (5;10)'. In fact, on the pictures which the teachers presented to the children, it could be seen that the character in the bed was the wolf, so that for the child the situation was ambiguous. This shortcoming was remedied in the two following experiments.

It can be seen from Table 1 that there were three different types of response, with a tendency for the youngest children to be either incorrect about the belief and emotion of Little Red Riding Hood or correct about the belief and incorrect about the emotion. With increasing age, there was a tendency for more children to adopt the correct and coherent view that Little Red Riding Hood would expect to see her grandmother in the bed and so would not be afraid as she, unsuspectingly, entered the house. The authors report that children who gave this mature response also gave a sound rationale for their view. The explanations of children who were correct about Little Red Riding Hood's belief but not her emotion gave explanations that invoked the wolf although they had correctly stated that she expected to see her grandmother in the bed.

Careful analysis of children's explanations suggested that the choice of the Little Red Riding Hood story may have introduced an additional level of ambiguity in that it involves a wolf dressing up in grandmother's clothes. The pictures that accompanied the story depicted the wolf in bed, still looking like a wolf in spite of his attempts at disguise. So, in the next experiment, this ambiguity was removed.

Of the 38 children who correctly said that Little Red Riding Hood believed the grandmother was in bed, 24 simultaneously thought that she was afraid of the wolf. From a logical point of view, this answer is surprising and this 64% raises an important theoretical problem. This response pattern varied with age in that only one child below 5 years of age provided the correct response with an appropriate justification.

A second experiment was conducted to eliminate the effect of the wolf's ambiguous disguise.

Experiment 2

Participants

A total of 40 participants, 22 girls and 18 boys (mean age = 59.7 months, SD = 10.7 months) took part in this experiment. All the children came from a French kindergarten.

Materials

A small house (40 × 40cm), two toy animals (a little goat and its mother, a nanny-goat) and a wolf puppet were used for the second story.

Procedure

The experimenter individually interviewed each child in a separate room. He told the child the following story. 'This is a little goat and this is his mother. They live here, in this house. The mother has to go out and leave the little goat alone in the house. She explains to him that there is a bad wolf living in the neighbourhood and that he likes to eat little goats. When his mother went out, the goat was told not to open the door unless his mother showed him her white leg through the hole in the door.' (The experimenter showed the child how the mother put her leg through the hole.) When the child had understood this first part of the story, the experimenter went on. 'When the goat was alone, since his mother had gone out, the bad wolf came [the wolf puppet is on the experiment hand] and said to him in a tiny voice: 'Open the door for me, I am your mother and I want to come inside.' The goat answered: 'I won't open unless I can see your white leg.' Then the wolf put white flour on his leg, showed it through the hole and said: 'See, I am your mother, open the door.' Then the goat opened the door, the wolf went in and ate the goat up.'

> Study 2 used a new story, involving puppets, which would have been unfamiliar to the children. The story was told once to the children and then the first part was repeated, stopping at the point where the wolf is about to put his leg through the hole in the door. Again, the children were not explicitly tested to ensure that they had understood the story.

After this first story the experimenter told the child that he would tell the story to him or her again to be sure the child knew it properly. The second time the experimenter told the story, he stopped at the point where the wolf has put its leg through the hold, and asked the child three questions: (1) 'Now, does the goat think his mother will come in or does he think the wolf will come in?' (order counterbalanced across the sample); (2) 'Now, before opening the door, is the goat afraid?' and (3) 'Why?'

The structure of the questions is identical to Experiment 1. Again, the order of mention of the two characters in Question 1 is counterbalanced to ensure that children are not guided towards one answer rather than the other. This order manipulation is not examined statistically to confirm that responses did not differ across the two versions of the question. It is a good idea to do this so that the results can then be conflated across the sub-conditions if there is no difference. Alternatively, if there is a difference, this can be taken into account in subsequent analysis.

Result

Table 2 shows the number of children in each age group giving the different response patterns. Ten of the 28 children who correctly said that the goat believed his mother wanted to come in simultaneously thought that he was afraid of the wolf. This percentage (37per cent) is lower than that in the Little Red Riding Hood story, perhaps because the ambiguity about the appearance of the wolf had been removed and the fact that the hero was acting (the goat opened the door) instead of being simply present as in the previous story. In addition, as in the Little Red Riding Hood story, the children knew the end of the story and this could have retroactively interfered with their assessment of the current situation.

The general pattern of responses was the same as in the previous experiment, with younger children being more likely to be incorrect about both belief and emotion and older children being correct about both. Overall, a higher proportion of children in Experiment 2 (45 per cent) were correct about both than in Experiment 1 (26 per cent), suggesting that the scenario in the second experiment was more transparent. The mean and standard deviation of age for the two samples of participants were very similar so a direct comparison is legitimate.

To use a weaker emotion than fear, to eliminate the stereotypes attached to the character of the wolf and to avoid using a typical deception scenario and its associated interference, a third experiment was conducted. This was a modification of the classical 'Maxi' task (Wimmer & Perner, 1983).

In the first two experiments, children knew the outcome of the story and, as the authors suggest, this may have biased their responses. Indeed, knowledge of the actual outcome increases the total number of representations of actual and possible events that children

Table 2   *Number of children in each age group giving three different response patterns*

Belief	Emotion	3 years	4 years	5 years	6 years	Total
Wolf	Afraid	6	4	1	1	12
Grandmother	Afraid	2	3	3	2	10
Grandmother	Not afraid	1	4	6	7	18

> have to entertain. Experiment 3 therefore used a variation on one of the standard ToM tasks, 'Maxi and the chocolate'.

Experiment 3

Method

Participants

A total of 55 participants, 26 girls and 29 boys (mean age = 67.8 months, SD = 6.3 months) took part in the experiment. All the children came from two French kindergartens. A sample with a higher mean age was selected because the previous experiments had shown that erroneous responses were found even after the age of 6 years.

> The participants were somewhat older than in the first two studies since the focus of Study 3 was on children who were making the transition from being correct about beliefs, but not emotions, to being correct about both.

Materials

The materials for this third story were: a toy house (40 × 40cm): two little toy figures, one yellow and one red (Maxi and his brother); two boxes (one blue and the other white); and two pieces of chocolate (plastic).

Procedure

> The variation on the original Maxi task involved the eating of most of Maxi's chocolate and the use of two boxes. In the original story, all the chocolate is eaten and Maxi returns to an empty box (Baron-Cohen et al., 1985).

The experimenter individually interviewed each child. He told them the following story. 'See. This is the story of a little boy called Maxi. This is Maxi [the experimenter pointed to the yellow figure]. Maxi is at home with his brother [the experimenter showed the house and the brother]. He has a piece of chocolate and he puts it in this blue box [the experimenter put the big piece of chocolate in the blue box]. Then Maxi goes outside to play [the experimenter showed Maxi walking away from the house]. While Maxi is playing outside, his brother opens the blue box, takes the piece of chocolate and begins to eat it. He eats almost all the chocolate and there is only a small piece left [the experimenter took the big piece and replaced it by the small piece]. Then, the brother puts the small piece in the white box.' At this point, the experimenter told the child he would tell the story a second time. After telling it a second time, the experimenter continued. 'Now Maxi wants to come home to eat his chocolate. He is hungry.' The experimenter showed Maxi walking into the house. Maxi stops in front of the door and the experimenter asked the child three questions: (1) 'Maxi is in front of the door, where will he look for his chocolate?' (2) 'When Maxi is in front of the door, is he happy?'; and (3) 'Why?'. In contrast to the previous experiments, the order of questions 1 and 2–3 were counterbalanced across the sample.

The three questions now probed action (rather than thought) and emotion. Perhaps surprisingly, in view of earlier comments, the entire story is told before the first part is repeated; and, again, there were no control questions to gauge understanding of the scenario.

Results

Table 3 shows the number of children in each age group giving the different response patterns. Remember that for half the children, the order of the questions was varied and the experimenter asked if Maxi was happy before asking where he would go to get his chocolate. All the children who gave the correct pattern justified their response by explaining that Maxi was happy because he did not know that his brother had eaten his chocolate. Children who said that Maxi was unhappy, even though he would look for his chocolate in the blue box, justified their response by explaining that the brother had eaten the chocolate.

Of the 48 children who correctly predicted that Maxi would go to the blue box, 38 also said that Maxi was unhappy because his brother had eaten the chocolate. Four of them added that Maxi was unhappy because there was nothing in the blue box (final outcome). In order to examine the reactions of older children in Expt 3, another investigation with the same procedure, but using the Piagetian method of counter-argument, was conducted.

In Experiment 3, 69 per cent of children were able to make a correct non-emotion judgment but were incorrect about the emotion, correctly saying that Maxi will look in the original location for his chocolate but incorrectly saying that he will not feel happy. The proportion of children being correct about both judgments is low at only 18 per cent, compared with 45 per cent in the previous study (even though the proportion of younger

Table 3 *Number of children in each age group giving three different response patterns*

Belief	Emotion	4 years	5 years	6 years	Total
White box	Not happy	4 (2+2)	3 (2+1)	0	7
Blue box	Not happy	3 (2+1)	21 (10+11)	14 (6+8)	38
Blue box	Happy	1 (0+1)	4 (2+2)	5 (3+2)	10

Between parantheses are the number of children who answered condition 1 (action question followed by the emotion question) and 2 (emotion question followed by action question)

> children was higher in Experiment 2). The authors do not comment on this difference but it may stem from the fact that an emotion like happiness is rather more diffuse than the fear that appears in the first two studies.

Experiment 4

Method

Participants

A total of 60 participants, 30 girls and 30 boys, aged from 6;4 to 8;7 (mean age = 85.65 months; SD = 5.48 months) took part in the experiment. All the children came from two French primary schools.

Procedure

The procedure was exactly the same as that in Expt 3, except for further questioning after the children's initial replies to the two test questions. When children succeeded on question 1, for both types of response to questions 2 and 3 (i.e. happy or unhappy) the experimenter gave a counter-argument in order to assess the robustness of the child's response. If the child said that Maxi was unhappy when he was in front of the door of the house because his brother had eaten the chocolate, he or she was asked if Maxi knew that his brother had eaten the chocolate and then he or she was asked if Maxi was happy or unhappy when he was in front of the door. If the child answered that Maxi was happy, possibly saying that he did not know that his brother had eaten the chocolate, he or she was questioned again: 'His brother has eaten the chocolate, do you really think that Maxi is happy about that?' Several counter-arguments occurred if the child changed his or her point of view during the questioning.

> Experiment 4 introduced a new procedure, that of counter-arguments. If children correctly answered the action question (indicating that they were aware Maxi did not know that the chocolate had been moved to a new location) they were offered a counter-argument after answering the question about how Maxi would feel. There are some important caveats to be made about the use of counter-arguments since, when children's responses are questioned implicitly by an experimenter, they are likely to change their response (Siegal, 1991). In this study, both correct and incorrect responses were challenged to compare the robustness of a child's response.

Results

Table 4 shows the number of children in each age group giving the different response patterns. It can be seen that 30 children did not answer both questions coherently. Moreover, they did not change their opinion about Maxi's emotion after having said that he did not know that his brother had eaten the chocolate. These results reveal a strong dissociation between a cognitive and emotional assessment of the situation and the difficulty of explicitly coordinating them. All these children succeeded, however, in correctly answering that Maxi did not know that his brother had eaten the chocolate. They showed, in their emotion attribution, the same pattern as that reported by Hogrefe, Wimmer & Perner (1986) concerning the action question in the classical task, i.e. they understood that Maxi did not know the actual state of affairs but, even so, they thought that he would react in accordance with that state of affairs. When this question led children to change their mind, a further counter-argument always provoked the reappearance of the erroneous emotion response. Thus, a spontaneous incorrect emotion response is a robust sign of the lack of logical mastery of the situation. By contrast, nine children who had initially given a correct answer to the emotion question were sensitive to the counter-argument and regressed in their reasoning.

The most common pattern was for children to say that Maxi would be unhappy when he arrived home (even though, at that point, he did not know that his brother had eaten his chocolate). Notably, none of the children who spontaneously made this incorrect judgment, changed their opinion in response to the experimenter's counter-argument. However, almost half the children who correctly said that Maxi would be happy when he arrived home changed to an incorrect response when put under pressure.

Table 4   *Number of children giving five different response patterns*

| | | Order of questioning | | |
		Action-emotion	Emotion-action	Total
Belief	**Emotion**			
White box	Not happy	5	5	10
Blue box	Not happy//Not happy	13	17	30
Blue box	Not happy//Happy	0	0	0
Blue box	Happy//Not happy	4	5	9
Blue box	Happy//Happy	8	3	11

The answer after//is the one which was given after the counter-argument.

If the false belief concept had been acquired around 4–5 years of age, 60 correct response patterns would have been expected in the present sample, but only 11 were actually observed. Seventy-eight per cent (39/50) of the children aged between 6;4 and 8;7 correctly answered the action question but incorrectly answered the emotion question. Obviously, 11/60 is different from 60/60 and 78 per cent is different from 0%.

The order of questioning had no observable effect on the responses, indicating the robustness of the results. In the pattern with correct action and emotion responses, the 13/17 distribution is not different from chance (i.e. 15/15) and in the pattern with a correct action response and an incorrect emotion response, the 8/3 distribution is not different from chance. (i.e. 5.5/5.5) (Sign test).

Three major conclusions can be drawn from both this experiment and the preceding one: (i) the combination of an incorrect action response and a correct emotion response was never observed, with the strong implication that success on the emotion question predicts success on the action question; (ii) the order of questioning had no effect on the response; and (iii) an initially incorrect emotion response revealed the inconsistency of the false belief concept, whereas an initially correct emotion response was robust only 50 per cent of the time.

> *Interestingly, the counter-argument to initially correct (i.e. 'happy') responses involved the use of 'really' as in 'Do you really think that Maxi is happy about that?'. The counter-argument to the 'not happy' response appears to have been worded in a more neutral manner so it is possible that the marked difference in the likelihood of the correct and incorrect responses being reversed was due to the wording of the counter-argument rather than a difference in the robustness of the children's view.*

A final experiment was conducted to replicate and extend the findings.

Experiment 5

Method

Participants

Forty-six children aged from 4;0 to 6;1 (25 boys and 21 girls) took part in the experiment. All the children came from two French kindergartens.

Procedure

This fifth control experiment was conducted in the same way as the third, but without varying the order of the questions, because this had had no observable effect on the responses (thus, the children were always asked the action question before the emotion question). Except for this modification, the procedure was exactly the same as that used in Expt 3, i.e. without the counter-argument introduced on Expt 4. In this control experiment, the experimenter was not the same as in the previous ones. He knew the standard false belief task and its administration, but he was not informed of the present paradigm and the expected results.

Experiment 5 replicated Experiment 3, apart from the use of a standard order for the questions. The main purpose of this final study, which is not clearly explained by the authors, was to increase the total sample of children tested. The larger sample (derived by pooling data from Experiments 3 and 5 with spontaneous judgments from Experiment 4) enabled the use of statistics to investigate age trends. This meta-analysis confirmed that there was a significant age trend from 4 to 6 years. It also confirmed that children who were correct about the emotion always made a correct judgment about where Maxi thought the chocolate was when he arrived home. No children showed the reverse pattern.

Results

Table 5 shows the number of children in each age group giving the different response patterns. The same general trend can be seen: 20 of the 26 children who correctly predicted Maxi's action failed to predict his emotion.

Given the absence of an order effect and for comparison purposes, the results of Expts 3, 4 and 5 can be combined, but only taking into account the spontaneous responses in Expt 4 and not those given after a counter-argument. Table 6 gives the results for the three experiments conducted on a total sample of 161 children aged from 4;0 to 8;7. There was a strong effect of age (Jonckheere's test gives an S value equal to 4.67 sigmas, $p < .0001$) on the level of response, but note that beyond even 6 years of age more than 50 per cent of the children still did not successfully answer the two questions. It should also be remembered that the successful emotion responses in Table 6 were spontaneous and that Expt 4 showed that about half of these responses were not robust.

Table 5   *Number of children in each age group giving three different response patterns*

Belief	Emotion	4 years	5 years	6 years	Total
White box	Not happy	13	6	1	20
Blue box	Not happy	7	8	5	20
Blue box	Happy	0	4	2	6

General discussion

One of the issues raised in the discussion is children's relatively delayed ability to judge another person's emotional state. In a recent paper De Rosnay and colleagues (De Rosnay, Pons, Harris & Morrell, 2004) argue against the view that the emotion attribution is generally more difficult than understanding of false beliefs. Their view is that children are seldom called on to make judgments about how someone will feel and that

---

there is a more natural (and observable) link between action and belief than emotion and belief. Thus, they argue, the opportunity to listen to people talking about how they feel provides essential experience that will promote an earlier understanding of belief-based emotion in others. They also suggest that children who are more linguistically able may find it easier to incorporate such information into their own thinking since, in their study, vocabulary scores independently predicted performance on a number of emotion attribution tasks.

The intermediate and contradictory patterns of responses observed in all the experiments confirm the general conception presented in the introductory test to this study. There is a gradual development that reflects improved communication among different assessments, (e.g. implicit, procedural, declarative, emotional) of a false belief situation and the progressive mastery of contradiction. In the introductory test, this was called the epistemological aspect of belief. Two separable, but related, issues need to be assessed: (i) the fact that the belief question is answered earlier than the emotion question, and (ii) the fact that children are inconsistent in their responses to logically related questions. The first issue is mainly related to the psychology of emotion, the second is more general and epistemological because it concerns the foundation of rationality, namely consistency.

The fact that emotion is more difficult to attribute accurately to a character than a more neutral mental state such as belief seems easy to explain: emotional cues are vivid whereas procedural inference is less so. If, for biological and phylogenetic reasons, the vividness of a stimulus renders it less penetrable because of the high priority attached to its message, the asymmetry reported in these experiments can be understood. Previous research (Ruffman & Keenan, 1996) has revealed children's understanding of belief and their understanding of a paradigmatic belief-based emotion, namely surprise, showing that an early conceptual analysis does not immediately trigger an appropriate emotion attribution. Moreover, Harris *et al.* (1989) showed that emotion attributions associated with false belief are difficult for children until the age of 6–7 years, even for simple desire-based emotions like joy or disappointment. The present study revealed that, when an emotion was provoked that did not fit the actual situation, the difficulty was pervasive; children formulated the contradiction without being able to overcome it. These findings reinforce the idea of a strong autonomy and lack of permeability for emotion attributions. A second reason for this *déclage* is linked to the action answer ('Where will Maxi look for his chocolate?'). This type of reply involves a form of realist facilitation (Mitchell, 1994) by incorporating the false belief into a behavioural pattern. By contrast, the emotion attribution does not facilitate this realist incorporation. It is suggested below that, in these circumstances, success on the Maxi task is not based on a completely mentalistic understanding of belief.

Table 6   *Number of children in each age group giving three different response patterns*

Action	Emotion	4 years	5 years	6 years	7 years	8 years	Total
Failure	Failure	17	9	9	2	0	37
Success	Failure	10	29	32	14	3	88
Success	Success	1	8	13	11	3	36
Total		28	46	54	27	6	161

The second issue concerns the conditions that make such an inconsistent and counter-intuitive analysis of the situation possible for the child. These fluctuations are not to be regarded as merely contingent fluctuations that depend on the format of the question or the context, but rather as genuinely logical failures. The standard Piagetian framework would invoke a lack of coordination between intuitions to account for such failures. Various contemporary accounts are based on a more precise concept of computation and mental load. For example, Frye, Zelazo, Brooks & Samuels (1996) explain interference, inconsistency and lack of inhibition in terms of the absence of meta or higher-order rules that allow a choice among lower-order rules. Zelazo, Carter, Reznick & Frye (1997) provide a more extensive study of the development of executive function. They make an inventory of all the functions implied in a problem-solving task and the specific difficulties associated with each.

The conceptual frame used here distinguished second- and third-person structures acquired respectively around 4–5 and 7–8 years of age. The first step around 4–5 years of age is characterized by the beginning of an explicit awareness of mental states, based on reflection. Reflection is taken to be synonymous with awareness as in the philosophical tradition: 'By reflection, I mean that notice which the mind takes of its operations and the manner of them; by reason whereof there come to be ideas of these operations in the understanding' (Locke, 1690). In this sense, many developmental facts reveal the beginning of such an awareness at 4 years of age. If there is a stage-link change at this age; it could be called the stage of reflection, after the stage of representation, which begins around 18 months according to Piaget, and before the stage of reason which begins around 7 years of age. With reflection, children become aware of their representational activity (cf. the concept of 'primary and secondary intention' of the scholastics (Brentano, 1874; Chisholm, 1986), and the concept of 'metarepresentation' (Perner, 1991)). They know, for example, that the state of affairs being considered is true or false, and know that they know, but they still cannot coordinate various pieces of explicit knowledge. This period contrasts dramatically with the previous one in which no such awareness is present. One can cite, for example, the notion of 'prelief (Perner, Baker & Hutton, 1994) or the studies of Harris (1994) and Harris, Kavanaugh & Meredith (1994) who maintained the simulationist thesis, which does not presuppose reflective awareness. They compared the young child who is pretending to the child (or to the adult) who is listening to a story. The child does not need to question the relationship between the truth of the episodes and the author's or narrator's belief in order to follow and enjoy the story and to understand it. Similarly, a person who dreams does not question the relationship between a dream and its reality. The question of whether a dream is fiction does not occur to the person who dreams. From the beginning of reflective knowledge to a first logical closure at around 7–8 years of age, numerous inconsistencies and *décalages* are observed in all domains of cognitive development. According to one's position, these inconsistencies should neither be taken as residual (equivalent to measurement error) nor as performance variations associated with contextual or linguistic variables. On the contrary, they are a major key to the understanding of the construction of rationality.

In the present case, two complementary explanations can be provided for the observed logical *décalage*. First, it is proposed that separate concepts of belief based on various peripheral systems and on a specific format of encapsuled information appear in the mind of the child at different periods. The development of rationality would then consist in the mind of the child at different periods. The development of rationality would then consist in the central communication among the outputs of these modules. A good analogy can be found in the mutual, shared and distributed knowledge theory (see e.g. Fagin, Halpern, Moses & Vardi, 1995; Sandu, 1997) which formalizes the different degrees of knowledge in a community of agents. Since Selfridge (1949) and Minsky (1986), the idea of distributed competences has progressed in psychology, but less than in computer sciences. The focus of this conception, which calls into question the Cartesian theory of mind and consciousness (see e.g. Dennett, 1991), concerns the elimination of a central locus of awareness and decision. Competence is not centralized or unified by a single agent, but is distributed among different agents (an agent could be defined as a module which comprises mental states, such as propositional attitudes, production rules or specific knowledge). The key to increasing competence in such a system is the development of communication among the different agents, insofar as this communication is linked to awareness and conceptualization.

The pre-belief state in the intermediate period – false belief attribution by a single mental agent (e.g. the action agent in the standard task) – can be explained by the absence of mutual knowledge among all the agents and, consequently, the attribution of the emotional agent is not informed and transformed by the procedural agent. In this case, the logical structure which allows a third-person point of view is, in fact, much more complex than accurate performance on the standard task in a second-person form. The latter only requires separating pre-beliefs, but not coordinating them (this is an analogy with the separation and coordination of perspectives as shown on Piaget's three mountains task; Piager & Inhelder, 1947). When the child reaches third-person psychology, at this final level, false belief is an invariant, or the fixed- point of the iteration of the operator to *know* among the mental agents who have moved from *distributed* to *mutual* knowledge (the procedural agent knows that the emotional agent knows the situation, and it knows that the latter knows that it knows, etc.). The products of this mutual knowledge are isotropic in Fodor's sense (Fodor, 1983) in that from any perspective, the point of view is the same; the inference cannot be modified by the way the problem is formulated or the belief embodied. Cognitive progress from distributed to mutual knowledge implies that the various responses of the agents must be encoded in a common language, and consequently in an amodal format. This raises the question for future research of how reason can speak to emotion and vice versa.

A second complementary explanation is to propose that, before reaching third-person psychology, the child has a only partial concept of belief, even if he or she succeeds on the standard task. This view leads logically to the conclusion that false beliefs attributed to the second-person standard are only partial mentalistic false beliefs; they are better described as pre-beliefs based mainly on behavioural cues. A very frequent justification given by the children who succeed on this task is not 'Because Maxi believes the chocolate is in this cupboard', but 'Because Maxi had put his chocolate in this cupboard'. In the latter case, Maxi's behaviour is not linked to his mental state, but to his past action. When the behavioural embodiment disappears, in the case of the comparison between action and emotion questions, the correct inference that it supported also disappears in the inconsistent children. Support for this interpretation could be provided by an analysis of the justifications given by the children: those evoking the past action failing the emotion question and those evoking the mental state (*via* 'he believes' or 'he thinks') succeeding. If this hypothesis were confirmed, the capacity to predict Maxi's behaviour would not be related to an understanding of belief, but more fundamentally to an understanding of the link between an action and its agent (the subject-verb link in language). The young child knows that the chocolate has changed places, but does not associate this fact with the action and the agent that brought it about. It is only when the first location of the chocolate is unambiguously attributed to Maxi and the second to the mother that a correct search prediction can be formulated.

This hypothesis needs further and careful verification. Of course, it does not contradict the first one because the coordination between different modular outputs necessarily produces, at the mutual knowledge level, a more complete and more powerful structure.

Paper 9   Preschoolers' understanding of number (Muldoon, Lewis & Towse, 2005)

The next paper is concerned with a specific aspect of cognitive development, namely understanding of one-to-one correspondence. The notion of one-to-one correspondence was first introduced by Piaget (Piaget & Szeminska, 1952) in relation to conservation problems. Conservation refers to the child's understanding that quantitative relationships between two objects are conserved, that is remain the same, despite irrelevant changes in the appearance of the objects. An irrelevant transformation is any change that does not involve addition or subtraction from the original quantities. There are a number of different conservation tasks, relating to the under-standing of physical quantities such as mass, weight, volume and number.

In the case of conservation of number, one-to-one correspondence involves understanding that one item in a set can be seen as corresponding to another item in a different set. Thus, if two sets have an equal number of items, one item in one set will correspond to one item in the other set and there will be no items that do not have a 'partner' in the other set. This one-to-one corre-spondence remains through changes in the physical arrangement of items in each set. However, children who are not at the stage of concrete operations, do not fully understand the implications of one-to-one correspondence. As Piaget showed, children will readily agree that two arrays of items, in which there is clear one-to-one correspondence, have the same number of items. However, when the spatial arrangement of one array is altered by increasing the distance between items, children who have not yet acquired conservation think that the two arrays no longer contain the same number of items.

One-to-one correspondence has also been seen as an essential principle of counting and the understanding of number (Gelman & Gallistel, 1978). Preschoolers show evidence of the first stage of understanding one-to-one correspondence when they can correctly relate counting number names (one, two, three …) to items in a set. This involves relating each number to one (and only one) item. This early understanding of one-to-one correspon-dence appears in the preschool years and Paper 9 investigates preschooler's ability to use this principle to compare the number of items in two sets.

Cognitive Development, 2005, 20, 472–491

Because it's there! Why some children count, rather than infer numerical relationships

Kevin Muldoon, Charlie Lewis, John Towse

Lancaster University, UK

1. Introduction

The development of children's numerical skills appears to incorporate several paradoxes. As Feigenson, Dehaene and Spelke (2004) note, mathematics is at once both obvious and obscure. On the one hand, young children show sophisticated insights into the preciseness of numbers (Sarnecka & Gelman, 2004) and infants distinguish both discrete and continuous quantities (see Feigenson et al., 2004). On the other hand, they also reveal some striking limitations, for example failing to discriminate between numerosities (Xu & Spelke, 2000). In the specific domain of children's counting too, there is a conundrum. Even by the age of approximately 3 years, children appear to possess a command of core principles that underlie counting behaviour (Gelman & Gallistel, 1978; Gelman & Meck, 1983). Yet there is often an exasperating reluctance among children to use the products of counting to draw legitimate and sensible conclusions about the relationship between sets (Michie, 1984a). In this paper, we present data from two experiments that help to understand why preschool children may fail to make the most of the numerical strategies that they implement. For this, we use a sharing task, and in so doing, we address and attempt to reconcile some apparent inconsistencies in the literature.

Sharing, like counting, is a skill that is acquired and practiced during early childhood (Pepper & Hunting, 1998). Preserving numerical correspondence among shares, through a scheme such as 'one-for-you, one-for-me', ensures that each recipient has an equivalent set. However, while this is an appropriate procedure to share out equally, and is a common strategy that appears fairly stable between preschool and school years (Miller, 1984), preschool children may have difficulty realizing what they have accomplished. In this sense, procedural mastery outstrips conceptual awareness of what has been achieved. That is, children below 8 years of age often insist that counting is necessary to reach a conclusion about the equality of the shares (Davis & Pitkethly, 1990; Frydman & Bryant, 1988). However, (and in contrast with this research) some findings suggest that, with conceptually paired items, 3-year-olds are able to recognize that corresponding sets are equivalent (Sophian, Wood & Vong, 1995). Why might children be inconsistent in these two situations?

The authors draw an important distinction between procedural mastery and conceptual understanding of what has been achieved by a procedure. Often, in development, children's ability to carry out a straightforward procedure may appear precocious and it is tempting to assume that they fully understand the implications of the procedure. In this case, children can use one-to-one correspondence to share out things equally when they are only three years old. However, this does not mean that they have a deeper, and more abstract, notion of the principle they have used which would enable them to transfer their knowledge to a range of different tasks. They also cannot use one -to-one correspondence to justify their sharing of objects in the same way that an older child, who has acquired concrete operations, is able to do.

Evidence that sharing has been carried out evenly, or fairly, ought to be sufficient for children to conclude that there are as many items in one set as there are in the other(s). Using a 'same/different' task, Cowan and Biddle (1989) found that 3-year-olds understood that distributing items using a 'one-for-you, one-for-me' rule results in sets that are the same, particularly if shares were small (i.e., <4 items) and visible. They were not tested on whether they knew how many items each set contained, however, and young children experience difficulty mapping the insights from quantitative equivalence onto number words. Frydman and Bryant(1988) exposed this difficulty when they asked 4-year-olds to share out sweets between dolls, then counted aloud one set for children, and asked how many sweets there were in the other. Even though most children had shared out successfully, none would infer (via the principle of cardinal extension) the numerosity of sweets in the second set. Without exception, every child started to count. Even when the set was hidden so as to preclude counting, less than half the children used equivalence to infer set size.

> *The three studies described in this paragraph and the next illustrate how much children's ability to succeed in a task is affected by what they are asked to do. In the first study (Cowan & Biddle, 1989), children shared out a small number of items so that, when asked if they contained an equal number of items, they could have judged without counting. In the second study (Frydman & Bryant, 1988), which also involved sharing, the experimenter counted aloud the number in one set and then asked how many there were in the other. Children who understand the concept of one-to-one correspondence, should be able to draw the logical conclusion that the number of sweets in the other set is identical. The third study (Sophian, Wood & Vong, 1995) used a different methodology that involved the initial setting up of pairs (frogs and boats) but also involved small numbers.*

Using cardinal extension to infer equivalent shares may be difficult for children, but they seem to have several conceptual building blocks in place to reach this milestone. First, children can use knowledge of cardinality when setting up corresponding sets (Becker, 1989; Sophian, 1988). Five-year-olds are able to count-out items and stop when they reach the number which ensures that two sets match (Russac, 1978). Secondly, they are also aware that cardinal extension is appropriate when inferring a number of conceptually paired items. Sophian et al. (1995) showed 3-year-olds pairs of frogs and boats (i.e., one frog per boat). These pairs were separated, by placing the frogs inside a box (a narrative explained that they were going to a party) while the boats were (moored) outside. The majority of children then successfully inferred the number of hidden frogs after counting the boats, at least so long as small sets (two or three) were used (consistent with Cowan & Biddle, 1989). Thus, many children apparently knew that correspondence between pairs of items implies identical cardinals.

There are important methodological differences between the Frydman and Bryant (1988), and Sophian et al. (1995), studies that may contribute to their divergent conclusions. First, Sophian et al.'s (1995) study started out with conceptually paired items; each frog had its own boat. Separating out six pairs of frogs and boats produces a set of six frogs and a set of six boats. In contrast, in Frydman and Bryant's (1988) task, sharing out six sweets gives two sets of three sweets. If conceptual pairs are thought of as whole (and not separate) entities, then the elements – the frogs and boats – become corresponding portions of these whole items. Making inferences about equivalence here need not be the same as making inferences when dividing up homogeneous items.

The authors highlight a number of important methodological differences between the three studies: use of a sharing or pairing task, set visibility and set size. These factors are systematically manipulated over two experiments.

Another difference concerns the visibility of the sets. Children could see the set-to-be inferred in the Frydman and Bryant (1988) but not the Sophian et al. (1995) study. In each case, children were essentially asked, "How many items are there in the first set?" followed by "How many items are there in the second set?" It may be that children count (rather then infer the numerosity of) a visible set simply because items are there. Children are prone to counting a single set in response to the question 'How many?' (Frye, Braisby, Lowe, Maroudas, & Nicholls, 1989), particularly when items are visible (Fuson, 1988; Wynn, 1990). Number conservation tasks also demonstrate that the perceptual impact from visible arrays can influence, even if not determine, children's appreciation of the situation (e.g., Piaget, 1952). Furthermore, children may opt to repeat a strategy (counting) on the second question that proved successful on the first. The principal aim of the present studies was to investigate the influence of these two contextual factors: – (1) sharing and (2) set-visibility – on children's developing ability to infer the number of items in a corresponding set.

We designed two play scenarios with which to examine the effects of these contextual variables. In one, that echoes Sophian et al.'s (1995) frog-boat task, children are shown toy animals that travel to school on their bicycles. Children are invited to pair animal with bicycles, before moving the pairs towards a schoolhouse. Upon arrival, the animals are placed inside the school, while the bicycles are placed in a separate bike shed. In the other scenario that echoes Frydman and Bryant's (1988) sweet-sharing task, children are asked to share out toy ice-creams between a toy ice-cream van and ice-cream shop. The questions put to children after allocating items are essentially the same in each scenario. Children are asked, 'How many animals are there in a school/How many ice-creams are in the ice-cream shop?' followed by, 'How many bicycles are there in the bike shed/How many ice-creams are in the ice-cream shop?' On half the trials, the bike shed/ ice-cream shop is covered, preventing children from seeing inside. If they are aware that corresponding sets have the same cardinal number, but prefer to count a target set rather than infer its numerosity, we expect children to make more inferences when the target set is hidden (hypothesis 1). If they know that sets of conceptually paired items (e.g., lions riding bicycles) have the same cardinal number, but do not understand that sharing sweets evenly produces equivalent sets, then we expect children to perform better when they are quizzed about the number of lions (hypothesis 2).

> *The two scenarios were designed to be similar in their use of objects and two locations but one involved the initial pairing of toy animals and bicycles and then their separation into two locations, whereas the other involved the sharing of ice creams between two locations. Children were asked how many items there are at each location, ensuring that questioning was essentially the same across the two paradigms. For each of the scenarios, one location was covered so that the children could not see inside to count the number of items. If children understand the logic of one-to-one correspondence, but are tempted to count just because they can, they should more likely to use inference to deduce the number in the second location when they are unable to count; and, if they understand one-to-one correspondence better in the pairing task than in the sharing task, then they should be better at using inference rather than counting in the former condition.*

We began to address these hypotheses with a relatively small-scale experiment. We restricted the number of trials to children, so as to minimize fatigue or carry-over effects, and consequently focused on a single set size and age group.

2. Experiment 1

2.1. Method

2.1.1. Participants

Forty children (3 years 5 months to 4 years 3 months, M = 3 years 9 months, S.D. = 2.6 months), from three pre-school playgroups in a predominantly White, urban population took part. None of the children had any identified learning difficulties.

2.1.2. Materials

Child-friendly materials similar to children's toys were used throughout. Two shoe-boxes, painted on one side to resemble a bicycle shed and a school, and on the other side an ice-cream van and a seaside shop. Two sets of toy animals (lions and dolphins) and two sets of toy food items (ice-creams and tins of soup). Matchboxes painted to resemble bicycles.

2.1.3. Procedure

The same male experimenter tested each child on two separate occasions (Sessions 1 and 2), approximately 1 week apart. Problems were presented in two scenarios; animals going to school and food being allocated to vendors to sell. In each scenario, the problem was presented in two levels of visibility: visible and hidden. Each child received two trials, one in each level of visibility, in each session. The order of presentation was counterbalanced.

2.1.4. Scenario 1 – animals going to school: warm-up phase

The experimenter introduced the child to the school and bicycle shed, then demonstrated how the animals got to school each day, saying, 'These lions go to school on their bikes. Look, each lion has his own bike, and he sits on it and pedals to school like this'. Lions were placed in matchboxes (one per matchbox) and slid across the table, whereupon each lion was placed in the school (by inserting them through a small hole in the roof) and the matchboxes lined up outside the bicycle shed. Dolphins swam to school en masse (hidden in the experimenter's hand). In the warm-up phase, children were asked only which type of animals the bicycles belonged to.

> *These tasks were designed to be engaging for preschool children. Choice of task is very important and has to be precisely targeted at the intended age group. School-aged children might well find that tasks using small toys are not age-appropriate since they no longer play with such toys at home.*

2.1.5. Test phase

A set of lions (7, 8 or 9) was placed on the table, along with the same number of matchboxes (bicycles). The experimenter asked the child to take the lions to school, reminding them that lions went one at a time. The experimenter moved the dolphins by hiding them in his hand and placing them inside the shoebox. The set of lions was the target set (i.e., the set in item-to-item correspondence with the bicycles) while dolphins acted as a control set (i.e., this set was not in one-to-one correspondence, and acted as a check against last-word-repetition using the cardinal number of bicycles). Once all the animals were in school, the experimenter asked, 'How many bicycles are in the bicycle shed?' followed by 'How many lions/dolphins are at school?' (the order in which children were asked about the target and the control sets was counterbalanced). If they said they did not know, children were asked to guess. The aim was to see if children would use cardinal extension to infer appropriately the number of lions from the number of bicycles, and refrain from extending the same cardinal to an unknowable number of dolphins.

> *The pairing task incorporated an additional control that is not fully explained. This involves the use of a second set of animals – dolphins – who also travel to school. Unlike the lions, they travel to school unseen, and are not in one-to-one correspondence with the bicycles. A child, who understands one-to-one correspondence, should correctly infer*

the number of lions from the number of bicycles but should not seek to do so for the dolphins. The reason for this additional control is that, having already said how many bicycles there were, the children might have been tempted to guess that there were the same number of lions just because it was the last number mentioned. However, a similar guess about the dolphins would be incorrect.

In the hidden condition the roof was left on ('because it is raining'), hiding the animals from view. In the visible condition the roof was removed ('because it is a nice day'), revealing the animals inside. If a child started to count the target set, the experimenter placed his hands over the shoebox and asked if they knew how many there were without counting. The bicycles were visible throughout both conditions. As an additional control against children succeeding through perceptual comparisons, all sets were arranged such that there was no spatial correspondence between any of them. Children readily rely on spatial cues to judge relative magnitude (e.g., Brainerd, 1979; Cowan, 1987; Michie, 1984a,b; Piaget, 1952; Saxe, 1977; Sophian, 1987), and we wanted to eliminate the potential for children to make comparisons this way.

Note that, if children attempted to count the number of animals, the experimenter stopped them and asked if they knew how many there were. This was intended to distinguish children who adopted a cautious strategy of counting (to confirm something they already knew) from those who saw counting as the only way to find out how many animals there were.

2.1.6. Scenario 2 – food being sold: warm-up phase

The child was asked to identify the ice-cream van and the shop, and then shown toy ice-creams. The experimenter then demonstrated how, as neither the shop nor the van had anything to sell (the shoeboxes were empty), it was necessary to share the ice-creams out so they both had the same. The child was invited to share them out after the experimenter had demonstrated how it could be done, and also shown some tins of soup (the experimenter explaining that when the weather got cold the shop needed to have soup in case people wanted something hot to eat).

2.1.7. Test phase

A set of ice-creams (14, 16 or 18) was placed on the table, and three to five tins of soup were retained in the experimenter's hand after being shown briefly to the child. The procedure was essentially the same as used for animals, with ice-creams being allocated to the shop (the target set) and van (corresponding set) except that children were told, 'Share out these ice-creams, so that the ice-cream shop and the ice-cream van have both got some ice-creams to sell. Put some in here (pointing) and some in here so they have both got the same.' Those placed in the shop became the target set and those in the van the corresponding set. Tins of soup acted as the control (unrelated) set. Once all the ice-creams had been shared out, the experimenter asked 'How many ice-creams does the ice-cream van have to sell?' followed by 'How many ice-creams/tins of soup does the shop have to sell?' (the order in which the experimenter asked about the target and control sets was counterbalanced). Again, the corresponding set – ice-creams in the van – was visible on all trials.

Scenario 2, involving sharing, also has a control condition involving soup cans. These function in the same way as the dolphins in the pairing scenario. Note that the set sizes were identical in the two conditions, ranging between 7 and 9.

2.2. Results

We start by addressing hypotheses 1 and 2 concerning the effects of set-visibility and scenario on the ability to infer corresponding numerosity. First, we take as our dependent variable the ability to make an appropriate inference spontaneously; that is without first attempting to count the target set. Next, we recode performance (on trials where the target set was visible). Following recoding, the dependent variable will include all correct inferences (i.e., spontaneous inferences and the inferences made after the experimenter had hidden the target set with his hand because the child initially attempted to count the set).

Table 1   *Number of children making inferences in each scenario*

Visibility	Visible		Hidden
	Spontaneous (no hiding)	**Inc. inferences made after hiding**	**Hidden**
Scenario			
Lions/bicycles (conceptual pairs)	5	11	16
Ice-creams (shared homogeneous items)	2	12	12

Notes: Spontaneous inferences are those where the child inferred without making any attempt to count items. The figures under 'inc. inferences made after hiding' refer to the total number of correct inferences made, including those made after the experimenter hid the target set because the child attempted to count. The possible maximum in each cell = 40.

For all analyses, a child was scored as correct when he or she inferred that the target (related) set, but not the unrelated set, shared the same cardinal as the counted set.[1] A preliminary analysis of the data revealed no effect of age (in months) or order of questioning (asking about the target/unrelated set first), and consequently, the data were pooled for all subsequent analyses.

> *The data are more complex for the visible condition since they show both the number of children making the correct inference without counting and those who made the correct inference after the experimenter covered the roof and prevented them from counting. There were 40 children in the study, each taking part in all four conditions across the two testing sessions. It can be seen that spontaneous performance was poor in the visible conditions for both scenarios but it improved when children were prevented from counting. Performance was best in the pairing scenario with hidden items. However, even in this condition, more than half the children were unable to infer how many lions there were from the number of bicycles.*

2.2.1 Spontaneous inferences

Table 1 shows the effect that set-visibility and scenario had on performance. Only 5 per cent of children inferred spontaneously a visible set of ice-creams, and 12.5 per cent inferred a visible set of lions (see left hand column of Table 1). These figures contrast sharply with the inferences made when the ice-creams and lions were hidden (30 and 40 per cent, respectively; see right hand column of Table 1).

Because the data failed to satisfy the criteria for parametric analysis, we used Sign tests[2] to examine the effects of visibility (visible versus hidden) and scenario (animals versus food items). Regarding visibility, 21 children scored equally on 'visible' and 'hidden' trials (e.g., they scored 0–0, respectively). Of the remaining 19 children, 17 made more inferences when the target set was hidden, with only two children showing the opposite pattern (i.e., making more correct inferences when the target set was visible); $p = 0.001$. Thus, children who knew that the numerosity of a related set could be inferred were more likely to display that knowledge when that set could not be counted. Turning to the effect of scenario, 26 children scored equally on 'lions/bicycles' and 'ice-cream' trials. Of the remaining children, 10 made more correct inferences when judging the number of bikes, with only four children making more correct inferences when asked about ice-creams. Although children were, therefore, more successful when judging paired rather than shared items, this difference failed to reach significance; $p = 0.180$.

> *The data here are binary since, in each condition, children either inferred or did not infer the number of items in the other set. This is a major reason for using Sign Tests as the data are also related rather than unrelated. The relatedness of scores is not reflected in Table 1 since this does not show how individual children performed across the different conditions. For this reason, the actual numbers of children performing better in one condition than another are reported within the text. For those responding differently in visible and invisible conditions, the majority were able to make an inference in the invisible condition but not the visible. However, the effect of scenario was not significant, probably because over half of the children responded similarly in both.*

We looked for reasons why only 35 correct inferences were made out of a possible total of 160. When the target set was visible, only seven correct inferences were made; on the remaining 'visible' trials children often attempted to count the target set (54/73). The incorrect responses in the 'hidden' condition were an approximately even mix of guesses (22 trials) and 'Do not know' (30 trials). We expected some children to try and remove the lid from the box when asked about hidden-sets and approximately half did so. When this happened, children were prevented from seeing inside and asked the question again.

This analysis of incorrect responses is revealing in showing that children who did not make an inference about the number of items in the other set either guessed or said that they did not know. This confirms that they did not understand the logic of one-to-one correspondence in relation to set size.

Whilst we were interested primarily in whether children would [1] infer or [2] try to count the target set, there was at least one other perfectly reasonable strategy open to the children, which was to recount the set they had just counted. However, none of the children resorted to this approach. We also accepted attempts to count the unrelated set – when that set was visible – as constituting correct responses. This was considered reasonable because the cardinal number for the counted set offered no clues as to the number of items in a set that was not in one-to-one correspondence. It is permissible, on logical grounds, to count one set and infer the numerosity of a corresponding set. There are no grounds for extending the cardinal from the counted set to an unrelated set. Thus, the unrelated sets of dolphins or tins of soup acted as a check on children's grasp of the logico-mathematical relationship between corresponding sets. Only two children successfully inferred the target set but failed to score because they made an incorrect inference about the unrelated set by extending the same cardinal to both sets.

One explanation for the pronounced influence of set-visibility might be that children were learning about the demands of the task on the earlier trials (i.e., on Session 1) and only later applying that knowledge. Although counterbalancing the order of presentation should have ruled this out, we checked by re-coding responses in terms of the chronological (first, second, third and fourth) order the children experienced the four trials. There were 15 correct inferences made on Session 1, and 20 made on Session 2: 8, 7, 9 and 11 on the first, second, third and fourth problems, respectively. None of these differences were significant.

> The authors rule out the possibility that children were learning how to do the task as they went along. This confirms the view that there was little understanding of the significance of one-to-one correspondence because children, who are on the verge of understanding something but are initially confused by the demands of a particular experimental task, are likely to get better as they gain experience.

2.2.2. Inferences made after hiding the visible set

In the previous analyses, children were scored as correct only if they inferred spontaneously, without making any attempt to count the target set. Frydman and Bryant (1988) found that 10/24 children in their study did make the correct inference after the experimenter hid the target set and asked if the child knew how many there were without counting. In order to assess whether a similar effect occurred here, scores on trials in the visible condition were recoded to account for an inference whether it was spontaneous or not (i.e., a child was scored correct if they made an inference before or after the set had been hidden by the experimenter). The total scores on trials in the visible condition rose from 7 to 23 (see the middle column of Table 1). Comparing the number of correct inferences made on hidden-sets trials with the number made on the recoded visible-set trials, McNemar's test revealed there was no longer an effect of set-visibility; $\chi 2$ $(1, N = 40) = 0.32$, $p > 0.05$. This reinforces the point that set-visibility was masking children's competence. One question is whether the increased scores following recoding were specific to a particular scenario. There were 27 correct inferences made when the target set consisted of lions inside the school and 24 when that set was the ice-creams inside the shop. Thus, following recoding, there was still no effect of scenario.

> Children's performance in the visible condition of each scenario was better when they were prevented from counting by the experimenter placing his hand over the items that were about to be counted. The number of inferences made under this condition was the same as in the invisible condition, showing the children were more likely to make an inference about set size when they were unable to count.

Although the small sample size in this first study precluded a statistical analysis of the roles that counting and sharing proficiency might play in children's ability to use cardinal extension, it is still interesting to note how well children were able to carry out these basic procedures. Whilst all children knew how to divide the paired sets of lions and bicycles by placing them in their appropriate locations, they were not as good at sharing the ice-creams out. Eleven children showed no ability to share evenly, 14 shared evenly on one trial and 15 children distributed equal shares on both trials. Sharing is an emerging skill for this age group. As a measure of counting proficiency, we looked at the number of times children counted the corresponding sets (i.e., the sets the experimenter asked the child to count before asking about the target and control sets) correctly across the two scenarios. Twenty-two out of 40 were accurate on all four trials. A further nine children counted accurately on three of the four trials. Thus, these 31 children counted accurately on 115 out of 124 trials, displaying little evidence that they had much difficulty enumerating the set sizes we used. The remaining nine children showed relatively poor counting skills, counting inaccurately on at least two of the four trials. This shows that counting, like sharing, was also an emerging skill for some of these children (counting proficiency was significantly correlated with sharing proficiency; r (39) = 0.41, $p < 0.01$). However, given the small number of inferences made spontaneously (35/160), and the finding that most children were good at counting the sets we used, we find no grounds for suspecting that a failure to infer was due to a lack of self-confidence in their counting accuracy. We explore this issue further in Experiment 2.

This discussion of children's proficiency in counting and sharing illustrates why keeping a very detailed record of children's responses is important. Clearly, there are a number of reasons why children may find both the pairing and sharing task difficult and it is important to try and understand how potential component skills might vary from child to child.

2.3. Discussion

Nearly half the children we tested showed no understanding that numerical equivalence could be inferred using cardinal extension when the target set was in one-to-one correspondence with a set already counted. The biggest influence on whether children would display this ability was the visibility of the sets. Few children resisted counting when it was a strategy available to them; being able to see the target set appeared to encourage them to count. In contrast, hiding the target set seemed to promote numerical inferences. Clearly, for some children, a reluctance to infer a corresponding numerosity cannot be accounted for by an absence of the requisite understanding. Children's knowledge may be underestimated if we take unnecessary counting as evidence that they have not yet grasped the relationship between correspondence and cardinal numbers.

We did not find reliable evidence that children were using the conceptual pairing of items as a cue to numerical correspondence, an association that is absent when homogeneous items are shared out. Both acts produce equivalent sets (when, as here, even numbers are used), and children did make more spontaneous inferences (albeit statistically non-significant) about paired sets than they did about sets that resulted from sharing, although this difference largely disappears when all correct inferences are considered. This is an issue we return to later.

3. Experiment 2

> One important change, introduced in Experiment 2, was the use of a greater number of trials to improve the scoring sensitivity. As we noted earlier, each trial offers a binary choice and so provides a gross measure. With more trials it is possible to distinguish between children who consistently make one kind of response and those who do not. The data are also more amenable to parametric analysis.

The results from Experiment 1 motivated a follow-up study that was more ambitious in scope, with the aim of replicating and extending the findings thus far. Hypotheses 1 and 2 were retained from Experiment 1 and re-assessed using more trials (and therefore, potentially greater power). An additional issue that we wanted to investigate concerned the sizes of the sets to be inferred. One possibility is that children in Experiment 1 were reluctant to make inferences about another set because they were sensitive to the limitations in their counting proficiency. We know that 3-year-olds are able to infer equivalence when small sets are used (two/three items: Cowan & Biddle, 1989; Sophian et al., 1995). But small numerosities – certainly up to four items – can be enumerated non-verbally (Chi & Klahr, 1975; Starkey & Cooper, 1980; Trick & Pylyshyn, 1994), and can be compared without verbal counting (Strauss & Curtis, 1984; but see also Mix, Huttenlocher, & Levine, 2002). The fact that young children judge more accurately when sets are small and visible raises the possibility that they are either making perceptual comparisons or enumerating the sets non-verbally. We therefore included small (two and three items) and larger sets (five and six items) in the stimuli. If children were less likely to make a numerical inference because they lack confidence in their counting ability (Gelman, 1972), we would expect larger sets to produce a different pattern of response (hypothesis 3). Determining children's counting proficiency permits an assessment of whether they can infer numerosity above their counting range. By including two different age groups (3- versus 4-year-olds), we hope to build a developmental model of children's abilities by looking at the interaction between these factors.

> The other change was to use both small sets and larger sets since 3-year-old children may not feel confident to count more than a very small number of items. If responses are affected by their counting skills, they should respond differently according to set size.

Finally, we wanted to examine whether either of the two core skills of counting and sharing are associated with the ability to draw appropriate numerical inferences. Children begin to grasp cardinality between the ages of 3 and 4 (Fuson, Pergament, Lyons, & Hall, 1985; Wynn, 1990), around the same time as they are learning that sharing is a numerical activity (Miller, 1984). Research into whether sharing competence is related to counting skill has found no association between the two (Pepper & Hunting, 1998). However, Mix (1999a, 1999b) and Saxe (1977, 1979) found children's counting accuracy correlates with the recognition of numerical equivalence on set-comparison tasks. The ability to maintain one-to-one correspondence between words and items when counting appears to offer a developmental advance particularly where there are perceptual differences (e.g., in size, colour, etc.) between sets being compared. However, it is less clear how the ability to count single sets accurately might help children gain the conceptual insight that sharing evenly produces sets with the same cardinal. It is intuitively appealing to suspect that the ability to maintain item-to-item correspondence between shares is a more likely predictor of this ability.

Experiment 2 also investigated the relationship of counting skills to task performance. The authors suggest that the ability to count per se may not be important but, rather, the ability to use one-to-one correspondence effectively when dividing items into two equal sets. In order to compare children with greater or lesser skills, the sample of participants included both 3-year-olds and 4-year-olds. Although these children differ in age by only one year, their counting skills are likely to have developed considerably over this period.

3.1. Method

3.1.1. Participants

Nineteen 3-year-olds (3 years 8 months to 4 years 0 months; $M = 3$ years 10 months, S.D. = 1.6 months) and twenty-six 4-year-olds (4 years 1 month to 4 years 8 months; $M = 4$ years 4 months, S.D. = 2.2 months) from two pre-school playgroups in a predominantly White, urban population took part. None of the children had any identified learning difficulties. None had taken part in Experiment 1.

3.1.2. Materials

As in Experiment 1 except there were three sets of toy animals (lions, pandas and ladybirds). Ladybirds that 'flew' to school always acted as the control set (in place of dolphins) in scenario 1, and lions and pandas were interchanged as the target set in an attempt to maintain children's interest in the tasks.

3.1.3. Procedure

The same as Experiment 1, except that in each scenario, the problems were presented with both small (two to three items) and large (five to six items) sets. Each child received 16 problems (eight in each Session), representing all the factorial combinations of the three factors. The order of presentation was counterbalanced using a Latin Square design. The control sets were only included on Session 2 in an attempt to reduce the time taken to administer the 16 trials and minimize the risk that children would withdraw from the study through fatigue or disinterest.

3.2. Results

3.2.1. Spontaneous inferences

There was no significant difference between the number of inferences made on Sessions 1 and 2 (182 versus 201), and so data were pooled across session. In the 'visible' condition, children tended to either infer spontaneously (141/360 trials) or attempt to count the target set (177/360), accounting for over 83 per cent of responses in this condition. The remaining responses were a mix of guesses (27) and 'do not know' (15). When the target set was hidden, children made many more inferences spontaneously (242/360). The incorrect responses in the 'hidden' condition were, again, a mix of guesses (78) and 'do not know' (39), but no attempts were made to count the target set. This was a surprise, as we expected some children to try and remove the lid from the box to see inside, but none did. Table 2 shows the mean number of times children made a spontaneous and appropriate[3] inference about the items in the target set for each set-type and set size.

The data satisfied the criteria for a parametric test, and ANOVA was therefore not only suitable but also corresponds with the analyses conducted by Sophian et al. (1995). A 2 (age: 3 versus 4) ´ 2 (scenario: animals versus ice-creams) ´ 2 (set size: small [2–3] versus large [5–6]) ´ 2 (visibility: hidden versus visible) repeated-measures ANOVA, with scenario, set size and visibility as within-subjects variables, confirmed hypothesis 1 in that the main effect of visibility was highly significant, $F(1,43) = 56.06$, $p < 0.001$; h_p^2 (i.e., partial Eta squared) = 0.57.

> *The use of more trials enabled an ANOVA to be carried out on the data. It also affects the way the data are reported in Table 2 which presents the mean number of inferences being made (ranging from 0 to 2). The main effect of visibility was significant but this interacted with scenario, with a more pronounced effect of visibility in the pairing task than the sharing task.*

Table 2   Mean number of correct spontaneous inferences and inferences made after hiding the visible set (maximum possible two in each condition)

| Set size | Hidden | | Visible spontaneous (after hiding) | |
Age/scenario	Small	Large	Small	Large
3-year-olds Ice-creams				
M	0.84	0.63	0.37 (1.00**)	0.32 (0.58)
S.D.	0.60	0.89	0.60 (0.67)	0.58 (0.69)
Animals				
M	1.74	1.11	0.74 (1.37**)	0.47 (0.95**)
S.D.	0.56	0.80	0.87 (0.68)	0.70 (0.78)
4-year-olds Ice-creams				
M	1.54	1.08	1.15 (1.50*)	0.58 (1.00**)
S.D.	0.58	0.84	0.83 (0.51)	0.76 (0.69)
Animals				
M	1.81	1.73	1.31 (1.73*)	1.00 (1.27*)
S.D.	0.49	0.60	0.84 (0.45)	0.80 (0.67)

Note: Asterisks denote significant differences between the number of correct inferences made after the experimenter had hidden the relevant set and the number of spontaneous inferences given for those sets.
  *$p < 0.05$.
**$p < 0.01$.

For every combination of scenario and set size, children made more spontaneous inferences when the target set was hidden from view. A significant interaction between scenario and visibility, $F(1,43) = 8.72$, $p < 0.05$; $\eta_p^2 = 0.17$, showed that the influence of set-visibility was greater on 'animals' problems than 'ice-cream' problems. There were also two significant three-way interactions, both including age.

There was an interaction between age, visibility and set size, $F(1,43) = 4.25$, $p < 0.05$, $\eta_p^2 = 0.09$. While all simple effects of visibility were significant on both small and large sets in both age groups, for 3-year-olds, the effect of visibility was most marked on small sets [$F(1,17) = 32.67$, $p < 0.001$ $\eta_p^2 = 0.65$ versus $F(1,17) = 9.92$, $p < 0.01$, $\eta_p^2 = 0.35$], whereas for 4-year-olds, the effect was most pronounced on large sets [$F(1,24) = 10.90$, $p < 0.005$, $\eta_p^2 = 0.30$ versus $F(1,24) = 34.41$, $p < 0.001 \eta_p^2 = 0.58$]. Three-year-olds are better at inferring small sets than large sets, especially when those sets are hidden. Conversely, 4-year-olds are generally able to infer small sets regardless of whether they are hidden or not, but some have difficulty inferring larger sets.

> *The three way interactions, involving age, are carefully interpreted by the authors. In both cases, the interactions stem from the different effects of set size on the younger and older children. One interesting finding was that the younger children were better at making inferences in the pairing scenario than the sharing scenario even with small set sizes whereas the older children performed very similarly in the two tasks but found the sharing task more difficult with the larger set size. Overall the effect of scenario was significant with the pairing task being easier.*

A second three-way interaction was found between age, set size and scenario, $F(1,43) = 12.52$, $p < 0.005$, $\eta_p^2 = 0.23$. All simple effects of scenario were significant for both small and large sets for each age group. Thus, although the effect of scenario failed to reach significance in Experiment 1, the greater power in the design of Experiment 2 has revealed this effect to be a reliable one. For 3-year-olds, the effect of scenario was most marked on small sets [$F(1,17) = 221.46$, $p < 0.001$, $\eta_p^2 = 0.54$ versus $F(1,17) = 5.59$, $p < 0.05$, $\eta_p^2 = 0.24$], whereas for 4-year-olds, the effect was most pronounced on large sets [$F(1,24) = 6.34$, $p < 0.05$, $\eta_p^2 = 0.20$ versus $F(1,24) = 22.27$, $p < 0.001$ $\eta_p^2 = 0.47$]. Three-year-olds are not as good at inferring equivalent shares as they are at recognizing that conceptually paired items share the same cardinal, even when smaller sets are used. In contrast, 4-year-olds are almost as good at recognizing the relationship between sharing and cardinality as they are at recognizing the relationship between cardinality and conceptually paired items, although they have greater difficulty in grasping that larger shares also have identical cardinals.

The other significant results were a main effect of age, $F(1,43) = 9.96$, $p < 0.005$, $\eta_p^2 = 0.19$; a main effect of Set size, $F(1,43) = 33.14$, $p < 0.001$, $\eta_p^2 = 0.44$; and a main effect of scenario, $F(1,43) = 38.23$, $p < 0.001$, $\eta_p^2 = 0.47$. In general, older children made more spontaneous inferences than younger children; the number of spontaneous inferences was greater when sets were small (supporting hypothesis 3); and children in both age groups were more likely to recognize the equivalence of paired items than they were to recognize the numerical equivalence that results from sharing things out evenly (supporting hypothesis 2).

We also investigated which, if either, of the core skills of counting and sharing, predicts the ability to infer the size of a corresponding set. Twenty-nine children (64 per cent) in the sample were consistently able to maintain item-to-item correspondence when they shared small sets of four and six items, although only 20 were able to do so with larger sets of 10 and 12 items. This change was significant as determined by a McNemar χ^2 test for significance of change, $\chi^2 = 6.4$, $p < 0.05$. Sharing was an emerging skill for these children, and 4-year-olds were significantly better than 3-year-olds,

$F(1,43) = 4.16$, $p < 0.05$, $\eta_p^2 = 0.09$. Similarly, children were better at counting small sets than large sets, $F(1,43) = 20.76$, $p < 0.001$, $\eta_p^2 = 0.33$, although 3-year-olds were in general just as good as the older children, $F(1,43) = 1.38$, $p = 0.25$, $\eta_p^2 = 0.03$. It seems that the ability to count sets of up of six items is in place by the age of three. Forty-one children (91 per cent of the sample) were able to count sets of two to three items without any difficulty, and over half (56 per cent) consistently counted larger sets accurately.

Hierarchical multiple regression was carried out using the number of spontaneous, correct inferences as the dependent variable.[4] Counting proficiency was measured as the number of trials [/16] where the child counted the corresponding set accurately ($M = 14.78$, S.D. $= 2.27$) and sharing proficiency as the number of trials [/8] where the child maintained item-to-item correspondence when sharing ($M = 6.13$, S.D. $= 2.07$).

Given that the previous analyses had revealed a significant main effect of age, this variable was entered first (see Table 3), and was confirmed as a significant contributor to the explained variance; $r(44) = 0.43$. Although the zero-order correlations between spontaneous inferences and both counting proficiency and sharing proficiency were significant (0.45 and 0.66, respectively), we entered counting proficiency next, followed by sharing proficiency. Together, these three variables explained over 50 per cent of the total variance (see Table 3). Moreover, the model shows that sharing proficiency is a unique predictor above and beyond the influence of age and counting proficiency (in contrast, counting proficiency failed to exert a similar effect once sharing proficiency had been entered; $\Delta R^2 = 0.30$, $p < 0.05$).

The relationship between counting and sharing skills and task performance was investigated using multiple regression. Given that age predicted performance (since older children were better than younger children) this was entered as the first variable in the regression analysis. Taking the second set of data in Table 3 (all correct inferences), age accounted for 17 per cent of the variance. Counting proficiency, entered as Step 2, accounted for a further 28 per cent of the variance and sharing proficiency a further 23 per cent when entered as Step 3. Overall, these three variables explained 68 per cent of the variance of the inference scores. Note that sharing proficiency remained a significant predictor of performance after counting had been entered into the regression analysis but the reverse was not true. This means that sharing proficiency was a more powerful, and unique, predictor of children's ability to infer set size using one-to-one correspondence.

3.2.2. Discriminating between the target and control sets

It is important to check that children were using cardinal extension to infer number because they knew that sets were equivalent and not simply using a last-word rule. Children could have made a correct inference about the target set by simply repeating the cardinal number for the counted set

Table 3 *Hierarchical multiple regression for variables predicting correct inferences*

Variable	B	S.E.B	β	ΔR²
Spontaneous correct inferences[a]				
Step 1				
Age	2.31	1.04	0.25*	0.19**
Step 2				
Counting proficiency	0.38	0.24	0.19	0.14**
Step 3				
Sharing proficiency	1.10	0.27	0.50**	0.19**
All correct inferences[b] (including those made after hiding the set)				
Step 1				
Age	1.70	0.82	0.19	0.17**
Step 2				
Counting proficiency	0.65	0.19	0.33*	0.28**
Step 3				
Sharing proficiency	1.16	0.21	0.54**	0.23**

[a] $R^2 = 0.52$.
[b] $R^2 = 0.68$.
*$p < 0.05$.
**$p < 0.01$.

without grasping why the two sets had the same cardinal number. We recoded the data from Session 2 such that a child was scored as correct only if he or she also understood that the target set and control set had different cardinal values. If children were basing their judgments on quantitative correspondence they should be more likely to use cardinal extension for that set than for another set they had no numerical knowledge of.

> The use of the control procedure (involving items that were not in one-to-one correspondence) allowed the authors to dismiss the idea that children may have appeared to infer the number of items in the corresponding set by merely repeating the last mentioned number. The critical finding is that in 91 per cent of cases children correctly stated the number of items in the corresponding set but did not give the same response to the control items.

There were 201 correct spontaneous inferences made during Session 2. On 182 of these trials (91 per cent), children discriminated between the related target set and the control set. There were only 26 instances of children extending the cardinal from the counted set to both the target and control sets, with 3-year-olds being more likely to make this mistake than 4-year-olds, $F(1,43) = 4.52$, $p < 0.05$, $\eta_p^2 = 0.10$. Other than the effect of age, there were no other significant influences on children extending the cardinal inappropriately; set size, scenario and visibility had no effect in this regard (all $ps > 0.05$). The control questions implied that only two children did not understand that the same cardinals apply only to equivalent sets. Thus, performance confirms that nearly all the children who used cardinal extension did so because they understood the relationship between cardinality and quantitative equivalence.

3.2.3. Inferences made after hiding a previously visible set

As in Experiment 1, scores on trials in the visible condition were recoded to discriminate between inferences made spontaneously and those made after the experimenter hid the items and repeated the question because the child went to count them. The relevant data are shown in Table 2. Hiding-then-repeating the question increased the number of inferences for almost every combination of age, scenario, set size and visibility. Overall, the number of valid inferences made rose from a total of 383 to a total of 488. This is striking given that children went to count the visible target set on only 145 trials. Thus, when they were prevented from counting, children went on to infer correctly over 70% of the time. The exception was when 3-year-olds were asked about large sets of ice-creams, and this led to a four-way interaction between scenario, set size, visibility and age, F $(1,43) = 5.10$, $p < 0.05$, $\eta_p^2 = 0.11$. Even when counting was prevented, by hiding the set, 3-year-olds were relatively poor at inferring large sets of shared items relative to small sets or paired sets. The interactions between scenario and visibility, $F (1,43) = 7.22$, $p < 0.05$, $\eta_p^2 = 0.14$, and between scenario, set size and age, $F (1,43) = 4.88$, $p < 0.05$, $\eta_p^2 = 0.10$, are both present as in the earlier analysis with similar estimates of effect sizes. We are not clear why hiding the targets sets (when children started to count them) reduced, but did not eradicate, the effect of set-visibility. It is possible that some children, when denied their first-choice strategy, fail to search for an alternative, although we concede that our data cannot shed any light on this matter.

> Preventing the children from counting had a very powerful effect in the second study, except in the case of the younger children in the sharing task with the larger set size. As this is the most difficult of the four tasks, it is not surprising that it was not amenable to prompting.

Recoding the data also retains all four significant main effects of set size, age, scenario and visibility (all $ps < 0.01$, all $\eta_p^2 > 0.08$). The estimates of effect size are similar to before except that a smaller effect of visibility $(\eta_p^2 = 0.09$ versus $0.57)$ confirms that being able to see a target set encouraged unnecessary counting. Attempting to count the target set was not associated with counting proficiency: $r (44) = 0.13$, $p > 0.05$. Furthermore, as Table 3 shows, it is still sharing proficiency that makes the biggest unique contribution to the model $(r [44] = 0.74)$ over and above the contributions of counting proficiency $(r [44] = 0.60)$ and age $(r [44] = 0.41)$.

In sum, the various analyses support the notion that important precursors to recognizing the link between corresponding sets and cardinal numbers are age-related developments in sharing and counting proficiency. Improvements in each of these basic skills are likely to be associated with the ability to draw appropriate inferences about numerical relationships, but this understanding often remains hidden when alternative strategies like counting are available or seen to be encouraged.

3.3. Discussion

> *The discussion points to the relatively good performance of the 3-year-olds in the pairing paradigm, especially with small sets. The authors conclude that the explicit pairing supports the younger children in recognising the significance of one-to-one correspondence. They argue that the perceptual support provided by the pairing scenario, together with developing sharing and counting skills, underpin the younger children's ability to make inferences about set size from one-to-one correspondence.*

As in Experiment 1, the visibility of arrays appears of act as a cue to counting. However, the introduction of an extra age group revealed some important differences. In contrast to Experiment 1, there was now much stronger evidence that the youngest children used conceptual pairing as a clue to numerical correspondence, and that the absence of this bond when homogeneous sets are shared out leads to something of an arithmetical *impasse* for 3-year-olds. Both acts produce equivalent sets, but younger children were more likely to infer equivalence if there was an established association between items. It is interesting to compare this finding with other evidence that suggests a pattern of gradual decontextualization in children's recognition of numerical correspondence. In set-matching tasks the degree of surface similarity (e.g., color, shape) is important; 3-year-olds recognize equivalence between homogeneous sets (e.g., one set of dots and another of shells) before they are able to recognize the relationship between sets of mixed objects around the age of four (Mix, 1999a). The level of perceptual support together with mastery of the counting routine helps very young children to make quantitative comparisons, at least when those sets are small (fewer than five items). Notwithstanding this association, it remains unclear how the ability to enumerate single sets helps children to grasp the fact that cardinal numbers have relative value.

Indeed, improvements in counting accuracy do not always correlate with the use of counting strategies to make numerical comparisons (Saxe, 1979). Moreover, counting proficiency appears insufficient to predict children's understanding of number conservation (Piaget, 1952), indicating that even accurate enumerators still have something fundamental to learn about the significance of cardinal numbers. Procedural mastery must be supplemented by conceptual insight if children are to apply their understanding of cardinality to simple arithmetical problems like set-comparison (Muldoon, Lewis, & Freeman, 2003). There are grounds for believing that conceptual knowledge of a procedure like counting, and its application as an arithmetical tool are linked (Sophian, 1997). Children need to learn the implications of cardinal numbers for judgments about relative quantity, not simply the connection between word-to-item correspondence and the cardinality of a single set (i.e., the one-to-one correspondence principle – Gelman & Gallistel, 1978), if they are to recognize why counting is a useful arithmetical tool.

Children appear to progress from being able to infer small conceptually related pairs of items before grasping the numerical significance of sharing, and this develops in tandem with age-related mastery of the sharing procedure. The use of small conceptually paired sets of items proved the least difficult of all our tasks and most children were able to infer appropriately. It is possible that conceptually paired sets, even pairs that are not found outside of children's games, as ours were, help children to access the fact that every item of one type has a corresponding item of another type. Items were 'paired' before being separated out. This is not usually the case when items are shared out. When sharing, set equivalence is established for the first time following the sharing routine, and item-to-item correspondence is solely the result of temporal correspondence between distributions.

We remain unsure whether the effect of set-type is due to the 'pairing' procedure or the conceptual link between items. This could be examined by adding a third scenario to the two we employed here. This would entail 'sharing' paired items out without establishing the conceptual link beforehand (i.e., without asking children to put lions and bicycles together before separating them out). Putting one lion in the school, and then one bicycle in the bike shed, followed by a lion in school and another bicycle in the shed and so on, would mirror the sharing routine but would result in sets of different items. Comparing performance on this scenario with the present lions/bicycles scenario would provide the effect of the original pairing procedure. Also, contrasting the inferences about 'shared' lion/bicycles in the new scenario with inferences about shared ice-creams would test the possibility that the greater success we observed with conceptually paired items was a result of them evoking a stronger 'equivalence' schema.

A further experiment is suggested in which implicit pairing is used. This points to the fact that the pairing and sharing scenarios differ in a number of ways, not least in their use of two sets of different items in the former and only one set of items in the latter.

Our findings also suggest why the children in Frydman and Bryant (1988) failed to show the level of success achieved by younger children in Sophian et al. (1995). The success rate of 77 per cent in Sophian's task was achieved only when sets were small (two/three items). When sets were larger – five/six items – performance dropped to less than 50 per cent. It is possible that the greater temporal demand of sharing large numbers of items prevents children from monitoring their own maintenance of item-to-item correspondence, leading to a decrease in confidence in their own sharing accuracy. The finding that age-related change in sharing proficiency was the best predictor of cardinal extension highlights the impact that an emerging mastery of temporal item-to-item correspondence has on children's awareness of sharing as a numerical activity. It is presumably easier to remember that each recipient has received the same if only 4 items are distributed than if 12 items are shared out. The fact that children made more correct inferences (albeit not to a statistically significant degree) with smaller shares supports this explanation.

The finding that children use an effective strategy one moment only to discard it the next is not a new one. Siegler (1995, 1996) offers a different explanation. Variability in performance is a characteristic of a transitional phase in the development from one state of knowledge to another. Knowledge of different strategies, whether explicit or implicit, has been viewed as a marker of developmental readiness. A child might use different strategies to solve two examples of the same mathematical problem on successive days (Siegler & Shrager, 1984). If children use ineffective strategies when they have effective strategies at their disposal, development is a shift in the frequency with which the competing strategies are selected for use.

The authors note that children's variable use of strategies is characteristic of a transitional stage of development as noted by Siegler (Siegler, 1998; Siegler & Alibali, 2005). (See also Chapter 2.)

4. General discussion

An important mathematical achievements for children is to recognize both [1] that corresponding sets have the same cardinal number, and [2] that sharing evenly produces such sets. It is clear that the recognition of numerical equivalence for conceptually paired items precedes the understanding that sharing also produces similar correspondence. Whilst 3-year-olds might be aware that sharing produces equivalent sets (Cowan & Biddle, 1989), and recognize the relevance of numerical values for correspondence relations (Becker, 1989; Sophian, 1988), our results provide further evidence that they have difficulty in connecting the two. Procedural mastery of counting is typically in place by the age of three, but age-related improvements in the ability to maintain item-to-item correspondence in a temporal action predict children's developing understanding of the connection between sharing, set equivalence and cardinality.

Of those who could make an appropriate inference, the visibility of the sets influenced whether they would display this understanding spontaneously. Many children were unable to resist counting when it was a strategy available to them. It is perhaps not surprising that being able to see a target set appears to encourage children to count (i.e., a familiar, 'direct' strategy) rather than infer (an 'indirect' strategy). Alternatively, it might be concluded that children tried to count items because they were not confident in the equivalence between the sets. We are less convinced by this possibility because having the target set hidden from the outset often revealed their confidence; the number of spontaneous inferences made when sets were hidden was over 70 per cent higher than when sets were visible. It is worth noting here that these inferences about hidden-sets were not tentative guesses; there was rarely, if ever, any suggestion that children were not confident in their judgments (even in the minority of cases when those judgments turned out to be wrong). It seems that some children possess a nascent concept of equivalence but circumstances can mask this. Consequently, children's knowledge may be underestimated if we take unnecessary counting as evidence that they have yet to grasp the link between quantitative correspondence and cardinal numbers. Children's abilities may be revealed one moment, but remain unexpressed the next if they do not feel it necessary to apply those particular skills.

There are at least five possible explanations why children might persevere with counting even when they are able to infer. First, children typically count when asked 'How many?' (e.g., Frye et al., 1989; Fuson, 1988; Wynn, 1990). Secondly, children may be encouraged to count by being asked 'How many?' for both sets; the effect of asking the same question twice has been clearly demonstrated on number conservation tasks (e.g., Rose & Blank, 1974; Samuel & Bryant, 1984). Thirdly, children may believe that counting is not merely a check, but essential if one is to know whether shares are fair (Davis & Pitkethly, 1990; Desforges & Desforges, 1980). Selective training where children are asked to make numerical inferences about hidden arrays might reduce this type of perseveration. Using small sets of two and three items offers the potential for even 3-year-olds to begin abstracting cardinal numbers in a way that perceptual cues to quantity often inhibit.

The results of the two experiments suggest that children may attempt to count items even when they can infer how many there are without counting. The authors suggest that a training study may show whether younger children can be encouraged to make inferences rather than count.

It is also possible, however, that performance was influenced by other domain-general information processing constraints. Working memory is needed for the active maintenance of temporary representations (Baddeley, 1986), such as the cardinal for the corresponding set in the present studies. Within-task forgetting is likely to impact on children's performance on mathematical tasks, and there is evidence that suggests that they employ a task-switching strategy when carrying out a counting span task that incorporates memory and processing requirements (Towse & Hitch, 1995; Towse, Hitch, & Hutton, 1998). That is, they engage either in memory operations, or counting operations, but not both simultaneously. Thus, a fourth explanation is that children simply forgot information encoded in memory when asked an additional question about a different set.

A fifth explanation is that the development of executive skills plays an important role. The results from Experiment 2 show that the ability to judge numerical equivalence using cardinal extension develops sometime between the ages of three and four. A concomitant growth in children's reflection on their own behaviour between these ages increases the amount of control they exert over their actions, but younger children are prone to ignore rules, even when they are able to verbally demonstrate appropriate rule-knowledge (Zelazo, Frye, & Rapus, 1996). Thus, executive limitations might account for the fact that many children in the present studies apparently knew the rule 'extend the cardinal from the corresponding set to the target set' but did not apply it across all trials. Further work is needed to resolve which, if any, of these alternative explanations is valid.

To summarize, we began by noting that children's numerical processing is often characterized by a perplexing mix of abilities and limitations (Feigenson et al., 2004). The present datasets show that, even within a particular paradigm (that is, with formally comparable tasks), there can be substantial differences in what children do. However, the data also help us to understand the basis of such variability. We argue that children can make inferences about numerical correspondence, but the physical presence of each set draws children towards counting in any case, and the set array contributes to this tendency too. We also argue, in line with others (Davis & Pitkethly, 1990; Desforges & Desforges, 1980; Frydman & Bryant, 1988) that 3-year-olds have yet to develop a full appreciation of the connection between sharing and cardinality. They are in a transitional stage, in which the concept of one-to-one correspondence, although central to mathematical reasoning and an understanding of what number represents (e.g., Piaget, 1952; Russell, 1960), is fledging in character. Although at this stage little is known about how children's understanding of sharing develops, we suggest that improvements in sharing proficiency are likely to be associated with a greater understanding of sharing as a quantitative exercise. Moreover, presenting children with arithmetical situations that preclude set enumeration may be especially helpful in directing them towards the conceptual realization that counting 'because it is there' is unnecessary.

Acknowledgements

We would like to thank the staff and children of Greaves Nursery, Lancaster and Morecambe College Playgroup, and St. Martin's Preschool Centre, Lancaster, for their generosity and commitment to this project. The first-named author also wishes to thank the Economic and Social Research Council, UK, for funding a post-doctoral fellowship during which this paper was produced.

Notes

1 Children were scored as correct if their inferred number matched the cardinal for the corresponding set irrespective of whether that set had been counted accurately or not. Children's grasp of cardinality can be masked by procedural errors. For example, if the corresponding set contained five items, but the child counted six, he or she was scored correct if they inferred the target set to be six. Three children scored on this basis on one occasion each.
2 The Sign test compares the number of positive and negative differences between two repeated measures. For example, comparing the number of children who are better at inferring hidden-sets (e.g., positive difference) with the number of children who are better at inferring visible sets (e.g., negative difference), where the Null hypothesis is that the number of positive and negative differences will be the same.
3 Children were scored as correct if their inferred number matched the cardinal for the corresponding set irrespective of whether that set had been counted accurately or not. Children's grasp of cardinality can be masked by procedural errors. For example, if the corresponding set contained five items, but the child counted six, he or she was scored correct if they inferred the target set to be six. Three children scored on this basis on one occasion each.
4 We combined performance on both scenarios into separate dependent variables for [1] spontaneous inferences and [2] all inferences (i.e., including those made after the target set had been hidden). Tests revealed a robust degree of reliability in each case; [1] = 0.89, [2] = 0.90.

Longitudinal studies

In Paper 9, the authors used regression analysis to identify predictors of inferential understanding of numerical relationships. Such predictors are concurrent in that they identify abilities that are associated with another ability at a single point in development. Analyses of concurrent predictors are useful in showing which specific abilities are relevant to the development of other abilities. From a developmental perspective, however, the most interesting questions concern how particular skills develop over time. Concurrent predictors may be implicated in development – and this is often the assumption of the researcher – but the best way to establish how early abilities are related to subsequent abilities is to use a longitudinal design in which the same children are followed over time and the relationship between early measures and later measures is examined. This is the design that was adopted in Paper 3 where features of mothers' speech to young children were related to the children's subsequent development of Theory of Mind understanding.

In the next paper, a longitudinal design is used to look at what predicts the development of reading ability between the ages of 5 (when formal reading instruction begins a school) and 7 (when clear individual differences in reading ability will be evident).

Paper 10   Longitudinal predictors of success in learning to read (Savage & Carless, 2005)

The aim of this study was to determine which particular components of phonological awareness – awareness of the sound structure of a language – are important for learning to read. The relationship between phonological awareness and learning to read has been the subject of many experimental studies. Over time, the tasks used to assess phonological awareness have become increasingly fine-grained and the questions asked about the relationships between performance in these tasks and learning to read have become, correspondingly, more specific.

As the authors explain, there are essentially two kinds of phonological tasks, those that measure awareness of rime and alliteration and those that measure the ability to manipulate phonemes. There has been considerable debate about whether each of these two tasks is causally related to learning to read English – since there are notable differences in learning to read, and the predictors of learning to read, across different scripts (Harris & Hatano, 1999). The authors describe two opposing views, those of Bryant and colleagues (Bryant, Maclean, Bardley & Crossland, 1990) and Muter and colleagues (Muter, Hulme, Snowling & Taylor, 1997). Bryant et al. argued that there were two routes from phonological awareness to reading, a direct route from rime awareness at age 4 and an indirect route that involved phoneme deletion ability at age 5. Muter et al. argued that only phoneme awareness predicted reading.

There were methodological differences between the two studies in that the Bryant et al. study did not measure both abilities at the same time. The debate about methodology and interpretation of the results continued across a series of papers (Bryant, 1988, 2002; Hulme et al., 2002; Hulme, Muter & Snowling, 1998; Muter, Hulme, Snowling & Taylor, 1988). The issue about the precise instructions given to children undertaking a task is an important one. Marked differences in performance can be found if children perceive their task in one way rather than another as a result of particular wording. Hulme and colleagues (Hulme et al., 1998) showed that instructions to choose a word that 'rhymes with' or 'rhymes with or sounds like' did not affect children's performance. However, performance in tasks is also affected by cognitive demands so that, in this case, one phonological awareness task might be a good predictor of reading because of its cognitive demands rather than because of the phonological units involved. The general point is that in comparing task performance, especially where one task is being used to predict performance on another task, it is important the tasks are comparable in all but the critical variable.

Journal of Child Psychology and Psychiatry, 2005, 46 (12), 1297–1308

Phoneme manipulation not onset-rime manipulation ability is a unique predictor of early reading

Robert Savage[1] and Sue Carless[2]

[1]McGill University, Montreal, Canada; [2]London Borough of Sutton, UK

There is now an enormous amount of convergent evidence from longitudinal, experimental and intervention studies of both good and poor readers suggesting that phonological awareness, or the ability to reflect upon the phonological structure of language, is closely and probably causally linked to successful reading (e.g., Adams, 1990; Brady & Shankweiler, 1991; Bradley & Bryant, 1983; Ehri et al., 2001; Wagner et al., 1997). While many agree that phonological awareness is a causal factor in reading acquisition and that it probably holds a necessary but not sufficient relationship to successful reading, there remains significant disagreement about the way different sorts of phonological skills should be understood and which of the many tasks used to operationalise phonological awareness best measures the construct (Anthony et al., 2002; Morais, 2003; Stanovich, Cunningham, & Cramer, 1984; Yopp, 1988).

Some researchers have sought to develop and refine psychological models that might explain the developmental emergence of different phonological skills in relation to reading and spelling acquisition. One influential model of this latter kind was advanced by Goswami and Bryant (1990). They argued that the whole literature on phonological awareness to date showed that rime detection skills were evident prior to children learning to read, whereas analytic phonemic skills such as phoneme segmentation and blending developed following exposure to alphabetic print systems, or following explicit tuition. Goswami and Bryant also argued that pre-existing rime detection skills also causally influence the development of explicit phoneme awareness skills when children start to learn to read. Bryant,

Maclean, Bradley, and Crossland (1990) measured rime and alliteration in pre-readers aged 4: 07, asking children to judge the 'odd one out' in spoken word sets such as 'peg', 'cot', 'leg'. Causal path analyses suggested that the pre-reading measure predicted reading and spelling performance through two routes: one route seemed to be *direct* from rime phonological performance at age 4 to reading and spelling performance at age 6, the other route was an *indirect* one that operated via sound deletion skill at age 5.

As the rime/alliteration and phoneme deletion measures were not taken at the same time, it is impossible to know whether phoneme awareness measures would also have predicted reading directly (Muter, 1994; Muter, Hulme, Snowling, & Taylor, 1997, 1998). Muter et al. thus measured rime and phoneme awareness at the same time. They found that phoneme awareness in year 1 predicted reading in years 2 and 3 whereas rime awareness did not predict later reading. Effects of rime awareness were found for spelling only at year 3. Muter et al. concluded that phoneme awareness predicts reading whereas onset-rime awareness does not.

Bryant (1998) noted in response that the instruction given in the rime detection task to identify the word that 'rhymes with *or sounds like*' the stimulus word presented may have meant that children chose onsets that were included as foils in some cases. For example, with the target word 'boat', and choice words 'foot', 'bike', 'coat', both 'coat' and 'bike' could be considered correct responses to the instruction given. On re-analysis, Muter et al.'s combined onset-rime measure incorporating these responses was a strong predictor of reading and spelling alongside phoneme awareness. Against this, Hulme, Muter, and Snowling (1998) demonstrated with a new sample of children that there was no effect of differential instruction (i.e., 'rhymes with' versus 'rhymes with or sounds like') on children's item selection.

Meaningful contrasts of phoneme awareness and rime matching may also be compromised because different tasks may have different extraneous cognitive and phonological demands (Bryant, 1998; Muter et al., 1997). Bryant (1998) thus argued that:

> If one wants to compare the predictive powers of onset-rime tasks and phoneme tasks, one should ensure that both sets of tasks involve exactly the same procedure apart from the difference in the phonological unit which the children have to detect. Any difference between the predictive success of the two tasks, then, would have nothing to do with the extraneous cognitive demands that these make. (p. 37)

This argument advanced by Bryant also applies to a recent re-analysis of the Muter et al. (1997) data and other longitudinal data from Wagner et al. (1997) undertaken by Anthony and Lonigan (2004). As the phoneme and onset-rime tasks were not at all comparable in terms of extraneous task demands in either the Muter et al. or the Wagner et al. studies, no strong conclusions can be drawn from re-analysis about the relative predictive validity of onset-rime versus phoneme awareness.

Other longitudinal research has, however, contrasted appropriately matched onset-rime and phoneme awareness tasks. Hulme et al. (2002) contrasted 72 normally developing 5- and 6-year-old children's phonological awareness using onsets and rimes and initial and final position phonemes on a series of detection, oddity and deletion tasks, matched on their extraneous demands. Hulme et al. provided corrective feedback on all phonological trials where children were inaccurate in their responses.

The study by Hulme et al. (2002) equated rime-onset and phoneme task in terms of cognitive demands and instructions. However, Bryant pointed out that the Hulme et al. study had used corrective feedback and this raised the possibility that what was being measured was not phonological awareness but phonological learning (Bryant, 2002). Thus the present study avoided the use of corrective feedback in order to rule out this possibility.

Regression analyses showed that, after control for extraneous variables, phonemic awareness but not onset-rime awareness measures uniquely predicted later reading. Furthermore, in a highly conservative analysis that also controlled for reading ability at the first point of testing, phoneme awareness but not onset-rime awareness predicted significant unique variance in later reading. This final analysis is important, as it shows that the predictive validity of phoneme awareness is not itself simply a consequence of early reading skills. Hulme et al. concluded that screening phoneme awareness is a practical measure for early identification of children who may be at risk of later reading difficulties.

Hulme's findings have also been evaluated in a series of commentaries that immediately followed publication of their paper. A number of theoretical and empirical questions were raised, many of which extend beyond their specific findings (see Anthony et al., 2002; Bowey, 2002; Bryant, 2002; Goswami, 2002; but see also Hulme, 2002 for replies). Two points are perhaps of central importance in evaluating the findings. Firstly, in theoretical terms, Bryant (2002) argues that the establishment of a strong link from phonemic awareness to reading is consistent with the view of phonemic awareness as an 'indirect route' originally described by Bryant et al. (1990), but concedes that the failure to find a direct link from onset-rime awareness to later reading is less consistent with the 'direct' route posited in his original 1990 paper. This latter route may have to be discarded. Secondly, Bryant (2002) pointed out that children were given corrective feedback on each experimental trial of the phonological tasks, rather than just in practice trials, so the Hulme phonological awareness measure may be one of 'phonological learning' rather than of phonological awareness per se.

Arguably, phonological learning might be an even more important indicator of the importance of a literacy variable than static phonological awareness measures (e.g., Spector, 1992). Indeed, a facility in rime- over phoneme-based learning tasks is also emphasised in transfer of learning tasks (e.g., Goswami, 1993; Goswami & Bryant, 1990). It might also be argued that for children with good phonological skills prior to testing, Hulme's task does not require phonological learning. Nevertheless, it may be important to demonstrate the differential predictive validity of phoneme awareness over onset-rime awareness, where the tasks used do not require phonological learning, before rejecting Bryant's direct route from rhyme awareness to reading. This paper seeks to extend the literature by carrying out such a study. In addition, as both Muter et al. (1997) and Bryant (2002) note that sample sizes in their studies may limit confidence in conclusions, we explored these questions using a substantially larger sample than reported previously.

> The sample size was considerably increased to provide stronger evidence of predictive patterns. Given that there are likely to be considerable individual differences in the early stages of learning to read, the use of a larger sample of participants potentially allows more scope for the significance of individual predictors to emerge. A large sample is particularly important for regression analysis as results are not reliable with a small sample. A minimum of ten participants is required for each variable entered into the analysis.

A second issue explored in this paper concerns the practical applicability of findings concerning rime and phoneme awareness. Hulme (2002) argues that a demonstration of superior predictive validity for phonemic over onset-rime awareness has important practical utility for screening and prevention. If true, then school-based phonological awareness screening ought to predict learning outcomes in schools. In England currently the National Literacy Strategy provides a nationally standardised system for assessing reading, spelling, writing, and mathematics performance at age 7 (and beyond) and provides teacher assessment of curricular progress in these domains as well as in science. Current predictors used to identify need and allocate resources to schools include proxy measures of socio-economic status (free school meals status), assessment of special educational need, and 'baseline assessment' (typically an academic and behavioural checklist rating given at school entry by teachers). Baseline measures are a modest but significant predictor of later performance (e.g., Strand, 1997, 1999). A combination of pupil background and baseline assessment measures predicts performance to a greater degree than baseline alone (Sammons & Smees, 1998).

Recently Savage and Carless (2004) screened a large sample of 435 five-year-old children using phonological awareness measures including rhyme generation, matching and segmentation and blending tasks. We trained schools learning support assistants (LSAs), employed to support teachers in classrooms, to undertake the phonological awareness screening of whole year 1 cohorts in 9 schools. Results showed that a combined phonological awareness measure was a strong unique predicator of performance at age 7 even *alongside* baseline performance, placement on a stage of a school's register of special needs and (more occasionally) gender. This work can be extended by exploring whether phoneme and/or onset-rime manipulation by school staff can also predict literacy outcomes at age 7, alongside other measures.

The factors that predict learning to read are not only of theoretical importance. Learning to read English can be difficult for some children – in part because English does not have high letter-to-sound correspondence in comparison to Spanish or Italian – and many resources are directed at children who find reading difficult. It is important that reading support targets the appropriate skills. The authors include more general measures that predict how well children get on at school in order to see whether, once these have been accounted for, specific skills still predict reading success. If they do, they are likely to be important at a practical level in the classroom.

Method

Design

All schools in one local authority (equivalent to school district) that had not participated in our previous longitudinal study were asked whether they were interested in taking part in this study. The schools were informed that the study was to be administered by learning support assistants. LSAs were members of staff prior to the study, employed to work with individuals, groups of children, or supporting teachers' whole class objectives. Schools were motivated to participate by the opportunity for their learning support assistants to receive training on phonologically based screening procedures and additional funded time to carry out the screening within schools to aid a programme of early literacy intervention planned in the authority. Involvement in the study was on a first-come-first-served basis.

In this study, the measures of phonological awareness were presented to the children by Learning Support Assistants (LSAs) who had received special training. In research with educational implications, this procedure is often adopted. It has a number of advantages. First, LSAs will be familiar to children in a class and so they will feel relaxed when they do the phonological awareness tasks which can be incorporated into normal classroom activities. Secondly, many more children can be tested because a number of LSAs, working in different schools, can be trained. A third advantage is that it involves schools very directly in the research, making them more likely to agree to participate and enabling them to feed back their experiences to the researchers.

All of the children in year 1 from 8 schools took part in the study. LSAs from participating schools were then given appropriate training on the use of phonological tests and explicit instruction on how to administer them. All phonological testing in the first phase was undertaken in November and December of year 1. Children had therefore experienced three months of formal teaching instruction in the National Literacy Strategy in year 1 at this point.

> Note that all children were tested at a similar time of the year. This is very important in studies of school-based learning where children may show rapid changes in their ability, especially in the early stages of acquiring a new skill. Note that, with the introduction of the National Literacy Strategy, children are given very similar instruction in reading and reading-related activities so effects should be similar from school to school.

For the children in the study, baseline data and additional pupil background data at the time of baseline assessment: a) special educational need (SEN) coding (from 1 – 'currently at-risk' – to 5 – 'statemented' for additional financial support), b) free school meal status, c) gender, and d) mother tongue of the family (each originally submitted in a standard form by all schools) were retrieved from centrally held statistical; records. This was then collated with the phonological awareness measures with support from staff from the statistics department of the local education authority. SEN (on versus not on the register), mother tongue (English or not English), gender, and free school meals (eligible or not eligible) were coded as dichotomous variables.

> There is no discussion of how ethical approval was obtained. The information that was included in the study on free school meal status, home language and statementing for a special educational need could be regarded as sensitive and agreement should be obtained from all parents for the inclusion of data about their child.

No measure of IQ was administered as the measure does not pertain to the research question concerning the relative predictive validity of rime and phoneme manipulation skills. Rime and phoneme manipulation skills are both already known to predict reading even after IQ is controlled (e.g., Bryant et al., 1990; Muter et al., 1997).

> IQ was not included as a measure in this study. The authors justify this by explaining that they are concerned with the relative predictive power of the different phonological awareness tasks. It is still possible that the relationship of IQ to each of the tasks might have been different although the attempt to make the tasks as similar as possible, in terms of their cognitive demands, should have reduced this possibility. Given that the phonological awareness tasks were administered by LSAs, it would have been impractical to gain standardised IQ measures as the administration of an IQ test requires specific training. There could also be ethical issues in making such information available to people who taught the children.

Participants

There were 419 children in the phonological awareness testing sessions. Their mean age was 5 years and 8 months when phonological awareness measures were taken. At the time of testing at age 7 years 3 months, when Key Stage 1 results were collected, 354 children were still available. Missing sample test scores at age 7 were initially cross-referenced with and collated across all participating schools to maximise the number of original sample children followed up. The modest loss in sample (15.5 per cent of the original sample over two school years) was thus due to children leaving the borough. There were 189 boys and 165 girls in this sample.

Materials

Measures administered at age 5

Baseline assessment for all children in these schools was collected using the Infant Index (Desforges & Lindsay, 1995), within 7 weeks of children entering school. The 'basic' sub-scale of this test rather than the combined baseline score (which includes a socio-behavioural rating) was used, as our previous research (Savage & Carless, 2004) showed that the basic subscale was a superior predictor of performance at age 7. The basic subscale asks teachers to rate early reading, writing, spelling and maths behaviour. In the Reading sub-section, for example, a low score of 1 is obtained if a child chooses to pick up books and 'works through them in the appropriate sequence', a score of 2 is achieved if letters within words can be identified correctly, whereas a high score of 3 is obtained if they can 'read from a simple scheme book or simple story book.' The test has acceptable reliability (Cronbach's alpha = .92, Lindsay & Desforges, 1999).

Given that 5-year-old children will vary considerably in their reading and other skills when they enter school, it is important to assess these at the start of the study and not assume that they will be the same. The baseline measures involve simple rating scales that are completed by the class teacher.

As some concerns about the reliability and construct validity of oddity and other detection tasks have frequently been raised (e.g., Hulme, 2002; Oakhill & Kyle, 2000; Snowling, Hulme, Smith, & Thomas, 1994), explicit phoneme and onset-rime segmentation and blending tasks were used to measure onset-rime and phoneme awareness. Such tasks are good predictors of early reading (Seymour & Evans, 1994). Seymour & Evans (1994) report that children find the phoneme segmentation tasks harder than the blending tasks. The present phonological awareness tests were generated by the experimenters. As children thus carried out the same kind of phonological operation on materials, extraneous factors are controlled. In order to control for possible linguistic aspects of the stimuli themselves, children segmented and blended exactly the same words in onset-rime tasks and phoneme teaks. A full list of stimuli is given in the appendix.

> *There are a number of different ways that phonological awareness can be assessed and these have been shown to place different cognitive demands on children. This study uses two types of task, segmentation and blending. These can be seen as mirrors of one another as segmentation involves splitting a word into its component sounds while blending involves putting together sounds to form a word. Both tasks can be used for onsets and rimes (/c/ + /at/) and for phonemes (/c/ + /a/ + /t/). Since both tasks can be difficult for children to understand, it is important to use practice trials and give feedback so that children are confident with the tasks before the experimental trials begin.*

Segmenting and blending

In the onset-rime blending task, children were told by their LSA: 'I'm going to pretend to be a robot and I can only say words in a funny way, like this: /m/–/at/'. Children were told:' I want you to slide the sounds together and see if you can make them into a word, like this/m/–/at/. Slide the sounds together and say/mat/'. If the child did not respond, then the LSA completed the task for the child. A similar procedure was followed for the next practice item. Twelve experimental trials then followed. Six of the blending tasks required blending onsets and rimes and 6 required blending phonemes. The phoneme blending task resembled the onset-rime blending task except that children were asked to blend all three phonemes (/m/–/a/ –/t/). Two additional practice trials were given prior to this task.

Unless otherwise stated, the protocol for the segmentation tasks was similar to that for the blending tasks. In the onset-rime segmentation task children were told: 'I want you to sound like a robot. I'm going to say a word and I want you to break the word into two parts. If I say 'pat' you would say/p//at/'. The LSA indicated the two parts by tapping their finger on the table. Children were then given the words 'pat' and 'bag' to segment into onsets and rimes. Similar instructions were given for phoneme segmentation, except that children were instructed to break the word into three parts. In all phonological awareness tasks, finger-tap cues were given if children did not respond, and feedback and modeling of successful answers were also given in the practice trials only, so that children understood the task. Unlike Hulme et al. (2002), no corrective feedback was given in the *experimental* phase of the task, so results here cannot be due to 'phonological learning'. Scores for blending and segmenting were combined to create phoneme manipulation scores and onset-rime manipulation scores. The Spearman-Brown internal reliabilities of the two tests were .83 and .89 respectively.

Early literacy screening

Three tests of early reading were also included: reading and spelling of six regular consonant-vowel-consonant words and pronouncing 12 CVC nonwords. The scores from the word and nonword reading and the spelling screening test were combined to create an early reading skills score.

A number of measures were used to see how well children could read and write when the phonological awareness measures were taken. For very early reading, standardised tests are not appropriate because they do not produce sufficient discrimination among children who can read and write a small number of words.

Nonsense-word reading

In the nonsense word reading task, children were asked to read twelve nonsense words. Six of these words were designed to be high rime neighbourhood non-words such as 'dat', sharing orthographic rimes with many real words (e.g., 'bat', 'cat', 'hat' etc.) and six were designed to be low or no-rime neighbourhood words such as 'tav'. They were constructed so that across the two non-word types exactly the same letter-to-sound correspondences occurred. Stimuli were chosen so that all short vowels were represented. The Spearman-Brown internal reliability of this test was .96 (see Savage, Carless, & Stuart, 2003, for further details on the construction of these items). In the screening phases of the study the non-words were presented on two pages, with six non-words per page in large bold font. Children were asked to read out loud these 'made-up' words after an example word was first modelled by the experimenter.

Reading and spelling

All children were asked to read six words (at, had, let, dig, cut, top) and to write six words (sat, hop, but, red, win, leg). Words were spoken one at a time by the experimenter. There were six experimental trials in each of the reading and spelling tasks. The Spearman-Brown internal reliabilities of the reading and spelling tests were .92 and .91 respectively.

Procedure

LSA training

The LSA training took place during a single morning. In each participating school, a class teacher also attended the training sessions, in order to familiarise them with the project and allow them to oversee implementation. All LSAs were assembled and first taught about the generic elements of the assessments, and the differences between onset-rime and phoneme assessment. Written step-by-step standard instructions for test administration were also disseminated. A strong emphasis was placed upon the need for integrity and accuracy in scoring correct answers for phoneme and onset-rime measures. LSAs then had an opportunity to explore and evaluate the materials, clarify the assessments and trial them informally. Researchers also visited schools before and during the assessments to clarify tasks as necessary.

Phonological and reading tests

Children were seen alone on two occasions at age 5. Tasks were presented by schools' own LSAs in one of two orders in this study; the LSAs were unaware of the theoretical purposes of the study. The design of this study thus provided a double-blind control. In session A the children completed the onset-rime blending and segmenting task and spelling. In session B children completed the phoneme segmentation and blending and word and nonsense word reading tasks. There was typically about five days between each assessment. Order of task presentation was counterbalanced: in half of the schools children experienced session A and then session B; in the other half of the schools they took session B then session A.

Measure administered at age 7

Key Stage 1 data at age 7 was collected by schools in the standard fashion for this national test. Most children complete a nationally standardised reading comprehension test, mathematics test, handwriting and spelling test under government-specified examination conditions. These tests are designed to have good psychometric properties, and are developed following 2 trials usually with a sample of over 2000 nationally representative children. The test content always relates directly to the relevant part of the National Curriculum which all teachers are currently instructed to plan and teach. All schools receive standardised instructions for explaining and using the tests, and test-administration is audited (Qualifications and Curriculum Authority, 2002).

> *Literacy measures at age 7 made use of Key Stage 1 assessments. These are used across all state schools (and some private schools) in England and Wales and they provide information about children's performance in literacy, maths and science in relation to peers. The authors make use of children's scores in these tests as well as teacher assessments.*

The reading comprehension test requires short answer and multiple choice responses to short passages above the questions. Typically, questions require retrieval or information from the text, but some questions require simple inferences about events and characters. This sort of test is appropriate as phonological awareness is an excellent predictor of reading comprehension and reading accuracy (e.g., Bradley & Bryant, 1985). Some children perceived by the teacher to be unlikely to succeed in the formal comprehension test are disapplied from the reading comprehension test and given a teacher-administered 'Reading Task' without examination conditions prevailing.

The reliability of this test (Cronbach's alpha) is .87 at level 2 and .78 at level 3. Some children may sit both reading tests. The spelling task involved accurately spelling frequent monosyllabic words such as 'book', 'tray', 'apple', 'plate' and occasionally multi-syllable words such as 'telephone' and 'happened'. The reliability of this test (Cronbach's alpha) is .94. The mathematics task assesses a basic range of operations and abilities, for example with number, shape, and logical relationships. The reliability of this test (Cronbach's alpha) is .90.

The Reading Task is a graded miscue analysis ('running record') of children's text reading with a teacher, evaluated against standard criteria. In addition at Key Stage 1, a teacher's assessment of each child's current global attainment in English, Maths and Science measured against the expected average performance of children in the National Curriculum is required. Data in the form of numbers of children achieving results at levels 'working towards 1', 1, 2 and 3 of the curriculum, alongside a sub-division of level 2 into A, B, and C (representing degree of 'security' of skills at this level), are recorded for the school and the local authority, A score of 2 would represent expected typical performance, a '3' represents somewhat above average performance, and '1' represents somewhat below average performance. The proportions of children sitting tests give a measure of the sample size for each measure and level.

Results

The first aspect of results was to explore the distribution of the data. The mean score for the baseline assessment was 11.46 (SD = 3.91). Consultation of the Infant Index norms showed that around 60 per cent of children in the standardisation sample would score below this point, suggesting a reasonably close match between the current and the standardisation sample. The Infant Index sample was also drawn solely from one English local education authority, rather than being a nationally representative sample. There was three missing data for the phoneme manipulation scores and two missing data for the onset-rime manipulation scores due to pupil absences. Scores are thus based on $n = 351$ across phonological manipulation tests. The mean score for the onset-rime manipulation task was 7.69 (SD = 4.07). For the phoneme manipulation task it was 7.62 (SD = 4.55). Scores on the two tests were therefore very similar, as might be predicted from a curriculum where onset-rime and phoneme awareness skills are both explicitly taught. A paired samples t-test showed that there was no significant difference between onset-rime and phoneme manipulation scores, $t (350) = .46$, n.s.

Scores on the baseline measure indicated that children in the sample were representative of children attending school in England.

The scores for the phoneme and onset-rime manipulation sub-tasks were also broken down by performance on the segmentation and blending tasks. Preliminary analyses showed no order effects on attainment in segmentation or blending tasks. Mean scores on the segmentation task were 3.07 (SD = 2.70) for onset-rimes and 3.37 (SD = 2.49) for phonemes. A paired samples *t*-test showed that this difference between onset-rime and phoneme manipulation scores was significant, t (350) = −4.82, p < .001. Mean scores on the blending task were 4.62 (SD = 2.03) for onset-rimes and 3.89 (SD = 2.33) for phonemes. A paired samples *t*-test showed that this difference between onset-rime and phoneme manipulation scores was significant, t (351) = 9.38, p < .001. This pattern of facility for onset-rimes in blending tasks and for phonemes in segmentation tasks replicates the pattern first reported by Seymour and Evans (1994).

> *For the segmentation tasks, scores on the phoneme task were significantly higher than for the onset-rime task but, for the blending tasks, there was a significant effect in the opposite direction. Such differences are likely to arise from the choice of stimuli.*

The distributions of test scores at age 7 on the Key Stage 1 tests are depicted in Table 1. The proportions of children achieving expected outcomes (level 2) at each stage of national testing was compared against national norms for 5 tested areas (reading comprehension, spelling, writing, maths and science teacher assessment). A χ^2 analysis was run comparing the observed proportions of children achieving at least a level 2 against national expected proportions of children achieving at least a level 2. Analysis showed there was no sign of significant difference between sample and national distribution of test results, χ^2 (4) = .96, n.s.

> *Like the baseline scores, the Key Stage 1 results were in line with national results, indicating that the sample in the study was representative.*

Concurrent prediction of reading

The means and correlations between onset-rime and phoneme awareness measures, baseline assessment ('basic' sub-scale) and early reading skills on the literacy screening measure are depicted in Table 2. Baseline basic scale scores, early reading skill scores and both phonological awareness test scores were moderately but significantly inter-correlated. The phoneme manipulation measure was the strongest predictor of early reading skill.

Table 1   *Percentages of children reaching different stages of Key Stage 1 reading, spelling, writing, science and maths assessments*

Assessment	Reading test	Reading task	Spelling	Writing
1	No test	15.0	No test	10.7
2	50.8	52.5	44.6	71.9
3 or above	29.4	No test	24.6	12.7
2/3 not given	19.8	32.5	30.8	4.3
Assessment test	Maths assessment	Science teacher-assessment	English teacher-assessment	Maths teacher-assessment
1	9.9	13.2	15.4	12.7
2	52.3	51.1	56.8	51.1
3 or above	35.6	33.6	24.3	34.2
2/3 not given	2.2	2.1	3.5	2.0

Table 2   *Correlations between phonological awareness and early literacy screening tasks at age 5*

	2	3	4
Phoneme manipulation	.76	.43	.81
Onset-rime manipulation	.49	.65	
Basic baseline score	.45		
Early literacy screening			

Note: All correlations are significant at $p < .01$.

The analysis is divided into two parts, looking at concurrent predictors of literacy and longitudinal predictors. As in Paper 11, a hierarchical regression analysis was used to determine concurrent predictors. Baseline scores were entered as Step 1, accounting for 20 per cent of the variance. Then onset-rime and phoneme manipulation scores (combining across the segmentation and blending tasks) were entered in two different orders. When onset-rime scores were entered second they accounted for a further 24 per cent of the variance and the addition of the phoneme manipulation scores accounted for a further 23 per cent of the variance. When the order was reversed, phoneme manipulation accounted for a huge 47 per cent of the variance and no further variance was accounted for when onset-rime scores were added.

In order to explore the relative ability of onset-rime and phoneme skills to predict concurrent reading ability, a hierarchical linear regression analysis was run considering all of the continuous variables. The combined early literacy measure was the dependent variable and the order of entry of phoneme and onset-rime manipulation entered at steps 2 and 3 was rotated after the 'basic' sub-scale of baseline assessment was entered at step 1. This analysis is displayed in Table 3.

This analysis shows that onset-rime and phoneme manipulation are significant predictors of reading at step 2, whereas only phoneme manipulation is a strong unique predictor of early literacy skills when entered at step 3 after onset-rime manipulation skills and baseline ability. This suggests that phoneme manipulation is a better predictor of reading at age 5 than onset-rime manipulation is.

Longitudinal prediction of reading, spelling and writing

The main issue was to explore the predictive validity of rime and phoneme-based phonological tests. Our previous research (Savage & Carless, 2004) had identified that gender, special educational needs (SEN) status, and the 'basic' (academic competencies) sub-scale of the baseline test score predicted aspects of outcomes at age 7 and so were included here. A measure of socio-economic status (free school meals) was also entered. Preliminary analyses of the present data also indicated that only 4 per cent of the sample did not have English as a mother tongue. Nevertheless, the 'mother tongue' variable also predicted some variance in later performance and so was included in this study as a dichotomous variable (English versus not English). These variables were entered in hierarchical regression analyses prior to entering onset-rime and phoneme awareness measures, allowing evaluation of the unique contribution of each variable at each step of regression analyses.

Table 3 *Hierarchical regression analysis predicting early literacy screening task at age 5 from phonological awareness and baseline measures*

DV: Step	IV	Early literacy R^2 change
1	Baseline	.20***
2	Onset-rime manipulation	.24***
3	Phoneme manipulation	.23***
2	Phoneme manipulation	.47***
3	Onset-rime manipulation	.00

*Note:*** = $p < .001$.

In order for analyses to attain appropriate goodness of fit – without the need to eliminate or amalgamate any independent variables in an unprincipled fashion resulting from the cross-tabulation of relatively small categories (such as SEN and free school meals) – binary rather then multinomial logistic regression analyses were run. This analysis required dependent variables to have a bivariate structure. Where necessary therefore, two analyses of National Curriculum performance were run, contrasting first level 1 versus level 2 and then level 2 versus level 3. For the purposes of these analyses, subdivisions of level 2 performance (2A, 2B, 2C) were ignored.

Since the outcome measures (dependent variables) were levels attained on the Key Stage 1 tests, a binary regression was used. Two versions of the regression analysis were carried out, one contrasting Level 1 (below average) with Level 2 (average) and one contrasting Level 2 with Level 3 (above average).

The predictors of Key Stage 1 test performance for reading tasks are depicted in section 1 of Table 4. Regression analyses show the two phonological awareness measures, baseline performance and all available pupil background data. Across analyses, it is clear that SEN and the baseline measure were frequently significant predictors of outcome, replicating patterns reported previously (Savage & Carless, 2004), while gender and free school meals (FSM) were modest and occasional predictors. Boys performed less well than girls, and children entitled to free school meals performed less well than those not entitled to free school meals.

In line with previous research, both gender and home background were modest predictors of literacy outcomes at age 7 and baseline measures and statement of special educational need were stronger predictors. All these measures were entered into the regression analyses and then the phoneme and onset-rime measures were entered in turn, again in the two possible orders.

Turning to the main contrast of interest – the phonological awareness measures – the three sub-sections of Table 4 show the results for the reading comprehension test, the reading task, and two teacher assessments of reading. Inspection of the analyses in each case shows that phoneme manipulation predicted all four measures of outcome in reading at step 6 after baseline assessment and pupil background measures were first controlled, and phoneme manipulation continued to predict all reading measures at step 7 after onset-rime manipulation was entered. In contrast, onset-rime manipulation, while a good predictor of reading measures at step 6 after baseline and pupil background data were entered, was not a significant predictor of outcome at step 7 for any reading measure after phoneme manipulation was first entered at step 6.

This table is complicated because it shows the pattern of predictions for children's scores on each of the literacy measures. The overall patterns are rather similar across outcome measures so I will use reading comprehension as an example. Here, the first five measures account for a total of 20 per cent of the variance. If onset-rime manipulation is entered as the next step, it accounts for an additional 7 per cent of the variance. Entering phoneme awareness as the final step accounts for a further 6 per cent. Both steps account for a significant increase in variance but it is striking that this pattern did not hold when the order of entering scores from the two phonological awareness tasks was reversed. Phoneme manipulation accounted for 12 per cent of the variance on its own

Table 4 *Hierarchical regressions predicting Key Stage 1 Literacy assessments at age 7 from measures at age 5*

Section 1: Reading

DV: Reading comprehension

Step	IV	R² change	DV: Reading task R² change	DV: Reading TA 1 vs. 2 R² change	DV: Reading TA 2 vs. 3
1	Gender	.03*	.01	.00	.05**
2	FSM	.01	.03*	.03*	.02**
3	M-Tongue	.00	.04	.01	.00
4	SEN	.07**	.24**	.31***	.06**
5	Basic	.09***	.07**	.06***	.15***
6	O-R	.07***	.03*	.05***	.07***
7	Phon	.06***	.05***	.03*	.04**
6	Phon	.12***	.07*	.08***	.10***
7	O-R	.01	.01	.00	.01

Section 2: Spelling and writing

DV: Spelling task

Step	IV	R² change	DV: Writing task level 1 vs. 2 R² change	DV: Writing task level 2 vs. 3
1	Gender	.02	.03*	.01
2	FSM	.00	.03*	.10
3	M-Tongue	.01	.02	.00
4	SEN	.04*	.17***	.06*
5	Basic	.12***	.03*	.08***
6	O-R	.07***	.01	.05**
7	Phon	.03**	.00	.03*
6	Phon	.09***	.01	.07**
7	O-R	.01	.00	.01

Note: * = $p < .05$. ** = $p < .01$. *** = $p < .001$.
Key: TA = Teacher-assessed; Gender = Gender of child; FSM = Free school meals eligibility; M-tongue = Mother tongue of family; SEN = Special Educational Need; Basic = Infant Index baseline 'basic' sub-scale; O-R = Onset-rime manipulation; Phon = Phoneme manipulation.

and entering rime-onset manipulation does not produce a significant increase. Looking across the entire table, it can be seen that this pattern is repeated for all of the literacy outcome measures except the comparison of Level 1 and Level 2 writing.

The predictors of Key Stage 1 test performance for spelling and writing are depicted in section 2 of Table 4. The three sets of analyses show the results for spelling and writing (levels 1 versus 2 and levels 2 versus 3 respectively). Inspection of the analyses shows that baseline assessment and SEN were significant predictors of spelling and writing outcome across the assessments, with children on the register of special educational needs less likely to achieve the higher grades in these tasks. Gender and free school meals predicted writing at levels 1 versus 2, with boys performing less well than girls and children eligible for free school meals performing more poorly than those not eligible for free school meals. Importantly, even after controlling for the effects of these variables, phoneme manipulation was a strong predictor for writing at levels 2 versus 3 and for spelling, when entered at step 6 and when entered after onset-rime manipulation at step 7. Onset-rime awareness was a significant unique predictor at step 6 of regressions, but was never a significant predictor, when entered after phoneme manipulation at step 7.

The predictors of Key Stage 1 test performance for maths are depicted in section 1 of Table 5 for the maths test, and maths teacher assessment (levels 1 versus 2 and levels 2 versus 3 respectively). Inspection of the table shows that baseline assessment and SEN status were again significant predictors of all maths assessments at age 7. Free school meals was also a significant predictor of maths test and teacher-assessment at the 1 versus 2 levels, with children not eligible for free school meals more likely to achieve higher grades in mathematics. After controlling for the effects of these extraneous variables, phonemic awareness entered at step 6 was also a modest but significant predictor of all maths test performance at step 6, and when entered after onset-rime manipulation at step 7. Onset-rime manipulation, while often predicting at step 6, was not a significant predictor of mathematics at age 7 after phoneme manipulation was first entered.

A somewhat similar picture existed for maths, with phoneme manipulation being a stronger predictor of attainment at 7 than onset-rime manipulation. When entered as the final variable in the regression analysis, the latter was not a significant predictor of any of the mathematics scores. Interestingly, the same pattern also existed for Level 2 versus Level 3 science.

The predictors of Key Stage 1 test performance for science teacher assessment are depicted in section 2 of Table 5. Inspection of this table shows that SEN and baseline assessment was a significant predictor of science proficiency ratings. Onset-rime manipulation but not phoneme manipulation score was a significant predictor of outcome at age 7 for teacher-rated science proficiency at level 1 versus level 2, with phoneme but not onset-rime manipulation predicting performance at level 2 versus 3.

In order to provide the most stringent test of the utility of a predictor of reading, the predictive validity of a measure can be evaluated after controlling for initial reading levels at age 5. Such analyses are highly conservative (e.g., Hulme, 2002) but are nevertheless useful in identifying possible causal predictors of reading (e.g., Wagner et al., 1997). This analysis also

Table 5 *Hierarchical regressions predicting Key Stage 1 maths assessments at age 7 from measures at age 5*

Section 1: Mathematics

Step	IV	DV: Maths test 1 vs. 2 R^2 change	DV: Maths test 2 vs. 3 R^2 change	DV: Maths TA 1 vs. 2 R^2 change	Maths TA 2 vs. 3 R^2 change
1	Gender	.00	.00	.00	.00
2	FSM	.06**	.00	.04*	.01
3	M-Tongue	.01	.02	.00	.02
4	SEN	.27***	.14***	.35***	.10***
5	Basic	.10***	.09***	.07***	.16***
6	O-R	.01	.04**	.05**	.02*
7	Phon	.04*	.02*	.03*	.02*
6	Phon	.04*	.05***	.08***	.04**
7	O-R	.01	.01	.00	.00

Section 2: Science teacher assessment

Step	IV	DV: Science teacher assessed level 1 vs. 2 R^2 change	DV: Science teacher assessed level 1 vs. 3 R^2 change
1	Gender	.00	.00
2	FSM	.04	.01
3	M-Tongue	.02	.00
4	SEN	.23***	.09***
5	Basic	.14***	.06***
6	O-R	.03*	.04**
7	Phon	.00	.02**
6	Phon	.02	.06***
7	O-R	.01	.00

Note: $* = p < .05$; $** = p < .01$; $*** = p < .001$.
Key: TA = Teacher-assessed; Gender = Gender of child; FSM = Free school meals eligibility; M-tongue = Mother tongue of family; SEN = Special Educational Need; Basic = Infant Index baseline 'basic' sub-scale; O-R = Onset-rime manipulation; Phon = Phoneme manipulation.

allows an evaluation of the specificity of the link between phonemic aware-ness and reading. In the analyses reported so far, phoneme awareness pre-dicts reading outcomes most strongly, but it also predicts several mathematics and science performance measures. An obvious explanation for this might be that all curricular tasks are linked to phoneme awareness indirectly through early reading ability.

> A further statistical control in longitudinal designs is to enter scores for the outcome vari-able at Time1 (age 5 in this study) into the regression model. This allows a researcher to test for specific and direct effects of a variable since the analysis assesses the extent to which a variable can predict the change from Time1 to Time2 in an outcome variable. It removes indirect effects such as the possibility that phoneme awareness affects read-ing at Time1 which, in turn, affects reading at Time2.

This theory suggests that controlling for reading ability should eliminate the link between phoneme awareness and mathematics and science tasks whereas the specific association between phoneme awareness and later reading (and possibly writing) should in some cases still be evident if phoneme awareness plays a causal role in reading acquisition. Table 6 therefore depicts regression analyses where the same individual and pupil variables reported above were again entered as steps 1–5 in analyses, but where additionally, early literacy screening score at age 5 is entered at step 6. Phoneme awareness and onset-rime awareness measures were then entered together as the final predictors at steps 7 and 8 of analyses.

Inspection of the results of this additional analysis in Table 6 showed that phoneme manipulation no longer predicts any of the maths or science tasks when entered after early reading. This finding is predicted from the view that maths and science performance is linked to phoneme awareness indirectly via the development of basic reading skills. In contrast, phoneme manipulation still predicted reading comprehension at age 7, teacher assessment of reading at level 2 versus 3 and writing at level 1 versus 2 even after early reading ability at age 6 was entered alongside baseline skills and pupil background data, consistent with the view that phoneme manipulation skills play a specific causal role in reading acquisition.

The effects of this final control of taking account of literacy at Time1 are very marked in that the predictive power of phoneme awareness remains for reading and writing (though the size of the effect is reduced as one might expect) but disappears for maths and science. As the authors note, this is a very stringent test which means that significant effects have to be very robust to remain.

Discussion

This research sought to establish whether explicit onset-rime manipulation predicts reading at age 7 independent of both phoneme manipulation and baseline skills and pupil background measures that are routinely used in schools. In order to establish findings with greater certainly we made sure to use the same segmentation and blending tasks to measure onset-rime and phoneme manipulation so that the effects of extraneous task demands on performance are minimised (Bryant, 2002). To this same end, children carried out onset-rime and phoneme segmentation and blending tasks with the same word stimulus set to control for potential confounds from the linguistic structure of the words manipulated. Our tasks did not require phonological learning but were 'static' measures of current ability. Furthermore, the order of phonological task administration was counterbalanced and task administrators as well as children themselves were blind to the theoretical purposes of the study. The phonological tasks both had good internal reliabilities. With these

Table 6 *Seven-step hierarchical regressions predicting Key Stage 1 at age 7 from measures at age 5 (controlling early literacy screening at age 5)*

Section 1: Reading

DV: Reading comprehension Step	IV	R² change	Reading task DV R² change	Reading TA 1 vs. 2 R² change	Reading TA 2 vs. 3 R² change
6	Early lilt	.30***	.09***	.11***	.25***
7	O-R	.00	.00	.00	.00
8	Phon	.02*	.00	.00	.02*
7	Phon	.02*	.00	.00	.02
8	O-R	.00	.00	.00	.00

Section 2: Spelling and writing

DV: Spelling task	IV	R² change	DV: Writing task level 1 vs. 2 R² change	DV: Writing task level 2 vs. 3 R² change
6	Early lit	.26***	.06**	.20**
7	O-R	.00	.00	.00
8	Phon	.01	.02*	.01
7	Phon	.01	.02	.01
8	O-R	.00	.00	.00

Section 3: Mathematics

DV: Maths test level 1 vs. 2 Step	IV	R² change	Maths test level 2 vs. 3 R² change	Maths TA 1 vs. 2 R² change	Maths TA 2 vs. 3 R² change
6	Early lit	.05*	.12***	.09**	.10***
7	O-R	.00	.00	.00	.01
8	Phon	.01	.01	.00	.00
7	Phon	.01	.00	.00	.01
8	O-R	.01	.00	.00	.00

Section 4: Science

DV: Science TA level 1 vs. 2 Step	IV	R² change	Science TA level 2 vs. 3 R² change
6	Early lit	.05**	.15***
7	O-R	.00	.00
8	Phon	.01	.01
7	Phon	.00	.01
8	O-R	.01	.00

Note: * = $p < .05$. ** = $p < .01$. *** = $p < .001$.
Key: Early lit = Early literacy screening; O-R = Onset-rime manipulation; Phon = Phoneme manipulation.

controls in place, our analyses were very clear in showing that while both onset-rime and phonemic manipulation abilities predicted reading at age 5, onset-rime manipulation did not predict early reading after phoneme manipulation was first entered in regressions after baseline, whereas phoneme manipulation predicted significant variance in early reading after onset-rime manipulation was first entered.

Longitudinally our analyses were also very clear in showing the relative predictive validity of onset-rime versus phoneme measures. Analyses showed that, after controlling for a range of individual and environmental pupil-related measures and baseline achievement tests routinely used by schools, and after control for onset-rime manipulation, phoneme manipulation predicted all four measures of later reading attainment, usually strongly. In contrast, the onset-rime manipulation measure did not predict any measures of reading at age 7 after pupil background, baseline data and phoneme manipulation were controlled. Regression analyses also showed that phoneme manipulation predicted all mathematics and some science assessments as well at age 7, though generally less strongly than they predicted reading. This profuse predictive power for phoneme manipulation for science and maths may be because teacher assessments of general 'ability' are often closely related to underlying literacy skills (Pretzlik, Olsson, Nabuco, & Cruz, 2003).

> The authors suggest that the predictive power of phoneme manipulation for maths and science scores at age 7 may lie in the fact that teacher ratings of ability are influenced by children's literacy skills. It is also likely that literacy skills are related in a general way to science and maths performance since being better at reading and writing makes it easier to do well in science and maths, both of which demand increasing literacy skills as children get older. Thus the link from phoneme manipulation to science and maths could be indirect via literacy. Such an indirect relationship will disappear when reading at Time1 is accounted for in the model.

Consistent with this explanation, stringent additional analyses controlling for early reading skills at age 5 showed that phoneme manipulation no longer predicted any mathematics or science assessments at age 7, but importantly did still predict reading comprehension, and teacher-assessed reading and writing at age 7. This finding that the effect of phoneme manipulation is evident in 2 of 4 reading measures at age 7, even in conservative analyses where reading ability at age 5 is also controlled, and after 5 pupil background and behaviour measures are also first controlled, is all the more impressive given the fact that the early reading screening measure was made up of nonsense words and regular CVC words that were themselves very strongly correlated with phonemic awareness at age 5. This analysis shows that the predictive association between phoneme manipulation skills at age 5 and reading at age 7 cannot simply be a consequence of early reading skills.

The results of this study are therefore consistent with the view that there is a strong and probably causal link between early explicit phoneme manipulation skills and later reading (Bryant, 2002; Hulme, 2002; Hulme et al., 2002). Our results are, however, less consistent with the view that there is an additional direct route between early onset-rime manipulation and later reading. In this sense our results accord with the views advanced by Hulme et al. (2002) on the basis of their findings. On the basis of the present data we cannot conclude that either phoneme awareness or rime awareness is a unique predictor of spelling ability at age 7. The reasons for the absence of an association here are somewhat unclear. Data from our other recent longitudinal study (Savage & Carless, 2004) nevertheless show that more general early screening measures that include *both* phonological awareness and word and nonsense word decoding tasks are amongst the strongest predictors of spelling available.

Our second more general aim was to look at the practical utility of phoneme and onset-rime manipulation tasks and early reading screening tasks as unique predictors of school literacy outcomes alongside a far wider range of pupil and environmental factors than has been explored before. The current results also confirm that phoneme manipulation (but not onset-rime manipulation) tasks are, alongside brief screening of early decoding skills, of practical utility in prediction and early identification of reading problems. Together, phoneme manipulation measures explained as much as 12 per cent of unique variance in outcome measures at age 7 reading comprehension, even after pupil background and baseline skills.

Another issue raised recently concerns the extent to which we can predict reading failure and intervene accordingly as well as predict reading success (Bowey, 2002). This is clearly a pressing issue for researchers and practitioners alike. We would argue that we probably need to cast our net as wide as possible to answer this question. Of the additional predictors we explored here, two predictors, baseline score and SEN status, were highly consistent in their effects. We confirm our recent finding that the Infant Index (Desforges & Lindsay, 1995) is a reliable predictor of later achievement across curriculum areas (English, Maths and Science) and mode of assessment (formal examination versus teacher-assessment). Teacher-screening, using well-designed and reliable early academic checklists, is clearly a helpful way of identifying possible future need. Similarly, early identification of children's possible special educational needs, signalled by placement on a school's 'register of special needs', is also an effective predictor of outcome. Modest–sized effects of gender and free school meal status were also sometimes evident, with boys and children eligible for free school meals performing more poorly.

Our combined data show that together with baseline and pupil background data, phonemic awareness is a very good predictor both of reading success *and* of relative reading difficulty. The hierarchical regression models we report, which included baseline data, pupil background, and phonemic skills, correctly predicted between 80 and 90 per cent of both the average versus above-average classifications of children at age 7 for reading. Similar proportions of correct classifications were evident in the average versus below-average reader comparisons. Thus, such combined information about cognitive, behavioural and pupil background data can inform early *preventative* interventions. These may include whole-school approaches as well as appropriate individual teaching and learning experiences.

The authors argue for a strong and direct link between the ability to manipulate phonemes and the development of literacy skills. Their measure of phoneme manipulation (segmentation and blending) at age 5, together with information about home background and baseline data on ability at school entry, correctly predicted which children would achieve Level 2 in their Key Stage 1 assessment and which would achieve Level 3 in over 80 per cent of cases; and there was similar success in predicting below average versus above average achievement. They go on to point out the potential diagnostic value of a measure of phoneme manipulation for identifying children who are likely to experience problems in learning to read.

Together the findings provide some optimism for those interested in early identification of learning needs. From a clinical perspective, results show which school-based assessments are important, what sorts of phonological assessment measures should be used in clinical assessment to predict risk of literacy difficulties, and possibly suggest ways consultants might support schools and teachers to develop *preventative* models of assessment and intervention. The evidence on the efficacy of early phonological awareness training on reading is strong (see Ehri et al., 2001, for a meta-analytic review). Our take-home point for clinical professionals is therefore that, alongside school-based assessments, assessing phoneme manipulation skills provides an accurate early identification system with the potential to prevent many literacy problems.

Correspondence to

Robert Savage, Department of Educational and Counselling Psychology, Faculty of Education, 3700 McTavish Street, McGill University, Montreal, Canada H3A 1Y2; Email: Robert.savage@mcgill.ca

Appendix

Onset-rime and phoneme blending		Onset-rime and phoneme setmentation	
win	keep	man	check
hot	shake	log	pun
red	cut	pit	meet

Nonsense words	
High *n*	**Low *n***
dat	tav
mip	pid
ved	dem
gop	pon
fug	gul
lan	gaf

6

EXPLORING ATYPICAL DEVELOPMENT

The three papers in this final chapter are all concerned with the abilities of children whose development is in some way atypical. I have chosen these papers because each raises rather different issues about atypical development.

The issues raised by the next study follow on from those discussed in Paper 10. This illustrated how early intervention can often reduce the severity of children's early reading problems. Children who find difficulty in learning to identify and manipulate phonemes and relate phonemes to letters can be supported in the development of these skills and, as a consequence, make better progress in learning to read than they might otherwise have done. However, such support will only work for some children. Other children will continue to have problems with reading. Indeed, some children may appear to be good readers at the outset but begin to fall behind as reading progresses.

One reason for such a developmental trajectory, in which an initially age-appropriate rate of progress is followed by a slowing down in progress, can occur when new skills are demanded in a task. Reading initially involves the recognition of single words which, in an alphabetic script like English, involves knowing about phonemes, letters and the relationship between them. However, as reading progresses, new skills become important. These include the ability to interpret complex clauses and to connect ideas across clauses and sentences in order to understand text. Some children are good are reading words or, as it is often expressed, they have good decoding skills. However, they find it difficult to understand text. This has serious educational consequences because, as children move up through school, they are required to understand more and more complex text. The next study investigates the difficulties encountered by children who are good at reading single words but struggle with text.

British Journal of Development Psychology, 1999, 17, 295–312

Ways of reading: How knowledge and use of strategies are related to reading comprehension

Kate Cain

University of Sussex

The main aim of this study was to investigate the use of metacognitive knowledge in the reading of text by children with a specific difficulty in reading comprehension. Such children are characterised as having normal (i.e. age-appropriate) reading at the single-word level and a good understanding of individual clauses (as evidenced by syntactic understanding) but they have a below-age ability to understand text. In particular, they find it hard to answer questions about a text they have just read. This paper considers whether children showing poor comprehension differ from matched controls in their knowledge of the goals and processes of reading and skill in applying such knowledge. The general idea is that children with less-skilled comprehension might have difficulty in varying their reading strategies from situation to situation, especially when a text is difficult to read.

Successful understanding of a text, the ultimate aim of reading, is dependent upon several different skills. As a result, many different sources of reading comprehension failure have been proposed, for example: phonological processing difficulties (Shankweiler, 1989); word-level deficits (Perfetti, 1985); sentence-level deficits (Cromer, 1970; Isakson & Miller, 1976); and higher level deficits such as poor inference-making ability (Oakhill, 1982, 1984). The population of interest in this study is children whose reading (and listening) comprehension difficulties appear to stem from the discourse level of processing. These children are fluent accurate readers who do not demonstrate any significant phonological (Stothard & Hulme, 1995) or syntactic difficulties (Yuill & Oakhill, 1991; but see Stothard & Hulme, 1992). However, such children do experience difficulty in answering questions about texts that they have just read (Yuill & Oakhill, 1991).

Skilled and less skilled comprehenders differ on a wide range of higher level reading-related skills (see Yuill & Oakhill, 1991, for a review). The purpose of the current study was to investigate precisely how one of these proposed higher level sources of comprehension failure, meta-cognitive aspects of reading, was related to comprehension ability. Previous work has examined the meta-cognitive knowledge of children with poor word reading skills and has not explored how such knowledge might specifically be related to comprehension ability. Two aspects of metacognitive knowledge were investigated in the current research: knowledge about the goals and processes of reading, and skill in applying such knowledge. This distinction has been used by various researchers who discriminate between knowledge about reading and regulation of reading (e.g. Baker & Brown, 1984; Kurtz, 1991).

Skilled and less skilled readers may hold different beliefs about reading. For example, younger and/or poorer readers' knowledge about reading appears to be quite limited, and they tend to focus on word reading rather than meaning construction aspects of the task (Myers & Paris, 1978; Paris & Jacobs, 1984). It is not surprising that beginner readers and poor readers place a greater emphasis on word reading accuracy than comprehension because the former is likely to be the more salient and/or emphasized feature of reading to them. There is also some evidence that an undue emphasis on the word-level aspects of reading is associated with poor comprehension. For example, poor comprehenders are more likely than good comprehenders to regard word reading accuracy as an indicator of reading skill (Garner & Kraus, 1981–1982; Yuill & Oakhill, 1991). Other tasks, however, do not reveal differences: when asked to choose the best of two fictional readers, both good and poor comprehenders demonstrate a preference for the one 'can read lots of long words' rather than the one 'who knows what things mean' (Yuill & Oakhill, 1991).

Knowledge about reading may affect the way that a reader reads a text. Older children appreciate that someone might read a story differently if their goal were to remember the story word-for-word than if the goal were to remember its meaning (Myers & Paris, 1978), and older high-ability readers know about sophisticated strategies to aid memory such as self-testing when reading, which less able readers rarely mention (Forrest-Pressley & Waller, 1984). More recent work has shown that good and poor comprehenders differ in their knowledge of which reading strategies are appropriate for different reading situations, e.g. studying or reading for pleasure (Pazzaglia, Cornoldi & de Beni, 1995), and such knowledge is related to the comprehension of expository (though not narrative) texts (Jetton, Rupley & Willson, 1995).

It is also important to know how to remedy problems that arise when reading. Better readers demonstrate greater awareness that particular strategies such as 'skip the parts you don't understand' can be detrimental to comprehension (Paris & Myers, 1981). Knowledge about strategies to repair word- and sentence-level comprehension failures differentiates high- and average-ability readers in the 11–12 year range, but similar differences have not been found among younger children and, where evident, the findings are somewhat contradictory. Forrest-Pressley & Waller (1984) found that average and good readers differed in their knowledge about sentence-level repair strategies but not word-level strategies, whereas Kirby & Moore (1987) report a relation between reading ability and knowledge about word-level repair strategies, but not sentence-level strategies. Furthermore, neither study addressed discourse-level failures of comprehension, such as not understanding a character's actions or a story event. This work demonstrates that good and poor readers differ in their knowledge about reading and indicates that comprehension skill may specifically be related to such knowledge, at least for older readers. However, although knowledge about reading processes and strategies may be necessary for skilled reading, it is not sufficient. Less skilled comprehenders may not only know less about the variables affecting comprehension, they may also be less able to adapt their reading style to suit the task demands. Indeed, Forrest-Pressley & Waller (1984) argue that skilled readers not only know *that* there are different ways of reading, but they also know *how* to monitor the efficiency and regulate the use of them. Forrest-Pressley and Waller assessed whether skilled readers were better able than less skilled readers to adapt their reading in different situations so that it was maximally efficient. They found that older and better readers were more flexible and were more likely than younger and poorer readers to adapt their reading style in accordance with task instructions: they remembered less of a story when required to skim it for a specified piece of information than when asked to study it.

In view of the wide range of declarative and procedural knowledge deficits found for young and poor readers, it is necessary to establish how such knowledge is specifically related to *comprehension* skill. Apart from the work of Yuill & Oakhill, and Pazzaglia et al., the studies discussed above did not control for differences in word recognition ability which is a widely recognized source of comprehension difficulties (e.g. Perfetti, 1985), but have instead used either non-standardized assessments of comprehension skill or composite measures of reading ability in which the comprehension score is highly dependent upon reading accuracy. Thus, it is possible that many of the effects found in this previous work are directly attributable to differences in word reading skill. Pazzaglia et al. *reiterate* Garner's (1987) suggestion that some children may emphasize word reading skills in these sorts of meta-cognitive assessments because they have experienced decoding difficulties and, indeed, they note that the poor comprehenders in their study demonstrated later decoding deficits. Individual differences in reading style may arise because poorer readers have to concentrate on reading each word at the expense of comprehension processing.

In order to investigate the hypothesis that metacognitive skills differ in children with skilled and less-skilled comprehension, with the implication that they are a causal factor in the text comprehension difficulties of the latter, it is important to rule out other sources of reading difficulty. In this case, the author identifies word-reading ability as an important lower-level factor, since children who find it difficult to identify words will also find it hard to make sense of sentences and text. Thus, in this study, children were matched for word reading.

If the relation between meta-cognitive knowledge about the reading strategies and comprehension ability is found to be an indirect one that is mediated by word reading difficulties, a good way to increase the (efficient) use of reading strategies would be to improve word reading accuracy. Alternatively, there may be a much more direct relation between such knowledge and comprehension skill: less skilled comprehenders may be less aware of different 'ways to read' and/or they may have less control over their reading and be less able to change their reading strategy. If the relation between knowledge and comprehension skill is found to be a direct one, it would be beneficial to teach and practice the necessary meta-cognitive skills. Meta-cognitive knowledge and skills have been successfully taught to populations of normal children (Paris & Jacobs, 1984; Paris, Saarnio & Cross, 1986) and also those with learning disabilities (Lucangeli, Galderisi & Cornoldi, 1995), but knowledge increments have been modest and experimental groups do not demonstrate superior performance on standardized assessments of comprehension (Paris & Jacobs, 1984; Paris, Saarnio & Cross, 1986). Thus it is important to establish whether the posited relation between comprehension skill and reading knowledge is a direct one.

The two studies reported in this research explored the relation between comprehension skill and meta-cognitive knowledge about reading and reading strategies in beginner readers. Skilled and less skilled comprehenders were matched for word reading accuracy using a standardized reading test that enabled the exclusion of any child whose comprehension problems might have arisen from word reading difficulties. Thus, if group differences on the experimental tasks arose, a 'word reading' explanation could be ruled out. However, if the less skilled comprehenders are found to be poorer on a task than their skilled peers, the direction of the relation is not clear. It may be that skilled comprehenders' superior strategy skills are a consequence of their greater experience of reading and understanding stories or, alternatively, that their superior strategy skills may be (in part) contributing to their reading comprehension success. The current study utilized a design analogous to the reading-level match design developed by Bryant and colleagues (see Bryant & Goswami, 1986, for a review) to determine which of the two explanations is the more plausible. In the comprehension age-match design used in the current work, the performance of the less skilled comprehenders is compared with that of a comprehension age-match group, comprised of younger normally developing readers of equivalent comprehension ability to the less skilled group (Cain & Oakhill, 1996; Stothard & Hulme, 1992). The comparison between the less skilled and comprehension age-match (CAM) groups provides a particularly strong test of the causation hypothesis. The argument here is that if the CAM group demonstrate superior strategy knowledge than the poor comprehenders, the difference cannot be said to be a product of a difference in the two groups' comprehension levels since the groups are matched for reading comprehension ability. A more plausible interpretation is that the difference is associated with the cause of the poor comprehenders' comprehension deficit. Thus, although causal links cannot be proven with this design, it provides valuable information on the most productive line to pursue in more costly and time-consuming training and longitudinal studies.

> *The children in the less-skilled comprehension group were matched (i) to a group of children of the same age but with age-appropriate (i.e. better) comprehension; and (ii) to a group of children who were younger but at the same level of comprehension. The rationale for this kind of design is to provide clearer evidence of the causal relationship of experimental task performance to reading comprehension. If metacognitive abilities are associated with reading comprehension ability then it would be expected that children with less-skilled comprehension would do less well on metacognitive tasks than peers with good comprehension. However, it is possible that lower performance on metacognitive tasks might be a consequence of less good reading comprehension rather than a cause. The comparison with the younger group at the same comprehension level provides further evidence: if metacognitive abilities are affected by reading level (rather than the other way round) then the younger children should also have poor performance on the metacognitive tasks. Note that this is a rigorous test of the causality hypothesis because one would expect the younger children to perform worse on the metacognitive tasks simply because they are younger – though the age difference is quite small.*

Study 1: The relation between declarative knowledge and reading comprehension

A structured interview was used to explore children's knowledge about aims of reading, and two different types of strategy knowledge: strategies for repairing difficulties encountered during reading and strategies that would assist memory of a story.

Method

Participants

Two samples of participants were selected. The first sample was asked questions about aims of reading and about strategies for repairing reading difficulties, and the second sample was asked the questions concerning strategies for remembering a story.

Each sample comprised three groups of children: 7–8-year-old skilled comprehenders and less skilled comprehenders, and a 6–7-year-old group matched with the older less skilled comprehenders for comprehension skill (the comprehension age-match, or CAM, group). Two tests were used in the selection process: the Gates–MacGinitie Primary Two Vocabulary Test (Gates & MacGinitie, 1965) and the Neale Analysis of Reading Ability (revised British edition) (Neale, 1989). The Gates–MacGinitie is a group-administered test, in which children have to select one out of four words to go with an accompanying picture. This test provides a measure of a child's sight vocabulary for words out of context.[1] The test was used to screen out 'exceptional' readers. Children who obtained either very high or very low scores were excluded, and the remaining 'average' readers were assessed individually on form 1 of the Neale Analysis. In this test children read a series of short stories out loud and any word reading errors are corrected. They are asked a set of comprehension questions after each story. The passages are graded in difficulty and testing stops once a prescribed number of reading accuracy errors has been made. The test provides separate scores for reading accuracy, based on the number of word pronunciation errors that a child makes, and reading comprehension, based on the number of comprehension questions that the child answers correctly. Performance on the Neale test was used to select and match the three groups.

The matching of the groups is very careful. All children were given both a single-word reading test (Gates–MacGinitie) to assess single-word reading comprehension and sight vocabulary and a text comprehension test (Neale Analysis). Table 1 shows that the less-skilled comprehenders had the same mean age as the age-matched group (and a similar SD). They also had a similar mean reading accuracy age and similar sight vocabulary. The two groups differed by nearly two years on comprehension age. The children in the comprehension-age match group were one year younger. Their single-word reading accuracy was also lower but reading comprehension was at the same level.

Sample 1

To select sample 1, 289 7–8-year-olds completed the Gates–MacGinitie test. Then, 140 children were individually administered the Neale test and 24 skilled comprehenders and 29 less skilled comprehenders were selected to participate in the experimental work. The skilled and less skilled comprehenders all obtained age-appropriate reading accuracy scores and did not differ significantly on this measure ($t(51) < 1.0$). However, the skilled groups' comprehension scores were at or above those predicted by their reading accuracy ability, whereas the less skilled groups' comprehension scores were below their chronological age and at least six months below their reading accuracy ages. The difference between the two groups' comprehension scores was significant ($t(51) = 14.15$, $p < .001$). In addition, the two groups were also matched for chronological age, sight vocabulary (measured by the Gates–MacGinitie), and the number of Neale stories that they had completed (all $ts < 1.0$). The latter measure was taken to ensure that the difference in comprehension scores was not because the less skilled group had read fewer stories and, therefore, obtained lower comprehension scores simply because they had attempted fewer questions. To select the comprehension-match children, 190 6–7-year-olds completed the Gates–MacGinitie test and 85 of these children were then assessed using the Neale. Twenty-seven children with age-appropriate reading accuracy and reading comprehension scores were selected to participate in further work. These children were selected so that the group's mean comprehension score was not significantly different from that of the less skilled comprehenders ($t(54) = 1.27$, $p > .10$; group means are shown in Table 1). This sample was asked the questions about the aims of reading and strategies for repairing reading difficulties.

Table 1   *Characteristics of sample 1*

	Skill group		
Measurement	**Less skilled comprehenders** (N = **29**)	**Comprehension-age match** (N = **27**)	**Skilled comprehenders** (N = **24**)
Chronological age[a]	7:8 (3.81)	6:8 (4.02)	7:8 (3.27)
Reading accuracy age[a]	7:11 (7.44)	6:8 (4.67)	7:10 (5.28)
Reading comprehension age[a]	6:7 (3.94)	6:8 (3.45)	8:2 (5.97)
Number of stories	3.31 (0.66)	2.37 (0.49)	3.33 (0.64)
Sight vocabulary (max. = 48)	37.14 (3.46)	33.59 (3.60)	37.88 (2.92)

[a] Ages given as years: months (standard deviations in months).
Note. The reading accuracy and comprehension scores are the age-equivalent scores provided in the Neale test, and the number of stories read refers to the stories that were completed during this assessment.

Sample 2

Sample 2 comprised 14 less skilled comprehenders, 12 skilled comprehenders and 12 comprehension age-match children. They were asked the questions about ways to remember a story (sample 2 means shown in Table 2). These children were selected according to the criteria described above from an initial screening of 110 7–8-year-olds and 106 6–7-year-olds. The skilled and less skilled groups were matched for reading accuracy, chronological age, Gates–MacGinitie sight vocabulary scores, and the number of Neale stories they had completed (all $ts(24) < 1.0$), but their comprehension ages were significantly different ($t(24) = 10.45$, $p < .001$). The comprehension age-match group were matched to the less skilled comprehenders for comprehension level ($t(24) < 1.0$).

Considerable care was taken to establish the comparability of the three groups on the target measures. Note that there were differences between younger and older children in the number of stories read on the Neale test and hence a likely difference in comprehension scores. In order to ensure that the comprehension scores of the younger, comprehension age-matched children were not being underestimated, scores using the same number of stories for older and younger children were also calculated. This was an important control which ruled out the possibility that the younger children were actually better comprehenders than children identified as less-skilled comprehenders. It also illustrates a more general problem in matching using this kind of design: older and younger children differ in a number of ways and it is important to ensure that such differences will not affect performance on the variable under investigation.

The comprehension abilities of the younger comprehension age-match groups in both samples may have been underestimated because they completed fewer stories during Neale testing than the older children who had better reading accuracy skills and were, thus, asked a lesser number of comprehension questions. Therefore the comprehension scores were re-analyzed, excluding the scores obtained by older children on stories that had been too difficult for the younger children to read (see Cain & Oakhill, 1996, for further detail on this procedure). The mean number of questions answered on this basis for sample 1 was: skilled = 12.33 (SD = 2.71); less skilled = 8.93 (SD = 1.96); CAM group = 9.30 (SD = 1.39). The less skilled and CAM groups did not differ on this more stringent test ($t(54) < 1.0$). Thus, we can be satisfied that, in this sample, the CAM group were an equivalent comprehension-level match for the less skilled comprehenders. Furthermore, when reanalysed in a similar way, the skilled comprehenders' scores were significantly better than those of the CAM group ($t(49) = 4.57$, $p < .001$), indicating that their superior comprehension skill was not simply due to their superior word reading ability. The question-answering data for sample 2 were analysed in the same way. In this more stringent test, the less skilled comprehenders and CAM group did not differ in the number of questions they answered correctly ($t(24) = 1.36$, n.s.), whereas the skilled comprehenders obtained significantly higher scores than the CAM group ($t(22) = 3.14$, $p < .01$).[2]

All of the children spoke British English as their first language and were selected from schools in socially mixed catchment areas. Good and poor comprehenders were drawn from the same classrooms and there was a similar proportion of boys and girls in each group.

Procedure

Children were interviewed individually and their responses were recorded and scored later. All open-ended questions were scored blind by a second marker. There was disagreement on less than 8 per cent of responses and

Table 2 *Characteristics of sample 2*

Measurement	Skill group					
	Less skilled comprehenders (*N* = 14)		Comprehension-age match (*N* = 12)		Skilled comprehenders (*N* = 12)	
Chronological age[a]	7:7	(4.44)	6:6	(3.88)	7:7	(4.04)
Reading accuracy age[a]	7:9	(5.17)	6:7	(4.98)	7:11	(5.73)
Reading comprehension age[a]	6:7	(3.87)	6:8	(3.11)	8:1	(5.14)
Number of stories	3.29	(0.47)	2.50	(0.52)	3.33	(0.65)
Sight vocabulary (max. = 48)	37.21	(4.00)	32.92	(2.91)	37.42	(3.00)

[a] Ages given as years : months (standard deviations in months).
Note. The reading accuracy and comprehension scores are the age-equivalent scores provided in the Neale test, and the number of stories read refers to the stories that were completed during this assessment.

these were resolved by discussion. Each interview question and the results pertaining to it are presented together in the following section. When chi-square analyses reached significance, the table was partitioned according to the guidelines in Siegal & Castellen (1988) so that the crucial comparisons between the less skilled and CAM group (partition 1), and between these two groups and the skilled comprehenders (partition 2) could be made. For sake of brevity, additional analyses are reported only where significant.

> *In Study 1, children were asked about three issues: the aims of reading, ways to remember a story, and strategies to employ when a text was difficult to read. The aim was to see if there were differences among the groups in awareness of reading strategies.*

Results and discussion

Aims of reading

A modified version of Yuill & Oakhill's (1991) task, described in the introduction, in which children had to choose between two fictional readers, was used. The question was changed from 'who is the best reader' to 'who is it best to be?' to avoid bias toward selection of the reader 'who could read the words'. There was a significant relation between skill group and choice of reader ($\chi^2(2,80) = 6.95$, $p < .05$). Whereas only 34.5 per cent of less skilled comprehenders selected the reader who could understand the words, 52 per cent of the CAM group and 71 per cent of the skilled group chose this option. When the chi-square was partitioned, the comparison between the less skilled comprehenders and the CAM group (partition 1) did not reach significance, but the comparison between these two groups and the skilled comprehenders (partition 2) did ($\chi^2(1,80) = 5.26$, $p < .05$).

When asked to pick out the best kind of reader, 71 per cent of the skilled comprehenders selected a reader who could 'understand the words' whereas only 34.5 per cent of the less-skilled comprehenders and 52 per cent of the CA match group did so. This suggests that poor comprehenders had relatively little awareness of the need to understand a story at a textual level.

Ways to remember a story

Children were presented with a similar scenario to one used by Forrest-Pressley & Waller (1984) to probe how they would try to remember a story for later recall. A different response classification was developed in order to distinguish between responses that emphasized memory for the gist of the text, such as 'think about the main points'; other 'non-memory' strategies, which included the use of external aids, such as 'copying the story down' (to read back to friend later); strategies that would not facilitate recall, e.g. 'say each word very clearly'; and 'don't know' responses (see Table 3 for the distribution of responses). To conduct the analysis, the data were pooled to compare gist responses with all other types. There was a significant relation between skill group and strategy ($\chi^2(2,38) = 7.46$, $p < .05$), which arose because the skilled comprehenders were more likely than the other two groups to suggest a gist strategy ($\chi^2(1,38) = 5.43$, $p < .05$).

When asked how they would try to remember a story, skilled comprehenders were more likely than the other two groups to suggest trying to remember the gist of the story; and, when asked to select one strategy from a choice of six, they were also more likely to choose a strategy that emphasised understanding and remembering the whole story (e.g. remembering the story as a film).

Table 3   *Responses in percentages to the question about ways to remember a story*

Response categories	Skill group		
	Less skilled comprehenders (N = 14)	Comprehension-age match (N = 12)	Skilled comprehenders (N = 12)
Don't know	57.1	41.7	33.3
Other responses	7.1	8.3	0.0
Non-memory strategy	21.4	8.3	0.0
Gist memory strategy	14.3	41.7	66.7

Note. Because of unequal sample sizes, the data are presented as percentages. The analysis was performed on the frequency data.

Strategy knowledge was also assessed using a forced-choice task in which children were presented with six different strategies, one at a time in a randomized order. Two options emphasized word-level aspects of reading: try to remember all the words in the story, and check that you can say all the words correctly. Two options selected from Paris & Myer's (1981) internal positive strategies emphasized comprehension aspects: imagine the story in your head like a film, and try to remember the main points of the story. Two options were considered neither to facilitate nor hinder memory for a text: read the story out loud, and make sure that you remember the names of all the people in the story.

One point was awarded when a child correctly responded that a 'comprehension' strategy would help them to retell a story and that 'word-level' strategy would not assist them in that task. No points were awarded for the 'neutral' items. Out of a possible total of four points, the group means were as follows: less skilled = 1.71 (SD = .75); skilled = 2.42 (SD = .62); CAM = 1.75 (SD = .75). A Kruskal–Wallis one-way analysis of variance revealed a significant effect of skill group: KW (2) = 9.01, $p < .02$ (corrected for ties). *Post hoc* comparisons revealed that the skilled comprehenders obtained significantly higher scores than the less skilled comprehenders ($p < .05$).

Strategies for repairing reading/comprehension failure

Children were asked to suggest repair strategies for five different types of reading problem, from word level to discourse level. Responses that included an independent remedy were compared to all others (asking for help, inappropriate strategies, and 'don't know' responses). The percentage of independent responses to each of the five types of question is shown in Table 4.

> A similar pattern was evident in the children's suggested strategies for dealing with problems encountered during reading. Children who were skilled comprehenders were better than the other two groups at suggesting appropriate strategies at all levels of reading difficulty (word, sentence and text). Thus all three measures suggested that good comprehenders had a sophisticated understanding of the requirements of text comprehension that was not evident in the less-skilled comprehenders or the younger children.

There was a relation between skill group and the ability to suggest an appropriate and independent remediation strategy for the following situations: when they encountered a word they could not read; when they did not understand the meaning of a sentence; and when they did not understand a character's actions. Additional analyses revealed that these effects arose because of differences between the responses of the skilled comprehenders and those of the other two groups (all $ps < .02$).

Summary

Less skilled and skilled comprehenders differed significantly in their knowledge about reading, demonstrating that there is a specific relation between

Table 4 *Percentage of each skill group who suggested an independent strategy for each type of problem*

| | Skill group | | | |
Reading problems	Less skilled comprehenders (N = 29)	Comprehension-age match (N = 27)	Skilled comprehenders (N = 24)	$\chi^2(2,80)$
Reading a word	41.4	37.0	75.0	8.68, $p < .02$
Understanding a word	20.8	18.5	20.7	< 1.0, n.s.
Understanding a sentence	6.9	18.5	37.5	7.74, $p < .05$
Understanding a character's actions	13.8	18.5	41.7	6.25, $p < .05$
Understanding an event	17.2	11.1	33.3	4.14, $p > .10$.

Note. Because of unequal sample sizes the data are presented as percentages. The analysis was performed on the frequency data. Independent strategies were compared to all other responses (asking for help, unsuitable strategies, 'don't know' responses).

comprehension skill and metacognitive knowledge which is not mediated by word reading ability. It should be noted that poor comprehenders were not simply poor in articulating a response: Responses to the 'aims of reading' question simply required selection of a fictional character, and they demonstrated a different selection preference to that of both other groups, although their performance was not significantly different to that of the CAM group. For other questions, the poor comprehenders often gave responses that were either inappropriate or, in the case of repair strategies, depended upon help from a more experienced individual (e.g. their teacher). It was unexpected that, in comparison to that skilled group, the less skilled comprehenders were so poor at suggesting an independent strategy for reading unfamiliar words, particularly when these two groups were matched for Neale word reading accuracy. This finding is puzzling because work by Stothard & Hulme (1995) and also our own unpublished data demonstrate that similarly selected groups of skilled and less skilled comprehenders perform comparably on non-word reading for which grapheme–phoneme conversion is essential.

The less skilled comprehenders' performance was, in general, very similar to that of the comprehension age-match group. The analyses did not reveal significantly poorer knowledge in the less skilled group and, in some cases, the less skilled comprehenders were more likely to suggest an appropriate strategy than the CAM group. The failure to find significant differences between the less skilled and CAM groups is a finding that is difficult to interpret, as Bryant & Goswami (1986) have pointed out. One possible interpretation is that the less skilled comprehenders and the comprehension age-match group do indeed possess comparable meta-cognitive knowledge. However, it is also possible that some other difference between the two groups is masking differential knowledge. Younger children may have less experience of answering questions and thus will be less able to fully articulate their knowledge. Indeed, their selection preference for the 'aims of reading' question, where they did not have to produce a descriptive response, was more similar to that of the skilled comprehenders than the less skilled group. Intelligence, which was not assessed in the current study, is another factor that may influence performance on such tasks. If, for example, all groups were at age-appropriate levels of verbal IQ, the CAM group would actually have obtained lower raw scores than the less skilled comprehenders. These poorer (though not deficient) verbal skills might limit their ability to articulate their superior knowledge. Another possibility is that the less skilled comprehenders are of lower intelligence than their skilled peers, which has limited their ability to acquire meta-cognitive knowledge, and/or to articulate such knowledge, making their knowledge appear similar to that of younger children. Unfortunately, because IQ data are not available for our groups, we cannot establish the degree to which IQ influenced the pattern of results. However, it should be noted that verbal IQ scores obtained for such populations (e.g. Stothard & Hulme, 1996) typically fall within the 'average' range on the Wechsler Intelligence Scale for Children (3rd ed., UK) (Wechsler, 1992, p. 34).

In summary, although these data confirm that metacognitive differences are related specifically to comprehension ability, they are ambiguous as to the direction of the relation, whether good meta-cognitive knowledge is (in part) a cause of reading comprehension success, or whether it is a consequence of experience at reading and comprehending text.

As stated in the introduction, whilst knowledge about optimal reading goals is important, it cannot guarantee good text comprehension. The ability to utilize such knowledge is also crucial. The experiment reported next set out to investigate the relation between comprehension skill and knowing *how* to adjust one's reading to meet different comprehension goals.

Study 2: The relation between procedural knowledge and reading comprehension

Study 2 employed a design adapted from Forrest-Pressley & Waller's (1984) project which demonstrated that older and better readers were better able to adapt their reading style for different goals. Two important modifications should be noted. In the original study, the reading measure did not distinguish between poor readers whose difficulties stemmed from poor word reading skills and those who experienced higher level deficits. In the current study, good and poor comprehenders were matched on a measure of reading accuracy to determine whether reading comprehension is *directly* related to flexibility in reading style, for reasons discussed previously. A comprehension age-match group was included to establish whether or not flexibility in reading style was simply a by-product of comprehension level.

In Study 2 a different approach was adopted. Instead of asking about strategies, children were given different reading tasks that emphasised either skimming the story, deciding on a title for the story, or reading carefully to answer the comprehension questions. The rationale was that, if metacognitive skills are important for good comprehension, then children with good comprehension should show a more flexible approach to reading and so should read the stories differently according to the instructions (and show differences in comprehension scores and reading speed).

Method

Participants

From an original sample of 207 children, 16 skilled comprehenders and 16 less skilled comprehenders were selected and matched in the same way as the groups described above. The two groups did not differ on the following measures: chronological age, Neale reading accuracy, Gates–MacGinitie sight vocabulary, number of Neale stories (all *t*s < 1.0), but the two groups obtained significantly different comprehension scores on the Neale Analysis ($t(30) = 13.27$, $p < .001$). In addition, 16 comprehension age-match children were selected from an initial pool of 170 children so that their mean comprehension score was not significantly different from that of the less skilled group ($t(30) = 1.36$, $p > .10$). The profiles of each group are presented in Table 5.

As in study 1, the reading comprehension data were reanalyzed to take into account the lesser number of stories read by the younger CAM group. The pattern of performance remained the same: the less skilled comprehenders and CAM group did not differ in the number of questions they answered correctly ($t(30) = 1.12$, $p > .10$), whereas the skilled comprehenders obtained significantly higher scores than the CAM group ($t(30) = 5.18$, $p < .001$).

Materials and procedure

Four short stories were adapted from a set of Indian folk tales, varying between 122 to 134 words in length. Eight comprehension questions, which could not simply be answered by verbatim recall of the text, were written for each one. Pilot work established that the vocabulary of the texts was suitable for this age group.

Table 5   Characteristics of skill groups who participated in study 2

	Skill group					
Measurement	Less skilled comprehenders (N = 16)		Comprehension- age match (N = 16)		Skilled comprehenders (N = 16)	
Chronological age[a]	7:8	(5.25)	6:8	(5.39)	7:9	(3.90)
Reading accuracy age[a]	7:10	(5.30)	6:11	(8.71)	7:11	(5.30)
Reading comprehension age[a]	6:7	(3.72)	6:8	(2.99)	8:3	(4.68)
Number of stories	3.31	(0.48)	2.63	(0.50)	3.31	(0.60)
Sight vocabulary (proportion correct)[b]	0.77	(0.08)	0.67	(0.07)	0.78	(0.07)

[a] Ages given as years : months (standard deviations in months).
[b] Two versions of the Gates-MacGinitie Vocabulary Test (Gates & MacGinitie, 1965; MacGinitie & MacGinitie, 1989) were used in this selection (each child completed only one). The two versions of the test comprised different numbers of items (45 and 48). Thus, the group means provided in Table 7 are the proportion correct rather than raw scores.
Note. The reading accuracy and comprehension scores are the age equivalent scores provided in the Neale test, and the number of stories read refers to the stories that were completed during this assessment.

There were four different instruction conditions: fun, skim, title and study. Children were asked to read the stories silently, to enable them to scan or skim-read the stories in the instruction condition which prompted that style of reading. They tapped on the table when they began reading and again when they finished, so that their reading time could be recorded. After each story they answered one condition-specific question before the eight comprehension questions. Thus, there were three dependent measures for each story: a comprehension score, based on the number of comprehension questions answered correctly, reading speed, and a response to the condition-specific question. The instructions and procedure were modified from those used by Forrest-Pressley & Waller (1984).

Title condition.   Children were told that it did not matter how long they took to read the story nor how well they did on the set of comprehension questions. The measure that was important was the answer to the special question: 'What do you think would be a good title for this story?' Titles were scored later for thematic relevance.

Fun condition.   The only difference between this condition and the title condition was the special question: 'How much do you think other children in your class would enjoy reading this story?' Children marked their response on a scale.

Skim condition.   Children were told that two things were important in this condition: they were instructed to read the story as quickly as possible and to find the answer to a special question, which always referred to a piece of information given in the story.

Study condition. Children were told that the only thing that was important in this condition was how well they answered the comprehension questions. In order to create a delay and distraction between the story reading and comprehension questions comparable to the other conditions, children estimated their performance on a rating scale before they were asked the comprehension questions.

Design

The experiment was a 3 × 4 design: skill group (skilled, less skilled, CAM) × instruction type (title, fun, skim, study). The stories and condition were counterbalanced within instruction condition and participant groups.

All children read under all four conditions and, to avoid the possibility that they would get better (or worse) over the course of the experiment, the order of conditions was randomised (as was the combination of story and reading condition).

Predictions

The primary predictions relate to the study and skim conditions. If less skilled comprehenders are not able to regulate their reading to meet the different aims of the different instruction conditions, they should obtain similar comprehension scores and reading speeds in these two conditions. The other two conditions were included in this experiment because all four subtasks were designed to provide additional information about reading. However, only the experimental comparisons which directly tested the validity of the experimental predictions were conducted on the comprehension and reading speed data. Predictions for performance on the subtasks relevant to the different conditions were as follows:

Title. The less skilled comprehenders were expected to produce less thematically relevant titles because their knowledge about the purpose of story titles is poor (Cain, 1996).

Fun. Differences in enjoyment ratings were not predicted because good and poor comprehenders express similar attitudes towards reading (Cain, 1994)

Skim. Accuracy in finding the specific piece of information reflects how well the child has established and monitored that goal, thus the less skilled group might plausibly be poorer at this.

Study. A discrepancy between estimated and actual performance was predicted for the less skilled group because previous work has demonstrated that less skilled comprehenders are not aware of their poor performance (e.g. Yuill & Oakhill, 1991).

Results

The experiment was a 3 (skill group: skilled, less skilled, CAM) × 4 (instruction type: title, fun, skim, study) design. Two analyses of variance were conducted on the data, one in which comprehension score was the dependent measure, and one in which reading speed was the dependent measure. These two analyses are presented next, in turn. The data from the four subtasks were analysed individually, and these results are presented at the end of this section.

Performance on the comprehension questions

An initial analysis of variance was conducted which included the order of instruction type as a factor. It revealed no effects of order and this factor was not involved in any interactions (all $Fs < 1.50$), indicating that none of the groups became increasingly oriented toward the comprehension questions during the course of the experiment. For brevity, order of presentation is not included as a factor in the analysis of variance that is reported.

> *There were no effects of order, so results were conflated across order in subsequent analysis. There were significant main effects of both Group and Condition and a significant interaction. When asked to provide answers to the comprehension questions (study condition), both the skilled comprehenders and the chronological age-matched group performed better than when they were asked to read the story quickly. The less-skilled comprehenders performed at a similar level in both conditions.*

The groups differed in how many questions they answered correctly (mean scores are presented in Table 6) and there was a main effect of skill group ($F(2,45) = 4.14$, $p < .025$) and also a main effect of instruction condition ($F(3,135) = 5.77$, $p < .002$). These effects were qualified by a significant interaction between the two factors ($F(6,135) = 2.34$, $p < .04$). Bonferroni *t*-tests to control for type I errors were conducted to test the predictions above. The skilled and CAM groups obtained significantly higher scores in the study condition than in the skim condition ($t^{|}(15) = 5.04$; $p < .05$; $t^{|}(15) = 2.78$, $p < .05$), but there was no significant difference between the less skilled comprehenders' scores for these two conditions ($t^{|}(15) < 1.0$ (significance values obtained from Appendix $t^{|}$, Howell, 1992).

Reading speed

The time taken in seconds to read each story was divided by the total number of words for each story. Thus, higher scores represent slower reading times (means in Table 7). These scores were the dependent measure entered into the analysis of variance (design as above). The means in

Table 6　Reading strategy experiment. Mean number of questions (and standard deviations) answered correctly by each skill group for the different instruction conditions (maximum = 8)

| | Skill group | | | |
| | Less skilled | Comprehension- | Skilled | |
Condition	comprehenders	age match	comprehenders	M
Study	2.53 (1.20)	3.69 (1.93)	4.88 (1.37)	3.70
Title	2.97 (1.49)	2.97 (1.34)	3.88 (2.07)	3.27
Fun	3.00 (1.59)	3.22 (1.46)	4.22 (2.12)	3.48
Skim	2.75 (1.39)	2.47 (1.32)	3.00 (1.45)	2.74
M	2.81	3.09	3.99	

Table 7　Reading strategy experiment. Mean reading speeds (and standard deviations) obtained by each skill group for the different instruction conditions. Reading time measure is seconds/words

| | Skill group | | | |
| | Less skilled | Comprehension- | Skilled | |
Condition	comprehenders	age match	comprehenders	M
Study	.471 (.17)	.636 (.21)	.539 (.16)	.549
Title	.483 (.21)	.558 (.15)	.441 (.17)	.494
Fun	.481 (.16)	.675 (.32)	.508 (.17)	.555
Skim	.426 (.14)	.531 (.16)	.452 (.20)	.469
M	.465	.600	.485	

Table 7 indicate that the CAM group read the stories more slowly than the other two groups; however the effect was only marginal ($F(2,45) = 2.84$, $p < .07$) and, thus, was not pursued further.

> For reading speed, there was a main effect of Condition but the Group x Condition interaction was not significant. Again, there were differences between reading conditions for the skilled comprehenders and younger children but there were no such differences for the children with less-skilled comprehension.

There was a main effect of instruction type ($F(3,135) = 9.19$, $p < .001$), but the interaction between skill group and instruction type did not reach conventional levels of significance ($F(6,135) = 1.89$, $p <.09$). Bonferroni t-tests were conducted to test the predictions made earlier. Both the skilled and CAM groups read faster in the skim condition than in the study condition (skilled, $t'(15) = 3.12$, $p < .05$; CAM, $t'(15) = 3.36$, $p < .05$). The difference between these two conditions for the less skilled group did not reach conventional levels of significance ($t'(15) = 2.16$, n.s. (critical value for $t'(15) = 2.69$, $\alpha = .05$)).

Subtasks

Title condition.   More than 80 per cent of children produced titles that simply listed the main story characters, e.g. 'The cat and the bird', so these data were not analysed further.

Fun condition.   A one-way analysis of the enjoyment ratings revealed that the three groups did not differ (less skilled = 4.13 (SD = 1.03); skilled = 3.56 (SD = 1.03); CAM = 3.44 (SD = .89): $F(2,45) = 2.21$, $p > .10$).

Skim condition.   The less skilled group were poorer, but not significantly so, at finding the specific piece of information (less skilled = 50 per cent, skilled = 69 per cent, CAM = 63 per cent).

Study condition.   The three groups provided comparable estimates of how well they thought they would do on the comprehension questions (less skilled = 3.25 (SD = 1.07); skilled = 3.25 (SD = 1.25); CAM = 3.63 (SD = 1.03)), but only the less skilled group overestimated their ability ($p < .002$).

> Interestingly, children in all three groups provided similar ratings of how well they thought they had understood the story but, in the case of the less-skilled comprehenders, this was an overestimate.

Discussion

The skilled comprehenders and the younger comprehension age-match group appeared to adapt their reading goals to those intended by the instructions, remembering more of the story in the Study condition, than in the Skim condition, whereas the less skilled group's understanding was not affected by the different task instructions. The less skilled group were also slightly poorer than the other groups at finding the specific piece of information in the Skim condition, another indication that they were not establishing different comprehension goals for their reading and/or that they were not monitoring how effectively they had achieved that goal. Unlike the skilled and CAM groups, the less skilled comprehenders did not read significantly faster in the Skim condition than in the Study condition, suggesting that they lacked flexibility and control over their reading. There was no indication that the less skilled group comprised less fluent readers: the CAM group had the poorest reading accuracy skills. Performance in the Fun condition was not compared to that obtained in the other conditions because, as stated earlier, only the experimental comparisons which directly tested the validity of the experimental predictions were performed. However, it should be noted that for both the skilled and CAM groups, comprehension in the Fun condition was superior to that obtained in the Skim condition, indicating that children do not necessarily need to be directed to study a text in order to comprehend it well.

The subtasks were designed to provide additional information about reading behaviour but only the Study condition yielded significant group differences, confirming that the less skilled comprehenders were not aware of their own limitations in understanding text.

The differences between the skilled and less skilled comprehender groups are an indication that the ability to adapt reading style in different circumstances is directly related to reading comprehension ability. The younger children were able to adapt their reading behaviour in an appropriate and similar manner to the older skilled comprehenders, in marked contrast to the less skilled group, demonstrating that flexibility and control over reading style are not simply by-products of good reading comprehension and, instead, should be considered as candidate skills for comprehension success.

General discussion

The aims of these two studies were to investigate precisely how knowledge about reading and regulation of the reading process are related to *comprehension* skill by controlling for word reading skill and by employing a design that could determine whether task performance differences were a by-product of differences in comprehension level.

Less skilled comprehenders were less likely than their skilled peers to describe comprehension-level aspects of reading, a difference that demonstrates a direct link between reading knowledge and comprehension skill because the groups were matched for word reading ability. Comparisons between the less skilled and younger children of equivalent comprehension skill did not reach significance and thus, as discussed earlier, the direction of the relation is not clear: good knowledge about reading may have arisen through good reading comprehension experience, or some other factor may have masked a true difference between the two groups.

Less skilled comprehenders did not demonstrate the same ability to adapt their reading to different task demands as either skilled comprehenders or the comprehension age-match group, indicating that this skill does not arise through reading comprehension experience. A more plausible interpretation is that it is an underlying factor of comprehension success. It cannot be determined whether or not the less skilled group's difficulties on this task stemmed from differences is knowing when it is appropriate to adopt a particular reading strategy or actual lack of control over the reading process, for the reasons discussed above.

If metacognitive deficits in reading regulation (and possibly knowledge about reading) are causally contributing to comprehension failure, training in such skills should improve reading comprehension. Previous studies have demonstrated that young children's knowledge about reading can be improved through instruction, but the benefits do not readily transfer to standardized reading and comprehension tests (Paris & Jacobs, 1984; Paris, Saarnio & Cross, 1986). The lack of transfer may be taken as a sign that metacognitive skills are not that crucial for discourse-level comprehension; however training populations who have learning disabilities has met with more success (Lucangeli, Galderisi & Cornoldi, 1995). Another possibility is that performance on the comprehension tests used in these earlier studies was restricted by word reading accuracy, improvement of which was not the focus of training. In addition, it may be that particular populations benefit from such training to a greater extent than others. It should be noted that the children in the Lucangeli et al. study were of normal intelligence, which may have facilitated their ability to take advantage of such training. IQ measures were not reported in the work by Paris and colleagues, but it is plausible that children of lower intelligence are less able to gain from training and to regulate their reading than peers. As mentioned in the Discussion of Study 1, it is not known whether IQ differences exist between the groups in the current studies and, thus, whether IQ influenced the pattern of data found. The different patterns of group performance found between the two current studies suggest that strategy use, rather than awareness about specific strategies, may be the crucial issue. Training programmes, which did not lead to transfer of skills, may not have addressed strategy *usage* sufficiently. Paris, Wasik & Turner (1991) make the point that application of a strategy can eventually become proficient and automatic, in which case it should be considered a 'skill', whose use is not controlled deliberately or effortfully, in much the same way that decoding is achieved by the skilled reader. Thus, training studies designed to test the possible causal link between comprehension skill and strategy use should ensure that strategy usage is taught so that it becomes an automatic component of everyday reading.

Acknowledgements

This work was conducted whilst the author was in receipt of an ESRC studentship. I am extremely grateful to Jane Oakhill for her discussion of this work and for her comments on an earlier version of this manuscript. Thanks also to Sarah Dunworth for acting as an independent marker of the interview data. I would also like to express my gratitude to the Brighton and Hove schools which participated in this work: Benfield, Hertford, West Hove and Whitehawk Junior schools, and St. Luke's and Stanford Infant schools.

Note

1 The Gates–MacGinitie, which is an American test, was chosen for this project because an equivalent British sight vocabulary test was not available. British sight vocabulary tests that are suitable for this age range use a cloze format and, thus, performance may be limited by sentence comprehension.

Cain concludes that the differences between skilled and less-skilled comprehenders are an indication that ability to adapt reading style in different circumstances is causally related to reading comprehension ability. This is a strong claim so it is legitimate to ask whether it is justified.

The matching of the three groups on reading comprehension and single-word reading was meticulous in both studies so the study cannot be criticised on those grounds. In Study 1, the CA matched group did not differ from the less-skilled comprehenders so the results were not clear cut, as the author recognises in the discussion. The main justification for the claim lies in the results of Study 2 where the reading of the less-skilled comprehenders was less flexible than that of both the other groups as evidenced by their similar levels of reading across all conditions.

It could be argued that children are less good at explaining strategies than at implementing them – and here the younger comprehension age-matched children would be at a disadvantage – but there are possible concerns about more fluent reading allowing better strategy control rather than the other way round. In other words, if children are finding it difficult to understand what they are reading, they may have fewer cognitive resources to enable them to control the reading process. The fact that the less-skilled comprehenders did not show a difference in reading speed across conditions may reflect the fact that they were unable to control their reading speed rather than the fact that they were unaware of the need to do so. A longitudinal study could disentangle the pattern of cause and effect.

The author suggests another possibility, namely, that children with skilled and less-skilled comprehension may have differed in IQ. This highlights the importance of ensuring the comparability of children with typical and atypical development on general measures.

Paper 12 Understanding Theory of Mind tasks by deaf and hearing children (Woolfe, Want & Siegal, 2002)

The next paper is concerned with differences in the understanding of Theory of Mind (ToM) tasks by two groups of children, one showing typical development and the other expected to show atypical development. The second group comprises children who were born with severe/profound hearing loss (or became deaf in the first months of life) but who are assumed not to be suffering from any specific cognitive impairment.

Over 90 per cent of deaf children are born into hearing families but a few are born to deaf parents. Many deaf children have considerable problems in acquiring spoken language but, for some, their home language is sign. Children in this group, who typically have deaf parents, grow up learning sign in the same way that hearing children grow up learning a spoken language (Marschark & Harris, 1996).

Many previous studies have found that deaf children from hearing families have difficulties with ToM tasks. For example, an earlier study by the previous author (Peterson & Siegal, 1998) used a modification of the standard Sally-Ann False Belief task (see Paper 3) and showed that typically developing 4-year-olds performed significantly above chance while younger typically developing children and older children, who were either deaf or autistic, did not. Peterson and Siegal have argued that deaf children's difficulty with understanding the thoughts, beliefs and desires of another person stems from their lack of language experience. They argue that children learn about the mental life of other people through conversation and, since many deaf children have very poor language and poor communication within their family, they have little opportunity to gain understanding of mental life. However, deaf children with deaf parents, who grow up using sign as their main language, should be as good as hearing children at understanding the mental life of others. This is the main hypothesis tested in this paper.

Child Development, 2002, 73 (3), 768–778

Signposts to development: theory of mind in deaf children

Tyron Woolfe, Stephen C. Want, and Michael Siegal

Introduction

The ability to understand that other people have mental states (thoughts, desires, and beliefs) that may be different from one's own, termed a 'theory of mind' (ToM; Flavell, 1999; Premack & Woodruff, 1978), is vital to everyday life. One central measure of ToM understanding involves knowledge that others can hold false beliefs about the location or contents of an object, and that these beliefs produce undesired behavioral consequences. There is a consensus that by the age of about 4 years, most typically developing children have a grasp of the consequences of holding false beliefs, and thus have ToM understanding (Perner, Leekam, & Wimmer, 1987; Surian & Leslie, 1999).

Although previous studies have shown that ToM understanding develops in tandem with aspects of language development (Tager-Flusberg, 2000), the nature of this relation is not yet clear. One proposal (e.g., Astington & Jenkins, 1999; de Villiers & de Villiers, 2000) is that ToM performance is closely tied to the development of children's language skills, particularly competence in syntax. Another proposal is that children's exposure to talk about mental states gives rise to ToM reasoning (Siegal, Varley, & Want, 2001). According to this view, the effects of language extend beyond syntax. Language is the medium through which children learn about the unobservable mental states of others; through immersion in conversation, children become aware of mental states and develop pragmatic knowledge in following the purpose and relevance of messages in conversation. They come to understand others' beliefs and communicative intentions and how these may differ from their own. Dunn (1994) has reported that preschoolers' success on ToM tasks is associated with the frequency with which they exchange mental state terms in conversations with parents, siblings, and friends. Similarly, Lewis, Freeman, Kyriakidou, Maridaki-Kassotaki, and Berridge (1996) found that the availability of exposure to mature speakers (adults, older children, and siblings) predicted children's performance on tasks involving ToM. These observations are consistent with the view that the more children are exposed to talk about thoughts and other invisible mental processes, the earlier they develop a ToM of other persons' mental states. Indeed, it has long been noted that children who are isolated in their contact with others have specific difficulty in adopting the perspectives of others (Hollos & Cowan, 1973).

A key test of these proposals comes from congenitally deaf children who are raised in hearing families and often have no easy means of communication with hearing family members and other children, especially about topics such as mental states, which may have no concrete referent (Marschark, 1993; Meadow, 1975; Morford & Goldin-Meadow, 1997; Power & Carty, 1990). An important question thus arises: given that developing a ToM may be dependent on hearing other people talk about mental states, does the restricted conversational world of some deaf children result in difficulties that are specific to understanding the (invisible) thoughts of others?

Previous studies have shown that on key tests of ToM understanding, deaf children of hearing parents lag several years behind hearing children of hearing parents, even when care has been taken only to include children of normal intelligence and social responsiveness in the deaf samples (Courtin & Melot, 1998; Deleau, 1996; Deleau, Guéhéneuc, Le Sourn, & Ricard, 1999; de Villiers & de Villiers, 2000; Figueras-Costa & Harris, 2001; Peterson & Siegal, 1995, 1997, 1998, 1999, 2000; Russell et al., 1998). These children acquire a sign language mainly outside the family and are thus 'late signers'. In contrast, deaf children who are born into families with a deaf communicative partner who uses a sign language are 'native signers'. They have access to language even before school owing to the presence in their household of at least one fluent user of a sign language, and they resemble typically developing hearing children in their ToM performance. This finding is in line with the observation that deaf preschoolers with deaf parents converse as readily about non-present ideas, objects, and events in sign as do hearing children in speech with hearing parents (Meadow, Greenberg, Erting, & Carmichael, 1981).

> This paper draws an important distinction between deaf children who are native signers, having learned to sign at home with their parents, and those who learn sign at school. Previous research on the acquisition of sign languages (Spencer & Harris, 2005) suggests that there are fundamental differences in the signing of those who are native signers and those who come late to signing. Note that the deaf children who are described as 'late signers' in this paper have not learned to sign after learning a spoken language. For these children, sign is their main mode of communication.

Nevertheless, there are significant issues that arise in interpreting existing research with deaf children. For example, tasks designed to test ToM understanding often rely on children giving a verbal or signed response. In samples of deaf late-signing children, it is not clear whether all possess sufficient verbal or sign language skills to either understand, or respond to, ToM tests of understanding how false beliefs may lead to an undesired outcome. Accordingly, the abilities of late-signing children may have been underestimated in previous research. For example, Peterson and Siegal (1999) reported a highly significant advantage in ToM performance to native-signing children over their late-signing counterparts. Yet the children in this investigation were given ToM tasks that can require significant verbal comprehension skills, and competence in communication was estimated solely on the basis of teacher ratings of deaf children's language.

> There is an important methodological issue here. Children who have poor language skills may fail ToM tasks just because of the high language demands.

The aim of the first study in the present investigation, therefore, was to test deaf children on false-belief tasks using 'thought pictures' (Custer, 1996). These minimize the need for verbal comprehension. Activation of perisylvian language zones, however, has been found in similar picture-based tasks that do not require language decoding or production (Brunet, Sarfati, Hardy-Bayle, & Decety, 2000), suggesting a role for language in mediating ToM performance that extends beyond a simple input/output function to central cognition. Consequently, despite the use of pictorial ToM tasks, deaf children's language skills were directly assessed using a newly developed test of receptive ability in the syntax and morphology of British Sign Language (BSL; Herman, Holmes, & Woll, 1999). The goal was to determine whether a difference in performance on pictorial tasks would emerge between late- and native-signing deaf children, and whether this difference would disappear when the children's abilities in syntax, as well as in spatial intelligence, were controlled.

The use of a non-verbal task does not reduce all of the potential confounds from language skill since previous studies have suggested that areas of the brain that are involved in language processing are also involved in the processing of 'thought pictures' of the kind used here. Thus, the sign language abilities of all the deaf children were assessed so that language skill could be included in statistical analyses as well as non-verbal intelligence.

Study 1

Method

Participants

Sixty prelingually profoundly deaf children, 4 to 8 years of age, of whom 40 were late-signing children (*M* = 6,8) and 20 were native-signing children (*M* = 5,10) participated in this study. Most of the late-signing children were recruited from five day schools in the United Kingdom (three mainstreamed schools with sign language provision and two special schools with bilingual communication in English and BSL). A small number of native-signing children were also recruited from such schools. It was necessary to recruit most native-signing children through direct contact with their parents, however, because native signers are rare among the deaf population as a whole.

All these children were profoundly, prelingually deaf. Being born deaf, or becoming deaf in the first months of life, is very different from becoming deaf after having learned to talk so it is important that all the children in the study were similar in this respect. The definition of 'late signing' is not given here but the term is used in the introduction to describe children who do not have deaf parents and so do not learn sign from birth. This may be an over-simplification because some hearing parents use sign right from birth (Spencer & Harris, 2005).

In addition to the deaf children, forty hearing children, twenty 3-year-olds (*M* = 3,7) and twenty 4-year-olds (*M* = 4,4) were recruited as controls. The hearing children attended five nursery schools in the United Kingdom.

Procedure

All deaf children were tested in BSL by a deaf experimenter who was himself a native BSL signer.

Children were first tested for their level of receptive skill in the syntax and morphology of BSL with the BSL Receptive Skills Test (Herman et al., 1999). This test begins with a vocabulary check (e.g., the signs for items such as 'apple' and 'umbrella') to ensure that children are able to both comprehend and produce the signs relating to objects and people that are subsequently used in the test proper. In the test proper, children watch a video of a deaf adult who presents three practice sentences followed by 40 test sentences in BSL. The sentences are designed to assess six grammatical features in BSL (Sutton-Spence & Woll, 1999): spatial verb morphology (e.g., 'box under bed'), number/distribution (e.g., 'lots apple'), negation (e.g., 'can't reach'), size/shape specifiers (e.g., 'curly hair'), noun/verb distinctions (e.g., 'boy drink'), and handling classifiers (e.g., 'hold umbrella open walk'). For each sentence children respond by selecting a picture to match the signed sentence from a choice of three or four alternatives in a picture booklet. Testing continues until four consecutive test sentences are failed. Children's raw scores on this test (out of 40) were converted to standardized scores and used to calculate their 'signing' age.

Following the BSL assessment, children's understanding of 'thought bubbles' was evaluated following the procedure of Wellman, Hollander, and Schult (1996). Two pictures were shown, one depicting a boy thinking about a dog (a boy with an attached thought bubble containing a dog) and the other depicting a boy with a real dog (a boy with a dog on a lead). Children were asked to point to the picture showing a boy thinking about a dog: 'Which (pointing to the two pictures) boy think dog?' in BSL syntax, or 'Which boy is thinking about a dog?' in English. All but one of the children gave the correct answer, and in all cases the correct answer was confirmed for the children: 'This (pointing to picture) boy think dog' in BSL syntax, or 'This boy is thinking about a dog' in English. The ToM task makes use of 'thought bubbles' so it was important to establish that children were able to understand what they meant. For this reason there was a pre-test in which children were asked to select a picture showing a boy thinking about a dog. Note that hearing children were also included in the study to ensure that the ToM tasks produced the expected pattern of performance with most 4-year-olds succeeding and most 3-year-olds failing the task. Since children's performance can vary so much from one testing situation to another, it is very important to have comparison data from typically developing children that were collected under exactly the same conditions, using identical stimuli.

Subsequently, children were shown four ToM 'thought pictures': two involved understanding a central character's True Belief (TB), and the other two involved a False Belief (FB). The four thought pictures were: (1) a boy fishing thinks he has caught a fish (TB = fish/FB = boot,) illustrated in Figure 1; (2) a girl thinks she sees a tall boy over a fence (TB = a tall boy/FB = a small boy standing on a box); (3) a man thinks he is reaching into a cupboard for a drink (TB = a drink/FB = a mouse); and (4) a man thinks he sees a fish in the sea (TB = a fish/FB = a mermaid). In each case, a flap on which was depicted some plausible obstruction (item 1, reeds; item 2, the fence; item 3, the cupboard door; item 4, reeds) covered the critical object from the central character's view. Thus in all stories some aspect of the scene was obscured from the central character's sight. For example, in the fishing scene, a flap depicting reeds concealed the end of the protagonist's fishing rod. In the TB version of the picture, removal of the flap revealed that the protagonist had caught a fish; however, in the FB version, removal of the flap revealed a boot on the end of his line. Children covered the central story character with their hand while the flap was removed, to emphasize the character's ignorance of the contents of the flap. Once the children had viewed the picture and had lifted and replaced the flap, they were shown a separate picture of the central character (from the original picture) with a blank thought bubble above his or her head. Next to this picture were four small pictures. For the FB tasks, two of these pictures were of distracter items, one showed the content of the protagonist's belief and the other showed the actual object. In the TB condition, the true content of the belief was represented together with three distracters. The deaf children were asked, through gesture and pointing, to indicate which of the four pictures showed what the character was thinking. Finally, children were asked to point to the picture of the actual object concealed by the flap. The four thought pictures were presented in a counterbalanced order to the children and the selection of an individual thought picture as an FB or TB item was randomized across subjects.

The use of a flap, to cover the 'real' object, and getting the children to put their hand over the protagonist while pulling back the flap, were both intended to reinforce the message that the protagonist was ignorant of the true state of affairs. Note that children were asked to select the actual object as well as the object that the character was thinking about; and all children were also given both True and False Belief conditions. These controls were important to establish that children understood the task so that failure to correctly identify a false belief could not be dismissed as a general failure to understand the task. (Reality questions in standard ToM tasks serve the same function – see Paper 3.)

Figure 1 *Central elements of the 'thought picture' presented in the theory of mind 'fishing' task (adapted from Custer, 1996). (A) The thought picture illustration as first presented to the child (with removable flap in place). (B) The False Belief (FB) version of the picture (with flap removed). (C) The True Belief (TB) version of the picture (with flap removed). (D) The four response cards, along with the thought bubble in which children had to place the card that illustrated the character's belief. The four cards are (from left to right); distracter 1, belief item, distracter 2, and actual object (FB only)*

To summarize, for each picture children were asked to identify what a character believed was behind the flap and what was truly there. They were only credited with passing the task if they answered both the belief and reality questions correctly. Each child therefore received an FB score from 0 to2 and a TB score from 0 to 2.

After receiving the thought pictures, children were given the colored version of Raven's Progressive Matrices (Raven, 1962). The purpose was to assess

Table 1 Mean Theory of Mind (ToM), spatial mental age, and British Sign Language (BSL) scores for children from study 1

Group	N	Age (months)	Age Range (months)	ToM (0-2)	Spatial Mental Age (months)	Standardized BSL	Raw BSL
Native signers	19	71.11 (15.78)	48–102	1.42 (.61)	86.21 (24.98)	109.95 (10.22)	27.37 (5.45)
Late signers	32	81.75 (13.79)	54–105	0.34 (.65)	76.97 (23.02)	90.03 (13.15)	24.03 (15.56)
Hearing 4-year-olds	20	51.75 (3.16)	48–57	1.30 (.86)	N.A.	N.A.	N.A.
Hearing 3-year-olds	20	43.05 (3.38)	38–47	0.35 (.67)	N.A.	N.A.	N.A.

Note: Values in parentheses are standard deviations. N.A. = not applicable.

their non-verbal (spatial) mental age. The hearing control children were tested by a hearing experimenter and were assessed on the thought pictures (as described above) to establish age norms for typically developing children.

Results

Eight of the late-signing deaf children in this study either had very minimal BSL ability, or did not understand the procedure for the BSL Receptive Skills Test and hence no measure of their language was possible. A single, native-signing child did not understand the procedure for Raven's Progressive Matrices and was also excluded. Therefore, the analysis was based on results from 32 late signers and 19 native signers. The mean ToM (FB only), mental age, and (standardized) receptive language scores for all groups of children arepresented in Table 1.

> There were two ToM tasks so the maximum score was 2. Table 1 shows that the hearing 4-year-olds, most of whom would be expected to pass a ToM task, had a mean score of 1.3. Three-year-olds, most of whom would not be expected to pass a ToM task, had a mean score of 0.35. This supports the use of the thought bubble task as a valid test of ToM understanding. Note that, in footnote 1, the authors report that the validity of the task was also established in relation to standard ToM tasks. In developing a new task, it can be valuable to compare it with well-established tasks that are thought to be assessing the same kind of ability.

The deaf native signers were significantly younger than their late-singing counterparts, $t(49) = -2.53$, $p < .05$. Nevertheless, as can be seen in Table 1, the native signers significantly outperformed the late signers on the ToM tasks, $t(49) = 5.84$, $p < .001$. The difference between the late and native signers was comparable with that between the hearing 3- and 4-year-olds, because the hearing 4-year-olds significantly outperformed the hearing 3-year-olds, $t(38) = -3.88$, $p < .001$.[1] The difference in spatial mental age between the deaf native and late signers was nonsignificant, $t(49) = 1.34$; although the native signers scored significantly higher than the late signers in their standardized scores on the BSL test, $t(49) = 5.66$, $p < .001$. When the children's raw BSL scores were considered, however, the two groups did not differ significantly, $t(49) = .90$.

> As predicted, native signers were significantly better at the thought bubble task than late signers. Note that the two groups were comparable in non-verbal IQ – so differences in understanding the task could not be attributed to differences in general intelligence – and they also had equivalent raw scores on the BSL test. This means that they succeeded on a comparable number of items – and so understood a roughly equivalent amount – but the BSL scores of the younger children were age-appropriate whereas those of the older children were not.

For the combined sample of native and late signers, or for the two groups alone, there were no significant correlations between ToM and chronological age or spatial mental age or between ToM and the raw BSL scores. For the combined sample only, there was a significant correlation between ToM and standardized BSL scores, $r = .31$, $p < .05$. The correlation between standardized BSL and spatial mental age was also significant, $r = .30$, $p < .05$.

Across the entire sample of deaf children, there was a relationship between standardised BSL score and performance on the ToM task. However, as reported, there was also a significant correlation between standardised BSL score and non-verbal IQ so it is not clear which was the most important relationship. A partial correlation could have clarified the relationship.

The results from this first analysis showed that deaf native and deaf late signers did indeed differ on ToM performance. However, the native and late signers also differed in their standardized BSL scores. Whereas the mean scores of both groups were within the normal range in BSL receptive skills for their age, the native signing group (ranging from 93 to 129 in their standardized scores) were somewhat more advanced and the late signers were somewhat delayed (66–119). Therefore, to investigate further the role of proficiency in BSL, an additional analysis of the scores of a smaller group of deaf native and deaf late signers was conducted; namely, on all those children who had standardized BSL scores between 90 and 110 ($N = 24$). All of these children passed both TB control tasks (all achieving a TB score of 2). The ToM, mental age, and BSL scores of these children are presented in Table 2.

Although there were control True Belief (TB) trials for all children, these were not taken into account in the analyses. In the sub-sample of deaf children who had BSL scores that were age-appropriate, there was maximum performance on the TB trials.

In this reduced sample of children, the native and late signers differed significantly on their ToM scores, $t(22) = 7.60$, $p < .001$, and (marginally) in their chronological age, $t(22) = -2.06$, $p = .051$. They did not differ significantly on their spatial mental age, $t(22) = .56$, or on their standardized, $t(22) = 1.88$, or raw, $t(22) = -.98$, BSL scores.

Discussion

Despite their younger age, the native-signing children outperformed the late-signing children who were matched for BSL proficiency and spatial mental age. In this sense, the ToM performance of the native signers was particularly impressive. The native-signing children were advanced for their age in spatial ability, in keeping with the advanced performance on measures of spatial cognition shown by deaf adult signers (Emmorey, Klima, & Hickok, 1998). Consistent with other studies that have used measures of nonverbal intelligence (Peterson & Siegal, 1999), however, there was no significant direct relation between the spatial measures and ToM. It should be noted that the ToM tasks used in this study minimized receptive language demands (and required only nonverbal, pointing responses).

The pattern of differences in ToM development between native and late signers demonstrated in Study 1 is consistent with the previous literature on ToM in deaf children. In terms of the entire sample of deaf children, there was a modest statistically significant correlation between the standardized BSL scores and ToM performance that was similar to the findings reported by Astington and Jenkins (1999) on the relation between syntax and ToM in hearing children. In the present study, however, it is important to note that children were assessed for their level of ability in a sign language using a new, standardized test of receptive ability in syntax and morphology. When the BSL Receptive Skills Test was used to match two groups of native- and late-signing deaf children for skill in BSL, the groups differed in terms of their ToM understanding, demonstrating that syntax alone (at least as shown on this standardized test) did not explain the difference in ToM ability between native and late signers.

> *Note that language skills alone cannot explain the difference in ToM performance for the early and later signers.*

Study 1 points to the native signers' familiarity with mental states as inferred from conversations with other signers as a major candidate explanation for the difference in ToM ability between the native and late signers. It could be argued, however, that a difference in 'executive functioning' (EF) – which involves the ability to plan and shift attention flexibly in problem solving – between the two groups was responsible. In recent research, some studies (e.g., Frye, Zelazo, & Palfai, 1995; Perner & Lang, 1999) have suggested that EF does play a role in the ToM performance of hearing children. It is possible that the ability to inhibit immediate responses (an ability dependent on proper EF) may help children to succeed on ToM tasks because it enables them to overcome any 'reality bias' present in the task (Mitchell, 1994). One might hypothesize that EF may play a greater role in the performance of late, rather than native, signers given the suggestion that late signers are more impulsive than native signers and typically developing children (R. I. Harris, 1978).

Study 2 was designed to examine the role of EF in a sample of native- and late-signing children. Additionally, Study 2 included a test of the children's

Table 2 Mean Theory of Mind (ToM), spatial mental age, and British Sign Language (BSL) scores for a subsample of children with standardized BSL Scores between 90 and 110

Group	N	Age (months)	Age Range (months)	ToM (0-2)	Spatial Mental Age (months)	Standardized BSL	Raw BSL
Native signers	12	72.17 (17.43)	50–102	1.58 (.52)	88.00 (25.60)	104.00 (6.18)	25.50 (5.30)
Late signers	12	85.17 (13.13)	62–104	.17 (.39)	83.00 (17.08)	100.17 (3.43)	32.17 (23.06)

Note: Values in parentheses are standard deviations.

ability to deal with representations that were physical (photographic) rather than mental. This test was added as a further control to determine whether the difficulties that late signers display with ToM tasks are specific to mental representation or apply to representation more generally.

> Executive functioning has been highlighted as a contributory factor in ToM task performance. The possibility remains that deaf children who do not acquire a language right from birth might show differences in their executive functioning when compared with native signers. The use of a task designed to measure executive functioning also allowed the investigators to see whether difficulties with understanding ToM are specific or part of a more general difficulty with complex tasks.

Study 2

Method

Participants

All 51 deaf children (of the original 60 from Study 1) who were included in the analyses from Study 1 were to have taken part in Study 2. Unfortunately, as a result of illness or absence, only 39 of the 51 deaf children from Study 1 could be retested. The sample therefore included 21 late signers ($M = 7,10$) and 18 native signers ($M = 6,0$).

Procedure

As in Study 1, all the deaf children were tested individually by a deaf native-signing experimenter, using communication methods appropriate to the individual child. In Study 2, children were given a measure of EF, along with a measure of their ability to reason about nonmental (photographic) representation. A version of the Wisconsin Card-Sorting Task, adapted for young children (see, Cole & Mitchell, 2000), was used to test children's EF.

> The Wisconsin Card-Sorting Task was used as a standard measure of executive functioning. The idea behind this task – which can be used with both adults and children – is that it involves changing from sorting a set of cards according to one dimension to sorting them along another dimension. There has been considerable debate about exactly what this test is measuring (Towse et al., 2000) but it is the most widely used experimental test of executive functioning.

The task involves sorting cards according to rules that change during the testing session. The largely nonverbal procedure of the card-sorting task makes it ideal for use with deaf children. For this task, a deck of cards was created that varied according to the shape and color on each card. In total, there were four different shapes (triangles, stars, squares, and circles) and four different colors (pink, brown, green, and blue). Before testing, all children were tested for their ability to discriminate all four shapes and colors; all children managed successfully.

> *The task itself is non-verbal since the response is card sorting. However, it can be difficult for children to understand what is required and so, as here, there was a practice session involving corrective feedback.*

The children and the experimenter were then given two different sets of 20 cards in which each set varied on shape and color. For example, a sample child's set might include 10 circles (5 blue and 5 green) and 10 squares (5 blue and 5 green). The corresponding experimenter's set would consist of 10 stars (5 pink and 5 brown) and 10 triangles (5 pink and 5 brown). Both sets of cards were shuffled into a random order prior to testing. In the initial phase, the experimenter sorted five of his cards according to one dimension (shape or color) and the children were asked to do the same to their cards ('You do similar me' in BSL syntax). During this initial phase, corrective feedback was given. After successfully sorting five consecutive cards according to this dimension, the experimenter indicated that the children were then to change the dimension on which the cards were to be sorted (from shape to color or vice versa). The experimenter then sorted five of his cards according to this new dimension. The children were asked to sort five of their cards according to this new dimension. In this part of the procedure, no corrective feedback was given. Finally, the sorting rule (sort by color or by shape) was changed again and the children were asked to sort five more cards. One point was given for each correctly placed card in each of the last two phases of the procedure (without corrective feedback). Each child was therefore given a combined score of 0 to 10.

The test of nonmental representation used was the False Photo task (Zaitchik, 1990) following closely the procedure used by Peterson and Siegal (1998). The children were first shown a Polaroid™ instant camera with which the experimenter took a photograph of each child. The children then watched as the photograph developed. Next, the children were shown two dolls, a mother and baby, and a toy bath and bed, placed on a white board with a white background. The baby was in the bath and the mother was placed next to it. The children observed as the experimenter took a photograph with the dolls in this position. While this second photograph was developing, the experimenter made the mother doll move the baby doll from the bath to the bed. With the developing photograph still face down, the children were then given two 'ready-made' photographs, one of the original setup (the dolls in their original places) and another with the altered setup (the dolls in their 'current' places). The children were asked to point to the ready-made photograph that matched the developing Polaroid photograph. The children were then asked the control question, 'Where was the baby before?' (signed as 'baby before where?') and had to point to the correct location. Finally the children were asked, 'Where is the baby now?' (signed as 'baby now where?').

> *The False Photo task has been shown to produce better understanding than a standard ToM task. There are a number of reasons why it is an easier task. First, it has a lower language requirement since children are asked to point to one of two pictures. Secondly, the task provides children with physical props that aid them in thinking about past and present events: the use of the photo provides children with a record of the original location of the baby.*

Results

> *There was a significant correlation between performance in the ToM task in Study 1 and in the executive function task in Study 2 across the sample of deaf children but not for each group individually. There was no difference in the executive function scores of the early and late signers. Note, however, that the scores on the executive function task are close to ceiling for both groups so it may be that this task was not sufficiently discriminating. In part, interpretation of this negative finding depends on how the scores of the two groups compared with hearing peers. If both groups are similar to hearing peers, this would suggest that deaf children have age-appropriate scores. However, as the Wisconsin task is not standardised it is not possible to tell from these data.*

The children's performance on the various measures in Study 2 is shown in Table 3. The mean scores of the late and native signers on the measure of EF were not significantly different, $t(37) = 1.30$. For the combined sample, EF was correlated with ToM scores, $r = .35$, $p < .05$, and spatial mental age, $r = 44$, $p < .01$. These correlations were nonsignificant for the late signers and only the correlation between EF and mental age remained significant for the native signers, $r = 50$, $p < .05$. For the combined sample or the two groups alone, EF scores did not correlate significantly with BSL scores (raw or standardized), chronological age, or spatial mental age. All children, whether late or native signers, succeeded on the False Photograph task, answering both the test and control questions correctly.

> *All children succeeded in the False Photo task, showing that they had no difficulty in understanding the difference between a past and present event, providing that they had an external cue to guide them.*

Table 3 *Mean Theory of Mind (ToM), spatial mental age, British Sign Language (BSL), and Executive Functioning (EF) scores in study 2*

Group	N	Age (months)	ToM	Spatial Mental Age (months)	Standardized BSL	Raw BSL	EF (out of 10)
Native signers	18	72.00 (15.73)	1.44 (.62)	87.67 (25.58)	109.94 (10.51)	27.78 (5.30)	9.06 (1.21)
Late signers	21	82.24 (14.24)	.33 (.66)	80.86 (23.95)	95.10 (10.16)	26.90 (18.47)	8.52 (1.33)

Note: Values in parentheses are standard deviations.

As in Study 1, the differences between the two groups of deaf children were not significant for the measure of spatial mental age, $t(37) = .61$, or raw scores on the BSL test, $t(37) = .19$. The two groups were significantly different in terms of chronological age, $t(37) = -2.13$, $p < .05$, standardized BSL scores, $t(37) = 4.48$, $p < .001$, and ToM scores, $t(37) = 5.41$, $p < .001$.

Discussion

Although native-signing children outperformed late-signing children on pictorial ToM tasks, they did not differ significantly on tests of either False Photographic reasoning or EF. Whereas in the combined sample, EF was correlated with ToM responses, this did not explain the overwhelming advantage of native signers in ToM performance. A recent study by Remmel (1999) also found that EF did not explain ToM differences between late- and native-signing children. Moreover, as was reported in Peterson and Siegal's (1998) study of representational abilities in late-signing deaf children, there was very good performance on the False Photograph task. Study 2, therefore, served to demonstrate that the differences between the native and late signers could not be seen in terms of general differences in representation or EF. Executive functioning may play a significant role in explaining the ToM performance of other groups of children, however, such as impulsive children with behavioral disorders (Hughes, Dunn, & White, 1998).

General discussion

In the sample of late-signing children, standardized scores on a measure of syntax and morphology in BSL were modestly associated with ToM responses and so in this sense, the data of the present research are consistent with the proposal that syntax has an initial role in performance on ToM reasoning tasks. However, compared with the late signers with whom they were equated for level of ability in syntax, the native signers in the present studies excelled in their ToM performance although they were actually younger in age. The advantage shown by native signers on standard ToM task (Peterson & Siegal, 1999) extended even to pictorial tasks that minimized the need for verbal comprehension skills.

> *The authors point to differences in the specific verbal abilities that are required for particular ToM tasks. This illustrates that there are no 'pure' measures of cognitive abilities or, arguably, of any abilities. It is always important to ask what was measured and how the measures were obtained.*

It is plausible that proficiency at syntax in the form of sentence complementation (e.g., understanding sentences such as 'John thought [falsely] that the cookies were in the cupboard') as described by de Villiers and de Villiers

(2000) may play an important role in performance on certain ToM measures. For example, deaf children have been shown a sequence of pictures that convey a story involving a 'changed-contents' false-belief task, in which the contents of a container have been changed without the knowledge of a central story character. The child is required to select either a surprised or not surprised facial expression for the character in the story as aided by the pictorial content. On such 'relatively nonverbal' tasks, measures of sentence complementation given to oral deaf children (who converse in speech rather than in a sign language) correlate significantly with performance (de Villiers, 2000; de Villiers, de Villiers, Schick, & Hoffmeister, 2000). The BSL Receptive Skills Test that was given to the signing children in the present investigation does not directly assess the syntax of sentence complementation. Astington and Jenkins (1999) incisively note, however, that children who fail standard verbal ToM tasks spontaneously produce object complements in their speech. Moreover, as Astington and Jenkins observed, on pictorial tasks very similar to those used in this investigation (namely, those employed by Custer, 1996), hearing 3-year-olds correctly answered questions involving sentence complementation if those sentences took the structure [person]–[pretends]–[that x]: for example, 'He pretends that his puppy is outside'. In contrast, hearing 3-year-olds did poorly when given sentences that took the form [person]–[thinks]–[that x]: for example, 'He thinks that his puppy is outside'. Both the 'think' and 'pretend' sentences use the same object complement, yet children answer correctly only when 'pretend' is used. Given these considerations, the syntax of sentence complementation falls short of providing a complete account of ToM performance, at least on pictorial tasks.

Because the two deaf groups in the present investigation were also equivalent in their spatial intelligence and EF, these findings can be seen as pointing to the powerful impact of early access to conversation on ToM performance. In contrast with deaf late-signing children, deaf children for whom sign is their native language have early opportunities to converse about the beliefs of others and to formulate an understanding of how these can be false. In related research, we have investigated whether these effects may alternatively be seen in terms of extralinguistic influences, such as the special quality of sibling relationships in the families of native signers, irrespective of the level of sign language abilities (Woolfe, Want, & Siegal, 2001). In this work, the perceived quality of the sibling relationship and proficiency on referential communication measures (namely, those of Lloyd, Camaioni, & Ercolari, 1995) significantly predicted deaf children's performance on pictorial ToM tasks independently of scores on the BSL Receptive Skills Test. In keeping with the results of recent studies with hearing children (Cole & Mitchell, 2000; Cutting & Dunn, 1999), ToM performance was unrelated to the number of siblings. Thus communication itself, rather than mere exposure to sibling relationships, is independently associated with ToM reasoning in both deaf and hearing children.

Although there appear to be no significant differences between the deaf and hearing in the quality of attachment and mother-toddler interaction (Lederberg & Mobley, 1990), deaf children of hearing parents receive much less communication than do deaf children of deaf parents. Hearing mothers of deaf 2- and 3-year-olds direct more visual communication to their children than do hearing mothers of hearing children but they still communicate primarily through speech to which the children often do not attend (Lederberg & Everhart, 1998). In contrast, through proficiency in visual communication, deaf mothers of deaf children can match the responsiveness of hearing mothers of hearing children (Spencer & Meadow-Orlans, 1966).

Further work is required to determine whether there is a sensitive or optimal period for displaying ToM reasoning and whether hearing families who strive to acquire a sign language early can serve to boost ToM in the deaf child. As a number of studies (M. Harris, 1992; Marschark, 1993; Vaccari & Marschark, 1997) have shown, most hearing parents do not have sufficient proficiency in manual communication to optimize social interactions with their deaf children and to converse freely about imaginary or unobservable topics such as others' beliefs. Moreover, they will often use the oral mode to converse with other hearing family members, innocently limiting a deaf child's access to informal conversations that may encourage ToM development as well as related skills in social cognition (Forrester, 1993). In the present investigation, the level of BSL attained by hearing family members of late-signing deaf children was highly variable. It should be noted that one 8-year-old late signer who failed the ToM tasks had family members who nevertheless were all actively learning BSL.

> The point in development at which particular external factors exert maximum effect is a key issue for developmental psychology. The Meins et al. study (Paper 3) suggests that the origin of children's developing understanding of the mental lives of others lies in the early interactions between infants and their parents.

Similarly, the schools of late signers cannot be relied on to provide a substitute for these kinds of conversations about the unobservable beliefs of others. Although attending signing all-deaf schools should promote more conversations in a sign language, the sign language fluency of adult figures in schools is variable and hence the quality of communication is not uniform. For late signers who attend mainstreamed schools, adults who have the responsibility to translate information to a sign language for deaf children (and to use complementary forms of visual communication) are often only present for the translation of curricular matter, and not for informal conversations in school that have the potential to stimulate development reflected in ToM reasoning. Few hearing children are taught to sign and, for those who do, this is usually extremely limited and is a mode of communication that is not used among their hearing peers.

The present studies converge with research on ToM in hearing children that points to the importance of conversational awareness in successful task performance. In research on hearing children, specifying that the ToM task is intended to refer to how a person with a false belief will initially be misled — rather than to the revised true belief of a person once a deception is discovered — facilitates children's correct responses (Joseph, 1998; Lewis & Osborne, 1990; Siegal & Beattie, 1991; Surian & Leslie, 1999). In contrast with hearing 3-year-olds, however, late-signing deaf children did not improve significantly on ToM tasks when the questions were explicitly 'conversationally supported' along these lines (Peterson & Siegal, 1995, 1999).

As noted elsewhere (Siegal, 1999), this pattern points to the importance of delineating two types of abilities in conversation. First is the ability to understand the pragmatic implications of questions (e.g., that they refer to an initial, rather than a final, search). A failure to follow these implications can mask hearing children's conceptual understanding, and that understanding only becomes apparent once the need to make specific conversational implications about the purpose and relevance of the task is removed. Second, there is the awareness involved in understanding the general shared grounding for commination in the mutual beliefs, knowledge, and assumptions underpinning conversational exchanges (Clark & Brennan, 1991). Deaf late-signing children are liable to be cut off from the early exchanges about similarities and differences in mental states with parents and siblings that are familiar to hearing children and native signers. Moreover, they are isolated from experience with the structure of well-formed conversation. This experience alerts normal hearing children by the age of 3 years that speakers are epistemic subjects who store and seek to provide information about the world (P. L. Harris, 1996). Thus, ToM is not simply a matter of vocabulary and syntax, but is the end result of social understanding mediated by early conversational experience. In the case of deaf late-signing children, limitations in conversational knowledge that involve the general shared grounding for communication may preclude good performance on ToM tasks. Late signers retain difficulties even when questions are conversationally supported in specifying that the tasks are intended to refer to how a person with a false belief will initially be misled.

Of course, the results of the present investigation do not mean that late signers are completely without insight into others' mental states. Marschark, Green, Hindmarsh, and Walker (2000) have recently reported that late signers age 8 to 13 years (considerably older than most children tested in the present studies) have the ability to attribute mental states correctly in generating stories about others with whom they have interacted hypothetically. Yet paradoxically Russell et al. (1998) found that problems on certain ToM tasks that require verbal story comprehension remain in deaf children of hearing parents even at the age of 13 to 16 years of age. Although performance on a wider range of tasks should be considered, this discrepancy may be reconciled in terms of Keil's (1989) observation with regard to children's lack of success on tasks in which they are required to reason about reality and the phenomenal world of appearances and beliefs. According to this account, it may be that children's difficulties do not necessarily reflect their intrinsic inability to deal simultaneously with two representations in general (i.e., of reality and false beliefs), but rather their lack of knowledge about how to deal with the apparent contradiction between the two in predicting behavior. In comparison with late-signing children even in adolescence, native-signing deaf children enjoy an early conversational access that facilitates acquisition of the specific ability to interpret the behavioral outcome of mental states (i.e., that behavior is determined by false beliefs rather than reality) on measures of ToM reasoning.

In this respect, more research is required to address processes by which children come to share others' beliefs in the conversational networks of deaf late- and native-signing children. There is a need to explore how the actual quality of communication between the deaf and their conversational partners influences their ToM understanding.

Acknowledgements

This article was prepared with support to T. W. from the Lord Snowdon Trust and the Wingate Scholarship Fund and by a Nuffield Foundation New Career Development Fellowship grant to S. C. W. and M. S. The authors thank the anonymous reviewers for their many helpful suggestions.

Notes

1   In conjunction with this study, another sample of twenty 3-year-old (M = 3,6) and twenty 4-year-old (M = 4,4) hearing children were given the same four pictorial tasks (two as FB versions and two as TB) as in Study 1 together with two 'standard' ToM tasks (the deceptive box and change-in-location, or 'Sally-Anne', tasks: Baron-Cohen, Leslie, & Frith, 1985; Perner et al., 1987). All children passed the two TB pictorial trials. The mean pass rate for the two types of FB tasks was highly similar to those of the children in Study 1, both for the 3-year-olds (pictorial = .55, standard = .53) and the 4-year-olds (pictorial = 1.37, standard = 1.45). For the entire sample of 40 children, the correlation between scores on the two types of FB tasks (pictorial and standard) was .42, p < .01. Call and Tomasello (1999) reported a similar association between children's performance on nonverbal and verbal ToM tasks.

Paper 13   Face-processing in children with Williams Syndrome (Karmiloff-Smith et al., 2004)

The final paper investigates another specific socio-cognitive skill in children showing an atypical pattern of development. The children have Williams Syndrome, a rare genetic disorder, and the task is recognising faces. Just as in the case of deaf and autistic children's understanding of Theory of Mind, there are reasons for investigating specific links between face-processing and Williams Syndrome. Children who have this disorder typically have a very good ability to process faces – and to interact socially with other people – that exceeds their cognitive capacities in other areas.

The paper begins by reviewing evidence on the development of face-processing abilities. These develop through infancy, beginning with a very general preference for stimuli with more information in the top than the bottom, through a marked preference for faces over other stimuli of similar complexity and, finally, to an ability to recognise specific faces. However, while infancy research supports the view of face-processing as a gradually unfolding skill, adult data on people who suffer from prosopagnosia suggests that face-processing is a pre-specified skill that operates independently from other kinds of cognitive processing. This is because one of the defining symptoms of prosopagnosia is an inability to recognise people's faces.

These two findings raise an important theoretical question about the interrelation of data from developmental and adult studies in the understanding of specific disabilities. Is evidence that a specific ability develops over time, rather than being innately specified from birth, compatible with evidence that this ability appears to be discrete in adulthood? The authors argue that a key issue is discovering the developmental trajectory of the ability to see how this might differ in children with an atypical pattern of development.

Journal of Child Psychology and Psychiatry, 2004, *45(7),* 1258–1274

Exploring the Williams syndrome face-processing debate: the importance of building developmental trajectories

Annette Karmiloff-Smith,[1] Michael Thomas,[2] Dagmara Annaz,[2] Kate Humphreys,[1] Sandra Ewing,[1] Nicola Brace,[3] Mike Van Duuren[4], Graham Pike,[3] Sarah Grice,[1] and Ruth Campbell[5]

[1]Neurocognitive Development Unit, Institute of Child Health, London, UK; [2]School of Psychology, Birkbeck College, London, UK; [3]The Open University, UK; [4]King Alfred's College, Winchester, UK; [5]Department of Human Communication, University College London, UK

In this article, we investigate the emergence of face recognition abilities in a rare genetic developmental disorder, Williams syndrome. The capacity for species recognition is one of the most fundamental abilities across the animal kingdom. One might therefore expect this to be a strong candidate for an innate ability in the case of the human infant. Yet the past couple of decades have revealed, at both the behavioural and brain levels, that the recognition of faces is a very gradual developmental process in both humans and other species such as the chick (Johnson & Morton, 1991). Indeed, brain localization and specialization in the processing of human faces, i.e., the gradual modularization of function over developmental time (Karmiloff-Smith, 1992, 1998), extends very progressively across the first 12 months of life and beyond (Johnson & de Haan, 2001). If infants start with anything resembling an innately specified template, it is unlikely to be face specific but rather in the form of a T-shape in which more information at the top of a stimulus parsed as an object is particularly attractive to the young infant's visual system (Simion, Macchi Cassia, Turati, & Valenza, 2001). With developmental time, however, the human face itself becomes increasingly the preferred stimulus (Johnson & Morton, 1991), enhanced not only by the massive input of faces but also by the fact that faces form a crucial site of attention for the social interactional patterns that develop over the first months of life.

Imaging experiments have shown that young infants' brains initially process upright human faces, inverted human faces, monkey faces and objects all in a relatively similar way across both hemispheres (Johnson & de Haan, 2001; de Haan, 2001). However, with development, brain processing of human upright faces becomes increasingly specialised and localised to the fusiform gyrus in the right hemisphere (Passarotti et al., 2003). Despite these developmental data pointing to very progressive specialization and localization of face processing, some theorists claim that the human brain is pre-specified with an independently-functioning face-processing module. Such claims are based on the fact that *adult* patients can present with prosopagnosia, i.e., a selective inability to recognize familiar faces, despite showing no obvious impairments elsewhere (Bruyer et al., 1983; de Renzi, 1986; Farah, Levinston, & Klein, 1995; Temple, 1997). So, there is still a debate concerning the extent to which face recognition abilities are part of the hardwired functional architecture of the infant brain versus the extent to which these emerge in adults mainly as a product of development. Can developmental disorders address this question, particularly those where face recognition appears to exceed general cognitive ability, such as in Williams syndrome?

Williams syndrome

Williams syndrome (WS) is a genetic disorder in which some 25 genes are deleted on one copy of chromosome 7, leading to serious deficits in spatial cognition, number, planning and problem solving (see Donnai &

Karmiloff-Smith, 2000, for full details). IQ scores are in the 50s to 60s range (Udwin & Yule, 1991). Of particular interest to cognitive neuro-scientists is the fact that two domains – language and face processing – show particular behavioural proficiency compared to the general levels of intelligence reached by this clinical group. Indeed, WS scores on some language and face-processing tasks fall in the normal range. When such findings first arose, they were heralded as demonstrating that, in the case of face processing, for instance, WS presents with an 'intact' or 'preserved' face-processing module (e.g., Bellugi, Sabo, & Vaid, 1988; Bellugi, Wang, & Jernigan, 1994; Wang, Doherty, Rourke, & Bellugi, 1995; though see Bellugi, Lichtenberger, Mills, Galaburda, & Korenberg, 1999, for more recent discussion). While some have rejected these claims (Karmiloff-Smith, 1997, 1998; Deruelle, Mancini, Livet, Cassé-Perrot, & de Schonen, 1999), others maintain that people with the syndrome display normal face process-ing (e.g., Deruelle, Rondan, Mancini, & Livet, 2003; Tager-Flusberg, Plesa-Skwerer, Faja, & Joseph, 2003). This is of course tantamount to claiming that face processing *develops* normally in WS.

Note the discussion of what it is for a process to be 'intact' or 'normal'. As noted in Chapter 1, development may take many different routes and, even though adult process-ing may appear to be similar across individuals, this similarity in the endpoint may dis-guise a number of different developmental pathways.

One of the problems with many of the WS face-processing studies is that terms like featural/piecemeal/componential/local/analytical versus config-ural/holistic/global/gestalt have been used interchangeably, as if they were synonymous, and thus have not been adequately specified. In this paper, we use the term 'featural' to refer to the ability to identify faces based on individual features (eyes, nose, mouth, chin), and the term 'con-figural' to refer to the ability to differentiate faces based on sensitivity to the spatial distances amongst internal features, i.e., second-order relational information. Configural face processing is associated with maturity of face recognition encoding and 'expert' recognition in adults. By contrast, the term 'holistic' is deemed to cover the gluing together of facial features (and hairline) into a gestalt, without necessarily conserving the spatial distances between features (Maurer, Le Grand, & Mondloch, 2002; Tanaka & Farah, 1993). In other words, the capacity to process information holistically does not involve the processing of second-order relational information. We start with a review of previous work on face processing in Williams syndrome, followed by three new experiments with this clinical population.

The authors identify a number of differences in the kind of face-processing tasks that have been used in different studies. They draw an important distinction between config-ural face processing, which involves the recognition and identification of specific faces using information about the relations among features, and featural face processing which allows the recognition that something, comprised of key features, is a face. The latter is present very early in infancy but the former develops over the first year of life and beyond.

Previous WS face-processing studies

There are no experimental studies of face processing in infants with WS to complement the studies of healthy infants discussed in our introduction. However, some observational work, as well as experiments indirectly tapping face processing, revealed that infants with WS spend significantly more time focused on faces than on objects (Bellugi, Lichtenberger, Jones, Lai, & St. George, 2000; Laing et al., 2002; Mervis & Bertrand, 1997). This has led many authors to assume that the WS infant's inordinate attention to faces explains why adults with WS end up achieving good behavioural scores on some face-processing tasks. But does such early attention to faces necessarily lead to configural processing in older individuals with WS?

> Studies of face processing in individuals with Williams Syndrome (WS) have used a variety of tasks. Standardised measures of face recognition tend to show responses within the normal range but more detailed analysis has revealed that the way that individuals with WS recognise faces may be unusual. Again, this reflects the idea that overall measures of performance may obscure strategic differences.

The initial claims that adolescents and adults with WS exhibit face recognition skills that are 'intact'/'spared' (i.e., developed normally) were based on findings that performance on the standardised face-processing tasks like the Benton Facial Recognition Test and the Rivermead Face Memory Task was at normal or near normal levels. However, several studies subsequently challenged the notion of an 'intact' face-processing module and suggested that people with WS achieve their normal scores by resorting to different strategies from controls. Karmiloff-Smith (1997) reported that on a face-matching task, adult participants with WS (N = 10) did not differ from chronological-age-matched controls with respect to featural analysis, but were significantly worse when items necessarily required configural analysis, i.e., taking account of second-order relations. These preliminary findings, the result of acknowledged post-hoc analyses, gained support from a later study by Deruelle et al. (1999). Twelve children and adults with WS, aged between 7 and 23, were compared against chronological-age (CA) and mental-aged (MA) matched controls in a task requiring participants to decide whether two pictures of faces were the same or different when presented in upright and inverted conditions (their second experiment). The clinical group was less subject to an inversion effect than the controls. The authors explained these results by a greater reliance of the WS participants on featural analysis in both the upright and inverted conditions, whereas the controls used predominantly featural processing for the inverted faces and configural processing for the upright faces. This led the authors to speculate that WS face processing is not merely delayed but follows a different developmental pathway. In a third experiment, Deruelle et al. (1999) investigated the processing of configurally and featurally modified schematic faces and geometric shapes. Yet again, the CA and MA matches produced significantly fewer errors than the WS group on configural items, but no differences emerged with respect to the featural ones. The 1999 Deruelle et al. study adds further support to the claim that people with WS are biased to process featural over configural information, regardless of the type of facial (real faces or schematic faces) or geometric stimuli.

The claim here is that individuals with WS process faces more at a featural level and less at a configural level and that this processing bias is present for other stimuli, not just faces.

Two recent papers have, however, challenged this now rather general conclusion and claimed that people with WS process faces in exactly the same way as controls (Deruelle et al., 2003; Tager-Flusberg et al., 2003).

Deruelle et al. (2003) sought to explore holistic face processing in WS. They compared 12 children and adolescents with WS (aged 6 to 17 years) against controls in their ability to match faces to either a low or high spatial frequency filtered target face. Two control groups were used, either matched individually on chronological age or on overall mental age. All groups tended to find face matching easier to a low spatially filtered target face (i.e., a face in which the broad patterns of light and dark were preserved but fine detail was lost) than a high spatially filtered face. WS performance fell between the CA and MA control groups but was not significantly different from either. While Deruelle et al. took these results to indicate that face-processing abilities develop normally in children with WS, the sensitivity of responses to the spatial frequency manipulation was unchanging with age across all the groups, despite the wide age range. This implies that, by the age of testing, any developmental change had already plateaued in terms of holistic face processing, making it impossible to assess the implications for the WS participants on the developmental trajectory.

In typically developing children, the major changes in face-processing ability occur over the first year of life. Accordingly, age-related changes are unlikely to occur several years later even in a population showing atypical development.

Tager-Flusberg et al. (2003) have also recently argued in favour of normally developing face processing in WS. That study had the merit of using a considerably larger sample than previous work, including 47 adolescents and adults with WS (aged 12 to 36 years) and 39 CA-matched controls. They were tested on the standardised Benton Face Recognition Test used in previous studies, as well as on a part-whole paradigm. This latter task involved matching individual face parts in two conditions, either in isolation or in the context of a whole face. The authors predicted that if the WS group were less influenced by the overall context of a face, they should show a reduced difference between the two conditions, whereas the controls should be aided in the recognition of individual features by their presentation in the context of a face. Face orientation was also varied to assess whether the ability to use the whole-face context was disrupted by inversion to the same extent in the control and WS groups. While the overall accuracy was better in the CA-matched control group than in the WS group, the presence or absence of surrounding face context had the same effect for upright presentation on controls and the clinical group. Tager-Flusberg et al. present their results as challenging previous WS data that pointed to atypical face processing and argue that earlier studies were underpowered because of small Ns. However, it is not clear that their task addresses the same aspect of face processing as previous studies. Their part-whole task (taken from Tanaka & Farah, 1993) concerns the processing of individual features recognized in isolation or in the context of a whole face. This taps, as the authors recognize, the processing of the face gestalt, i.e., first-order holistic processing, rather than second-order configural processing. Indeed, throughtout their article, Tager-Flusberg et al. contrast featural processing with 'holistic' processing rather than with configural processing. Yet the Deruelle et al. (2003) study indicates that individuals with WS are not markedly impaired on holistic processing and none of the existing research, including our own, has claimed that individuals with WS are incapable of first-order holistic processing. The debate is about second-order configural processing. Of importance, too, is the fact that in the Deruelle et al. study holistic processing assessed by spatial frequency manipulations exhibited no developmental change across the age range employed by Tager-Flusberg and colleagues. Similarly, when these researchers examined developmental change across their (wide) age range, they also found no correlation between age and performance in either the WS or CA groups. If the part-whole task targets holistic processing, and if holistic processing is at ceiling in both normal and clinical populations in the age ranges examined, then the conclusions than can be drawn regarding the typicality or atypicality of face-processing development in WS are obviously limited.

Note the specificity of the face-processing task used in the Tager-Flusberg study and the age range of the participants, the youngest of whom was 12 years old.

As noted, claims of atypicality in Ws face processing revolve around the extent to which these individuals make use of *second-order configural relations* when recognising faces. This is a capacity that emerges over developmental time in healthy controls. Therefore, it is the inversion condition used by Tager-Flusberg et al. that is potentially more informative here, since inversion causes disruption particularly to configural processing (Diamond & Carey, 1986). Unfortunately, Tager-Flusberg and colleagues' WS data are uninterpretable in this regard, because the clinical group is at floor on inverted stimuli. By contrast, two previous studies from separate laboratories have found significantly less difference between upright and inverted face recognition in WS groups compared to controls (Deruelle et al., 1999; Rossen, Jones, Wang, & Klima, 1995), again supporting the claim that this clinical population is atypical with regard to configural processing. The possibility that inconsistent findings in the WS face-processing literature are a result of confounding holistic and configural processing is one to which we will return. For the moment, we focus on further investigating configural processing in WS face recognition.

> There is an important design issue here that hinges on the notion of developmental change. A traditional way to examine differences between typical and atypical groups is to select participants from the atypical population and then select carefully matched controls. After matching, overall group comparisons are made to see if the two groups differ. Such matching does not take into account the possibility that the pathways – trajectories – of development in the two groups might be different since age is not included in the comparison. This possibility is not taken into account even when there are two control groups, one matched on age and the other on mental age.

The importance of developmental trajectories

Since the major theoretical dispute concerns whether face recognition develops normally in WS, it will be our contention that explanations must be couched in terms of developmental trajectories (see discussions in Karmiloff-Smith, 1998, and Thomas & Karmiloff-Smith, 2002). Indeed, this stance will influence our analytic techniques. It will cause us to move from comparisons of the WS group against individually-matched controls which we and other groups have used in the past (where the relation of performance to age is discarded in analyses once control participants are selected) to the construction of functions specifically linking performance with age. Our comparisons will relate performance to chronological age in both the control and clinical samples and, in the latter, also between our face-processing tasks and developmental stages on a number of standardised tests, including face recognition, visuospatial processing, and language (see Thomas et al., 2001, for a similar analytical approach). We believe that our new trajectory approach to disorders offers more insight with respect to the way in which development may have proceeded *over time* in a deviant fashion, even though the behavioural proficiency, measured by matching controls at a specific CA or MA, may end up similar to controls. Moreover, individual variability is as much a problem for individual matching as it is for building trajectories. Each participant exhibits individual variation from each group norm. In addition, we try to show in this paper that comparing trajectories has a marked advantage over individual matching with regard to MA comparisons. In an individually matched comparison, everything rides on the choice of MA measure and this is typically theoretically laden. However, if one builds a task-specific typical developmental trajectory, one can then evaluate whether the atypical group fits on the typical developmental trajectory according to a range of metrics. These can be theoretically neutral (does each individual fit *anywhere* on the trajectory), or according to CA, or according to a variety of MA measures. Finally, where wide age ranges are a problem for studies matching on CA or MA and age is ignored in subsequent analyses, the wide age range can actually be exploited positively when building developmental trajectories.

> *Mental Age matching is particularly problematic because there is no single way to measure mental age. Sometimes matching is done on the basis of verbal mental age but often, as is the case where children are likely to have language difficulties, matching is done on the basis of non-verbal mental age. As the authors note, the choice of measure is never neutral since a researcher will always have an implicit or explicit theory about precisely which variables should be matched.*

Our aim in this article is threefold. In our first experiment we aim to produce clearer evidence of the configural processing deficit and reduced inversion effect in a WS group, by using real faces in a task specifically tailored to this purpose. In our second experiment, we concentrate on the inversion effect. We establish a cross-sectional, task-specific developmental trajectory for a wide age range of normal controls on a task that embeds the recognition of inverted faces in the naturalistic context of a story-book. We then derive and contrast the trajectory on this task for a group of individuals with WS. In Experiment 3, we concentrate on sensitivity to configural vs. featural transformations of schematic faces and geometric patterns, once more building and contrasting developmental trajectories for the typical and atypical groups. In contrast to the findings of Deruelle et al. (2003) and Tager-Flusberg et al. (2003), our tasks allow us to chart developmental change in performance across our age ranges in both groups. In each case, we will reveal patterns of atypicality in WS face recognition over developmental time, even when accuracy levels are broadly similar.

Hypotheses

Experiment 1: If face recognition in WS has developed normally, individuals with WS should show no difference in accuracy compared to controls in discriminating a target face from a featurally or configurally transformed version of the target; moreover, if WS face processing has developed normally, then performance should be similarly influenced by the nature of the transformation and by inversion.

Experiment 2: When required to recognize contextualised faces in a storybook task, presented in upright or inverted orientation, we expect controls to become increasingly accurate and rapid with age with respect to upright faces, but also to show increased sensitivity to inversion (since this disrupts configural processing). If face recognition in WS has developed normally, the clinical group should show the same pattern as the controls with increasing chronological age. By contrast, if the developmental trajectory is simply delayed, then performance should be predicted by developmental age on the standardised Benton face recognition test, or on a standardised test of visuospatial ability (but possibly not on a standardised test of vocabulary). Finally, if face processing in WS follows a deviant trajectory then these predictions should not hold.

The trajectory of atypical development may be different from that of typical development or it may be delayed. In the former case, one would expect that the pattern of performance across tasks at any age (or at least most ages) would be different for typically and atypically developing children whereas, if development is delayed, the pattern will be similar to that of younger children. One way of finding out whether trajectories are different or merely delayed is to look at what predicts performance. If the same factors predict performance in typically and atypically developing children, this suggests that development is following a similar pathway in both groups. If different factors are predictive in the two groups, this implies that development is following a different path in the two groups. However, in order to draw such a conclusion, it is important that development across the same part of the trajectory is being compared since, at different stages of development, different skills may predict performance.

Experiment 3: We expect controls to demonstrate an emerging skill in detecting configural transformations in upright faces with increasing age. If face recognition in WS has developed normally, the clinical group should show the same pattern as the controls when matching schematic face and non-face stimuli transformed configurally or featurally. By contrast, if the developmental trajectory is merely delayed, then it should be predicted by developmental age on the Benton task, or on a standardised test of visuospatial ability. Finally, if face processing in WS follows a deviant trajectory, then these predictions should not hold.

Experiment 1: Investigating configural and featural processing of real faces

Experiment 1 provides detailed data on featural and configural face processing in adults with WS. The aim of this study was to determine whether the endpoint of face processing is the same in adults with WS as it is in normal adults. This is a starting point for investigating a developmental trajectory since it is important to know whether two developmental processes have ended up in the same place in typically and atypically developing individuals.

We begin by assessing the presence of differences in configural processing and in the inversion effect in WS using real faces in a test specifically designed for this purpose by Mondloch and colleagues (Mondloch, Le Grand, & Maurer, 2002).

Method

Participants[1]

Fourteen adult participants with WS were tested on this task. Two did not fully understand the instructions and their data were excluded from the analyses. The 12 remaining participants had a mean CA of 30;0 (SD: 11;11, range: 16; 3–51; 0). Language ability was assessed using the Peabody Picture Vocabulary test (Dunn & Dunn, 1981) for which their mean test age was 13;10 (SD: 6; 7, range: 8; 2–30; 8). Visuospatial ability was assessed using the Pattern Construction subtest of the British Abilities Scale (BAS-II; Elliot, Smith, & McCulloch, 1996). The mean spatial test age of the WS group was 5; 4 (SD: 1; 7 range 3; 7–8; 9). Thus the WS group exhibited the characteristic disparity between these two abilities (language greater than visuospatial skill: paired *t*-test, *t* = 5.42, df = 11, *p* < .001), alongside overall delay. A control group was individually matched to each participant in the WS group, based on chronological age, gender and socio-economic status. The choice of a chronological age match was based on the claims that face processing is an independently-functioning, intact ability in this clinical population, as well as to equate to the best extent possible for life experience with faces in the two groups. MA controls could have been interesting, too, but were not our main focus here. The CA matches were on average within 4.5 months of each of the participants with WS, with the mean CA of the control group being 29; 11 (SD: 11; 6, range 16;6–51;0). A comparison of the CAs of the control and WS groups revealed no significant difference (paired *t*-test, *t* = .19, df = 11, *p* = .856).

Note that matching was done on the basis of chronological age, gender and socioeconomic status. The authors explain their rationale for matching in this way, which is appropriate here because individuals with WS are thought to have age-appropriate face matching skills. This matching is also appropriate because of the predicted differences between featural and configural face processing, the latter becoming better with age and experience of faces. (Interestingly, by the age of 4 months, face recognition tends to be better for faces of individuals from familiar racial groups [Sangrigoli & de Schonen, 2004] suggesting that experience has an important role to play.)

Stimuli

A photo of a real face (called Jane) was used to create featural and configural sets of new faces. In the featural set, new faces were created by replacing the original features (eyes and mouth) with the features of different faces. In the configural set, features were moved up or down within the face contour, or moved closer together or further apart in relation to the original positions of the features (for more detailed description of the task used with a different population, see Mondloch, Le Grand, & Maurer, 2002; note the 'contour' condition of that study was not employed here).

The featural and configural face processing were chosen to be rather similar to one another in that they both involve the manipulation of features within a face.

Procedure

The procedure employed a well-tested paradigm for directly differentiating between featural and configuring processing of real faces (Mondloch et al., 2002). Participants were presented sequentially with two faces and asked to determine whether the two faces were the same or different. Trials were blocked into upright and inverted trials, and within those, separate blocks where faces were featurally altered or configurally altered (referred to as 'spacing' in Mondloch et al.). Trials were blocked to encourage participants to adopt specific face-processing strategies (Mondloch et al., 2002).

Testing involved the presentation of two faces and asking if they were the same or different. Note that trials were blocked so that faces were either upright or inverted and either a featural or configural change was made. It is unusual to block trials in this way but the aim here was to increase the use of strategies. If people do the same task several times in a row, they are likely to develop an effective strategy.

The testing session began with 12 practice trials, to ensure that all participants understood the instructions and meaning of the words 'same' and 'different'. During the task proper, each participant was presented on a computer laptop with 30 trials from the featural and configural sets respectively. For each participant, the upright block was always presented before the inverted block. The order of configural and featural blocks within these was counterbalanced. Each block consisted of 15 'same' and 15 'different' randomised trials. During each trial, the target face was presented for 400 ms and the second face, to which the participant had to respond on the keyboard with 'same' or 'different', was displayed until the response button was pressed. The inter-stimulus interval was 300 ms, a delay chosen to prevent apparent-motion cues from the presentation of a different face (Mondloch et al., 2002).

There were 12 practice trials to familiarise participants with the task since they were unlikely to have encountered such a task before.

Bright yellow Velcro pads were stuck on the two relevant keys to make it easy for participants to respond. For each trial a target face was followed by a test face that could either be identical to the target face or transformed configurally or featurally. The dependent variables were reaction time and accuracy.

Note that the time between the presentation of items for the same/different judgment was carefully chosen to remove the possibility that one face would appear to 'move' to become the second face.

For the analysis, we divided the task into two components: *Identity Recognition* (for all items where no change had been made between target and test face and the participant correctly responds 'same'), and *Difference Detection* (where the participant correctly spots that the test face differs from the target, either due to a configural or featural transformation, and responds 'different'). We consider the two sets of responses separately, because transformations are only relevant to difference detection.

Results

Identity Recognition

A comparison of accuracy levels in identity recognition revealed no significant difference between the groups (ANOVA: main effect of group: $F(1,22) = 1.38$, $p = .253$, $\eta_p^2 = .059$). In addition, both groups performed equally well on upright and inverted faces. Prior to analysis, response time data were cropped so that outliers that fell two standard deviations away from each individual's mean time were eliminated. This removed 4.7 per cent of the data points from the WS group and 4.4 per cent of the data points from the CA control group.

Outlying scores were removed before data analysis.

For identity recognition, individuals with WS tended to respond more slowly than CA controls, but this effect was not reliable ($F(1,22) = 3.38$, $p = .081$, $\eta_p^2 = .132$). Where the WS were slower (in mean scores), they were also less accurate than the control group, suggesting that there were no speed–accuracy trade-offs at work.

> When participants who are slow are also less accurate, this suggests that both speed and accuracy are reflecting performance in the same way. If participants who are slower are more accurate, this suggests that there is a trade-off between speed and error, which can pose problems for the analysis.

Whether identity recognition trials fell within configurally transformed or featurally transformed blocks had no effect on performance (effect of transformation block: errors, $F(1,22) = 1.02$, $p = .323$, $\eta_p^2 = .044$; response times, $F(1,22) = .43$, $p = .519$, $\eta_p^2 = .019$). No significant interactions of transformation block emerged with any of the other variables, implying that trial blocking of featurally vs. configurally transformed faces did not induce specific face-processing strategies sufficient to affect identity recognition. The mean accuracy levels and response times are provided in Table 1.

Difference Detection

The difference detection condition includes the additional variable of manipulation type: configural or featural. Accuracy and response times for difference detection are also included in Table 1. Once more, there was no significant difference in accuracy levels between the groups (effect of group: $F(1,22) = 2.03$, $p = .168$, $\eta_p^2 = .085$). Analysed in isolation, the CA control group exhibited a characteristic pattern in the difference detection task, whereby it turned out to be harder to detect configurally changed faces than featurally changes faces (main effect of transformation: $F(1,11) = 26.89$, $p < .001$, $\eta_p^2 = .710$), and whereby inverting the face added to the difficulty only for configurally changed faces (interaction of transformation ´ orientation: $F(1,11) = 61.97$, $p < .001$, $\eta_p^2 = .849$). Overall, the WS group experienced the same effects of transformation, i.e., configurally transformed faces were not additionally harder for the participants with WS (main effect of transformation in the WS group: $F(1,11) = 33.61$, $p < .001$, $\eta_p^2 = .753$, between-group comparison, interaction of group ´ transformation: $F(1,22) = .57$, $p = .457$, $\eta_p^2 = .025$). However, the clinical population did exhibit a differential effect of inversion on the face transformation compared to the control group. In particular, they demonstrated a larger inversion effect on featurally transformed faces than the CA control group and a smaller inversion effect on configurally transformed faces (between-group comparison,

Table 1 *Means and standard errors (SE) for accuracy (%) and response times (ms) in Identity Recognition and Difference Detection*

| | 'Featural' | | | | 'Configural' | | | |
| | Upright | | Inverted | | Upright | | Inverted | |
Identity Recognition Group	**Mean**	**(SE)**	**Mean**	**(SE)**	**Mean**	**(SE)**	**Mean**	**(SE)**
WS								
Accuracy	72%	(6%)	67%	(10%)	81%	(4%)	74%	(9%)
RT	1702	(355)	1531	(249)	1630	(377)	1565	(306)
Control								
Accuracy	80%	(6%)	83%	(4%)	74%	(5%)	87%	(5%)
RT	880	(101)	1011	(136)	1115	(147)	992	(87)

	Transformation							
	Featural				Configural			
	Upright		Inverted		Upright		Inverted	
Difference Detection Group	**Mean**	**(SE)**	**Mean**	**(SE)**	**Mean**	**(SE)**	**Mean**	**(SE)**
WS								
Accuracy	86%	(5%)	74%	(7%)	51%	(6%)	31%	(8%)
RT	1701	366	1569	333	1766	371	1895	444
Control								
Accuracy	85%	(5%)	83%	(6%)	75%	(4%)	29%	(7%)
RT	873	73	874	62	1033	99	1136	112

interaction of group 'transformation' orientation: $F(1,22) = 14.73$, $p = .001$, $\eta_p^2 = .401$). Inspection of Table 1 (lower panel) suggests that this interaction was driven most strongly by a greater disparity between WS and CA control groups in detecting configurally transformed upright faces. Indeed, in a direct comparison of detecting configural transformations in upright faces, the WS group were significantly worse than controls, but showed no difference when these stimuli were inverted (independent-sample t-tests comparing groups, Upright: $t(22) = 3.34$, $p = .003$; Inverted: $t(22) = .16$, $p = .878$). In other words, the normal configural expertise for upright faces found in the CA-matched controls was not apparent in the WS group, despite broadly equivalent overall levels of accuracy. The WS group responded more slowly than the CA control group but, as with Identity Recognition, this did not reach significance (main effect of group: $F(1,22) = 4.09$, $p = .056$, $\eta_p^2 = .157$).

Detailed analysis of the data from the difference detection task showed that there was a subtle difference between the two groups. This lay in the response of the WS group to upright faces with a configural change. With these stimuli, participants from the WS group were noticeably less accurate than controls at detecting transformations and they were also, on average, over 700 ms slower in responding.

Discussion

The clinical group turned out to be as accurate as the CA controls on both identity recognition and difference detection and, although they tended to respond more slowly, the difference was not significant in either condition. By these measures alone, one might conclude that face recognition had developed normally in the WS group. However, the groups diverged in other important ways, in particular on transformations in the difference detection task. While configural transformations were harder to detect than featural transformations, the key condition that separated the groups was performance on upright configural faces, where controls were significantly more accurate. Sensitivity to second-order configural differences in upright faces is a hallmark of face recognition expertise (Yin, 1969). It is most disrupted by inversion, and the WS group demonstrated a qualitatively different response to inversion that stemmed particularly from weaker performance on upright configurally transformed faces.

The configural processing of upright faces is the task that is closest to everyday recognition of faces. So the fact the WS participants found this more difficult than controls, suggests that there may be a fundamental difference in the way that faces are being processed by the two groups. This prepared the way for an investigation of development in the next two studies.

Experiment 2: Face recognition in a story-supported task

In Experiment 2, we consider the progressive developmental emergence of the inversion effect, using a task that embeds the recognition of inverted faces in the more naturalistic setting of a storybook. Here, we introduce a novel approach to controls, by building a full task-specific developmental trajectory.

Since it is the difference between the configural processing of upright and inverted faces that distinguished the WS and Control participants, this is the difference that was investigated. The task used in Experiment 2 involved more naturalistic face recognition of upright and inverted faces.

Method

Participants

Seventeen adolescent and adult participants with WS were tested. Three participants failed to correctly identify either a single upright face or a single inverted face and were excluded from subsequent analyses. The 14 remaining participants with WS had a mean CA of 26;3 (SD: 11; 11, range: 12; 0–54; 10). Language ability was assessed using the British Picture Vocabulary Scale (BPVS) (Dunn, Whetton, & Pintilie, 1997), for which the mean test age was 11; 2 (SD: 3; 6, range: 7; 4–17; 6). Visuospatial ability was assessed using the Pattern Construction subtest of the British Abilities Scale (Elliot et al., 1996). The mean test age of the WS group was 5;6 (SD: 1; 2, range 3; 4–8; 9). Thus, this new WS group exhibited the characteristic disparity between these two abilities (language greater than visuospatial skill: paired *t*-test, *t* = 7.51, df = 13, *p* < .001), alongside overall delay. Participants were also given the Benton Face Recognition Test. Mean Benton score was 42.2 (SD: 4; 5, range: 35–51), corresponding to performance within the normal adult range (41–54; Benton, Hamsher, Varney, & Spreen, 1983). Using the age norms from the Benton, these scores were translated into age equivalents (Benton et al., 1983), taking a ceiling score to be reached at 14 years. This gave the WS group a mean Benton age equivalent of 11; 4 (SD: 2; 7, range: 6; 6–14; 0).

> There was a wide age range in the WS participants. This is common in studies of populations who suffer from a rare disorder. Note that the youngest participant was 12 years old and so, from a developmental perspective, on the verge of adulthood.

Data from 111 control children were also analysed. These data were collected by Brace et al. (2001), with group means derived for separate age bins. We reanalysed the data for this sample, using each child's CA to build a task-specific cross-sectional developmental trajectory. The control group had a mean CA of 8;0 (*SD*: 2;8, range: 2;8–11;5). There were 12 children between 2;8 and 4;4, 20 children between 5;2 and 6;11, 26 children between 7;2 and 8; 8, 28 children between 9;2 and 10;2 and 25 children between 11;1 and 11;5. This age range enabled us to build a full trajectory of typical developmental changes on this specific task.

> Unlike Experiment 1, there was no matched control group. Instead, the performance of the participants with WS was compared with data from typically developing children, grouped according to age, who had carried out the same inverted faces task. These data provided an indication of the trajectory of developmental changes in performance in this task against which to compare the performance of the WS group.

Stimuli

The stimuli were taken from Brace et al. (2001) and were modified for use with a touch-screen monitor using Superlab 2.0. The stimuli consisted of two parts: a Storybook and a computer game. The Storybook was a hand-painted story about two boys, called Tom and Jamie. One of the boys is kidnapped by a witch and taken to her castle. The witch turns the boy into a variety of objects, such as a robot that retains only the boy's face, and hides him in amongst 8 other boys that she has kidnapped. The only way for the other boy to rescue his friend is to play a game of hide and seek in order to spot his friend amongst the other boys/objects, which are either upright or hung upside-down. In the first two pages of the book, pictures of Jamie and Tom are present, whereas in the next five pages the story continues without any pictures of the boys, to ensure that subsequent recognition of the faces is delayed by about three minutes. The hide and seek computer game includes upright and inverted pictures of one of the two target faces (Tom or Jamie) among 8 distractor faces. Two versions of the task were run with different target faces. Each participant saw one of the two versions (for further details, see Brace et al., 2001).

Note that both the stimuli and the task were identical to the Brace study.

Procedure

In the first part of the study the experimenter (or the participant if s/he read easily) read a story aloud, during which the participant was asked to point to the pictures of the two boys and to repeat their names after the experimenter. On completion of the first part of the story, the participant was asked if s/he would like to play a computer game of finding the lost boy (Tom or Jamie). Eight trials were run, including two practice trials. For each trial, a picture was presented on the touch-screen with the target face hidden amongst 8 distractor faces of varying similarity to the target face. The position and orientation of the target face within the array of 9 faces was systematically varied. Once the detection game was completed, the story reading was continued to achieve a happy ending. Participants' data were only included if they correctly recognised at least one upright and one inverted instance of the target face. In most cases, performance accuracy was much better.

Note that three participants failed to meet the minimum criterion of correctly identifying at least one upright and one inverted face. The reason for such an exclusion criterion is that participants who failed to recognise at least one face in each condition would not have provided reliable data. It is important, from a statistical point of view, to ensure that participants score above chance. In part, this has to do with designing a task of the right level of difficulty. However, in a special population, it is likely that some participants will not be able to do a task and so exclusion criteria are needed.

Results

The wide age and ability range of the WS and control groups was exploited to generate developmental trajectories on the story task, i.e., to create a function relating increase in performance (either accuracy or response time) against increasing age. For the WS group, 'age' was for each analysis either their chronological age, their Pattern Construction equivalent, their Benton equivalent or their BPVS equivalent. The WS developmental trajectory was compared against the developmental trajectory for the controls, constructed from over one hundred typically developing children between 2;8 years and 11;5 years.

> *A number of different comparisons were made between the developmental trajectory for typically developing children and those for the participants with WS, involving various measures of the 'age'. This is because, in theory, a number of different indicators of age might be appropriate (such as face recognition in a standardised test, or language age). In typically developing children, different measures of age will tend to be rather similar although it is not unusual for there to be some small discrepancies between different abilities. In an atypical group, it is common for some abilities to be better than others; and this is the case here since one hallmark of WS is the disparity in abilities across domains.*

WS performance on Benton Facial Recognition Test

First, we establish that the scores of this group of participants with WS generally fell 'in the normal range', according to a standardised test of face recognition. Figure 1 depicts the Benton scores for the WS group plotted against individuals' chronological age, on the one hand, and against their Pattern Construction age equivalent, on the other. This figure includes the 15 of the 17 participants for whom Benton scores were available. Scores on the Benton were also converted into a Benton age equivalent (Benton et al., 1983) for later use. Several points are of note. First, as in previous studies, many of the WS group fell within the normal range on the Benton task and, indeed, the overall WS group mean was in the normal range. Second, WS performance was nevertheless *delayed* compared to the typical developmental profile, so that scores-in-the-normal-range do not imply here entirely normal development. Third, while the WS scores broadly increased with age, this relationship was not significant ($r^2 = .000$, $p = .954$, or with 2 outliers removed, $r^2 = .153$, $p = .167$). This was because of the cross-sectional nature of the sample: severity of expression of the disorder varies independently of age. Fourth, the Benton scores were in excess of the level that would be predicted by the Pattern Construction ability of the WS group. Lastly, there was no correlation between performance on Benton and test age on the Pattern Construction subtest in the WS group ($r^2 = .000$, $p = .967$), suggesting that these two tasks tap (at least in part) different processes. While Brace et al. (2001) had no Benton and Pattern Construction data for their children, we collected indicative data in our laboratory for a sample of 21 healthy children between 3;6 and 11;2 (mean 6;9, SD 2;7) who performed both these tests. For these children, Pattern Construction test age strongly predicted Benton scores, with a correlation of $r = .873$ ($r^2 = .763$, $p < .001$).

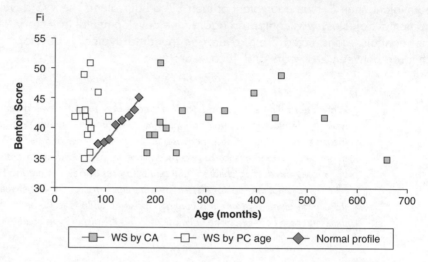

Figure 1   *Benton face recognition scores for participants with WS (N = 15), plotted either against Chronological Age (CA) or against Patterns Construction (PC) age equivalent score. Also shown are normative scores from Benton age equivalent (Benton et al., 1983)*

The disparity in the abilities of the WS participants is illustrated in Figure 1. For typically developing children (indicated by the diamond), Benton scores increased in line with chronological age in a consistent manner. (Note that this is because the Benton test is a standardised test that has been designed to produce this trajectory in a typically developing population.) For the participants with WS, age was not significantly related to Benton scores. In part this may because the majority of participants were beyond the age at which the greatest changes occur (ceiling is taken to be 14 years). However, the data also suggest that something other than age predicts how well individuals with WS do on a standardised test of face recognition. Data for pattern construction age (non-verbal spatial cognition) shows a different pattern. As might be expected, all the WS participants are poor at this task and there was no relation to Benton scores. Note that such a relationship is present for typically developing children.

The normal developmental trajectory

Trajectories were analysed using an analysis of co-variance (ANCOVA). This test requires the relationship between performance and age to be roughly linear. To linearise the relationships, accuracy was plotted against one-over-age squared (in months) (see Thomas et al., 2001, for details). The log of reaction time was plotted against the log of age (in months).

> *The underlying model of development used here is one of linearity, in other words, the assumption of a uniform change in ability as age increases. The assumption of linearity is demanded by the statistical tests and so the data were transformed to produce linearity before the analysis was carried out.*

For the control sample, accuracy rates on upright and inverted faces (each out of 3) were compared to chronological age. Controls exhibited a significant improvement in accuracy with age $(F(1,109) = 27.01, p < .0001)$ and a significant accuracy cost of recognising inverted faces $(F(1, 109) = 4.56, p = .035)$. The size of the inversion effect did not alter significantly across the developmental profile $(F(1,109) = .153, p = .697)$. Figure 2(a) depicts this relationship (note that, for clarity, accuracy is plotted against chronological age in this figure, rather than the transformed age variable used in the analysis). Chance performance in this face identification task was 11 per cent.

Mean reaction times for upright and inverted face recognition on correct trials were compared to chronological age. Controls exhibited a significant reduction in reaction time with age $(F(1,109) = 38.50, p < .001)$ and a significant time cost of recognising inverted faces $(F(1,109) = 4.50, p = .036)$. Moreover, the cost of recognising inverted faces significantly increased with age, consistent with the emergence of configural face-processing expertise $(F(1,109) = 5.93, p = .016)$. This trajectory is depicted in Figure 3(a).

> *The first stage in the analysis was to look at developmental trajectory for recognition of upright and inverted faces in the control sample. Key things to note are that accuracy increased with age and that, at all ages, the inverted faces were more difficult to recognise than the upright faces. Speed of recognising the faces decreased with age but the difference between upright and inverted faces remained constant. The accuracy scores for upright and inverted faces are shown in Figure 2a (lines in bold) where it can be seen that the trajectories for performance on the upright and inverted faces are parallel to one another.*

WS developmental trajectory

For the relationship between performance and chronological age, direct comparisons between the WS and control groups must be interpreted with caution, because the samples have differing variability and are non-overlapping in terms of CA. The direct comparison revealed no overall significant group difference in either accuracy or reaction time when the performance of the WS group was compared to this much younger typically developing control group.

When considered on its own, the WS group revealed no significant relationship between accuracy or reaction time with increasing chronological age (accuracy: $F(1,12) = 1.13$, $p = .309$; RT: $F(1,12) = 2.33$, $p = .153$). Unlike the significance levels in the controls, there was only a trend in the direction of an inversion cost in the accuracy data ($F(1,12) = 4.34$, $p = .059$), and no effect in the RT data ($F(1,12) = .00$, $p = .999$). There was no indication that the inversion effect altered across chronological age (interaction of orientation and age: accuracy, $F(1,12) = 1.33$, $p = .271$; RT: $F(1,12) = .01$, $p = .908$). These trajectories are shown in Figures 2(b) and 3(b).

The next stage was to establish the developmental trajectory for the participants with WS. As already indicated, there was no significant increase with age. There was also no significant effect of inversion for either accuracy or speed and no change in the difference between recognition of upright and inverted faces with age. The trajectory for this group was thus very different from the typically developing children.

The next step was to explore whether any of the standardised measures – Benton, Pattern Construction, or BPVS – was a good predictor of performance on the Storybook task. Performance was compared against WS test age equivalents for each of these measures.

Having established that chronological age did not predict task performance in the WS group, the final stage of analysis was to see if any of the other measures of 'age' was a better predictor. Each of the other three measures of 'age' – Benton scores, Vocabulary scores and Pattern Construction – showed a different pattern of prediction. Vocabulary did not predict either accuracy or speed whereas Benton scores predicted speed but not accuracy and Pattern Construction scores predicted accuracy but not speed.

Performance on the Benton did not predict accuracy ($F(1,11) = .62$, $p = .447$) but did successfully predict reaction time on the Storybook task ($F(1,1) = 5.26$, $p = .043$; inversion effect non-significant; $F(1,12) = 3.23$, $p = .100$). By contrast, performance on the BPVS predicted neither accuracy nor reaction time. Performance on the Pattern Construction sub-test of the BAS-II did not predict reaction times but did successfully predict accuracy levels in the WS group (accuracy: $F(1,12) = 10.33$, $p = .007$; RT: $F(1,12) = .90$, $p = .362$). The trajectories are shown in Figures 2(a) and 3(a). The accuracy trajectory revealed an unusual pattern in the WS group. There was a marginally non-significant inversion effect in the WS group ($F(1,12) = 4.54$, $p = .055$) but a significant interaction whereby the inversion effect became *smaller* as Pattern Construction ability increased ($F(1,12) = 12.91$, $p = .004$). The reaction time data replicated this pattern but differences were not reliable (inversion effect: $F(1,12) = 1.32$, $p = .273$; interaction: $F(1,12) = 1.13$, $p = .308$).

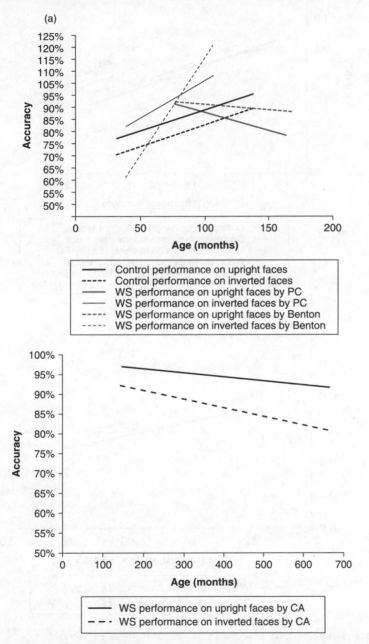

Figure 2 *Developmental trajectories for accuracy on the Picture-book face recognition task: (a) trajectories for accuracy against age for controls and for the WS group plotted according to their Pattern Construction age equivalent and separately according to their Benton age equivalent; (b) accuracy against chronological age for the WS group*

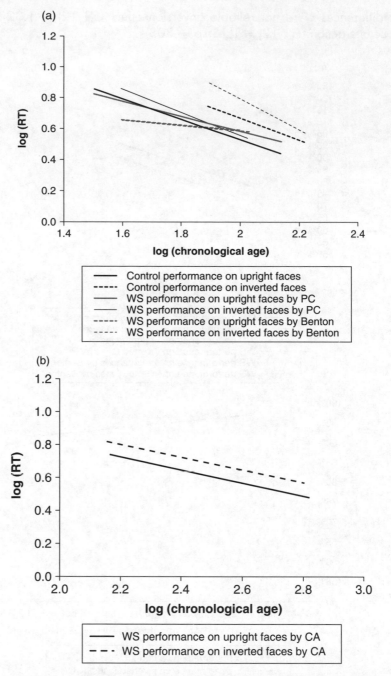

Figure 3 *Developmental trajectories for response times on the Picture-book face recognition task: (a) response time against age for controls and for the WS group plotted according to their Pattern Construction age equivalent and separately according to their Benton age equivalent (log-log plot); (b) response time against chronological age for the WS group (log-log plot)*

Comparison to the control group revealed that WS accuracy on the Storybook task was in excess of what would be expected for Pattern Construction ability (main effect of group: $F(1,121) = 4.21$, $p = .042$). The differential modification of the inversion effect with increasing age was not significant in the combined analysis (3-way interaction of group by age by orientation: $F(1,121) = 2.78$, $p = .098$).

Discussion

As in previous studies, we found that WS Benton scores fell within normal range and better than would be expected by their performance on a standardised visuospatial constructive task. Experiment 2 also yielded novel findings, because we built a full trajectory of typical developmental changes over time for this particular task. Indeed, between the ages of 3 and 12, the normal developmental trajectory reveals increasing accuracy and faster response times for upright faces, as well as the progressive emergence of an inversion effect in terms of reaction times. Most theorists concur that this is the signature of an emerging specialisation for configural processing of upright faces. While the WS group did not differ from the control trajectory in terms of accuracy or speed of response, their developmental trajectory failed to show the progressive emergence of a face inversion effect. In other words, as was suggestive of the findings from Experiment 1, the WS *behavioural* proficiency of some face-processing tasks, e.g., the Benton, seems to stem from an atypical developmental trajectory. In terms of relating WS performance to their other skills, increasing ability on the Benton task predicted an increase in reaction time in the WS group, but again, no emergence of an inversion effect. Benton performance did not significantly predict accuracy on the Storybook task. Ability on BPVS bore no relation to increasing performance on our task. Increasing ability on Pattern Construction predicted an increase in accuracy in the WS group and a modification of the inversion effect, but the modification was unusually in the reverse direction: better Pattern Construction predicted a smaller inversion effect.

> The key finding from Experiment 2 was that the WS participants did not show an inversion effect whereas, in the typically developing children, there was evidence of an increasing effect of inversion from the age of 3 years onwards. What this means is that typically developing children get increasingly better – more accurate and faster – at identifying a face they have seen before when it is in its canonical (upright) orientation. Remember that, in Experiment 1, control adults were much more accurate at recognising an upright over an inverted face when they were making a configural judgment, that is, a judgment about the face as a coherent set of features. This is the judgment that is required in the Storybook task.

Experiment 3: Configural and featural processing of schematic stimuli

A major implication of the results of Experiment 2 was that individuals with WS differ from controls in the way that they process faces. Typically developing older children and adults show evidence of configural processing – and hence a difference in the processing of upright and inverted faces – whereas individuals with WS do not make use of configural processing to the same extent. This hypothesis is explored in the final experiment which uses schematic faces to enable tight control over features and their interrelation and thus allows the researchers to contrast a featural change with a configural change in pairs of faces.

The aim of this experiment was to assess whether adults with WS show a configural or featural bias in their perceptual processing of schematic faces and geometric patterns. The use of schematic faces allows tighter control of stimulus attributes and the closer matching of face and non-face stimuli. Participants once again were required to make similarity judgements about transformed stimuli. In one condition, they judged which of two test patterns differed most from a previously presented target pattern, where one test pattern was identical to the target and one was transformed. This task is similar to the *Difference Detection* condition in Experiment 1. In a second condition, both test stimuli were transformed, one configurally, one featurally. This *Judgement Preference* task allowed us to assess the relative salience of the two types of transformation for the participants. In addition, the coexistence of normally developing performance on Difference Detection but atypical performance on Judgement Preference would point to a preferred processing strategy in WS rather than an underlying deficit.

Method

Participants

Twelve adolescents and adults with WS were tested on this task. Their mean CA was 27;1 (SD: 11;11, range: 15;1–52;3). Language ability was assessed using the British Picture Vocabulary Scale (Dunn et al., 1997), for which the mean test age was 12;2 (SD: 3; 10, range: 7;0–17;6). Visuospatial ability was assessed using the Pattern Construction subtest of the British Abilities Scale. The mean spatial test age of the WS group was 5;8 (SD: 1;3, range 4;1–8;9). Thus as in the previous experiments, the new WS group exhibited the characteristic disparity between these two abilities (language greater than visuospatial skill: paired *t*-test, *t* = 6.88, df = 11, *p* < .001), along with overall delay. Performance on the Benton for this group yielded a mean of 42.0 (SD: 3.4, range: 35–47) corresponding to performance within the normal adult range (41–54; Benton, Sivan,

Hamsher KdeS., Varney, & Spreen, 1994). Once more, the age norms from the Benton were used to convert these scores into age equivalents, taking a ceiling score to be reached at 14 years. Employing this method, the WS group had a mean Benton age equivalent of 11;3 (SD: 2;5, range: 6;6–14;0). For comparison with Experiment 1, once more Pattern Construction test age failed to reliably predict Benton score in the WS sample, Pearson correlation = .264 (r^2 = .070, p = .408).

Sixty-one control children, adolescents and adults, covering the mental and chronological age spans of the clinical group, were also tested in order to build a developmental trajectory specifically for this task. Their overall mean CA was 12;5 (SD: 9;3, range: 5;5–53;1). There were 12 children between 5;4 and 6;5, 12 children between 7;0 and 7;5, 12 children between 8;10 and 9;9, 13 children between 12;2 and 12;10, and 12 adolescents and adults between 14;11 and 53;1. For the children, BPVS data were also collected to ensure that they fell within the normal range.

Stimuli

Three sets of stimuli were displayed on a computer screen: schematic faces, scrambled faces and geometric shapes. The stimuli all comprised four black elements within a yellow circle of 7 cm. Two featurally modified and two configurally modified versions of each stimulus were created. For the schematic and scrambled faces, featural changes were made by replacing the eyes, since this is the most salient feature of a face: round eyes were replaced with squares or diamonds of a similar size as the original feature. By contrast, since all features have equivalent salience for geometric patterns, all four features were replaced to avoid disrupting symmetry. Configural changes were made by stretching or squashing the set of features towards or away from the centre by 20 pixels, thereby creating new, second-order configural relations between the features. Configural changes to the scrambled face could not be made by displacing the elements vertically without breaking the symmetry of the arrangement, so they were made by displacing all the elements horizontally towards or away from the centre of the pattern by 20 pixels.

> Note that a detailed description is provided of the featural and configural changes to the schematic faces.

Procedure

In each trial, a target pattern was presented followed by, or simultaneously with, two test patterns. In the *Difference Detection* task, one of the test patterns was identical to the target pattern while the other was a version that had undergone either a featural or a configural transformation. In the

Judgement Preference task, both of the test patterns were transformed versions of the target pattern: one featurally transformed, the other configurally transformed. For both tasks, the participant had to decide as quickly as possible which test pattern (left or right) differed the most from the target patterns.

There were two different tasks, one involving a comparison of two faces (as in Experiment 1) and a new task in which a target is presented and then two manipulated variants, one involving a featural change and one involving a configural change. Both sequential and simultaneous presentation were used for both types of manipulation.

The stimuli consisted of two blocks of 48 trials. One block had sequential presentation, with the target presented in isolation, to be replaced by the two test patterns. The second block had simultaneous presentation, with target and two test patterns appearing on the screen at the same time. There were 16 schematic faces, 16 scrambled and 16 geometric pattern trials. The order of these blocks was the same for all participants. Within each of these blocks there were 8 difference detection and 8 judgement preference (4 configural and 4 featural) trials, which appeared in a randomised order. Participants indicated which image they thought was most different by pressing the response key on the same side as the picture. Velcro pads were attached to the two relevant keys on the computer keyboard to assist participants with remembering which keys should be pressed. Each participant was tested individually and given 8 practice trials. For the Difference Detection trials the dependent variables were accuracy of response and response time, whereas for Judgement Preference trials it was the number of featural responses.

Results

As in the previous experiment, the results were analysed by building and comparing task-specific cross-sectional developmental trajectories for the control group and the WS group. For the WS group, the trajectory linking age and performance employed a variety of age measures: either their CA, their Benton age equivalent, their Pattern Construction age equivalent, or their BPVS age equivalent. As before, analysis of covariance was used to compare developmental trajectories. Unless otherwise noted, these involved the same data transformations to improve linearity discussed for Experiment 2.

Note that the statistical analysis carried out here follows the same rationale as Experiment 2.

The typical developmental trajectory

A comparison of control accuracy, levels for all stimuli (face-like, scrambled, geometric), transformation types (featural vs. configural), and presentation conditions (simultaneous vs. sequential) against age was carried out. Presentation condition had no main effect ($F(1,58) = .21$, $p = .648$) and the same held for an overall analysis of response times ($F(1,58) = 1.07$, $p = .305$). There did appear to be a face-specific effect of simultaneous presentation, a point to which we will return shortly. For the remainder of the analyses, performance was averaged over simultaneous and sequential presentation conditions. A comparison of the two non-face-like patterns revealed that scrambled face features were harder than geometric patterns (accuracy: $F(1,58) = 3.96$, $p = .051$; RT: $F(1,58) = 1.92$, $p = .171$) but there were no interactions with other variables. For the remainder of the analyses, we will focus on comparisons between face-like stimuli and geometric patterns.

Difference Detection

The relationship between accuracy and age for the typically developing controls on face-like stimuli is depicted in Figure 4(a). An ANCOVA revealed significant improvement in accuracy with age ($F(1,59) = 4.88$, $p = .031$). There was no differential response to face-like stimuli and geometric patterns ($F(1,59) = .74$, $p = .392$), although there was an indication that performance on geometric patterns increased more rapidly with age (interaction of stimulus type and age: $F(1,59) = 3.95$, $p = .051$). Transformation type had no overall effect, but this turned out to be a consequence of averaging across presentation conditions.

A comparison of the accuracy data in the simultaneous vs. sequentially presented conditions revealed one unexpected effect. In the simultaneous condition, the controls responded more accurately to configurally transformed stimuli than featurally transformed stimuli. This held only for face-like stimuli and not for geometric patterns ($F(1,58) = 4.21$, $p = .045$) and was not present in the sequential conditions (interaction with condition: $F(1,58) = 3.96$, $p = .050$). An analysis of the sequential condition on its own revealed an interaction of transformation type with age, such that detection of configural transformations was less accurate than featural transformations, but the disparity decreased with age (interaction of transformation and age: $F(1,59) = 6.37$, $p = .014$). This effect was the same for both faces and geometric patterns. It is therefore possible that under the low-memory load conditions of simultaneous presentation, configural expertise for face processing emerges more easily in typically developing children than for sequential processing.

An analysis of reaction times revealed that responses became faster with age ($F(1,59) = 47.36$, $p < .001$), shown in Figure 4(b). Configural transformations were detected significantly more slowly than featural transformations but this disparity disappeared with age (main effect of transformation: $F(1,59) = 9.96$, $p = .003$; interaction with age: $F(1,59) = 6.90$, $p = .011$).

The key finding to emerge from this experiment was that, for the typically developing group, responses became faster with age but the differences between the featural and configural changes decreased with age; and, in the preference task, a configural change to a face was seen as more different than a featural change, with increasing age. The two tasks produced converging evidence in support of the view that configural processing of faces changes with age.

Judgement Preference

Which transformation type was more salient to typically developing children? Comparison of preference data was restricted to accuracy, because when participants' preferences were exclusively for one transformation type, no response times were available for the non-preferred transformations. Figure 5(a) demonstrates how preferences change with age. The relationship between choice type and age was best fitted by a linear relationship, and so choice was compared against untransformed chronological age. The analysis was carried out for a single choice type, since configural vs. featural choices co-specify each other in the forced choice paradigm. An ANCOVA revealed a significant effect of age on choice type ($F(1,59) = 11.35$, $p = .001$) whereby in typical development, individuals increasingly see configurally transformed stimuli as more different from the target and decreasingly choose featurally transformed stimuli. Let us now turn to the trajectory of the clinical group.

The WS developmental trajectory: Difference Detection

Did the WS group demonstrate a normal facility for recognising each transformation type? Dealing with accuracy first, a between-group comparison of WS developmental trajectory with the typical trajectory revealed no overall effect of group ($F(1,69) = .216$, $p = .643$). The trajectories are shown in Figure 4(a). Importantly, however, the WS group exhibited worse performance on configurally transformed stimuli while the control group did not (interaction of group and transformation type: $F(1,69) = 8.27$, $p = .005$). Moreover, when the trajectory of the WS group was constructed according to their Benton test age equivalent, a comparison with controls revealed that the disparity in configural processing in WS persisted ($F(1,69 = 8.07$, $p = .006$), depicted in Fig 4(b). In neither case is this pattern modified by presentation condition. Importantly, then, for their level of performance on a standardised face recognition task (which generally fell in the normal adult

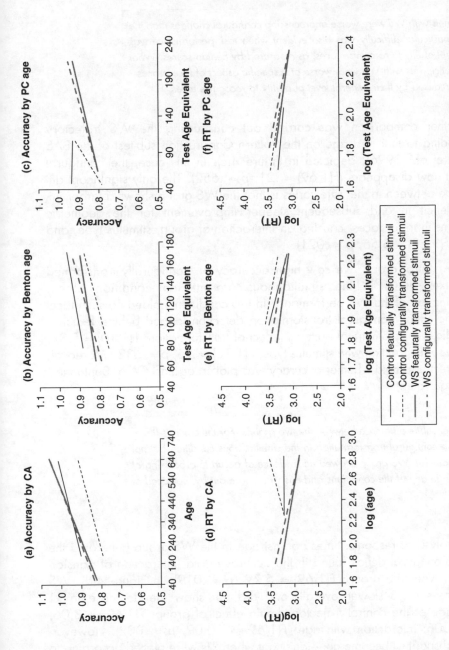

Figure 4   Cross-sectional developmental trajectories for the WS and control groups on the schematic faces task, for detecting featural vs. configural transformations. Trajectories for accuracy and reaction time across age are plotted according to the chronological age of the participants (CA), Benton face recognition test age equivalent (ceiling age 14;0), or Pattern Construction (PC) test age equivalent (ceiling age 18;0). See text for details

range), the WS group exhibited a differential pattern of response to featural vs. configural transformations.

As a group, participants with WS were worse at processing configural changes than the control group. This particular difficulty was also evident when task performance was plotted against general ability to recognise faces, as measured by Benton scores. What this means is that participants with WS were worse at a specific aspect of face processing than would be predicted by their general level of ability to recognise faces.

A further comparison was carried out constructing the WS trajectory according to their test age on the Pattern Construction sub-test of the BAS (Elliot et al., 1996), depicted in Figure 4(c). In this case, the configural deficit now disappears $(F(1,69) = .21, p = .652)$. The only significant difference between in the trajectories is that the WS group shows a larger initial deficit in and subsequent steeper improvement for the geometric patterns than for faces, causing an interaction of group, stimulus type, and age $(F(1,69) = 5.56, p = .021)$.

In the control group, we saw high accuracy on configurally transformed face-like stimuli in the simultaneous presentation condition alone. Examination of the WS performance in this condition yielded no such face-specific effect: configural transformation detection lagged behind featural, as it did with geometrical patterns (effect of transformation: $F(1,10) = 5.87$, $p = .036$; interaction with stimulus type: $F(1,10) = .25, p = .632$). Moreover, the effect also held whether accuracy was plotted against CA or Benton test age equivalent.

There was also another subtle difference between the two groups. For the controls, there was high accuracy on configural transformation in the simultaneous condition but not the sequential condition. The WS group showed no evidence of accurate processing of configural information in any of the conditions and this was borne out by the speed of response data.

An analysis of response times against age in the WS group generated the same configural deficit found in the accuracy data (interaction of transformation type and group: $F(1,69) = 5.79. p = .019$), in Figure 4(d). WS responses were slower overall, and did not show the decrease in RT with age of the control trajectory (main effect of group: $F(1,69) = 8.06$, $p = .006$; interaction with age: $F(1,69) = 10.09, p = .002$). However, these disparities became non-significant when RTs were plotted according to Benton test age, depicted in Figure 4(e). Plotting the WS trajectory according to Pattern Construction ability also caused the WS group to be indistinguishable from the normal trajectory, in Figure 4(f). However, somewhat

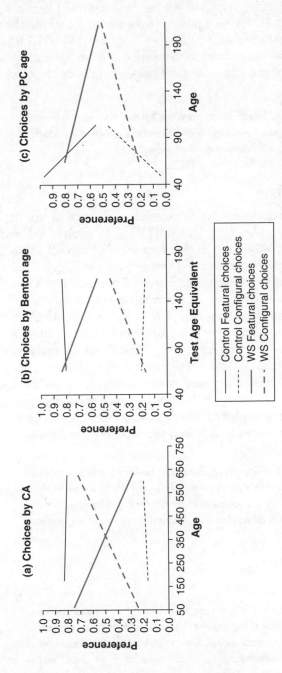

Figure 5 Cross-sectional developmental trajectories for the WS and control groups on preferences for featurally vs. configurally trans-formed face schematics, in a forced choice task to determine which stimulus is most different from the target. Trajectories are plotted accord-ing to the (a) chronological age of the participants (CA), (b) Benton face recognition test age equivalent (ceiling age 14;0), or (c) Pattern Construction (PC) test age equivalent (ceiling age 18;0). See text for details

unexpectedly, plotting performance against BPVS age equivalent produced a strong interaction with transformation type, such that increasing vocabulary age in the WS group (but not the control group) was associated with a divergence in RTs for recognising featurally and configurally transformed stimuli, with configural recognition slowing ($F(1,69) = 10.85$, $p = .002$). While this pattern appeared in the response times for both face-like stimuli and geometrical patterns, it did not appear in the accuracy data.

There was an unexpected relationship with vocabulary age for the WS group in that participants with higher language ages showed more of a difference between the speed of processing of featural and configural manipulations of faces.

Judgement Preference

Did the WS group reveal the same relative salience of transformation type as the typically developing controls? Figures 5(a) to (c) summarise the responses of the WS group in deciding whether a configurally or featurally transformed stimulus was more different than the target. These are plotted against CA, Benton test age, and Pattern Construction test age respectively. The WS group demonstrated no alteration in choice with CA ($F(1,10) = .02$, $p = .880$) or Benton test age ($F(1,10) = .42$, $p = .534$; controls: $F(1,59) = 8.31$, $p = .005$). Plotting the WS performance according to level of Pattern Construction ability produces a more typical-looking pattern, although the effect of age on choice does not yet approach significance ($F(1,10) = 1.91$, $p = .197$). The implication here is that sensitivity to the configural-featural dimension in WS is in line with Pattern Construction ability; yet this dimension is not the one exploited when participants with WS achieve their high face recognition scores in standardised tasks like the Benton.

Data from the judgment preference task also supported the view that the WS participants did not show age-related changes in face processing. This is very clearly shown in Figure 5a where the controls (in bold) show a characteristic cross over in preferences with age but the WS group show a consistent preference for a featural change as being more different than a configural change.

Discussion

Although all three experiments pointed to differences in featural relative to configural processing of faces in the two groups, Experiment 3 produced better performance of configural manipulations than of featural manipulations. This supports the point made by the authors in their introduction about the effect of quite small changes in task on performance and the need for convergence of results across a series of studies using different paradigms.

Although in Experiment 1 scores were poorer in the configural than in the featural trials in the upright condition, in this third experiment configural processing turned out to be easier than featural processing in upright condition. Why is this? A possible explanation is that the transformation types had different relative salience in the two tasks, i.e., configural transformations were more obvious with the schematic stimuli (stretched or compressed faces) than featural transformations (diamonds instead of squares for eyes), whereas in the Jane real faces, the configural changes involve quite subtle rearrangements compared to the more obvious change of different eyes in a face. Hence the importance of avoiding premature conclusions from a single study. Our focus, however, is on change over time in the sensitivity to the two transformation types, and particularly in the cross-group comparison, leading to several important differences between the WS group and the controls. First, the clinical group display a developmental delay in configural processing for their CA, but importantly, this also holds with respect to their level of face recognition performance on the Benton, which suggests atypical underlying processes. Second, when memory load is completely reduced due to simultaneous presentation of the target and test stimuli to be compared, then the controls, but *not* the participants with WS, display a face-specific sensitivity to configural transformations. Third, the clinical population is significantly slower than the controls, with a particular deficit in RTs for configurally transformed stimuli. While this holds for chronological age, the trajectory of RTs is not distinguishable from the normal trajectory when plotted according to their Benton or Pattern Construction age equivalents. Plotting the WS data according to their BPVS language test age does point to some indication of verbally mediated strategies that have been identified in other areas like number (Ansari et al., 2003), suggesting that the WS individuals may use their language proficiency to bootstrap other domains.

General discussion

What have we learnt from these three experiments? In our first experiment with real faces, we hypothesized that if face processing in WS had developed normally, then individuals with the syndrome should show no difference in accuracy or response time in discriminating a target face from a featurally or configurally transformed version of the target. At first blush, our overall results suggest this to be the case: the clinical group was as accurate as the controls on both identity recognition and difference detection, albeit somewhat slower. However, a key condition separated the groups' performance; for upright configural faces, the controls were significantly more accurate than the WS group. Yet, sensitivity to second-order configural differences in upright faces is the hallmark of face-processing expertise (Yin, 1969), lacking in the WS group. In our second experiment with real faces embedded in a story, we hypothesised that if face processing in WS had developed normally, then like the controls they would become increasingly accurate and rapid with age with respect to upright faces, but also show increased sensitivity to inversion, which disrupts configural processing. Our results showed that although again the WS group did not differ from the controls in terns of accuracy or speed of response, their developmental trajectory failed to show progressive emergence of the face inversion effect, again lacking the hallmark of face-processing expertise (Yin, 1969). Moreover, despite normal scores on the Benton, these latter did not predict accuracy on the storybook task. Finally, in our third experiment with schematic faces, we hypothesised that if face processing in WS had developed normally, then like controls they would demonstrate an emerging skill in detecting configural transformations in upright faces with increasing age. Our results showed not only a delay in configural processing with respect to CA, but importantly with respect to their level of face-processing performance on the Benton, suggesting not only delay but atypicality. Moreover, when memory load was reduced in the simultaneous presentation condition, the controls, but *not* the participants with WS, showed an increase in their sensitivity to configural transformations in faces.

A number of our findings, particularly the lack of progressive emergence of the inversion effect, only became obvious from the comparison of the developmental trajectories. Plotting the WS data with respect to their levels over time on several other developmental criteria (standardised measures of face processing, pattern construction or language) brought forth differences than were not detectable in accuracy or speed alone. Comparisons of behavioural scores at specific ages (CA or MA) often suggested no difference between WS and controls. But these are static comparisons that do not elucidate the trajectory by which people reach their proficiency. So, in our view, there is a distinct advantage of building task-specific developmental trajectories. In general, many studies of developmental disorders fall within the theoretical framework of adult neuro-psychology. In such an approach researchers ask whether an ability in an atypical group is 'intact' or 'impaired' and draw their inferences on the basis of whether the clinical group does or does not differ from normal controls matched, say, on mental age. Delay is often ignored or implicitly dismissed as irrelevant, with statements such as 'the clinical group did not differ significantly from the controls', omitting to recall in the discussion that the MA-controls were, say, 20 years younger than the atypical participants! Here and elsewhere we have argued that delay cannot be simply ignored because the dynamics of a developing system over time are vital influences on final outcome (Karmiloff-Smith, Scerif, & Ansari, 2003). But this doesn't merely hold for mental-age-matched controls. Even if a clinical population reached the same scores as their chronological controls, it is still an open question as to whether they display those *behavioural* scores via the same *cognitive* processes as the controls and whether the trajectory by which they moved from childhood to adulthood followed the same *developmental trajectory* as controls (see discussion in Karmiloff-Smith, 1998). In other words, the vital issue for an in-depth comparison of two groups is whether the developmental trajectory shows the same pattern *over time*. Merely demonstrating the equivalence of two groups at Time Z tells us about Times X and Y and thus nothing of the route by which each group reached that level. Furthermore, even when Benton scores fell within the normal range, our trajectories showed that WS performance was nevertheless delayed compared to the typical trajectory, meaning that even 'scores-in-the-normal-range' does not imply entirely normal development. And in many cases, Benton scores for face processing in WS did not predict success levels on configural processing in our face-processing tasks.

We have argued in this paper that building full normal developmental trajectories of each specific task, and subsequently plotting the atypical trajectory on the trajectory, is a more informative way in which to address developmental questions. What we deem to be particularly interesting in our studies is that the broad pattern of scores in the end state was often not reliably distinguishable from chronological age, and yet the trajectory of development was atypical. In addition, by placing the clinical group at different points on the typically developmental trajectory of different standardised measures, we overcome the problem of having to recruit numerous different individually matched control groups for each and every standardised measure. In sum, our approach focuses on change over time rather than performance at a particular moment in development.

The important question for developmental disorders must always be, in our view, 'does it (face processing, language, number, and the like) *develop* normally or atypically? We have tested this by asking: 'Is face recognition in WS in step with developmental markers established in the control sample?' While a truly longitudinal approach would obviously be ideal (but take some two decades!), our cross-sectional task-specific trajectories of a very large number of controls addresses this question more directly than groups matched statistically on either mental or chronological age. For the practical purposes of the present set of experiments, and because of the claims in the literature that we were attempting to address, our youngest participants were 12 years of age. However, our lab is currently working on the featural/configural face-processing distinction in infants, toddlers and children, to complete the trajectories of both typically developing controls and those with developmental disorders. These are clearly very labour-intensive studies.

In conclusion, we agree that the extant literature has identified a proficiency with respect to holistic processing in WS (Deruelle et al., 2003; Tager-Flusberg et al., 2003). But, contrary to the claims of these authors, this work is not inconsistent with our claim that second-order configural processing is indeed impaired in WS in both face processing and general visuospatial processing . Our work measuring brain potentials (Grice et al., 2003) also points to particularly deficient integration of features into a configural whole in WS, suggesting that both face processing and visuospatial processing suffer from similar deficits. Yet, for two decades, the literature has claimed that face processing and visuospatial processing are independent of one another in WS, with the former 'spared' and the latter seriously impaired (Bellugi et al., 1988, 1994). Our findings suggest that this may not be the case. Although scores on the Benton were better than predicted by Pattern Construction scores, it was these latter that were more in line with our face-processing experimental tasks targeting directly the featural/configural distinction. And, whereas people with WS show improvements with age for the Benton, the same improvements are not apparent for tests where configural processing is essential. When configural processing is crucial, people with WS show a deficit (Deruelle et al., 1999), but when global/holistic processing is needed such as in the Navon task, then the WS resemble typically developing controls (Farran, Jarrold, & Gathercole, 2003). It is *second-order configural processing*, demonstrated by the lack of an emergent inversion effect, that yields an atypical developmental trajectory in this clinical population. In our view, spatial cognition is simply more vulnerable to second-order configural impairments in WS development, and many face-processing tasks can be solved by featural or holistic strategies, thereby camouflaging any configural deficit. In other words, while scores in one domain (face processing) may outstrip scores in the other domain (visuospatial cognition), both domains may be affected by similar deficient processes but one reveals this impairment more subtly than the other. Seeming dissociations in the outcome, then, do not necessarily entail dissociations all the way along the developmental pathway (Karmiloff-Smith, 1998).

In conclusion, we argue that the developmental approach taken here, highlighting the importance of building developmental trajectories, is an essential, additional methodology for uncovering the subtleties of the causes of developmental disorders in general, and of face processing in particular.

Acknowledgements

We should like to thank the Williams Syndrome Foundation, UK, for putting us in touch with families and particularly all the clinical and typically developing participants for their contribution. This research was supported by MRC Programme Grant No. G9715642 NIH Project Grant R21TW06761-01 to AK-S. We especially thank Daphne Maurer and Cathy Mondloch of MacMaster University, Canada, for making the Jane Faces Task available to us.

Note

1 All participants with WS across the three experiments (a different opportunity sample each time because of the great distances) had been diagnosed clinically and by means of the FISH probe for the deletion of the elastin gene. Because of the rarity of Williams syndrome and the size of the United Kingdom, numbers are necessarily somewhat low, ranging from 12 to 17 participants with WS per experiment. However, this is well above many of the published papers on this syndrome and is comparable, for instance, to the study of Deruelle et al. (2003), which was viewed by these authors as sufficient to make claims about 'normal' development in WS face processing.

REFERENCES

Bailey, T. M., & Plunkett, K. (2002). Phonological specificity in early words. *Cognitive Development, 17*, 1265–1282.

Baillargeon, R. (1999). Young infants' expectations about hidden objects: a reply to three challenges. *Developmental Science, 2*(2), 115–163.

Baillargeon, R., Needham, A., & DeVos, A. (1992). The development of young infants' intuitions about support. *Early Development and Parenting, 1*, 69–78.

Baron-Cohen, S., Leslie, A. M., & Frith, U. (1985). Does the autistic child have a theory of mind? *Cognition, 21*, 37–46.

Benenson, J. F., & Schinazi, J. (2004). Sex differences in reactions to outperforming same-sex friends. *British Journal of Developmental Psychology, 22*, 317–333.

Bennett, A. J., Lesch, K. P., Heils, A., Long, J., Lorenz, J., Shoaf, S. E., et al. (2002). Early experience and seratonin transporter gene variation interact to influence primates. *Molecular Psychiatry, 7*, 118–122.

Bowerman, M. (1973). *Early syntactic development: a cross-linguistic study with special reference to Finnish*. Cambridge: Cambridge University Press.

Bradmetz, J., & Schneider, R. (1999). Is Little Red Riding Hood afraid of her grandmother? Cognitive vs. emotional response to a false belief. *British Journal of Developmental Psychology, 17*(4), 501–514.

Brown, R. (1973). *A first language: the early stages*. London: George Allen & Unwin.

Bryant, P. E. (1982). The role of conflict and of agreement between intellectual strategies in children's ideas about measurement. *British Journal of Psychology, 73*, 243–251.

Bryant, P. E. (1988). Sensitivity to onset and rhyme does predict young children's reading: a comment on Muter, Hulme, Snowling and Taylor (1997). *Journal of Experimental Child Psychology, 71*, 29–37.

Bryant, P. E. (2002). It doesn't matter whether onset and rime predicts reading better than phoneme awareness or vice versa. *Journal of Experimental Child Psychology, 82*, 41–46.

Bryant, P. E., & Kopytnyska, H. (1976). Spontaneous measurement by young children. *Nature, 260*, 773.

Bryant, P. E., Maclean, M., Bardley, L. L., & Crossland, J. (1990). Rhyme and alliteration, phoneme detection and learning to read. *Developmental Psychology, 26*, 429–438.

Bunce, L., & Harris, M. (submitted). 'I saw the real Father Christmas!': Children's everyday uses of the words real, really and pretend. *British Journal of Developmental Psychology*.

Butterworth, G. E. (2001). Joint visual attention in infancy. In G. Bremner & A. Fogel (Eds), *Blackwell Handbook of Infant Development* (pp. 213–240). Malden, MA: Blackwell.

Butterworth, G. E., & Itakura, S. (2000). How the eyes, head and hand serve definite reference. *British Journal of Developmental Psychology, 18*(1), 25–50.

Butterworth, G. E., & Jarrett, N. L. M. (1991). What minds have in common is space: spatial mechanisms serving joint visual attention in infancy. *British Journal of Developmental Psychology, 9*, 55–72.

Cain, K. (1999). Ways of reading: how knowledge and use of strategies are related to reading comprehension. *British Journal of Developmental Psychology, 17*, 295–312.

Case, R. (1985). *Intellectual development; A systematic reinterpretation*. New York: Academic Press.

Christophe, A., & Morton, J. (1998). Is Dutch native English? Linguistic analysis by 2-month-olds. *Developmental Science, 1*(2), 215–219.

Cowan, R., & Biddle, S. (1989). Children's understanding of one-to-one correspondence in the context of sharing. *Journal of Experimental Child Psychology, 9*, 133–140.

Cutting, A. L., & Dunn, J. (1999). Theory of mind, emotion understanding, language and family background: individual differences and interrelations. *Child Development, 70*, 853–865.

De Rosnay, M., Pons, F., Harris, P. L., & Morrell, J. M. B. (2004). A lag between understanding false belief and emotion attribution in young children: relationships with linguistic ability and mothers' mental state language. *British Journal of Developmental Psychology, 22*, 197–218.

Deak, G. O., Flom, R. A., & Pick, A. D. (2000). Effects of gesture and target on 12- and 18-month-olds' joint visual attention to objects in front of or behind them. *Developmental Psychology, 36*(4), 511–523.

Elman, J. L., Bates, E. A., Johnson, M. H., Karmiloff-Smith, A., Parisi, D., & Plunkett, K. (1996). *Rethinking innateness: a connectionist perspective on development*. Cambridge, MA: MIT Press.

Fenson, L., Dale, P., Resnick, S., Bates, E., Thal, D., Reilly, J., et al. (1990). *MacArthur Communicative Development Inventories: technical manual*. San Diego: San Diego State University.

Fernald, A. (2001). Hearing, listening and understanding: auditory development in infancy. In G. Bremner & A. Fogel (Eds), *Blackwell Handbook of Infant Development* (pp. 35–70). Oxford: Blackwell.

Flavell, J. H. (1992). Cognitive development: past, present and future. *Developmental Psychology, 28*, 998–1005.

Flavell, J. H., Green, F. L., & Flavell, E. R. (1986). Development of knowledge about the appearance reality distinction. *Monographs of the Society for Research in Child Development, 51*(1), 1–68.

Flavell, J. H., Miller, P. H., & Miller, S. A. (1993). *Cognitive development* (3rd edn). Englewood Cliffs, NJ: Prentice-Hall.

Flynn, E., Pine, K., & Lewis, C. (2006). The microgenetic method: time for change? *The Psychologist, 19*(3), 152–155.

Freeman, D. (1983). *Margaret Mead and Samoa: the making and unmaking of an anthropological myth*. Cambridge, MA: Cambridge University Press.

Frydman, O., & Bryant, P. E. (1988). Sharing and understanding of number equivalence by younger children. *Cognitive Development, 3*, 323–339.

Gelman, R., & Gallistel, C. R. (1978). *The child's understanding of number*. Cambridge, MA: Harvard University Press.

Goodall, J. (1986). *The Chimpanzees of Gombe: patterns of behavior*. Boston: Bellknap Press of the Harvard University Press.

Gottlieb, G. (2007). Probabilistic epigenesis. *Developmental Science, 10*(1), 1–11.

Grégoire, A. (1937). *L'apprentissage du langage. Vol 1: les deux premières années*. Liège: Bibliothèque de la Faculté de Philosophie et Lettres.

Grosskurth, P. (1988). *Margaret Mead: a life of controversy*. London: Penguin.

Halliday, M. A. K. (1975). *Learning how to mean: explorations in the development of language*. London: Edward Arnold.

Harris, M. (1992). *Language experience and early language development*. Hove, East Sussex: Erlbaum.

Harris, M., & Butterworth, G. (2002). *Developmental psychology: a student's handbook*. Hove, East Sussex: Psychology Press.

Harris, M., & Chasin, J. (1999). Developments in early lexical comprehension: a comparison of parental report and controlled testing. *Journal of Child Language, 26*, 453–460.

Harris, M., & Hatano, G. (Eds). (1999). *Learning to read and write: a cross-linguistic perspective*. Cambridge: Cambridge University Press.

Harris, P. L., Johnson, C. N., Hutton, D., Andrews, G., & Cooke, T. (1989). Young children's theory-of-mind and emotion. *Cognition and Emotion, 3*(4), 379–400.

Harris, M., Jones, D., & Grant, J. (1983). The nonverbal context of mother' speech to children. *First Language, 4*, 21–30.

Harter, S. (1988). *Manual for the self-perception profile for adolescents*. Denver, CO: University of Denver.

Hesketh, S., Christophe, A., & Dehaene-Lambertz, G. (1997). Non-nutritive sucking and sentence processing. *Infant Behavior and Development, 20*(2), 263–269.

Hood, K. (2005). Development as a dependent variable: Robert B Cairns on the psychobiology of aggression. In D. M. Stoff & E. J. Susman (Eds), *Developmental psychobiology of agression* (pp. 225–251). New York: Cambridge University Press.

Hughes, C., Oksanen, H., Taylor, A., Jackson, J., Murray, L., Caspi, A. and Moffitt, T. E. (2002). 'I'm gonna beat you!' SNAP!: an observational paradigm for assessing young children's disruptive behaviour in competitive play. *Journal of Child Psychology and Psychiatry, 43*(4), 507–516.

Hulme, C., Hatcher, P. J., Nation, K., Brown, A., Adams, J., & Stuart, G. (2002). Phoneme awareness is a better predictor of early reading than onset-rime awareness. *Journal of Experimental Child Psychology, 82*, 2–28.

Hulme, C., Muter, V., & Snowling, M. J. (1998). Segmentation does predict early progress in learning to read: a reply to Bryant. *Journal of Experimental Child Psychology, 71*, 39–44.

Inhelder, B., & Piaget, J. (1958). *The growth of logical thinking from childhood to adolescence*. New York: Wiley.

Karmiloff-Smith, A. (1979). *A functional approach to child language: a study of determiners and reference*. Cambridge: Cambridge University Press.

Karmiloff-Smith, A., Thomas, M., Annaz, D., Humphreys, K., Ewing, S., Brace, N., Van Deuren, M., Pike, G., Grice, S., & Campbell, R. (2004). Exploring the Williams syndrome face-processing debate: the importance of building developmental trajectories. *Journal of Child Psychology & Psychiatry, 45*(7), 1258–1274.

Klahr, D., & Wallace, J. G. (1976). *Cognitive development: an information-processing view*. Hillsdale, NJ: Erlbaum.

Leman, P. L., Ahmed, S., & Ozarow, L. (2005). Gender, gender relations, and the social dynamics of children's conversations. *Developmental Psychology, 41*, 64–74.

Lerner, R. M. (1998). Theories of human development: contemporary perspectives. In R. M. Lerner (Ed.), *Handbook of Child Psychology* (5th ed., Vol. 1, pp. 1–24). New York: Wiley.

Lewis, M. (1990). Models of developmental psychopathology. In M. Lewis & S. M. Miller (Eds), *Handbook of developmental psychopathology* (pp. 15–26). New York: Plenum.

Marschark, M., & Harris, M. (1996). Success and failure in learning to read: the special (?) case of deaf children. In C. Cornoldi & J. Oakhill (Eds), *Reading comprehension difficulties: Processes and intervention* (pp. 279–300). Hillsdale, NJ: Lawrence Erlbaum Associates Inc.

Mead, M. (1928). *Coming of age in Samoa: a psychological study of primitive youth for Western civilization.* New York: William Morrow.

Meins, E., Fernyhough, C., Fradley, E., & Tuckey, M. (2001). Rethinking maternal sensitivity: mothers' comments on infants' mental processes predict security of attachment at 12 months. *Journal of Child Psychology and Psychiatry, 42,* 637–648.

Meins, E., Fernyhough, C., Russell, J., & Clark-Carter, D. (1998). Security of attachment as a predictor of symbolic and mentalising attitudes: a longitudinal study. *Social Development, 7,* 1–24.

Meins, E., Fernyhough, C., Wainwright, R., Das Gupta, M., Fradley, E., & Tuckey, M. (2002). Maternal mind-mindedness and attachment security as predictors of Theory of Mind understanding. *Child Development, 73*(6), 1715–1726.

Milgrom, J., Westley, D. T., & Gemmill, A. W. (2004). The mediating role of maternal responsiveness in some longer term effects of postnatal depression on infant development. *Infant Behavior and Development, 27,* 443–454.

Muldoon, K., Lewis, C., & Towse, J. N. (2005). Because it's there! Why some children count, rather than infer numerical relationships. *Cognitive Development, 20*(3), 472–491.

Murray, L., Woolgar, M., Cooper, P., & Hipwell, A. (2001). Cognitive vulnerability to depression in five year old children of depressed mothers. *Journal of Child Psychology and Psychiatry, 42,* 891–900.

Muter, V., Hulme, C., Snowling, M. J., & Taylor, S. (1988). Segmentation, not rhyming predicts early progress in learning to read. Erratum. *Journal of Experimental Child Psychology, 71,* 3–27.

Muter, V., Hulme, C., Snowling, M. J., & Taylor, S. (1997). Segmentation, not rhyming predicts early progress in learning to read. *Journal of Experimental Child Psychology, 65,* 370–396.

Overton, W. F. (1998). Developmental psychology: philosophy, concepts, and methodology. In R. M. Lerner (Ed.), *Handbook of Child Psychology* (5th edn, Vol. 1, pp. 107–188). New York: Wiley.

Peterson, C. C., & Siegal, M. (1998). Changing focus on the representational mind: Deaf, autistic and normal children's concepts of false photos, false drawings and false beliefs. *British Journal of Developmental Psychology, 16,* 301–320.

Piaget, J., Inhelder, B., & Sizeminska, A. (1960). *The child's conception of geometry.* London: Routledge and Kegan Paul.

Piaget, J., & Szeminska, A. (1952). *The child's conception of number.* London: Routledge & Kegan Paul.

Rutter, M. (2007). Gene-environment interdependence. *Developmental Science, 10*(1), 12–18.

Sangrigoli, S., & de Schonen, S. (2004). Recognition of own-race and other-race faces by three-month-old infants. *Journal of Child Psychology & Psychiatry, 45,* 1219–1227.

Savage, R., & Carless, S. (2005). Phoneme manipulation not onset-rime manipulation ability is a unique predictor of early reading. *Journal of Child Psychology & Psychiatry, 46*(12), 1297–1308.

Siegal, M. (1991). *Knowing children: experiments in conversation and cognition.* Hove: Lawrence Erlbaum Associates.

Siegler, R. S. (1976). Three aspects of cognitive development. *Cognitive Psychology, 8*, 481–520.

Siegler, R. S. (1998). *Children's thinking* (3rd edn). Upper Saddle River, NJ: Prentice-Hall.

Siegler, R. S. (2007). Cognitive variability. *Developmental Science, 10*(1), 104–109.

Siegler, R. S., & Alibali, M. W. (2005). *Children's thinking* (4th edn). Upper Saddle River, NJ: Prentice-Hall.

Sirois, S., & Mareschal, D. (2002). Models of habituation in infancy. *Trends in Cognitive Science, 6*(7), 293–298.

Smith, N. V. (1973). *The acquisition of phonology: a case study*. Cambridge: Cambridge University Press.

Sophian, C., Wood, A. M., & Vong, K. I. (1995). Making numbers count: the early development of numerical inferences. *Developmental Psychology, 31*, 263–273.

Spencer, P. E., & Harris, M. (2005). Patterns and effects of language input to deaf infants and toddlers from deaf and hearing mothers. In M. Marschark & P. E. Spencer (Eds), *Sign language development* (pp. 71–101). Oxford: Oxford University Press.

Thelen, E., & Smith, L. B. (1994). *A dynamic systems approach to the development of cognition and action*. Cambridge, MA: MIT Press.

Towse, J. N., Redbond, J., Houston-Price, C. M. T., & Cook, S. (2000). Understanding the dimensional change card sort: perspectives from task change and failure. *Cognitive Development, 15*, 347–365.

Valsiner, J. (1998). The development of the concept of development: historical and epistemological perspectives. In R. M. Lerner (Ed.), *Handbook of Child Psychology* (5th edn, Vol. 1, pp. 189–232). New York: Wiley.

van Geert, P. (1998). We almost had a great future behind us: the contribution of non-linear dynamics to developmental science in the making. *Developmental Science, 1*, 143–159.

Vygotsky, L. S. (1961). *Thought and language*. Boston, MA: MIT Press.

Waddington, C. H. (1975). *The evolution of an evolutionist*. Ithaca, NY: Cornell University Press.

Watson, J. B. (1919). *Psychology from the standpoint of a behaviorist*. Philadelphia, PA: J.B. Lippincott.

Watson, J. B., & Rayner, R. (1920). Conditioned emotional responses. *Journal of Experimental Psychology, 3*, 1–14.

Westermann, G., Mareschal, D., Johnson, M. H., Sirois, S., Spratling, M. W., & Thomas, M. S. C. (2007). Neuroconstructivism. *Developmental Science, 10*(1), 75–83.

Wimmer, H., & Perner, J. (1983). Beliefs about beliefs: representation and constraining functions of wrong beliefs in young children's understanding of deception. *Cognition, 13*, 103–128.

Woolfe, T., Want, S. C., & Siegal, M. (2002). Signposts to development: Theory of Mind in deaf children. *Child Development, 73*, 768–778.

Zelazo, P. D., & Müller, U. (2002). The balance beam in the balance: reflections on rules, relational complexity, and developmental processes. *Journal of Experimental Child Psychology, 81*, 458–465.

INDEX

Please note that entries in bold refer to the author's text and all other entries refer to the journal papers.

Wilcoxon signed ranks test *cont.*
    chronological age (CA) 297, 298, 299,
        301, 305–308
    **configural and featural processing
        of real face 303–308**
    description of syndrome 295–297
    developmental trajectories 313–317,
        322, *323*, 324, *325*
        importance of **300**–301
        and normal trajectory 312–313
        Picture-book face recognition *315*, *316*
    identity recognition 305–**306**, *307*
    mental age (MA) 297, 298, **301**
    Pattern Construction **314**, *315*, 317,
        320, 327
    previous face processing studies **297**–302
    problems with studies 296
    stimuli **304**, 309–**310**, **319**
    **story-supported task, face
        recognition 308–317**
Wisconsin Card-Sorting Task **285**–286
words, phonological specificity *see*
    **mispronunciations, researching young
    children's ability to detect**
work, women's behaviour at 109
WPPSI (Wechsler Pre-School and Primary
    Scales of Intelligence)
    behavioural problems 37, **44**
    postnatal depression study 57, **59**

young children, experimental studies
    see also infants and toddlers,
        experimental studies
    disruptive behaviour *see* **disruptive
        behaviour in young children,
        assessment**
    outperforming friends, researching
        reactions to *see* **friends,
        outperforming, sex differences
        in reactions to**
    postnatal depression, effect on infant
        development *see* **postnatal
        depression, experimental study**
    segregation of interactions with peers,
        by sex 92
    visual attention to objects *see* **visual
        attention in mothers and
        infants, joint**
    words, detection of mispronunciations *see*
        **mispronunciations, researching
        young children's ability to detect**

Zelazo, P. D. 19
zone of proximal development, concept 15